SELECTIONS FROM
The Female Spectator

D0863160

WOMEN WRITERS IN ENGLISH
1350–1850

SELECTIONS FROM

The Female Spectator

by Eliza Haywood

Edited by

Patricia Meyer Spacks

New York   Oxford

Oxford University Press

1999

Oxford University Press

Oxford   New York

Athens   Auckland   Bangkok   Bogotá   Buenos Aires   Calcutta
Cape Town   Chennai   Dar es Salaam   Delhi   Florence   Hong Kong   Istanbul
Karachi   Kuala Lumpur   Madrid   Melbourne   Mexico City   Mumbai
Nairobi   Paris   São Paulo   Singapore   Taipei   Tokyo   Toronto   Warsaw

and associated companies in
Berlin   Ibadan

Published by Oxford University Press, Inc.
198 Madison Avenue, New York, New York 10016

Oxford is a registered trademark of Oxford University Press.

Library of Congress Cataloging-in-Publication Data
Haywood, Eliza Fowler, 1693?–1756.
Selections from The female spectator / by Eliza Haywood;
edited by Patricia Meyer Spacks.
p.   cm.—(Women writers in English 1350–1850)
Includes bibliographical references and index.
ISBN 0-19-510921-X; ISBN 0-19-510922-8 (pbk.)
1. Women—Literary collections.   2. Women—Great Britain—Conduct
of life—History—18th century—Sources.
I. Spacks, Patricia Ann Meyer.
II. Title.   III. Series.
PR3506.H94A6   1999
824'.5—dc21   98-18306

1 3 5 7 8 6 4 2

Printed in the United States of America
on acid-free paper.

CONTENTS

FOREWORD

Women Writers in English 1350–1850 presents texts of cultural and literary interest in the English-speaking tradition, often for the first time since their original publications. Most of the writers represented in the series were well known and highly regarded until the professionalization of English studies in the later nineteenth century coincided with their excision from canonical status and from the majority of literary histories.

The purpose of this series is to make available a wide range of unfamiliar texts by women, thus challenging the common assumption that women wrote little of real value before the Victorian period. While no one can doubt the relative difficulty women experienced in writing for an audience before that time, or indeed have encountered since, this series shows that women nonetheless had been writing from early on and in a variety of genres, that they maintained a clear eye to readers, and that they experimented with an interesting array of literary strategies for claiming their authorial voices. Despite the tendency to treat the powerful fictions of Virginia Woolf's *A Room of One's Own* (1928) as if they were fact, we now know, against her suggestions to the contrary, that there were many "Judith Shakespeares" and that not all of them died lamentable deaths before fulfilling their literary ambitions.

This series offers, for the first time, concrete evidence of a rich and lively heritage of women writing in English before the mid–nineteenth century. It grew out of one of the world's most sophisticated and forward-looking electronic resources, the Brown University Women Writers Project (WWP), with the earliest volumes of the series derived directly from the WWP textbase. The WWP, with support from the National Endowment for the Humanities, continues to recover and encode for a wide range of purposes complete texts of early women writers, and it maintains a cordial relationship with Oxford University Press as this series continues independently.

Women Writers in English 1350–1850 offers lightly annotated versions based on single good copies or, in some cases, collated versions of texts with more complex editorial histories, normally in their original spelling. The editions are aimed at a wide audience, from the informed undergraduate to professional students of literature, and they attempt to include the general reader who is interested in exploring a fuller tradition of early texts in English than has been available through the almost exclusively male canonical tradition.

Susanne Woods
Elizabeth H. Hageman

INTRODUCTION

Eliza Haywood did not want us to know much about her. Alexander Pope notoriously slandered her during her lifetime, repeatedly implying her sexual promiscuity. (In Book II of *The Dunciad,* for instance, Haywood figures as a prize for the winner of a booksellers' race, implicitly as a whore, posing with "Two babes of love close clinging to her waist" [l.158].) But Pope was only one of many who cast sexual aspersions on Haywood. Perhaps as a consequence, she apparently wished no record of herself after her death. In the words of her contemporary, David Erskine Baker: "from a supposition of some improper liberties being taken with her character after death, by the intermixture of truth and falsehood with her history, she laid a solemn injunction on a person who was well acquainted with all the particulars of it, not to communicate to any one the least circumstance relating to her."[1] Two centuries later, many important facts about Haywood's life remain in dispute.

Possibly she was born in 1693 to Francis and Elizabeth Fowler of London, about whom nothing beyond their names and place of residence is known. Or her parents may have been Robert and Elizabeth Fowler of St. Peter's Cornhill in London, whose daughter Elizabeth was christened in 1689. In that case, her father would have been a prosperous hosier, and she would have had four siblings, two of whom attended Oxford. She also claimed a close relationship to Sir Richard Fowler of Shropshire, whose sister Elizabeth was christened in January 1692/3; perhaps, then, she belonged to a family of some distinction. But how nearly, if at all, she was related to this family remains obscure.

The confusion deepens around the subject of her marriage. Biographers and critics have long accepted the claim that she married—and subsequently left—a clergyman named Valentine Haywood. Re-

---

1. Entry for "Eliza Heywood," in *Companion to the Play House,* 2 vols. (London, 1764), 1: Qrv; quoted in Christine Blouch, "Eliza Haywood and the Romance of Obscurity," *Studies in English Literature* 31 (1991): 536.

cent research, however, indicates that this clergyman actually married one Elizabeth Foord, who left him in 1721.[1] No one has yet claimed any knowledge about the name or nature of another candidate for the role of Haywood's real, probably nonclerical, husband. On the basis of slender evidence (the only kind available to us), George Whicher characterizes her in her young matronhood as "evidently a lively, unconventional, opinionated gadabout fond of the company of similar She-romps, who exchanged verses and specimen letters with the lesser celebrities of the literary world."[2] Haywood herself asserted her motherhood of two children. Were they, as Pope suggested, illegitimate? One can argue plausibly for that possibility—or for its converse.

Marriage and children, however, did not interfere with Haywood's public achievement. Perhaps she left her husband; perhaps he died, as she alleged in one letter, adding that the sudden death of her father had intensified her need.[3] In any case, economic necessity apparently provided the impetus for some of her efforts: like many of her female contemporaries, she conducted her life in the public eye partly because she needed money. She acted in numerous plays and wrote plays of her own. She wrote novels, political pamphlets, periodicals, conduct books (addressed variously to servants, wives, and husbands), and poetry and made translations from French. Her first novel, *Love in Excess* (1719), vied for popularity with Daniel Defoe's *Robinson Crusoe*, published the same year. It appeared quickly in four editions, one of the great best-sellers of the eighteenth century, and attracted huge audiences, as did most of the many novels Haywood published during the 1720s.

Those novels, typically short, adapted the techniques and structures of romance.[4] Telling their stories at breakneck speed, they often use

---

1. I am indebted for this information, and for my general survey of biographical facts, largely to Christine Blouch's essay.

2. George Frisbie Whicher, *The Life and Romances of Mrs. Eliza Haywood* (New York: Columbia Univ. Press, 1915), 4.

3. The undated (and possibly inauthentic) letter is printed by Gabrielle M. Firmager, "Eliza Haywood: Some Further Light on her Background?" *Notes and Queries* 236, no.2 (1991): 181–83.

4. Another volume in the *Women Writers in English* series, edited by Paula Backscheider, publishes selections from Haywood's plays and short fiction.

exotic settings, favoring Mediterranean countries, and fairly implausible plots. Their heroes and heroines have stock names out of the pastoral, romantic, and classical traditions, names that often recur in Haywood's fiction and in that of her contemporaries. Like their names, the characters often seem more or less interchangeable. Although the novels sketch rather than fully develop character, they reveal the writer's intense interest in the predicaments of women, predicaments typically caused by men, and in possible expedients for confronting them. Haywood's heroines pursue their amorous desires, rely on female alliances, employ deliberate techniques of disguise and deception, display extraordinary persistence. Twentieth-century readers should not find it difficult to understand why these fictions attracted such a large audience—especially, one might speculate, a female audience.

In the 1730s Haywood concentrated mainly on other-than-fictional forms, returning in the 1740s to her focus on the novel. By then, in the wake of Samuel Richardson's *Pamela* (1740), popular taste had shifted. Richardson's novel avoided the high-born heroines and implausible predicaments of romance to concentrate on the career of a virtuous servant girl who finally achieves marriage with her aristocratic master. It inaugurated the domestic fiction that flourished throughout the rest of the century, fiction that made private households the arena of action and assigned importance to the dilemmas of private persons, particularly young women. Haywood's fictional productions of the 1740s moved in the same direction, taking the form of longer, less ostentatiously fanciful works than those she had written earlier. Her novels of this decade generally proclaim their morals with some insistence. *Betsy Thoughtless* (1751), published only five years before Haywood's death, exemplifies the methods of her later fiction. The novel's title telegraphs its message: Haywood imagines in meticulous detail the career of a young woman who acts on the basis of impulse and desire (avoiding, however, serious sexual contamination) and consequently finds herself married to an unpleasant man and separated from the good man who truly loves her. All turns out well in the end, though, as Betsy learns the error of her ways and reforms sufficiently to earn a happy marriage.

Although this kind of plot, and the leisure of its development, differs markedly in structure and pace from Haywood's earlier fiction, the central concern with female difficulties remains constant. Haywood adapted her method to her audience's preferences and expectations while preserving the integrity of her own preoccupations. Her thematic concentration on women's situations persists through all her generic experimentation.

The *Female Spectator* (1744–46) belongs to the middle of the decade that saw publication of many of Haywood's domestically oriented novels. Periodicals intended specifically for women had appeared occasionally in England since 1693, when the entrepreneurial publisher John Dunton issued the *Ladies' Mercury* as a spin-off of his successful *Athenian Mercury,* which had already flourished for two years.[1] Although the *Ladies' Mercury* proclaimed female authorship and appealed to a female readership, it was almost certainly written, edited, and produced by men. Haywood's journal was in fact the first periodical for women actually written by a woman.

Facts about eighteenth-century readership remain hard to come by.[2] Although one can peruse publishers' lists and subscription lists from certain circulating libraries, they may reveal more about who had money than about who actually read books. The readership of periodicals remains particularly obscure, since magazines not only appeared periodically (once a month, in the case of the *Female Spectator*) but were also collected into annual volumes that libraries might circulate. Contemporaneous received opinion held that women composed the main readership for novels, and such general-interest periodicals as the *Tatler* and the *Spectator* openly and insistently proclaimed their concern for women as readers and as recipients of moral instruction. Joseph Addison and Richard Steele, authors of these earlier periodicals, had evolved a brilliant formula for success, producing individual magazines consisting typically of a single informal essay written in a con-

---

1. For a fuller account of early women's magazines, see Ros Ballaster, Margaret Beetham, Elizabeth Frazer, and Sandra Hebron, *Women's Worlds: Ideology, Femininity and the Woman's Magazine* (London: Macmillan, 1991).

2. For a particularly useful treatment, see J. Paul Hunter, *Before Novels: The Cultural Contexts of Eighteenth Century English Fiction* (New York: Norton, 1990). Also valuable is Lawrence Stone, "Literacy and Education in England 1640–1900," *Past and Present* 42 (1969): 69–139.

versational tone about subjects of immediate general interest—the nature of a fashionable young man's brain and of his female equivalent's heart, for instance; or, for more intellectual substance, the appeal of *Paradise Lost* and the nature of the imagination. Addison and Steele made literary and philosophic subjects accessible; they provided lessons in manners and morals as well as considerable entertainment; they aroused interest in a fictional cast of characters from whom many of their utterances allegedly emanated. Everybody read the *Tatler* and the *Spectator*: its authors by no means wrote *only* for women. Haywood ostensibly did just that—although men, of course, may also have read what she wrote.

Like the *Tatler* and *Spectator,* the *Female Spectator* consisted of a single long essay composing each issue. Haywood probably wrote all, or virtually all, of these essays, although many allegedly originate in letters from readers. The essays provided an ideal forum for direct and indirect discussions of the kind of issue their author had investigated in her longer fiction: the problem of female opportunity and limitation. More specifically, Haywood concerned herself with how women might operate effectively within the social restrictions that enveloped them. She knew the difficulties of female life within a patriarchal system, but she refused to accept those difficulties as fully definitive of women's possibilities.

The governing idea of the *Female Spectator* is the urgency of *experience* for middle-class women. Eighteenth-century convention dictated that most such women would lead relatively confined domestic lives, cut off from the possibility of remunerative work and even from wide social opportunity. The wise countess in Charlotte Lennox's 1752 novel, *The Female Quixote,* summarizes the female situation in a way that applies to many real-life women throughout the century. Speaking to Arabella, who asks for an account of her "Adventures," the countess explains that good women nowadays do not have adventures. Arabella, interpreting the world in terms derived from her reading of romance, expects excitement everywhere. The countess uses her own life to try to disabuse the girl of such fantasy:

> When I tell you . . . that I was born and christen'd, had a useful and proper Education, receiv'd the Addresses of my Lord _____ through the

> Recommendation of my Parents, and marry'd him with their Consents and my own Inclination, and that since we have liv'd in great Harmony together, I have told you all the material Passages of my Life, which upon Enquiry you will find differ very little from those of other Women of the same Rank, who have a moderate Share of Sense, Prudence and Virtue.[1]

She does not convince Arabella that adventures are no longer a viable possibility for respectable women, but the likely readers of Haywood's magazine would have taken for granted the conditions to which the countess alludes.

To such readers, Eliza Haywood offered vicarious experience. Long tradition had established that reading history, with its accounts of large patterns of human events, could provide a counterpart for and supplement to direct encounters of the world. Some critics, a little uneasily, thought that novels (as opposed to romances) might, by fictional history, supplement female experience in particular. (Their uneasiness registered anxiety that women would acquire the wrong lessons from literary works that represented mixtures of vice and virtue in their characters and frequently emphasized love as a motivating force.) Haywood set out to provide a combination of fiction, information, and didacticism that would convey a realistic impression of women's lives yet make the possibilities of such lives interesting despite social restriction.

Establishing her authorial persona at the beginning of her periodical, the Female Spectator emphasizes her own wide and varied experience of "a Hurry of promiscuous Diversions." She has kept company with many sorts of people and from them learned about "many Occurrences, which otherwise I had been ignorant of." Moreover, she claims, she has come to understand the roots of those "Occurrences," to "see into the secret Springs which gave rise to the Actions I had either heard, or been Witness of." But she does not assign herself an exemplary moral position or altogether comprehensive knowledge. Setting out to record the consequences of her experience, she immediately

---

1. Charlotte Lennox, *The Female Quixote, or The Adventures of Arabella,* ed. Margaret Dalziel (Oxford: Oxford Univ. Press, 1989), 327.

discovers her own insufficiencies, so she decides to supplement her information with that provided by three female friends: a harmoniously married woman of great "Wit," a wise widow, and a virtuous young unmarried woman. Together, the four may be able to gratify the "Curiosity" that the Spectator declares omnipresent among human beings, but they will not know everything or discuss everything—not, for instance, war or politics. Still, the Female Spectator as persona hopes to realize her ambition "to be as universally read as possible."

Her delineation of herself and her friends on the basis of their age, virtue, and marital condition foretells her emphasis in the periodical as a whole on conventional definitions of women and their opportunities. Many of the lessons she teaches belong to received wisdom. They also vividly reflect her historical moment. She inveighs, for instance, against gambling and excessive tea drinking, both common pastimes of upper-class women in particular, and both understood as forms of financial extravagance. Many eighteenth-century writers worried about "luxury," meaning extravagant self-indulgence, particularly in imported products, as a destructive force in the culture.[1] Haywood joins their number. Tea, an expensive import from Asia, had only relatively recently become fashionable. By the time Haywood wrote, upper-class women made a common practice of social tea drinking. The *Female Spectator* calls attention to the physical dangers of this habit, but more insistently to its moral perils as a form of self-indulgence and laziness, infecting even servants. The many forms of social gambling, equally fashionable, offer comparable hazards. Haywood also warns women against the less specifically contemporary temptations of jealousy and gossip. She recommends compliance to husbands, for the practical reason that women have no other plausible recourse, given legal and social actualities. Her warnings and recommendations alike would have sounded familiar in her period. Yet the variety of her methods, the energy of her common-sense approach, and the manifest intensity of her convictions all lend freshness to her

---

1. For an excellent discussion of this subject, see John Sekora, *Luxury: The Concept in Western Thought, Eden to Smollett* (Baltimore: Johns Hopkins Univ. Press, 1977).

message even now. And that message is, after all, not altogether pre-dictable.

Haywood's devices for maintaining the curiosity and the interest of her readers include purported letters from correspondents who report their personal problems or complain about social ills; frequent inter-spersed narratives, some of them unusually long; and extensive dis-quisitions on social and personal aspects of the female situation. The letters, although often of considerable interest in themselves, also stim-ulate wide-ranging reflection by the Female Spectator, who, even when she offers predictable answers to the questions asked her, justifies them by inventive and persuasive logic. Haywood imagines, for instance, a letter from a flirtatious young woman who asks for help in deciding which of three suitors she should choose (Bk. VI). She esteems one of them, pities another, and loves the third. The Spectator, of course, goes for esteem. But she makes the argument in negative as well as positive terms. Not only does she specify the value of the worthy man who fails to flatter his beloved but possesses the qualities that foretell happy married life, she also makes vivid the dangers of the more friv-olous possible choices. Memorably characterizing the recipient of pity as a "whining *Strephon*" ("Strephon" being one of those stock names from pastoral poetry, typically applied to a lovelorn shepherd), she dismisses his professed feeling as superficial or fraudulent. More elab-orately—because she considers him more dangerous—she spins out a scenario of what married life might be like with the man her corre-spondent professes to love. "The Heart is a busy, fluttering, impudent Thing," the Spectator observes: "It will not lye still when one bids it." So she worries about the emotional appeal of the narcissistic man whom she imagines, in compelling detail, as continuing in marriage to love only himself and as causing great suffering to his wife.

The letter of inquiry thus becomes a pretext for narrative, and the narrative in turn provides a pretext for moral instruction. Similarly, the longer stories frequently included, which display the gusto and inventiveness also manifest in Haywood's novels, invariably serve to make or emphasize a moral point. Here Haywood reveals her common sense as well as her psychological astuteness. She tells the story of a wife who finds her husband in an unambiguously compromising situation with another woman (Bk. X). The wronged wife expresses all her rage, berating her husband and proclaiming her injuries. The husband knows and feels his own culpability, but he cannot tolerate what he perceives as his wife's attempt to dominate him. Consequently, although he had been quite ready to give up his mistress and confess his guilt, he hardens his position. The wife ends up alone and lonely. The moral is not that men should not stray, although that can be assumed, but that women, in their own interests, should control their self-expression. Men *will* stray, Haywood knows. The significant question is how women, given their limited social resources, should cope with such actualities.

Marriage, the Female Spectator announces, figures among the most important human concerns:

> There is no one Thing, on which the Happiness of Mankind so much depends; it is indeed the Fountain-Head of all the Comforts we can enjoy ourselves, and of those we transmit to our Posterity.—It is the Band which unites not only two Persons, but whole Families in one common inseparable Interest.—It is that which prevents those numberless Irregularities and Confusions, that would else overthrow all Order, and destroy Society. (Vol. 1, Bk. II)

If Haywood eschews public politics as subject, she reveals in such passages as this one a clear understanding of the relation between personal and public interest. Love is a feeling, she understands, and a dangerous one at that. Marriage is a social institution as well as a personal arrangement. Many of her stories concern women's choices in and before marriage. She warns against marrying too young, telling of a girl who insists on marrying a man whom her parents have warned her against, only to discover a genuine passion later for one who seduces her, impregnates her, and causes the destruction of her marriage and her life (Bk. I). The point of this story, Haywood makes clear, is less to denounce the young woman's wickedness than to criticize the parents who keep a girl from any knowledge of men and thus dispose her to believe herself in love with the first man who presents himself. The Female Spectator praises the generosity of parents who allow daughters their own informed choices, telling of a model family in which the children all concern themselves with their siblings' welfare and the father wishes only his daughter's happiness. She tells a rather unexpected tale about a young man, trapped in an unwanted match because his inheritance depends on it, who steadfastly refuses to consummate his marriage although his beautiful, virtuous, compliant wife gives every evidence of adoring him (Bk. II). Happiness depends on mutuality of inclination, the story implies.

The accumulation of such stories conveys a complicated and comprehensive view of marriage as lure, trap, financial arrangement, venue for display, and locus of happiness. As even my brief summaries should suggest, the narratives display considerable intricacy and inventiveness. Often they seem to miniaturize entire novels, adumbrating elaborate plots and sketching multiple possibilities of character. One might readily surmise that the stories alone would suffice to engage and hold a considerable audience. Equally compelling, though, are the straightforward disquisitions on moral, social, or psychological issues in which Haywood conveys the full intensity of her concern for the situation of women as possessors of individual consciousness and as members of society. Some of the issues she investigates hold potential interest for men as well as women: the moral as well as aesthetic implications of "taste," for instance, or the dangers of prejudice—a subject treated by others in the eighteenth century, and most memorably by Jane Austen. Some of Haywood's subjects, such as the evils of stepmothers, implicate women in particular. The single matter that appears to involve Haywood most profoundly—she recurs to it repeatedly, although the present selection contains only two extended examples—is female education. This woman who preaches compliance to husbands, the social necessity of women's subordination, also believes passionately in the life of the mind. Women should learn about the natural sciences, she argues. Such learning helps them to appreciate divine power and their ordained place in the world; there is nothing subversive about it. But Haywood makes an enthusiastic allusion to "Donna Lawra," who not only argues with but actually confutes the learned men of Italy (Bk. X). (She is probably referring to Laura Bassi, an eighteenth-century Italian scientist who was professor of anatomy at the University of

Bologna.) The reference clearly conveys Haywood's sense of knowledge as personal power, a perception that underlies all her discussions of female education. She claims that knowledge makes women better wives and mothers, but she also implies that it gives them more sense of control over themselves and their environments.

Haywood's argument for a woman's right to know may lure twentieth-century readers into believing her a protofeminist. Indeed, her precise awareness of the limits on female power and scope suggest the kind of consciousness now associated with feminism. But all of Haywood's explicit recommendations to women urge them to work within the existing system, which she takes for granted almost as though it constituted part of the natural order. The pages of the *Female Spectator* reveal that she wants the greatest possible autonomy for individual women, the greatest possible personal fulfillment. But she is severely realistic in her assessment of likelihoods and possibilities. She understands that female freedom exists within externally established limits.

As James Hodges has pointed out, the insistent practicality of Haywood's approach accounts for much of her periodical's method and tone. Comparing the *Female Spectator* with the courtesy books that preceded it, Hodges writes that Haywood's journal "offers advice which is entirely practical in character and is based not upon any academic theorizing about life but upon a real appreciation of its actual difficulties and problems."[1] I agree with Hodges's judgment but would add that Haywood's heavy reliance on narrative lends her advice a kind of concreteness and specificity largely missing in the conduct books. When, for instance, Haywood tells the story of a young woman, Barsina, jilted by a fortune-seeking cad, she dwells on the details of Barsina's revenge, which involves making her erstwhile lover believe that he has drunk poison (Bk. XIII). Terrified of death, he endures drastic medical treatment—emetics and purges to induce evacuation— that actually bring him close to death. Recovering in rural seclusion,

---

1. James Hodges, "The Female Spectator, a Courtesy Periodical," *Studies in the Early English Periodical,* ed. Richmond P. Bond (Chapel Hill: Univ. of North Carolina Press, 1957), 154.

he chances upon Barsina and believes her a ghost. The terror of this
apparition completes his chastisement. As for Barsina, she goes on to
live, loverless, in utter serenity.

The story is fanciful, but its message is not. Haywood vividly conveys her conviction that women can always find the resources to assert
their dignity and self-sufficiency, even when custom and convention
declare them humiliated and helpless. If the cards are stacked against
them, they can find their own stacked decks to play with.

Twentieth-century women (and, with different parameters,
twentieth-century men) also exist within social constrictions. A sur-
prising aspect of the *Female Spectator* is the degree to which it conveys
insights relevant beyond its own time and place. In obvious respects
it belongs utterly to mid-eighteenth-century England. The profound
assumed connection between money and marriage; the repeatedly revealed power of fathers; the concern about "luxury," about tea drinking, about gambling; the reminiscences of the "South Sea Bubble";
the allusions to swords and hoops and to the power of the British navy
and of British merchant ships—all the magazine's assumptions, allusions, and attitudes help locate a rich cultural context. Haywood writes
within a patriarchal and capitalist society. The South Sea Bubble epit-
omizes its values. In 1721 the London stock market crashed, with dis-
astrous financial results for many who had overinvested in hope of a
quick fortune. The South Sea Company, a trading firm with invest-
ments in the Far East, had assumed the national debt, with promises
that its financial resources and connections would ensure endless profit.
Men and women from all social classes rushed to invest, possessed by
their conviction that money meant power, and acquiring it implied
social success. The scheme had been ingenious, apparently rescuing the
British government (which owed a hundred million pounds to private
creditors) and making fortunes possible for anyone willing to take a
slight risk. The collapse of the South Sea Company and of the market
it supported not only endangered livelihoods; it also revealed the greed
on which much of the nation's life was predicated. Greed, free enter-
prise, capitalism, belief in the possibility of something for nothing—
it may all sound familiar to late-twentieth-century Americans.

Haywood understood and used knowledge about such matters, connecting the fashionable female pastime of social gambling with the national financial debacle. She also (perhaps more importantly) revealed her understanding of the intricate ways in which women in particular can serve or undermine their own self-interest and of the difficulty of ascertaining exactly where self-interest leads in any particular case. Such understanding belongs to the novelist's awareness of how social and personal concerns intersect and complicate one another. It is a kind of understanding that extends far beyond the eighteenth century.

The present selections comprise perhaps a third of the whole. Chosen to indicate the range of Haywood's concerns and methods, they come from many parts of the collected edition. No single book of the twenty-four composing Haywood's original collection is printed in its entirety, but this volume contains substantial excerpts from most of the books. It is designed to allow either haphazard or sequential reading. One can browse among the essays and stories, pausing on what strikes the fancy, or one can read straight through from beginning to end. Either way, Haywood offers—as she would have hoped—much in the way both of entertainment and enlightenment.

Selected Bibliography

Adburgham, Alison. *Women in Print: Writing Women and Women's Magazines from the Restoration to the Accession of Victoria.* London: Allen and Unwin, 1972.

Ballaster, Ros, Margaret Beetham, Elizabeth Frazer, and Sandra Hebron. *Women's Worlds: Ideology, Femininity and the Woman's Magazine.* London: Macmillan, 1991.

Blouch, Christine. "Eliza Haywood and the Romance of Obscurity." *Studies in English Literature* 31 (1991): 535–52.

Browne, Alice. *The Eighteenth Century Feminist Mind.* Brighton: Harvester, 1987.

Firmager, Gabrielle M. "Eliza Haywood: Some Further Light on her Background?" *Notes and Queries* 236, no. 2 (1991): 181–83.

Hodges, James. "The *Female Spectator*, a Courtesy Periodical." *Studies in the Early English Periodical.* Ed. Richmond P. Bond. Chapel Hill: Univ. of North Carolina Press, 1957. 151–82.

Koon, Helene. "Eliza Haywood and the *Female Spectator*." *Huntington Library Quarterly* 42 (1978): 43–55.

Schofield, Mary Anne. *Eliza Haywood.* Boston: Twayne, 1985.

Shevelow, Kathryn. "Re-Writing the Moral Essay: Eliza Haywood's *Female Spectator*." *Reader: Essays in Reader-Oriented Theory, Criticism, and Pedagogy* 13 (1950): 19–28.

Todd, Janet. *The Sign of Angellica: Women, Writing and Fiction, 1660–1800.* London: Virago, 1989.

Whicher, George Frisbie. *The Life and Romances of Mrs. Eliza Haywood.* New York: Columbia Univ. Press, 1915.

Note on the Text

The present edition is based on the Huntington Library copy of the first collected edition of the *Female Spectator* (1745). Eighteenth-century practices of paragraphing, punctuation, spelling, and capitalization have been retained, with a few exceptions: principally, the substitution of quotation marks for italics to identify quotations, the normalization of long *s,* and the elimination of small caps at the beginning of paragraphs. Indented poetic passages originally printed in an italic font have been printed here in a roman font; passages of indirect quotation, on the other hand, remain in italic. Multiple layers of emphasis, particularly in headings, have been reduced. The first line of poetic passages has not been indented; salutations and closings in letters printed within the text have been regularized. The basetext is remarkably free of mistakes. I have silently corrected the few obvious printers' errors: such matters as turned, transposed, or omitted letters. All notes are mine, with a single exception identified in brackets as Haywood's.

Acknowledgments

The arduous initial work on this text was performed by Julia Flanders and supported by the Women Writers Project. I am most grateful to the project and its workers, and especially to Carol Barash, Elizabeth H. Hageman, Erika Olbricht, and Susanne Woods for editorial help.

SELECTIONS FROM
The Female Spectator

TO

HER GRACE

THE

DUTCHESS

OF

L E E D S.[1]

May it please Your GRACE,

    As the chief View in Publishing these Monthly Essays is to rectify some Errors, which, small as they may seem at first, may, if indulged, grow up into greater, till they at last become Vices, and make all the Misfortunes of our Lives, it was necessary to put them under the Protection of a Lady, not only of an unblemish'd Conduct, but also of an exalted Virtue, whose Example may enforce the Precepts they contain, and is Herself a shining Pattern for others to copy after, of all those Perfections I endeavour to recommend.

---

1. **Dutchess of Leeds:** Mary (d. 1764), a direct descendant of the famous seventeenth-century Duke and Duchess of Marlborough, married to Thomas Osborne, Duke of Leeds, a fellow of the Royal Society and a distinguished political figure. Haywood dedicated each volume of the collected edition of the *Female Spectator* to a different member of the nobility—presumably for the possible financial advantage of their patronage.

It is not therefore, Madam, that You are descended from a *Marlborough*[1] or a *Godolphin,*[2] dear as those Patriot Names will ever be while any Sense of Liberty remains in *Britons;* nor on the Account of the high Rank You hold in the World, nor for those Charms with which Nature has so profusely adorn'd Your Person; but for those innate Graces which no Ancestry can give, no Titles can embellish, nor no Beauty attone for the Want of, that Your G RACE has an undisputed Right to this Offering, as the Point aim'd at by the Work itself gives it in some measure a Claim to Your Acceptance.

That Promise which the first Years of Life gave of a glorious Maturity, we have seen compleated long before Your G RACE arrived at an Age, which in others is requisite to ripen *Wit* into *Wisdom,* and concile[3] the sparkling *Ideas* of the *one* with the correcting *Judgment* of the *other.*—We beheld with Admiration, how *Reason* outstrip'd *Nature* even in the most minute Circumstances and Actions; but the Crown of all, was the happy Choice of a Partner in that State which is the chief End of our Beings.—There shone Your Penetration, when among so many Admirers, You singled out Him who alone was worthy of You.—One, who *Great* as he is, is yet more *Good* than *Great,* and who has given such Instances how much it is in the Power of Virtue to ennoble Nobility, as all must admire, tho' few I fear will imitate.

Marriage, too long the Jest of Fools, and prostituted to the most base and sordid Aims, to You, Illustrious Pair! owes its recovered Fame, and proves its Institution is indeed divine!

But this is no more than what every one is full of; and in entreating your G RACE' S Protection to the following Sheets[4] I can only boast

---

1. **Marlborough:** John Churchill, first Duke of Marlborough (1650–1722), famous general and diplomat.

2. **Godolphin:** Sidney Godolphin, first Earl of Godolphin (1645–1712), statesman who served with distinction as Lord High Treasurer.

3. **concile:** reconcile.

4. **Sheets:** of paper. Although this dedication belonged to the collected edition, the journal had originally appeared in issues consisting of a single large page.

of being one among the Millions who pray that Length of Days and uninterrupted Health may continue that Happiness to which nothing can be added, and that

I am,
With the most profound Duty and Submission,
May it please your GRACE,
Your GRACE'S,
Most Humble,
Most Obedient, and most
Faithfully Devoted Servant,
The FEMALE SPECTATOR.

THE

Female Spectator.

FROM BOOK I.

It is very much, by the Choice we make of Subjects for our Entertainment, that the refined Taste distinguishes itself from the vulgar
and more gross: Reading is universally allowed to be one of the most
improving, as well as agreeable Amusements; but then to render it so,
one should, among the Number of Books which are perpetually issuing
from the Press, endeavour to single out such as promise to be most
conducive to those Ends. In order to be as little deceived as possible,
I, for my own part, love to get as well acquainted as I can with an
Author, before I run the risque of losing my Time in perusing his
Work; and as I doubt not but most People are of this way of thinking,
I shall, in imitation of my learned Brother of ever precious Memory,[1]
give some Account of what I am, and those concerned with me in this
Undertaking; and likewise of the chief Intent of the *Lucubrations*[2]

---

1. **my learned Brother . . . Memory:** the Spectator, from the journal of that title edited in
1711 and 1712 by Joseph Addison (1672–1719) and Richard Steele (1672–1729). The phrase
"of ever precious Memory" is conventionally used with reference to the dead; it may refer
to the fact that Addison and Steele are dead or to the presumed demise of the fictitious
Spectator.

2. **Lucubrations:** intensive studies.

hereafter communicated, that the Reader, on casting his Eye over the four or five first Pages, may judge how far the Book may, or may not be qualified to entertain him; and either accept, or throw it aside as he thinks proper: And here I promise, that in the Pictures I shall give of myself and Associates, I will draw no flattering Lines, assume no Perfection that we are not in reality possessed of, nor attempt to shadow over any Defect with an artificial Gloss.

As a Proof of my Sincerity, I shall, in the first place, assure him, that for my own Part I never was a Beauty, and am now very far from being young; (a Confession he will find few of my Sex ready to make:) I shall also acknowledge, that I have run through as many Scenes of Vanity and Folly as the greatest Coquet[1] of them all.—Dress, Equipage, and Flattery, were the Idols of my Heart.—I should have thought that Day lost which did not present me with some new Opportunity of shewing myself.—My Life, for some Years, was a continued Round of what I then called Pleasure, and my whole Time engrossed by a Hurry of promiscuous Diversions.—But whatever Inconveniences such a manner of Conduct has brought upon myself, I have this Consolation, to think that the Public may reap some Benefit from it:—The Company I kept was not, indeed, always so well chosen as it ought to have been, for the sake of my own Interest or Reputation; but then it was general, and by Consequence furnished me, not only with the Knowledge of many Occurrences, which otherwise I had been ignorant of, but also enabled me, when the too great Vivacity of my Nature became tempered with Reflection, to see into the secret Springs which gave rise to the Actions I had either heard, or been Witness of,—to judge of the various Passions of the human Mind, and distinguish those imperceptible Degrees by which they become Masters of the Heart, and attain the Dominion over Reason.—A thousand odd Adventures, which at the Time they happened made slight Impression on me, and seemed to dwell no longer on my Mind than the Wonder they occasioned, now rise fresh to my Remembrance, with this Advantage, that the Mystery I then, for want of Attention,

---

1. **Coquet:** habitual flirt.

imagined they contained, is entirely vanished, and I find it easy to account for the Cause by the Consequence.

With this Experience, added to a Genius[1] tolerably extensive, and an Education more liberal than is ordinarily allowed to Persons of my Sex, I flattered myself that it might be in my Power to be in some measure both useful and entertaining to the Public; and this Thought was so soothing to those Remains of Vanity, not yet wholly extinguished in me, that I resolved to pursue it, and immediately began to consider by what Method I should be most likely to succeed: To confine myself to any one Subject, I knew, could please but one kind of Taste, and my Ambition was to be as universally read as possible: From my Observations of human Nature, I found that Curiosity had, more or less, a Share in every Breast; and my Business, therefore, was to hit this reigning Humour in such a manner, as that the Gratification it should receive from being made acquainted with other People's Affairs, should at the same time teach every one to regulate their own.

Having agreed within myself on this important Point, I commenced Author, by setting down many Things, which, being pleasing to myself, I imagined would be so to others; but on examining them the next Day, I found an infinite Deficiency both in Matter and Stile, and that there was an absolute Necessity for me to call in to my Assistance such of my Acquaintance as were qualified for that Purpose.—The *first* that occured to me, I shall distinguish by the Name of *Mira,* a Lady descended from a Family to which Wit seems hereditary, married to a Gentleman every way worthy of so excellent a Wife, and with whom she lives in so perfect a Harmony, that having nothing to ruffle the Composure of her Soul, or disturb those sparkling Ideas she received from Nature and Education, left me no room to doubt if what she favoured me with would be acceptable to the Public.—The *next* is a Widow of Quality,[2] who not having buried her Vivacity in the Tomb of her Lord, continues to make one in all the modish Diversions of the Times, so far, I mean, as she finds them consistent with Innocence and Honour; and as she is far from having the least Austerity in her

---

1. **Genius:** natural aptitude (not extraordinary gifts).

2. **Quality:** high rank or position in society.

Behaviour, nor is rigid to the Failings she is wholly free from herself, those of her Acquaintance, who had been less circumspect, scruple not to make her the Confidante of Secrets they conceal from all the World beside.—The *third* is the Daughter of a wealthy Merchant, charming as an Angel, but endued with so many Accomplishments, that to those who know her truly, her Beauty is the least distinguished Part of her.—This fine young Creature I shall call *Euphrosine,*[1] since she has all the Chearfulness and Sweetness ascribed to that Goddess.

These *three* approved my Design, assured me of all the Help they could afford, and soon gave a Proof of it in bringing their several Essays; but as the Reader, provided the Entertainment be agreeable, will not be interested from which Quarter it comes, whatever Productions I shall be favoured with from these Ladies, or any others I may hereafter correspond with, will be exhibited under the general Title of *The Female Spectator;* and how many Contributors soever there may happen to be to the Work, they are to be considered only as several Members of one Body, of which I am the Mouth.

It is also highly proper I should acquaint the Town, that to secure an eternal Fund of Intelligence,[2] Spies are placed not only in all the Places of Resort in and about this great Metropolis, but at *Bath, Tunbridge,* and the *Spaw,*[3] and Means found out to extend my Speculations even as far as *France, Rome, Germany,* and other foreign Parts, so that nothing curious or worthy of Remark can escape me; and this I look upon to be a more effectual way of penetrating into the Mysteries of the Alcove, the Cabinet, or Field,[4] than if I had the Power of Invisibility, or could with a Wish transport myself wherever I pleased, since with the Aid of those supernatural Gifts, I could still be in no more than one Place at a Time; whereas now, by tumbling over a few Papers from my Emissaries, I have all the Secrets of *Europe,* at least such of them as are proper for my Purpose, laid open at one View.

---

1. **Euphrosine:** Euphrosyne, one of the three Graces.

2. **Intelligence:** information.

3. **Bath . . . Spaw:** fashionable resorts where visitors "took the waters," bathing in natural warm springs.

4. **Alcove . . . Field:** the bedroom, boudoir, or hunting field.

I would, by no means, however, have what I say be construed into a Design of gratifying a vicious Propensity of propagating Scandal:— Whoever sits down to read me with this View, will find themselves mistaken; for tho' I shall bring real Facts on the Stage, I shall conceal the Actors Names under such as will be conformable to their Characters; my Intention being only to expose the Vice, not the Person.— Nor shall I confine myself to modern Transactions:—Whenever I find any Example among the Antients which may serve to illustrate the Topic I shall happen to be upon, I shall make no scruple to insert it.—An Instance of shining Virtue in any Age, can never be too often proposed as a Pattern, nor the Fatality of Misconduct too much impressed on the Minds of our Youth of both Sexes; and as the sole Aim of the following Pages is to reform the Faulty, and give an innocent Amusement to those who are not so, all possible Care will be taken to avoid every thing that might serve as Food for the Venom of Malice and Ill-nature. Whoever, therefore, shall pretend to fix on any particular Person the Blame of Actions they may happen to find recorded here, or make what they call a Key to these Lucubrations, must expect to see themselves treated in the next Publication with all the Severity so unfair a Proceeding merits.

And now having said as much as I think needful of this Undertaking, I shall, without being either too greatly confident, or too anxious for the Success, submit it to the Publick Censure.

> Of all the Passions giv'n us from Above,
> The noblest, softest, and the best is Love,[1]

Says a justly celebrated Poet; and I readily agree that Love in itself, when under the Direction of Reason, harmonizes the Soul, and gives it a gentle, generous Turn; but I can by no means approve of such Definitions of that Passion as we generally find in Romances, Novels, and Plays: In most of those Writings, the Authors seem to lay out all their Art in rendering that Character most interesting, which most sets

---

1. **Of all . . . Love:** quotation unidentified.

at Defiance all the Obligations, by the strict Observance of which Love can alone become a Virtue.—They dress their *Cupid* up in Roses, call him the God of soft Desires, and ever-springing Joys, yet at the same time give him the vindictive Fury, and the Rage of *Mars*.[1]—Shew him impatient of Controul, and trampling over all the Ties of Duty, Friendship, or natural Affection, yet make the Motive sanctify the Crime.—How fatal, how pernicious to a young and unexperienced Mind must be such Maxims, especially when dressed up in all the Pomp of Words! The Beauty of the Expression steals upon the Senses, and every Mischief, every Woe that Love occasions, appears a Charm.—Those who feel the Passion are so far from endeavouring to repel its Force, or being ashamed of their Attachment, however opposite to Reason, that they indulge and take a Pride in turning into Ridicule the Remonstrances of their more discerning Friends. But what is yet more preposterous, and more evidently shews the ill Effects of writing in this manner is, that we often see Girls too young, either to be addressed to on the Score of Love, or even to know what is meant by the Passion, affect the Languishment they read of,—roll their Eyes, sigh, fold their Arms, neglect every useful Learning, and attend to nothing but acquiring the Reputation of being enough a Woman to know all the Pains and Delicacies of Love.

Miss *Tenderilla* is one of those I have described: She was the other Day invited to a Concert, and as soon as the Music began to strike up, cried out in a kind of dying Tone, yet loud enough to be heard by a great Part of the Assembly,

If Music be the Food of Love, play on.[2]

A young Lady happened to be near her, who is supposed to be very near entering into the Marriage-State, but contents herself with discovering[3] what Sentiments she is possessed of in favour of her intended

---

1. **Mars:** god of war in Roman mythology.

2. **If Music . . . play on:** the first line of Shakespeare's *Twelfth Night*.

3. **discovering:** revealing.

Bridegroom only to those interested in them.—She blushed extremely at the Extravagance of her Companion, and the more so, as she found the Eyes of every one turned upon her, and by their Smiles and Whispers to each other, shewed that they imagined *Miss* had burst into this Exclamation merely on her Account. A smart[1] Gentleman, on the next Bench to them, took this Opportunity of rallying[2] her very wittily, as he thought, on the Discovery the young Confidante had made; and the poor Lady was in the utmost Confusion, 'till she who had occasioned it being vexed to find what she had said so much mistaken,[3] and that no Notice was taken of herself, behaved in such a manner as left no room to doubt which of them was the proper Object for Ridicule.

How easy were it now for a designing Fortune-Hunter to make a Prey of this Bib-and-Apron Heroine![4]—The less qualified he was to render her Choice of him approved, and the more averse her Friends[5] appeared to such a Match, the more would she glory in a noble Obstinacy of contemning[6] their Advice, and sacrificing her Person and Fortune to an imaginary Passion for him; and one has no need of being a very great Prophet to foretel, that if she is not speedily removed from those who at present have the Care of her, and some other Methods taken than such as hitherto have been made use of, to give her a more rational way of thinking, that Wealth her frugal Parents hoarded up, in order to purchase for her a lasting Happiness,[7] will only prove the Bait for her Destruction.

I am sorry to observe, that of late Years this Humour has been strangely prevalent among our young Ladies, some of whom are scarce entered into their Teens before they grow impatient for Admiration,

---

1. **smart:** clever, witty.

2. **rallying:** teasing.

3. **mistaken:** misunderstood.

4. **Bib-and-Apron Heroine:** child heroine (a bib and apron composed part of the dress of a very young child).

5. **Friends:** relatives.

6. **contemning:** despising, disdaining.

7. **Wealth . . . Happiness:** money her parents have saved to provide a lavish dowry that will make their daughter attractive to rich suitors.

and to be distinguished in Love-Songs and Verses, expect to have a great Bustle made about them, and he that first attempts to perswade them he is a Lover, bids very fair for carrying his Point.[1]—The Eagerness of their Wishes to be addressed, gives Charms to the Address itself, which otherwise it would not have; and hence it follows, that when a young Creature has suffered herself to fall a Victim to the Artifices of her pretended Lover, and her own giddy Whim, and is afterwards convinced of her Error, she looks back with no less Wonder than Shame on her past Conduct, detests the Object of her former imaginary Passion, and wishes nothing more than to be eternally rid of the Presence of him she once with so much Eagerness pursued.

It is not, therefore, from that Inconstancy of Nature which the Men charge upon our Sex, but from that romantic Vein which makes us sometimes imagine ourselves Lovers before we are so, that we frequently run such Lengths to shake off a Yoke we have so precipitately put on.—When once we truly love, we rarely change: We bear the Frowns of Fortune with Fortitude and Patience:—We repent not of the Choice we have made, whatever we suffered by it; and nothing but a long continued Series of Slights and ill Usage from the Object of our Affection can render him less dear.

To be well convinced of the Sincerity of the Man they are about to marry, is a Maxim, with great Justice, always recommended to a young Lady; but I say it is no less material for her future Happiness, as well as that of her intended Partner, that she should be well assured of her own Heart, and examine, with the utmost Care, whether it be real Tenderness, or a bare Liking she at present feels for him; and as this is not to be done all at once, I cannot approve of hasty Marriages, or before Persons are of sufficient Years to be supposed capable of knowing their own Minds.

Could fourteen have the Power of judging of itself, or for itself, who that knew the beautiful *Martesia* at that Age, but would have depended on her Conduct!—*Martesia,* descended of the most illustrious Race, possessed of all that Dignity of Sentiment befitting her high Birth, endued by Nature with a surprizing Wit, Judgment, and Pen-

---

1. **bids . . . Point:** is very likely to win what he wants.

etration, and improved by every Aid of Education.—*Martesia,* the Wonder and Delight of all who saw or heard her, gave the admiring World the greatest Expectations that she would one Day be no less celebrated for all those Virtues which render amiable the conjugal State,[1] than she at that Time was for every other Perfection that do Honour to the Sex.

Yet how, alas, did all these charming Hopes vanish into Air! Many noble Youths, her Equals in Birth and Fortune, watched her Increase of Years for declaring a Passion, which they feared as yet would be rejected by those who had the Disposal of her; but what their Respect and Timidity forbad them to attempt, a more daring and unsuspected Rival ventured at, and succeeded in.—Her unexperienced Heart approved his Person, and was pleased with the Protestations he made her of it.—In fine,[2] the Novelty of being addressed in that manner, gave a double Grace to all he said, and she never thought herself so happy as in his Conversation. His frequent Visits at length were taken notice of; he was denied the Privilege of seeing her, and she was no longer permitted to go out without being accompanied by some Person who was to be a Spy upon her Actions.—She had a great Spirit, impatient of Controul, and this Restraint served only to heighten the Inclination she before had to favour him:—She indulged the most romantic Ideas of his Merit and his Love:—Her own flowing Fancy invented a thousand melancholly and tender Soliloquies,[3] and set them down as made by him in this Separation: It is not, indeed, to be doubted, but that he was very much mortified at the Impediment he found in the Prosecution of his Courtship; but whether he took this Method of disburthening his Affliction, neither she nor any body else could be assured. It cannot, however, be denied, but that he pursued Means much more efficacious for the Attainment of his Wishes. By Bribes, Promises, and Entreaties, he prevailed on a Person who came frequently to the House to convey his Letters to her, and bring back her Answers.—This Correspondence was, perhaps, of greater Service to him, than had

---

1. **conjugal State:** state of marriage.

2. **In fine:** in short.

3. **Soliloquies:** speeches made to oneself, the word possibly implying some theatricality.

the Freedom of their Interviews not been prevented:—She consented to be his, and to make good her Word, ventured her Life, by descending from a two Pair of Stairs Window,[1] by the Help of Quilt, Blankets, and other Things fastened to it, at the Dead of Night.— His Coach and Six waited to receive her at the End of the Street, and conveyed her to his Country Seat, which reaching soon after Break of Day, his Chaplain made them too fast[2] for any Authority to separate.

As he was of an antient honourable Family, and his Estate very considerable, her Friends in a short time were reconciled to what was now irremedible, and they were looked upon as an extreme happy Pair.—But soon, too soon the fleeting Pleasures fled, and in their room Anguish and Bitterness of Heart succeeded.

Martesia, in a Visit she made to a Lady of her intimate Acquaintance, unfortunately happened to meet the young *Clitander;* he was just returned from his Travels, had a handsome Person, an Infinity of Gaiety, and a certain Something in his Air and Deportment which had been destructive to the Peace and Reputation of many of our Sex.—He was naturally of an amorous Disposition, and being so, felt all the Force of Charms, which had some Effect even on the most Cold and Temperate.—Emboldened by former Successes, the Knowledge *Martesia* was another's, did not hinder him from declaring to her the Passion she had inspired him with.—She found a secret Satisfaction in hearing him, which she was yet too young to consider the Dangers of, and therefore endeavoured not to suppress 'till it became too powerful for her to have done so, even had she attempted it with all her Might; but the Truth is, she now experienced in *reality* a Flame she had but *imagined* herself possessed of for him who was now her Husband, and was too much averse to the giving herself Pain to combat with an Inclination which seemed to her fraught only with Delights.

The House where their Acquaintance first began, was now the Scene of their future Meetings:—The Mistress of it was too great a Friend

---

1. **two Pair of Stairs Window:** third-floor window.

2. **fast:** firmly knit (i.e., married).

to Gallantry[1] herself to be any Interruption to the Happiness they enjoyed in entertaining each other without Witnesses.—How weak is Virtue when Love and Opportunity combine!—Tho' no Woman could have more refined and delicate Notions than *Martesia,* yet all were ineffectual against the Sollicitations of her adored *Clitander.*— One fatal Moment destroyed at once all her own exalted Ideas of Honour and Reputation, and the Principles early instilled into her Mind by her virtuous Preceptors.[2]

The Consequence of this Amour was a total Neglect of Husband, House, and Family.—Herself abandoned, all other Duties were so too.—So manifest a Change was visible to all that knew her, but most to her Husband, as most interested in it.—He truly loved, and had believed himself truly beloved by her.—Loth he was to think his Misfortune real, and endeavoured to find some other Motive for the Aversion she now expressed for staying at Home, or going to any of those Places where they had been accustomed to visit together; but she either knew not how to dissemble, or took so little Pains to do it, that he was, in spite of himself, convinced all that Affection she so lately had professed, and given him Testimonies of, was now no more.—He examined all his Actions, and could find nothing in any of them that could give occasion for so sad a Reverse.—He complained to her one Day, in the tenderest Terms, of the small Portion she had of late allowed him of her Conversation:—Entreated, that if by any Inadvertency he had offended her, she would acquaint him with his Fault, which he assured her he would take care never to repeat.—Asked if there was any thing in her Settlement or Jointure[3] she could wish to have altered, and assured her she need but let him know her Commands to be instantly obeyed,

To all this she replied with the most stabbing Indifference.—That she knew not what he meant.—That as she had accused him with nothing, he had no Reason to think she was dissatisfied.—But that

---

1. **Gallantry:** amorous intrigue.

2. **Preceptors:** teachers.

3. **Settlement or Jointure:** financial provisions made for a woman at the time of her marriage.

People could not be always in the same Humour, and desired he would not give himself nor her the Trouble of making any farther Interrogatories.[1]

He must have been as insensible, as he is known to be the contrary, had such a Behaviour not opened his Eyes; he no longer doubted of his Fate, and resolving, if possible, to find out the Author of it, he caused her Chair[2] to be watched wherever she went, and took such effectual Methods, as soon informed him of the Truth.

In his first Emotions of his Rage he was for sending a Challenge to this Destroyer of his Happiness; but in his cooler Moments he rejected that Design as too injurious to the Reputation of *Martesia,* who was still dear to him, and whom he flattered himself with being able one Day to reclaim.

It is certain he put in Practice every tender Stratagem that Love and Wit could furnish him with for that Purpose; but she appearing so far from being moved at any thing he either said or did, that, on the contrary, her Behaviour was every Day more cold; he at last began to expostulate with her, gave some Hints that her late[3] Conduct was not unknown to him, and that tho' he was willing to forgive what was past, yet as a Husband, it was not consistent with his Character to bear any future Insults of that nature. This put her beyond all Patience.—She reproached him in the bitterest Terms for daring to harbour the least Suspicion of her Virtue, and censuring her innocent Amusements as Crimes; and perhaps was glad of this Opportunity of testifying her Remorse for having ever listened to his Vows, and cursing before his Face the Hour that joined their Hands.

They now lived so ill a Life together, that not having sufficient Proofs for a Divorce,[4] he parted Beds, and tho' they continued in one House, behaved to each other as Strangers: never eat[5] at the same Table

---

1. **Interrogatories:** interrogations.

2. **Chair:** sedan chair; a covered vehicle for one carried on poles by two bearers.

3. **late:** recent.

4. **Proofs for a Divorce:** adultery was the only ground for divorce; the husband lacks the kind of hard evidence he would need to substantiate an accusation of adultery.

5. **eat:** an eighteenth-century form used for the past as well as the present tense.

but when Company was there, and then only to avoid the Questions that would naturally have been asked had it been otherwise; neither of them being desirous the World should know any thing of their Disagreement.

But while they continued to treat each other in a manner so little conformable to their first Hopes, or their Vows pledged at the Holy Altar, *Martesia* became pregnant: This gave the first Alarm to that Indolence of Nature she hitherto had testified; her Husband would now have it in his Power to sue out a Divorce; and tho' she would have rejoiced to have been separated from him on any other Terms, yet she could not support the Thoughts of being totally deprived of all Reputation in the World.—She was not ignorant of the Censures she incurr'd, but had Pride and Spirit enough to enable her to despise whatever was said of her, while it was not backed by Proof; but the glaring one she was now about to give struck Shame and Confusion to her Soul.—She left no Means untried to procure an Abortion; but failing in that, she had no other Resource[1] than to that Friend who was the sole Confidante of her unhappy Passion, who comforted her as well as she could, and assured her, that when the Hour approached she need have no more to do than to come directly to her House, where every thing should be prepared for the Reception of a Woman in her Condition.

To conceal the Alteration in her Shape, she pretended Indisposition, saw little Company, and wore only loose Gowns.—At length the so much dreaded Moment came upon her at the dead of Night; and in the midst of all that Rack of Nature, made yet more horrible by the Agonies of her Mind, she rose, rung for her Woman,[2] and telling her she had a frightful Dream concerning that Lady, whom she knew she had the greatest Value for of any Person upon Earth, ordered her to get a Chair, for she could not be easy unless she went and saw her herself. The Woman was strangely surprized, but her Lady was always absolute in her Commands.—A Chair was brought, and without any other Company or Attendance than her own distracted Thoughts, she

---

1. **Resource:** probably a mistake for "Recourse."
2. **Woman:** lady's maid.

was conveyed to the only Asylum where she thought her Shame might find a Shelter.

A midwife being prepared before, she was safely delivered of a Daughter, who expired almost as soon as born; and to prevent as much as possible all Suspicion of the Truth, she made herself be carried Home the next Morning, where she went to Bed, and lay several Days under Pretence of having sprained her Ancle.

But not all the Precautions she had taken were effectual enough to prevent some People from guessing and whispering what had happened.—Those whose Nearness in Blood gave them a Privilege of speaking their Minds, spared not to tell her all that was said of her; and those who dared not take that Liberty, shewed by their distant Looks and reserved Behaviour, whenever she came in Presence, how little they approved her Conduct.—She was too discerning not to see into their Thoughts, nor was her innate Pride of any Service to keep up her Spirits on this Occasion.—To add to her Discontents, *Clitander* grew every Day more cool in his Respects, and she soon after learned he was on the Point of Marriage with one far inferior to herself in every Charm both of Mind and Person.—In short, finding herself deserted by her Relations, and the greatest Part of her Acquaintance, without Love, without Respect, and reduced to the Pity of those, who, perhaps, had nothing but a greater Share of Circumspection to boast of, she took a Resolution to quit *England* for ever, and having settled her Affairs with her Husband, who by this Time had entered into other Amusements, and, it is probable, was very well satisfied to be eased of the Constraint her Presence gave him, readily agreed to remit her the Sum agreed between them, to be paid yearly to whatever Part of the World she chose to reside in, she then took leave of a Country of which she had been the Idol, and which now seemed to her as too unjust in not being blind to what she desired should be concealed.

Behold her now in a voluntary Banishment from Friends and Country, and roaming round the World in fruitless Search of that Tranquillity she could not have failed enjoying at Home in the Bosom of a Consort[1] equally beloved as loving.—Unhappy charming Lady, born

---

1. **Consort:** husband.

and endued with every Quality to attract universal Love and Admiration, yet by one inadvertent Step undone and lost to every thing the World holds dear, and only more conspicuously wretched by having been conspicuously amiable.

But methinks it would be hard to charge the Blame of indiscreet Marriages on the young Ladies themselves:—Parents are sometimes, by an over Caution, guilty of forcing them into Things, which otherwise would be far distant from their Thoughts. I am very certain it is not because the *Italian, Spanish,* or *Portuguese* Women are so much warmer in their Constitutions than those of other Nations, but because they are so cruelly debarred from all Conversation with the Men, that makes them so readily accept the first Offer that presents itself.— Where Opportunities are scarce, they are glad to speak their Minds at once, and fear to *deny* lest it should not be in their Power afterward to *grant.* Even in *Turkey*, where our Travellers boast of having had such Success among the Women, I have known several that were married to *English* Gentlemen, and permitted to live after the Custom of our Country, who have made very excellent Wives.—In *France,* the People are, questionless, the gayest and most alert in the World, and allow the greatest Liberties to their Women; yet to hear of a clandestine Marriage among them is a kind of Prodigy,[1] and tho' no Place affords Scenes of Gallantry equal to it in any Degree of Proportion, yet I believe there is none where fewer false Steps are made, or Husbands have less Reason to complain of the want of Chastity in their Wives. Nature in all Ages is abhorrent of Restraint, but in Youth especially, as more headstrong and impetuous, it will hazard every thing to break through Laws it had no Hand in making. It therefore betrays a want[2] of Policy, as well as an unjust Austerity, to seclude a young Lady, and shut her up from all Intercourse[3] with the Men, for fear she should find one among them who might happen to please her too well.—Chance may in a Moment destroy all that the utmost Care can do; and I say a Woman is in far less Danger of losing her Heart, when every Day surrounded with a Variety of gay Objects,

---

1. **Prodigy:** amazing or marvelous thing.

2. **want:** lack.

3. **Intercourse:** social communication.

than when by some Accident she falls into the Conversation of a single one.—A Girl, who is continually hearing fine Things said to her, regards them but as Words of course;[1] they may be flattering to her Vanity for the present, but will leave no Impression behind them on their Mind: But she, who is a Stranger to the gallant Manner with which polite Persons treat our Sex, greedily swallows the first civil thing said to her, takes what perhaps is meant as a mere Compliment for a Declaration of Love, and replies to it in Terms which either expose her to the Designs of him who speaks, if he happens to have any in reality, or if he has not, to his Ridicule in all Company he comes into.

For this Reason the Country-bred Ladies, who are never suffered to come to Town for fear their Faces should be spoiled by the Small-Pox,[2] or their Reputations ruined by the Beaux,[3] become an easier Prey to the Artifices of Mankind, than those who have had an Education more at large: As they rarely stir beyond their Father's Pales,[4] except to Church, the Parson, if he be a forward Man, and has Courage to throw a Love Song, or Copy of Verses to Miss over the Wall, or slip it into her Hand in a Visit he pays the Family, has a rare Opportunity of making his Fortune; and it is well when it happens no worse; many a 'Squire's Daughter has clambered over Hedge and Stile,[5] to give a rampant Jump into the Arms of a young jolly Hay-maker or Ploughman.

Our *London* Ladies are indeed very rarely laid under such Restrictions; but whenever it happens to be the Case, as Nature is the same in all, the Consequence will be so too.—Would Miss *Eagaretta* have ever condescended to marry the greasy Footman that run before her Chair, had he not been the only Man her over-careful Father permitted her to speak to?—Or would *Armonia* have found any Charms in a

---

1. **of course:** merely conventional or customary.

2. **Small-Pox:** a common and disfiguring disease at this time; dependable inoculation was not introduced until late in the century.

3. **Beaux:** dandies, gallant young men.

4. **Pales:** enclosures.

5. **Stile:** an arrangement of steps allowing passage over a fence.

Mousetrap or *Leathern Apron*, had she been indulged the Conversation of a *White Staff?*[1]

*   *   *

FROM BOOK II

When first myself and Assistants set about this Undertaking, we agreed to lay down certain Rules to be observed among us, in order to preserve that Harmony, which it is necessary should exist in all Societies, whether composed of a great or small Number.—One of the most material of which is to devote two Evenings in every Week to the Business we have engaged in.—In the first of these Meetings we communicate to each other what Intelligence[2] we receive, and consider on what Topicks we shall proceed.—In the second, we lay our several Productions on the Table, which being read over, every one has the Liberty of excepting against, or censuring whatever she disapproves; nothing being to be exhibited to the Publick, without the joint Concurrence of all.—The Rendezvous is kept at my Lodgings, and I give strict Orders, that no Person whatever shall be admitted to interrupt our Consultations; but you may as well attempt to exclude the Lightning, as the Impertinence of some People.—I dare say, there are few of my Readers who have not, some Time or other in their Lives, been plagu'd with a buzzing, fluttering kind of Animal, whose Love, for the Time it lasts, is more troublesome, than the Hate of any other created Being that I know of.—I mean a Race of Mortals, who will tell you all their own Secrets in two Hours Acquaintance, and from thence imagine, they have a Right to expect you should be as communicative to them.—They will see one, whether one will or not; —there is no shutting one's self from them;—they burst in upon one at all Hours, and pursue one wherever one goes;—they come galloping to repeat every thing they see or hear of; and one must either be wholly

---

1. **White Staff:** the badge of a chief officer of the Crown.

2. **Intelligence:** news.

rude, or banish all Thoughts of one's own, however agreeable or necessary, to listen to the vociferous Trifle they are big[1] with;—and the
only Consolation one has, is the Certainty of getting rid of them the
next new Acquaintance they make.

It was lately[2] my Misfortune to be fasten'd upon by one of those
Tempo-Amyarians,[3] (if I may venture to call them so, without offending
the Criticks) and during the Zenith of her Fondness of me, had not
a Moment I could call my own.—She came one of those Evenings we
had set apart for the Entertainment of the Publick, and in spite of the
Charge I had given, forced her Passage through my Servants, and flew
directly to the Room where we were sitting.—As she enter'd without
Ceremony, so she made no Apology for the Abruptness, tho' she found
I had Company, and might easily have seen by my Countenance, how
little I was pleas'd with her Visit, if she had not been too tenacious of
a Welcome for the News she brought, which she told me, was of so
much Consequence, that she could not have slept all Night, without
making me Partaker of it.

As it was not from a Lady of her degree of Understanding, that I
expected any Intelligence fit for my Purpose, and was very much out
of Humour at her Presence, I return'd no Answer to the Compliment
she made me; but she seem'd to take no Notice of my Indolence in
this Point, and without waiting to see whether I should grow more
inquisitive or not, began immediately to unlade herself of the Fardle[4]
she had brought with her.

She inform'd us she had been at Court that Day, had seen the fine
Lady *Bloometta,* it being the first Time of her Appearance there since
her Marriage,—describ'd every Article of her Dress,—told us how
charming she look'd,—how all the young Peers envy'd the Happiness
of old *Pompilius,* yet at the same Time sneer'd at the unequal Match,
and seem'd to promise themselves some agreeable Consequences from

---

1. **big:** pregnant.

2. **lately:** recently.

3. **Tempo-Amyrians:** a coinage that may combine a Greek word suggesting obscurity and
confusion with a Latin one indicating speed: those who are quick at spreading disinforma-
tion. I owe this interpretation to Gordon Braden.

4. **unlade . . . Fardle:** unburden herself of the load.

it.—How some, as he led her to the Presence, cry'd out—"May and December"!¹—others, "Fire and Frost!"and a thousand such like petty Reflections, which the new-wedded Pair could not but expect, and any one might be assur'd would be made, without being an Ear-witness of.

After having said all she could on this Affair, she started up, and with a Promise, neither wish'd nor requested by me, of calling upon me early the next Morning, took her Leave with as little Ceremony as she had come in, and left us the Liberty of pursuing our own Discourse.

However, as Good springs sometimes out of Evil, this very Interruption occasion'd the Conversation to turn on a Subject, which never can be too much attended to, and the too great Neglect of which is the Source of almost all the Evils we either feel, or are witness of in private Life.

I believe I shall easily be understood to mean Marriage, since there is no one Thing, on which the Happiness of Mankind so much depends; it is indeed the Fountain-Head of all the Comforts we can enjoy ourselves, and of those we transmit to our Posterity.—It is the Band which unites not only two Persons, but whole Families in one common inseparable Interest.—It is that which prevents those numberless Irregularities and Confusions, that would else overthrow all Order, and destroy Society; but then not to pervert the Intention of so necessary and glorious an Institution, and rob it of every Blessing it is full of, lies only in ourselves.—No violated Vows, before pledg'd to another,—no clandestine Agreements made up by hasty and ungovern'd Passion,—no sordid Bargains, where Wealth, not Merit, is the chief Inducement,—no notorious Disparity of Years, of Family, or Humours, can ever be productive of a lasting Concord, either between the Principals themselves, or those in Alliance with them. *Dirges,*² rather than *Epithalamiums,*³ should be sung at

---

1. **May and December:** a traditional way to designate the marriage of a young woman and an old man.

2. **Dirges:** songs sung at funerals, laments.

3. **Epithalamiums:** marriage songs.

Nuptials such as these, and their Friends pity, not congratulate their Lot.

Pompilius had lived in very good Harmony with his former Lady, and none would have condemned him for paying his Vows a second Time at the Altar of *Hymen*,[1] provided he had made Choice of a Partner more agreeable to his present Years.—His Inclinations might not, indeed, have been gratify'd to so exquisite a Degree, but then his Judgment had not been arraigned,[2] nor had he forfeited in Age, that Reputation of good Sense he had acquired in Youth. How great a Pity is it then, that he should give way to the Dictates of a Passion, the Gratifications of which can afford him but a short-liv'd Joy—must be injurious to his own Character, and doubly so to the Object of his Affections.

What, if the charming *Bloometta* had been disappointed in her first Wishes—What if the too insensible *Palemon* had preferr'd a little sordid Dross to the Possession of the finest Woman upon Earth, and her Resentment at the Indignity offer'd to her Youth and Beauty, joined with the Ambition of her Parents, had set the Pretentions of *Pompilius* in an advantageous Light, a Moment's Reflection might have served to convince him of the Motives, and if he truly loved, have made him chuse to recommend some noble Youth of his own Family, whose Merits might have obliterated whatever Sentiments she had been possess'd of in Favour of *Palemon:* This indeed would have been a Proof of the most generous Affection, and at the same Time of that Command over himself, which is expected from Persons in his Station.

But how much soever the united Joys of Love and Wine, may be able to lull all Thoughts of Remorse in a Heart, which seems intent only on indulging its own Desires, be they ever so extravagant, that of the sweet *Bloometta* must endure Pangs, which every Day will become more severe, by the Efforts of her Prudence to conceal them;—what Conflicts between Sincerity and Duty must rend her gentle Breast, when her doating Lord exacts from her a Return of his Endearments!—How must she regret the sad Necessity of being oblig'd

---

1. **Hymen:** god of marriage.

2. **had not been arraigned:** would not have been accused.

to feign what Nature will not grant!—Those tender Languishments, which when mutual, afford mutual Transport,[1] seem awkward and nauseous in the Man we do not love; and instead of more endearing him to us, turn the Indifference we before had to him, into Aversion and Contempt.—In fine,[2] there are no Words to express the Miseries of a loath'd Embrace; and she who sacrifices to Pride or Pique the Pleasures of her Youth, by marrying with the Man she hates, will soon, tho' too late to repair the irremedable Mischief, repent in the utmost Bitterness of Soul what she has done.

Methinks it is with great Injustice that the Generality of the World condemn *Aristobulus* of Ingratitude, Perfidiousness, and Cruelty; he is indeed an Instance, that Love is not in our Power, and tho' his Lady's Fate is much to be commiserated, his own is, in reality, no less deserving our Compassion. This Nobleman, who, for the Graces of his Person had few Equals, made many Conquests, without the Artillery of one single Sigh or Protestation:—*Celinda,* to his great Misfortune, was among the Number—*Celinda,* of illustrious Race, Heiress to vast Possessions, and endu'd with many Perfections of Mind and Body; yet *Celinda,* whose Love has been the Bane of all his Happiness—long did she conceal the Secret of her Passion from the whole World, as well as from him who was the Object of it; yet indulging the Pleasure of seeing him as much as possible, frequented all Places where there was a Probability of meeting him, 'till finding that he paid her no other Civilities, than what her Rank demanded, those soft Emotions, which in the Beginning afforded only delightful Images, now degenerated into Horrors, as they approached nearer to Despair.—She fell sick,—the Physicians soon perceiv'd her Disorder was of the Mind, and perswaded those about her, to use their utmost Endeavours for discovering the Cause.—In vain were all the Intreaties of her Friends, in vain the Commands of the most tender Father; her Modesty resisted all, and it was not 'till she was judg'd by every one that saw her, as well as by herself, to be at the Point of Death, that she was prevail'd upon to confess, that she desired Life only to behold *Aristobulus.*

---

1. **Transport:** rapture.
2. **In fine:** in short.

Her Father, who had before suspected the Disease, tho' not the Person from whom the Infection came, was rejoiced to find, that her Inclinations had not disgraced his Dignity; and assured her, that if to see *Aristobulus* was of so much Consequence, she should not only see, but live with him, 'till Death should put a Period to that Happiness.

He made this Promise, in Confidence that the Father of *Aristobulus* would gladly accede to the Union of their Families; nor was he deceiv'd in his Conjecture; the Proposal he made was receiv'd with the utmost Satisfaction, and the Marriage Writings[1] were drawn between them, before the young Lord, who happen'd at that Time to be on a Party of Pleasure in the Country, knew that any such Thing was in Agitation.

Celinda was immediately made acquainted with this Agreement, and from that Moment the long absent Roses resumed their Places in her Cheeks, her wonted Strength and Vivacity return'd, and she was again the Joy of all who knew her.

But a far different Effect, alas! had the News of this Affair on him, who was with so much Vehemence beloved by her.—A special Messenger being dispatch'd to bring him up to *London,* he no sooner was inform'd of the Occasion, than he was seiz'd with the most mortal Anguish;—he threw himself at his Father's Feet, and with all the moving Rhetorick of dutiful Affection, conjur'd him by that paternal Tenderness he had ever treated him with, and which he had never been guilty of doing any thing to forfeit, not to insist on his fulfilling an Engagement, than which Death could not be more terrible.

Never was Surprize greater than that of the Father of *Aristobulus,* to hear him speak in this manner; but it yet received a considerable Increase, when on demanding the Reasons of his Refusal, and what Objections he had to make against becoming the Husband of so well descended, so rich, so virtuous, and so young a Lady, he had none to offer, but that he was not inclined to marry, or if he were, had something in his Nature, which oppos'd any Inclination in her Favour.

The Match was too advantageous to their Family, for the old Peer to be put off with what seem'd to him so trifling a Motive, as mere

---

1. **Marriage Writings:** financial settlements.

want of Love; he therefore resolved, that his Son should comply with his Commands, and to that End enforced them by the most terrible Menaces of never seeing him more, and of cutting him off from all his Inheritance, excepting what was entail'd upon the Title, which was very small, and little able to support it.

This was a very great Shock to one, who had the highest Notions of Grandeur, and a Relish for all the expensive Pleasures of the Young and Gay.—He knew his Father rigid, and obstinate to be obey'd by all who had any Dependance on him; and doubted not, but his Resentment would sway him to do as he said: he therefore repented he had irritated him so far, and began to feign a less Aversion to the Marriage;—he begg'd to be forgiven, and promised to visit *Celinda,* in the Hope, he said, that he should discover more Charms in her Conversation, than he yet had been sensible of. His Father seem'd somewhat pacify'd with this Assurance, and bid him go and offer her a Heart she well deserved, and he had too long delayed bestowing.

He did not, it is certain, deceive his Father in this Point;—he went, but went with a View very different from what any one could have imagin'd he would ever have conceiv'd:—In the room[1] of entertaining her with soft Professions, which, perhaps, are sometimes made by those, who mean them as little as himself could have done, he frankly confess'd, he had an Aversion to the married State; that it was not in his Power to make a Husband, such as she had Reason to expect; and entreated that she would order[2] it so, that the Nuptials, which his Father seem'd so bent on compleating, might be broke off on her Side.

How alarming such a Request must be to one who loved as she did, any one may judge; but the Excess of her Tenderness over-ruled all that Pride and Spirit, which is so natural to Women on such Occasions;—she paus'd a while, probably to suppress the rising Sighs, but at length told him, that what he desired was the only thing she could refuse him;—that her Father was no less zealous than his own for an Alliance, and that she had been too much accustom'd to Obedience, to dare to dispute his Will in a Thing he seem'd so bent upon.

---

1. **In the room:** in place.

2. **order:** arrange.

As nothing but his eternal Peace could have enforc'd him to have acted in this manner, with a Lady of her Birth and Fortune, and whose Accomplishments, in spite of the little Effect they had upon him, he could not but acknowledge, he was astonished at the Calmness with which she bore it; and judging by that, her Affection could not be less tender than he had been told, he left no Arguments untry'd to make that very Affection subservient to his Aim, of being freed from all Engagement with her;—but she still pleading the Duty she owed to him who gave her Being, he grew quite desperate, and throwing off that Complaisance he had hitherto behaved with, told her, that if for the Preservation of his Birthright he were compell'd to marry her, he neither could, nor would even endeavour to love her as a Wife;—that she must expect only uncomfortable Days, and lonely widow'd Nights; —and that it was not in the Power of the Ceremony, nor in either of their Fathers, to convert an utter Dislike into Inclination.

To this cruel Declaration she reply'd coldly, that as they were destin'd for each other, by those who had the sole Power of disposing their Hands, it was a very great Misfortune their Hearts could not comply with the Injunction; but as for her Part, she was determined to follow Duty, tho' she fell a Martyr to it.

Tho' under the Obedience of a Daughter, she had the Opportunity of veiling the Fondness of a Lover, the Honour of our Sex greatly suffered by such a Behaviour; but, poor Lady, the Excess of her Passion hinder'd her from seeing into the Meanness[1] of it, and at the same Time flatter'd her with the Belief, that in spite of the Aversion he now expressed, her Treatment of him, and the Tenderness she should make no Scruple of revealing to him in all its Force, when she became his Wife, would make an entire Change in his Sentiments, and it would not be in his Power to avoid recompensing, with some degree of Affection, so pure, so constant, and so violent a Flame, as he would then be convinced she long had felt for him.

Aristobulus, after he had left her, again essay'd to work upon his Father's Mind; but all he could urge being ineffectual, he yielded to be a *Husband,* rather than suffer himself to be cut off from being an *Heir.*—A Day was appointed for the Celebration of their Nuptials,

---

1. **Meanness:** small-mindedness.

and they were married with a Pomp more befitting their Quality, than the Condition of their Minds.—At Night they were put to Bed, with the usual Ceremonies; but the Moment the Company withdrew, he rose, and chose rather to pass the Hours 'till Morning on a Couch alone, than in the Embraces of a Woman, who had indeed Perfections sufficient to have made any Man happy, who had not that Antipathy in Nature, which there is no accounting for, nor getting rid of.

It is not to be doubted but *Celinda,* not only that Night, but for a long Time afterward, continued to put in Practice every tender Stratagem, and used every Argument that her Love, and the Circumstances they now were in, could inspire, but all were equally in vain, as the Poet says,

Love scorns all Ties but those that are his own.[1]

Aristobulus remain'd inflexible, and obstinately bent, never to be more of a Husband than the Name:—Neither Time, nor her patient enduring the Indignity put upon her, have wrought the least Alteration in her Favour.—They live together in one House, but lie not in the same Bed; eat not at the same Table, rarely see each other, and their very Servants appear as if of different Families.—Years after Years have rolled on in this Manner, yet she continues still a Virgin Bride; while he, regardless of her Love or Grief, endeavours to lose in the Arms of other Women, the Discontent which a forced Marriage has involved him in.

Few Men, indeed, have acted with that early Sincerity, and openly declared their Hatred, like *Aristobulus,* before Marriage; but too many have done it afterwards, and prov'd by their Behaviour, that they look'd upon the sacred Ceremony but as a Thing necessary to be done, either for the sake of propagating their Families, or for clearing their Estates from Mortgages,[2] or for the Payment of younger Children's Fortunes.[3] These, and various other Motives might be assigned for the

---

1. **Love . . . own:** unidentified.

2. **clearing . . . Mortgages:** getting money from the marriage to enable the bridegroom to pay off mortgages on his family estate.

3. **Payment . . . Fortunes:** Since the prevailing system of primogeniture meant that only the eldest son of a family ordinarily inherited significant amounts of money, marriage to a rich woman might provide means for a man to provide wealth for his siblings.

Alliances daily on Foot; but to hear of one that promises an Accomplishment of all the Ends proposed by the first Intention of this Institution, is a kind of Prodigy, and to say, there goes a truly happy Pair, after the first Month, would call the Speaker's Veracity in Question.

Fame[1] either swells the Number beyond its just Extent, or there are now no less than Twenty-three Treaties of Marriage either concluded, or on the Carpet,[2] between Persons of Condition, of which scarce the odd Three afford the least Prospect of Felicity to the Parties concern'd.

Can Mrs. *Tulip,* in the Autumn of her Age, tho' in her Dress gaudy as the Flower whose Name she bears, imagine her antiquated Charms will be able to reclaim the wild, the roving Heart of young *Briskcommon?* Not but that Gentleman has Sense, Honour, and Good-nature, Qualities which could not fail of making him know what was due to the Merits of *Claribella,* had the Condition of his Fortune permitted him to marry her.—But his intended Bride must become more contemptible in his Eyes, than even her grey Hairs could make her, when he reflects on the Vanity which infatuates her so far, as to deprive her lovely Neice of what might have made the Happiness of her Life, only to purchase to herself the Name of Wife, to one young enough to be her Son.

Who sees *Philimont* and *Daria* together, without perceiving that nothing can be more adored by *Philimont,* than *Daria;*—nothing more dear to *Daria* than *Philimont?*—Do not the equally enamour'd Pair seem to shoot their very Souls to each other at every Glance?—Is *Daria* ever at the Opera, the Park, the Play, without her *Philimont?*—Or does *Philimont* think any Company entertaining, if *Daria* is absent?—Yet *Philimont* is on the Point of Marriage with *Emilia,* and *Daria* has been long betroth'd to *Belmour:*—Strange Chequer-work of Love and Destiny!

What Reason has *Sabina* to boast of Charms superior to the rest of her Sex, or flatter herself with being always the Object of *Theomene*'s Wishes?—Have not his Vows been prostituted to half the fine Women in Town, and if he persisted in those he made to her so far as Marriage,

---

1. **Fame:** rumor.

2. **on the Carpet:** under negotiation.

is it not because her Fortune is larger than theirs, and more enables him to discharge those Debts his Extravagancies had contracted!

How bitterly does *Dalinda* repent her giving way to an inconsiderate Passion, which hurried her to throw herself into the Arms of the mean-born, but meaner-soul'd, ill-natur'd *Macro*.—She imagin'd, as she has since confess'd, that by marrying one so infinitely beneath her, she would have been sole Mistress of herself and Fortune; that he would never dare to take any Privileges with the one, without her Permission, nor pretend to have the least Command over the other; and that instead of being under the Authority of a Husband, she should have found in him an obsequious Slave:—But, poor mistaken Woman! *Macro* no sooner was possess'd of the Power, than he made her see a sad Reverse to all her Expectations:—He was so far from regulating the Affairs of her Estate and Family according to her Pleasure, or as she had been accustom'd to do, that he plainly shew'd he took a Pride in contradicting her;—he consulted her Inclinations in nothing, and even before her Face gave Commands, which he knew would be the most disagreeable to her, and which if she offer'd to oppose, told her in the rudest manner, that he was Master, and as such would be obey'd.—At first she rav'd, reproach'd him with Ingratitude, and vow'd Revenge;—but what, alas! could she do!—she had taken no Care that proper Settlements,[1] in case of Accidents, should be made, and was asham'd to have recourse to any of her Kindred, whom she had disgraced and disobliged, by so unworthy a Match.—The Resentment she testify'd therefore only served to render her Condition worse, and add new Weight to the galling Yoke she had so precipitately put on;—he retrench'd her Equipage and Table;[2] set Limits even to her Dress;—would suffer her neither to visit, nor be visited, but by those he approved, which were all Creatures or Relations of his own, and such as she had been little used to converse with;—deny'd her even Pocket-Money;[3]—took every Measure he could invent to break her Spirit, and make her wholly subservient to his Will, 'till at last his

---

1. **Settlements:** legal arrangements ensuring that property is available for the wife in the event of separation, divorce, or the death of her husband.

2. **Equipage and Table:** carriage and horses and allowance for food.

3. **Pocket-Money:** money allowed a woman for her personal use.

Tyranny got the better, and has now reduced her to the most abject Slavery.

Tremble *Mariana,* lest your Father's Clerk should prove another *Macro*, and rather endure the short-liv'd Pangs of combating an unhappy Inclination, than by yielding to it, run the Hazard of Miseries, which Death alone can put a Period to.

*　　*　　*

FROM BOOK III

Methinks it is with great Impropriety that People, when they see an unsocial Person, cry out, How ill-natur'd such a one is!—Nature in itself delights in Harmony, is loving, grateful, benevolent, pleased in itself, and pleased to see others so.—Every one is born with Qualities suited to Society; and when they deviate, it is not the Effect of Nature, but of the Influence of those vicious Passions which by their ill Conditions corrupt Nature, and render it no longer what it was:—Avarice, Ambition, Rage, Envy, and Jealousy are the Weeds that grow up in the Soul; and, if indulged, will by degrees choak all the nobler Principles.—How beautiful is Nature in Infancy, before those turbulent Passions gather Strength! and how beautiful would she also be in Maturity, could those Passions be always under the Government[1] of Reason!

Some may perhaps object, that I pretend[2] to divide what Heaven in our Composition has thought fit to blend:—That Passions are in reality a Part of Nature, and that none are born without some Share of them.—They may say, that in Childhood we are no less affected for such Trifles as are conformable to our Years than at a riper Age we are for what we then look on as more substantial Benefits.—They will quote against me this Line of one of the most excellent of our *English* Poets,

---

1. **Government:** control.

2. **pretend:** presume.

Men are but Children of a larger Growth.[1]

To all this I readily agree; but then the Passions of Childhood are too weak to hurry us to any thing that can be called a Vice, unless strongly indulg'd indeed by those who have the Care of us; and as they increase in Strength, our own Reason, which is given us for a Guide, increases in proportion also; so that it is the undoubted Business of our Parents and Governors[2] to keep all dangerous Propensities in us under the greatest Subjection, and preserve Nature in its Purity while we are young; and our own to do it afterward, since the infallible Consequences of any Neglect on this score are no less than to render us obnoxious to the World, and irksome to our selves.

I would not here be thought to mean that the Reserved, the Sullen, the Peevish, or even the Morose, are always under the Dominion of vicious Passions.—A continued Series of Disappointments, Calamities, Ill-usage, (which, I am sorry to say, is the sure Attendant on Misfortune) or a long Fit of Sickness, may in time make sour the sweetest Temper; but then the Gloom which they occasion will not render the Person, so affected, cruel, base, covetous, perfidious, or in fine[3] any way wicked:—Such a one may be tiresome, and look'd upon as a dead Weight in Company, but will never be found dangerous, and the only Mischief he does is to himself.

But where Avarice prevails, all that is injurious to Mankind may be expected: I think under this Head almost whatever is pernicious to Society may be ranged,[4] since where it does not find other bad Qualities, it certainly creates them.—It indeed destroys the very End of our Being.—A mean Distrust, Envy, Hatred, and Malice, will neither suffer us to enjoy a Moment's Peace ourselves, nor allow it to others, when but suspected of a bare Possibility of standing between us and our darling Interest.—Concord, that universal Good, is entirely abolish'd by it;—every publick Virtue, every private Obligation of Duty,

---

1. **Men . . . Growth:** John Dryden, *All for Love* 4. 1.

2. **Governors:** tutors.

3. **in fine:** in short.

4. **ranged:** organized.

Gratitude, and natural Affection, are sacrificed to particular Views, which center all in Self, and to attain, neither secret Fraud nor open Violence are spared. How many Wars have been render'd unsuccessful!—how many well laid Schemes disconcerted!—how many Communities broken and dissolved!—how many once-flourishing Families reduced to Beggary, meerly by the Avarice of one Person, who found his Interest in the Ruin of the whole.—Nothing is more known than this Truth, and we often see that those of the same Blood, nay who have suck'd the same Milk, have proved the most cruel and inveterate Enemies to each other.—Shocking Reflection!—let us quit it and turn our Eyes on the Contrast.

The worthy Family, of which *Euphrosine* is a Part, has in a very late Instance given us a most amiable one, and will, I hope, be an Example for many others to imitate.

This beautiful young Lady was address'd by a Gentleman immensely rich, but of more than twice her Age, and besides had nothing either in his Person or Conversation capable of rendering him agreeable to a delicate and refin'd Taste, such as hers. He made his Court to her Father before he mentioned any thing of his Passion to herself, and at the same Time accompanied his Declaration with Offers of a nature few Parents but would have readily accepted.—But he referr'd him to his Daughter's Inclinations, only assuring him that he would lay his Commands on her to receive his Visits; and that if she consented, he for his Part should be extremely proud of his Alliance.

With this the old Lover was oblig'd to be content; and since he found it must be by his Rhetoric his Point was to be gain'd, endeavour'd to prove his Passion, and inspire one in her by those Ways he thought most likely to succeed:—He entertain'd her with all the amorous Speeches he could remember out of Plays;—brought her all the favourite Airs in the *Opera* for her Spinet,—carryed her to *Vaux-Hall-Gardens* and *Ruckholt*,[1]—and told her, that wherever she came she was the *Venus*[2] of the Place.

---

1. **Vaux-Hall-Gardens and Ruckholt:** fashionable places of amusement in London where members of different social classes mingled to talk, eat, walk, and listen to music.

2. **Venus:** goddess of love and beauty.

Euphrosine, who is all Obedience, knowing her Father authorized his Suit,[1] durst neither repulse nor make a Jest of it, but accepted his fine Speeches, Treats, and Presents, as coming from a Man, who, in all probability, she was destined for:—The Contempt she had for him she kept as an inviolable Secret; and never spoke of him to her dearest Companions, nor even her Brothers and Sisters, but with all imaginable Respect. The Constraint she put on herself by this Behaviour, however, took away great Part of that Chearfulness and Vivacity which had used to sparkle in her Eyes;—she grew much more reserved in Company than she had been, and was often surprized with Tears running down her Cheeks, when she had thought herself alone.

She was too dear to all belonging to her for so visible a Change not to be taken notice of, yet none mentioned the least Word to her concerning it; and the Courtship continued for near a Month, when the Impatience of the Lover, emboldened by his Mistress's obliging Reception, made him very pressing for a Day being fixed to consummate his Happiness:—The Answers she gave him on that Head were, that she was entirely at her Father's Disposal, and that it would not be becoming in her either to anticipate or delay his Pleasure.—When he talked to her Father, he told him, that he had not yet examined his Daughter's Heart; but when he had done so, he would either hasten or prolong the Time, according as he found her in a Disposition for it:—always concluding with reminding him, that to render them both happy, it was necessary nothing should have the least Air[2] of Constraint on either Side.

This did not satisfy the other; for, as Lovers naturally flatter themselves, he took all the Civilities paid him by *Euphrosine,* in Obedience to her Father, for so many Proofs of her liking of his Person; and as he doubted not but she was no less desirous than himself for a Conclusion of this Affair, seemed to resent these Delays, as much as he durst, to him who had the sole Disposal of his Mistress: He became

---

1. **Suit:** courtship.

2. **Air:** appearance.

however so urgent, that the Father of *Euphrosine* at length promised him to sound her Inclinations the next Day, and that he should then know his Resolution.

Accordingly he sent for her to his Closet,[1] and having made her sit down by him, told her how impatient her Lover[2] was for the Completion of his Wishes, and the Promise he had given him of a definitive Answer,—set forth the Passion he had for her in much better Terms than he had ever done for himself, and added, that he was so far from desiring any Portion[3] with her, that on the first Declaration he had made to him of his Love, he had protested he would accept of nothing from him but his Consent.

"This *Euphrosine*," continued he, "is the State of the Case, and such the disinterested Kindness he has for you:—You know that I have several Children, and that Part of my Fortune, which I should give with you to a Man who required it, will be a considerable Addition to their Portions:—You may believe also, that there are not many Fathers who would consult your Inclination in this Point; but, my dear Child, I am not one of those:—I am sensible[4] that true Felicity does not consist in Wealth alone, and think it both unjust and cruel to make those wretched to whom I have given Being:—Tell me, therefore, without Reserve, or Fears of offending me, what your Thoughts of this Gentleman are, and whether you can love him, as it will be your Duty to do if you become his Wife?"

The virtuous Maid hung down her Head at these Words, and faintly replied, that the Education she had received would always instruct her to fulfil her Duty.

Her Father on this told her, there were two ways of fulfilling a Duty;—the one merely because it was so; and the other, because it afforded a Pleasure to oneself:—"and," resumed he, "I should be sorry to see you sacrifice your Peace to the former.—The Melancholly I have observed in you ever since this Gentleman has had my Permis-

---

1. **Closet:** small private room.

2. **Lover:** suitor.

3. **Portion:** dowry, the money a woman brings to her husband in marriage—provided, of course, by her father.

4. **sensible:** aware.

sion to visit you as a Lover, makes me think that the Proposal is far from being agreeable; but as I may possibly be mistaken, I would be convinced by your laying open your whole Heart to me on this Occasion."

Emboldened by so much Goodness, she at last ventured to declare, that if she never happened to see a Man more agreeable, she would chuse always to live single: "However, Sir," continued she, "as the Match affords some Conveniency to you, and you approve it, I resolved from the first Moment to offer nothing in Opposition to your Will, but to endeavour to merit, in some measure, the Indulgence you have treated me with by an implicit Obedience."

"No, no, my dear Child," replied this excellent Father, "you well deserve to be left to the Freedom of your Choice, by your Readiness to resign it.—You shall no more be troubled with the Sollicitations of a Person whom I never expected you could regard in the manner his Vanity has made him hope.—This Day shall put an End to all your Disquiets on that score."

Euphrosine was about to thank him, as the Consideration he had of her Peace deserved from her, when the sudden Entrance of her two Brothers and three Sisters obliged her to delay it.—They had heard of the Proposal her Lover had made of relinquishing her Portion; and finding she was now sent for by their Father, and shut up with him, doubted not but it was in order to enforce her, by his Command, to make a Choice it was easy for them to perceive was utterly against her Inclinations. Urged by the Necessity they thought there was of their Interposition, they came together in a Body, and all at once falling at their Father's Feet, conjured him not to suffer any Considerations of Interest to them to prevail on him to render a Sister, so justly dear to them, unhappy, by a Match which they were well convinced, tho' never from herself, could not be agreeable to her.—Some hung about his Feet, some kissed his Hands, and all lifted up their Eyes, streaming with Tears, as dreading the Answer he should give to this Request.

The tender Father listened to so uncommon a Testimony of fraternal Affection with a Transport[1] mixed with Astonishment; but unwilling to indulge the Pleasure he took in seeing them thus, at the

---

1. **Transport:** ecstasy.

Expence of the Pain Suspense inflicted on them;—"Rise!—Rise, my dear, my worthy Children!" cried he, embracing them one after another, "your Suit is granted before you thought of asking it:—Neither *Euphrosine,* nor any one of you, shall ever be compelled by my Authority, as a Father, to give your Hands where your Hearts do not first lead the way."

Nothing could equal the Joy they felt at hearing him speak in this manner, except the Satisfaction their mutual Tenderness to each other afforded him.—*Euphrosine,* on her Part, knew not how to express her Gratitude and Love either to the one or the other.—In fine, there was nothing to be seen among this endearing Family, but Embraces, Kisses, and all the Demonstrations of the most fond, unfeigned Affection, flowing from Minds perfectly at Ease and satisfied with each other.

Oh! what could the greatest Acquisitions of Fortune bestow, in any degree of Competition with those pure and unmixed Raptures, which arise from the disinterested Love and Friendship between Persons of the same Blood!—It is sure a Pleasure which no Words can paint;— no Heart unfeeling it conceive!—A Pleasure inspired by Nature, confirmed by Reason, heavenly in itself, and laudable before God and Man.

But besides this Satisfaction we feel within ourselves, and the Esteem we acquire in the World by living with our Kindred in Concord, there is a Policy in it, even as to the Gratification of our most sordid Views, which I wonder any body can be so blind as not to see, I mean that of fulfilling the old Proverb,—"Laying up against a rainy Day."[1]— There are few Families so unfortunate as to have none among them prosper; and when all are governed by one common Interest, will not the Success of one be the Advantage of the other?—Life is an uncertain Ocean, numberless, nameless Dangers lurk beneath the fairest Surface: —None, at his first Embarkation, can promise to himself he shall go through his Voyage unruffled with the Storms which from above, below, and every where impend.—Who then would not be glad

---

1. **Laying . . . Day:** The proverb means that one should provide in good times for possible bad times ahead.

to secure some friendly Bark[1] at hand, whose kind Assistance, in case of a Wreck, might save him and the Remnants of his scattered Fortune!

How well known, yet how little attended to, is that excellent Story of him, who having many Children, and finding the Hour of his Dissolution approaching, sent for them all to come to his Bed's Side; then ordered a Bundle of Sticks well tied up to be brought, and giving it into the Hands of the eldest, commanded him to break it; which having vainly essayed to do, the second Brother took it; then the third, and so on, till they had all tried their several Strengths with equal Success.—"The Thing is impracticable," said one of them, "unless we cut the Bandage;—singly we may easily break them." "True," replied the Father; "and so my Sons will it be impossible to hurt any of you, while you continue in the Bandage of Love and Unity; but if that should be once dissolved, your Strength is lost, and you are in danger of becoming a Prey to every Artifice of designing Men."

Love and Friendship, they say, will admit no Sharers in the Heart;— where either are sincere and without Reserve, it must be between two Persons;—when a third comes in for any Part, that Interest which ought to be entire is divided, weakened, and perhaps, by different Views, thrown into Confusion: The Maxim questionless is just as to the general, but has nothing to do with the Union which ought to subsist among those of the same Family, who, like so many young Branches of the same Tree, if closely knit together, are best defended from the Inclemency of the Weather for being numerous.

It is odd, methinks, that even Pride of Blood should not influence those descended from an illustrious House, to support, in some measure answerable to the Dignity of their Birth, those of their own Kindred who may have happened to fall into Misfortunes:—Are they not sensible that all the Contempt they are treated with by mean-soul'd Creatures, points obliquely at themselves? And can they know the miserable Shifts to which they are frequently reduced to for Bread, without reflecting that the Grandeur of the whole Family suffers in these unhappy Branches?

---

1. **Bark:** boat.

Strange Infatuation! To what can be ascribed so total a Neglect of that which we owe to Heaven, ourselves, and those belonging to us?—Where is the fatal Spell that stops up all the Avenues of the Soul, and suffers neither the Dictates of Religion, the Pleas of soft Compassion, nor the more powerful Impulses of Nature to our own Flesh and Blood, to gain the least Admittance?—Where but in Luxury, and a false Pride of being able to outvye each other in those expensive Vices former Ages would have blushed to be found guilty of?

Did not the once discreet and virtuous *Lucillia* refuse so poor a Gift as half a Guinea[1] to a very near Relation, who once had been her Equal in Fortune, but now in the extremest Exigence took the Liberty of petitioning her, yet went the same Evening to an Assembly, where she lost a thousand Pistoles[2] at Play![3]

Wonderful are the Changes which Difference of Times create! A few Years since,[4] a Gamester[5] was the most despicable Character in Life;—now whose Society more coveted than People of that Profession!—All who had any Reputation to lose, or desired to be thought well of by their Neighbours, took care, whenever they indulged themselves in that Diversion, to do it with as much Privacy as possible.—But *now*, not to love Play is to be unpolite:—Cards were then made use of only as the Amusement of a tedious Winter's Evening:—*Now* all Seasons are alike, they are the Employment of the Year; and at some of our great Chocolate-Houses,[6] many thousand Acres are often swallowed up before Dinner.—Persons, who were observed to have superior Skill in Play, were *then* distinguished by the odious Name of *Sharpers,* and as such avoided by all Men of Sense:—*Now* they are complimented with the Title of great *Connoiseurs,* applauded for their

---

1. **half a Guinea:** A guinea, in British currency, was one shilling more than a pound. Although it is impossible to arrive at precise monetary equivalents in twentieth-century terms, half a guinea might be worth approximately thirty dollars in today's currency.

2. **Pistoles:** old gold European coins. A thousand pistoles was perhaps equivalent to $60,000.

3. **at Play:** gambling.

4. **since:** ago.

5. **Gamester:** gambler.

6. **Chocolate-Houses:** Like coffee houses, chocolate houses provided places for informal socializing and newspaper reading—as well as for gambling, as the present context suggests, and for drinking chocolate.

Understanding in all the Niceties of the Game, and that is looked upon as the most useful kind of Learning, which teaches how to circumvent an Adversary at the important Business of *Whist.*[1]

This Vice of Gaming, originally descended from the worst of Passions, is certainly the most pernicious of any to Society.—How great a Misfortune is it therefore that it should become the *Mode,* and by being encouraged by Persons of Figure and Condition,[2] render the lower Class of People (who are always fond of imitating their Superiors) ambitious, as it were, of being undone in such good Company.

To this unhappy Propensity is greatly owing that so many Shops lately well stock'd and flourishing, are now shut up even in the Heart of the City,[3] and their Owners either Bankrupts or miserable Refugees in foreign Parts:—Nor is it to be wondered at, when the honest Profit that might be made of *Trade* is neglected, for the precarious Hopes of getting more by *Play;* the Citizen will have but little Share with the Courtier, and, to add to his Mortification, will find that the Misfortunes which attend this going out of his own Sphere, serves only as a Matter of Ridicule to those very Persons who reap the Advantage of his Folly.

We may date this extravagant Itch of Gaming, which, like the Plague, has spread its Contagion through all Degrees of People, from the fatal Year 1720.[4] The alluring Prospect of making a great Fortune at once, and without any Labour or Trouble, so infatuated the Minds of all the Ambitious, the Avaricious, and the Indolent, that for a Time there seemed an entire Stagnation of all Business but what was transacted by the *Brokers* in *Change-Alley.*[5]—Then it was that Sharping[6] began to flourish in the Nation, and has ever since continued under various Shapes.—The great Bubble of the *South- Sea* dissipated, a

---

1. **Whist:** a popular card game.

2. **Figure and Condition:** good appearance and high rank.

3. **the City:** the commercial center of London.

4. **the fatal Year 1720:** when the stock market crashed after extensive speculation in the South Sea Company, a trading firm that had taken over the national debt.

5. **Brokers in Change-Alley:** stock brokers, who functioned in the commercial center of London.

6. **Sharping:** gambling.

thousand lesser ones, tho' equally destructive to honest Industry, sprung up:—New Modes of Ruin were every Day invented: *Lotteries* on *Lotteries* were continually drawing, in which few beside those who set them up had any thing but *Blanks.*[1]—These the Wisdom of the Legislature thought fit to put a Stop to, but had not Power to extirpate the unhappy Influence which a long Inattention to Business had gained.—The People had been too much accustomed to Idleness to return with any Spirit to their former Avocations:—They wanted the golden Fruit to drop into their Laps, and fresh Opportunities of renewing those chimerical Expectations, by which already three Parts in four of the middling Class had been undone.—*Chance* was the Idol of their Souls, and when any of their more sober Friends remonstrated to them the Madness of *quitting* a *certain settled* way of getting a *moderate Living,* for the *fleeting visionary* Schemes of a *luxurious one*,— they all returned this common *cant*[2] Answer, that *they were willing to put themselves in Fortune's Way,*—and, *that they might possibly be as lucky as some others, who, being very poor before, had now set up great Equipages,*[3] and made a fine Figure in the World.

This it was that converted Gaming from an Amusement into a Business, it being the only Matter now remaining out of which their so much-beloved Castles in the Air could be formed:—One Night's good Run at Cards, or a lucky Cast of the Dice, would repair all that had been lost in other Ventures, and every one thought it worth his while to stake his last Remains.

There are always a Set of artful People who watch to take Advantage of any public Frenzy.—These soon discovered the general Bent, and to humour it with Novelty, contrived various kinds of Gaming, which never had before been dreamed of; by which every one, if it so happened, might arrive at the End of his Desires. Numbers, by this Stratagem, were taken in, who otherwise perhaps, by a conscious Want of Skill in the old Games, would have been restrained, since it requires

---

1. **Blanks:** blank lottery tickets, which paid nothing.

2. **cant:** the jargon of a particular social or occupational class.

3. **Equipages:** horses and carriages, with their attendant servants.

neither Thought nor Ingenuity to be successful at these new-invented Tables.[1]

I could name a certain Spot of Ground within the Liberties of *Westminster,*[2] which contains no less than fourteen public Gaming-Houses in the Compass of two hundred Yards; all which are every Night crowded with a promiscuous Company of the great Vulgar and the Small, as *Congreve* elegantly and justly calls all such Assemblies.

To hurl the *Tennis-Ball,* or play a Match at *Cricket,* are certainly robust and manly Exercises;—they were originally invented to try and preserve Strength and Activity, and to keep those of our Youth, who were not born to meaner Labours, from Idleness and Effeminacy.—The playing at the latter also, County against County, was designed to inspire a noble Emulation to excel each other in those Feats which might render them more able to serve their King and Country, when the Defence of either required them to take up Arms.—No mercenary Views had any Share in the Institution of these Games:—Honour was the only Excitement,—Applause the only End proposed by each bold Attemptor. These, alas! of later Days, are but empty Names;—a thousand Pound[3] has more real Charms than any are to be found in Glory:—Gain, sordid Gain, is all that engrosses the Heart, and adds Transport to Success. Without that, Numbers, who throng to give Proofs of their Activity, would rather chuse to pass the Time away in lolling over a Lady's Toilet[4] while she is dressing, or in his own Easy-Chair at Home, listening to the Music of his Footman's *French* Horn.

Will any one say that this is true Nature?—No, it is the Vices which deform Nature, and only by being too general and customary, may be called a second Nature.—Would Nature ever direct us to search into the Bosom of the Earth for Gold!—Or when found, to idolize the Ore our Hands had dug!—to pride ourselves more or less according

---

1. **Tables:** gaming tables.

2. **Liberties of Westminster:** the district subject to the authority of the borough of Westminster, which contains the Houses of Parliament and Buckingham Palace.

3. **a thousand Pound:** a thousand pounds, a large amount of money, perhaps equivalent to $60,000 or more.

4. **Toilet:** dressing table.

to the Quantity of the shining Pelf[1] we are Masters of, and to place all Honour, Virtue, and Renown in being rich!

However, since the World is so much altered from what it was in the true State of Nature, and there is now no subsisting without some Portion of this Gold, we must not affect to despise it too much: But as we ought not to listen to the Calls of Avarice, in acquiring it by any indiscreet or scandalous Means, so when possessed of it, we ought not to lavish it away in Trifles we have no Occasion for, and perhaps had better be without.—We should reflect, that our Posterity will have need of it as well as ourselves, and look on every Extravagancy we are guilty of as a Robbery of them; that we are no more than Tenants for Life in whatever descends to us from our Parents; and that we should leave it as entire and unembezled as we received it from them.—Nor is the Injustice less when we needlesly, and to gratify any inordinate Appetite, dissipate those Goods of Fortune we may have acquired by our own Industry.—Children, being Part of ourselves, are born to share in our Possessions; and nothing is more absurd, in my Opinion, than the Saying of some People, that *their Children may labour for themselves as they have done.*—How are such Parents certain they will be able to do so? A thousand Accidents may happen to render the utmost Efforts they can make of no effect; and when that is the Case, how hardly must a Son think of a Father, who, by a profuse and riotous manner of Living, has reduced to starving those who derive their Being from him!

Not that I would wish any one to deny himself the Necessaries, nor even the Pleasures of Life, for the sake of his Posterity; but in all these Things there is a golden Mean to be observed, which is indeed no other than to follow Nature, enjoy ourselves while we live, and prudently reserve something for those to enjoy who are to live after us.

It is certain that no Age, no Nation ever were equal to us in Luxury of all kinds.—The most private low-bred Man would be a *Heliogabalus*[2] in his Table; and too many Women there are, who, like

---

1. **Pelf:** money.

2. **Heliogabalus:** (ca. 205–222 B.C.) Roman emperor notorious for indecency and indulgence.

Cleopatra, would not scruple to swallow a whole Province at a Draught.[1]

Then as to Dress, they seem to study now not what is most becoming, but what will cost the most:—No Difference made between the young Nobleman and the City-Prentice,[2] except that the latter is sometimes the greater Beau:[3]—Gold-headed Canes, Watches, Rings, SnuffBoxes, and lac'd Wastcoats,[4] run away with the Fortune that should set him up in Business, and frequently tempt him to defraud his Master, who perhaps also, taken up with his own private Pleasures, examines too little into his Shop-Affairs, and when the Till is drained, borrows a while to support his darling Pride, then sinks at once to Ruin and Contempt.

Our Sex is known to be so fond of appearing fine and gay, that it is no wonder the Tradesmen's Wives should even exceed their Husbands in the Article of Dress; but it is indeed prodigious that so many of them should, merely for the sake of being thought able to afford any thing, destroy the reasonable End of Finery, and render themselves awkward, nay preposterous, instead of genteel and agreeable.—When a Gold and Silver Stuff,[5] enough to weigh a Woman down, shall be loaded yet more with heavy Trimmings, what Opinion can we have either of the Fancy or Judgment of her that wears it?—And is not her Neighbour, whom to out-shine, perhaps, she has strained her Husband's Purse-Strings for this costly Garment, infinitely more to be liked in a plain *Du Cape* or *Almazeen!*[6]

I am sorry to observe that this false Delicacy in Eating, Drinking, Apparel, Furniture and Diversions, so prevalent among us, has not only undone half the Nation, but rendered us extremely ridiculous to

----

1. **Cleopatra . . . Draught:** At a banquet during her time with Antony, Cleopatra allegedly drank a pearl of immense value that had been dissolved in wine.

2. **City-Prentice:** young man apprenticed to a merchant in the City, the commercial center of London.

3. **Beau:** dandy.

4. **lac'd Wastcoats:** waistcoats adorned with lace.

5. **Stuff:** fabric.

6. **Du Cape, Almazeen:** plain, stout fabrics.

Foreigners who are Witnesses of it.—Thus Avarice introduced Luxury, Luxury leads us to Contempt, and Beggary comes on apace.

I fear what I have said on these Topics will be but ill relished by a great many of my Readers; but if I have the good Fortune to find it has had an Effect on any one of them, so far as to cause them to see the Error they have been guilty of, I shall be the less chagrin'd at the Resentment of the wilfully Blind.—Times like these require Corrosives, not Balsams[1] to amend:—The Sore has already eaten into the very Bowels of public Happiness, and they must tear away the infected Part, or become a Nusance to themselves and all about them.

*   *   *

I have somewhere read of an antient Philosopher, who, whenever any very ill Accident befel him, made Invitations to his Friends, entertained them in the most chearful Manner, and appeared extremely happy in his Mind.—And, on the contrary, on the Arrival of any thing for which other People expect Congratulations, he shut himself up in his Chamber, fasted, wept, and in his whole Deportment had all the Tokens of a Person under some inconsolable Affliction. On being asked the Reason of a Behaviour so contradictory to that of all Mankind besides, he replied, "Those who wonder to see me merry in Adversity, and sad in a more prosperous Condition, do not consider what Fortune is, or do not rightly understand the Nature of that fickle Deity.—Is she not ever fleeting,—ever changing, and generally from one Extreme to the other?—How then, when any Good befals me, can I avoid being under the most terrible Apprehensions that an adequate Evil will immediately ensue?—And when any Mischief has happened to me, have not I Reason to rejoice in the Expectation that the same Proportion of Happiness is at Hand?"

The Humour of this Philosopher was very extraordinary indeed, and one may justly say he strained the Point beyond what it will well bear;

---

1. **Balsams:** aromatic preparations applied externally for soothing wounds or healing pain.

yet upon the whole there is somewhat of Reason in it, according to Mr. *Dryden,*

> Good unexpected, Evil unforeseen,
> Appear by Turns as Fortune shifts the Scene.[1]

But not to have Recourse to Caprice or Fiction to enable us to support the Calamities which Heaven sometimes inflicts on us, we ought to consider, that by well-bearing them we have the better Claim to hope an Alternative in our Favour. A desponding Temper is, of all others, the least pleasing both to God and man; it shews a Diffidence in the *one,* and to the *other* a Want of that Complaisance which is due from us to Society.

Can any thing, if we consider rightly, be more rude than to disturb the Chearfulness of whatever Conversation we come into, with the melancholly Detail of our private Misfortunes?—They are our own, and ours alone, and a Man ought no more to wish to infect others with his Griefs than with his Diseases.

Those who imagine they find Ease in complaining are of a very mean and selfish Disposition.—A great Spirit is almost as much ashamed of Pity as of Contempt; and a generous one will never endure to excite that Sorrow from which Pity naturally flows.

Indeed, where Proximity of Blood, or the more binding Ties of Friendship afford a reasonable Expectation of Relief in any Exigence of Fortune, it would be a foolish Pride to withhold the Knowledge of it, and what they might justly suspect was owing to a Want of that Confidence which is the only Cement of a true Affection, and also betrays somewhat of a Despondency, which it is much better to try every thing, depend on every thing, and even cheat ourselves into a Belief of Impossibilities, rather than give way to.

Foreigners will have it, that there is somewhat in our Climate which renders this unhappy Propensity more natural to us than to any other Nation; and I believe the frequent Changes in the Weather, and a certain Heaviness in the Air at some Seasons of the Year, may indeed

---

1. **Good unexpected . . . shifts the Scene:** John Dryden, trans., Virgil, *Aeneis* 11. 656–57.

contribute greatly to it; but I fear there may also be other Causes assigned, which it lies solely in ourselves to remove, and which, if we do not speedily do, the Reflections made upon us Abroad will carry a severer Sting than we are yet aware of.

Our Climate, I suppose, is the same it ever was:—Our Hemisphere is no more clouded with Vapours:—Our Winds no more variable than some Ages past:—Yet I challenge any of the foreign ones to produce half the Number of sad Examples of Despondency that these latter ones have done.

Let us not therefore lay the whole Blame of those unhappy Actions we daily hear of, on elementary[1] Causes, nor depreciate a Climate which has, and, I hope, again may be productive of the brightest Genius's,[2] and bravest Spirits that ever any Country had to boast of.—It is not the ill Aspect of the *Stars,* nor the unkindly Influence of the *Moon* has wrought this Effect on us, but our falling off from the Virtues of our Ancestors:—The Change is in ourselves;—and while all seem eager to *undo,* or be *undone,* it is not to be wondered at that the Horrors of conscious Guilt on the one Hand, and the Contempt and Miseries of Poverty on the other, should hurry many of us to Deeds of Desperation.

The fatal Source of all the Calamities we labour under is an Indulgence of those destructive Passions, which in their Beginnings might be easily rooted out; but once suffered to get Head,[3] not all our Resolution will have Power to subdue.—Avarice, Ambition, Luxury and Pride are the very Tyrants of the Mind, they act without Council, are above all Restraint, and having once deposed Reason from her Throne, render her even subservient to their basest Aims.

How then can those who have the Care of Youth answer to themselves the Neglect of so material a Point, as not inculcating early into them an Abhorrence of these destructive Vices?—This is a Duty which principally belongs to Parents, but when other no less indispensable

---

1. **elementary:** pertaining to the forces of nature.

2. **Genius's:** In the eighteenth century, plurals of words ending in *s* were frequently formed with the apostrophe.

3. **get Head:** advance, press forward.

Avocations deny them Leisure for discharging it.—Sickness or old Age renders them unable, or Indolence unwilling, to do it; the least they can do is to chuse Persons properly qualified for this mighty Trust.

Few People of Condition, indeed, but take care that those they set over their Children shall be such as are capable of instructing them in all the modish Accomplishments of Life; but however necessary that may be towards procuring them a Character of *good Breeding,* it ought not to come in Competition with that of *good Reputation.* Governors and Governesses, therefore, should not so much be chose for their Skill in Languages,—for Fencing,—Dancing,—Playing on Music, or having a perfect Knowledge of the *Beau-Monde,*[1] as for their Sobriety, Morality and good Conduct.—Their Example ought to be such as should enforce their Precepts, and by shewing the Beauty of a regular Life in themselves, make their Pupils fall in Love with it, and endeavour an Imitation.

It were almost as well, if not entirely so, to leave a young Gentleman to his own Management, as to put him under the Care of one who, to endear himself to him, shall flatter his Vices, because it is giving him a Sanction, as it were, for all the Irregularities he may take it in his Head to commit.—Too many Instances of this may be found among those who are at an infinite Expence in travelling for Improvement, yet bring Home little besides the worst Part of the Nations where they have been.

Would People of Fashion but give themselves Time to reflect how great an Ascendant the very Name of Governor has over their Children, they would certainly be more cautious on whom they conferred it. Methinks the Story of the young rich *Mercator,* yet recent in every one's Memory, should be a Warning not only to the Friends, but even to every Gentleman himself who is going to travel, to be well acquainted with the Character and Principles of him who is to attend him in the above-mentioned Quality.

He was the only Son of a wealthy foreign Merchant, who losing both his Parents while he was yet an Infant, he was left to the Guardianship of two Persons, of whose Integrity his Father had many

---

1. **Beau-Monde:** fashionable world.

Proofs.—Nor had the young *Mercator* any Reason to complain of their deceiving the Trust reposed in them.

They used[1] him with the same Tenderness they could have done had he been their own Son:—They put him to the best Schools:—They saw that the Masters did their Duty by him; and when he had finished all that a Home-Education[2] could bestow, they thought fit to send him for his greater Improvement to make the Tour of *Europe.*

The only Care they now had upon their Hands, was to find a Person whose Abilities for a Governor were well attested.—It is certain they spared no Pains for that Purpose, and were at last recommended to one who had all the Appearance of a sober Gentleman,—had travelled before in that Capacity, and was well acquainted both with the Languages and Customs of those Places which they intended their young Charge should see.

It gave them a very great Satisfaction to imagine they had found one who so well answered their Desires; but *Mercator* much more, to be under the Direction of a Person who he was well convinced would not be severe on his Pleasures. This young Gentleman was of an amorous Constitution, and had contracted an Intimacy with a Woman, who tho' far from being handsome in her Person, and of a Character the most infamous that could be, he was nevertheless fond on to a very great degree. He had happened to be in Company with the Person who was afterwards made Choice of for his Governor, at the Lodgings of this Prostitute, and some others of the same Profession, and when he saw him with his Guardians, tho' he had now assumed a very different Air, well remembered he was the same with whom he had passed more than one Night in Rioting and Debauchery.

In fine, they soon came to a perfect Understanding of each other; and when the Time arrived for their Departure, the complaisant Governor was far from opposing his Pupil's taking this *Fille de Joy*[3] with him.

---

1. **used:** treated.

2. **Home-Education:** education in his native country.

3. **Fille de Joy:** prostitute; literally, "daughter of joy."

Paris was the first Place at which they stayed any time; and our young Traveller was so taken up with the Gaieties he found there, that he was in no Haste to quit it, which his Governor perceiving, thought fit to humour him in, and accordingly they took a fine Hotel,[1] lived in the most voluptuous manner, and *Marian,* for so I shall call the Partner of the looser Pleasures of the unhappy *Mercator,* shared with them in all the wild Frolics they were continually inventing for the passing away those Hours, which the careful Guardians at Home flattered themselves were employed in a far different way.

After having wasted near a Year in this manner, *Mercator* was taken suddenly sick; whether the Disease he laboured under was brought on him by his Excesses, or by any other more secret Cause, I will not take upon me to determine, nor do I hear of any one that can be more positive; but this is certain, that his Disorder lay greatly in his Head, and he was often very delirious.

It is to be supposed that in one of these Fits it was that the Governor wrought on him to send for a Priest and a Notary-Public at the same time; the one married him to *Marian,* and the other drew up a Testament, in which he bequeathed that Woman, by the Name and Title of his Wife, the Sum of 60,000*l.*[2] and 40,000*l.* which was the whole Remainder of his Fortune, to his dear Friend and Governor, as a Recompence for the great Care he had taken both of his Soul and Body.

These were the Words of the Will, which being signed, sealed, and in all Points duly executed in the Presence of several Witnesses, the Testator, as having no more to do with Life, or those he was among having no more for him to do, expired, as I have been told, in the most intolerable Agonies.

Marian, in those altered Circumstances, soon after returned to *England* with him who shared in poor *Mercator*'s Fortune, and whom she married the Moment the Decency she now affected in her new Grandeur would permit.

---

1. **Hotel:** large private residence.
2. **60,000l.:** sixty thousand pounds.

The Guardians, and other Friends of the deceased Gentleman, made all imaginable Enquiry into this Business, but could only receive dark Hints, and such Conjectures as were not sufficient to commence a Process[1] upon: But with what Vexation they see this wicked Pair roll in their Coach and Six, and triumph in their Guilt, any one may imagine.

It will not be expected I should comment on this Action, because I have already said the Truth of the Particulars is yet hid in Darkness: What Time may produce I know not, but at present every one is at Liberty to judge as they think most agreeable to the nature of the Thing. All I propose by relating it, is to remind all those who have any young Gentlemen to send Abroad, that they cannot be too scrutinous into the Principles of the Persons entrusted with the Direction of them.

End of the THIRD BOOK.

FROM BOOK IV

How glorious a Privilege has Man beyond all other sublunary Beings! who, tho' indigent, unpitied, forsaken by the World, and even chain'd in a Dungeon, can, by the Aid of Divine Contemplation, enjoy all the Charms of Pomp, Respect, and Liberty!—Transport himself in Idea to whatever Place he wishes, and grasp in Theory imagin'd Empires!

Unaccountable is it, therefore, that so many People find an Irksomeness in being alone, tho' for never so small a Space of Time!—Guilt indeed creates Perturbations, which may well make Retirement horrible, and drive the self-tormented Wretch into any Company to avoid the Agonies of Remorse; but I speak not of those who are *afraid* to reflect, but of those who seem to me not to have the *Power* to do it.

---

1. **Process:** law suit.

There are several of my Acquaintance of both Sexes, who lead Lives perfectly inoffensive, and when in Company appear to have a Fund of Vivacity capable of enlivening all the Conversation they come into; yet if you happen to meet them after half an Hour's Solitude, are for some Minutes the most heavy lumpish Creatures upon Earth: Ask them if they are indispos'd? they will drawl out—*No, they are well enough.*—If any Misfortune has befallen them? still they answer—*No,* in the same stupid Tone as before, and look like Things inanimate till something is said or done to reinspire them.—One would imagine they were but half awoke from a deep Sleep, and indeed their Minds, during this Lethargy, may be said to have been in a more inactive State than even that of Sleep, for they have not so much as dream'd; but I think they may justly enough be compar'd to Clock-work, which has Power to do nothing of itself till wound up by another.

Whatever Opinion the World may have of the Wit of Persons of this Cast, I cannot help thinking there is a Vacuum in the Mind;—that they have no Ideas of their own, and only through Custom and a genteel Education are enabled to talk agreeably on those of other People.—A real fine Genius can never want Matter to entertain itself, and tho' on the Top of a Mountain without Society, and without Books, or any *exterior* Means of Employment, will always find that *within* which will keep it from being idle:—*Memory* and *Recollection* will bring the Transactions of *past* Times to View;—*Observation* and *Discernment* point out the *present* with their Causes; and *Fancy,* temper'd with *Judgment,* anticipate the *future.*—This Power of Contemplation and Reflection it is that chiefly distinguishes the *Human* from the *Brute* Creation, and proves that we have Souls which are in reality Sparks of that Divine, Omniscient, Omnipresent Being whence we all boast to be deriv'd.

The Pleasures which an agreeable Society bestows are indeed the most elegant we can taste; but even that Company we like best would grow insipid and tiresome were we to be for ever in it; and to a Person who knows how to think justly, it would certainly be as great a Mortification never to be alone, as to be always so.

Conversation, in effect, but furnishes Matter for Contemplation;—it exhilerates the Mind, and fits it for Reflection afterward:—Every new thing we hear in Company raises in us new Ideas in the Closet or on the Pillow; and as there are few People but one may gather something from, either to divert or improve, a good Understanding will, like the industrious Bee, suck out the various Sweets, and digest them in Retirement. But those who are perpetually hurrying from one Company to another, and never suffer themselves to be alone but when weary Nature summonses them to Repose, will be little amended, tho' the Maxims of a *Seneca*[1] were to be deliver'd to them in all the enchanting Eloquence of a *Tully*.[2]

But not to be more improved, is not the worst Mischief that attends an immoderate Aversion to Solitude.—People of this Humour, rather than be alone, fly into all Company indiscriminately, and sometimes fall into such as they have Reason to repent their whole Lives of having ever seen; for tho' they may not possibly reap any Advantage from the *Good,* their Reputations must certainly, and perhaps their Morals and Fortunes too, will suffer very much from the *Bad;* and where we do not give ourselves Leisure to chuse, it is rarely we happen on the former, as they being infinitely the smaller Number, and also less easy of Access to those whose Characters they are unacquainted with.

Many young Persons of both Sexes owe their Ruin to this one unfortunate Propensity of loving to be always in Company; and it is the more dangerous, as nobody takes any Pains to conquer it in themselves, but on the contrary are apt to mistake it for a laudable Inclination, and look on those who preach up the Happiness of a more retir'd Life, as phlegmatic and vaporish.[3]—I doubt not but I shall pass for such in the Opinion of many of my Readers, who are too volatile to consider that it is not a sullen, *cynical,* total avoiding of Society that I recommend, but a proper Love of Solitude at *some Times,* to enable us to relish with more Pleasure, as well as to be essentially the better for Conversation at *others,* and also to select such for our Companions as may be likely to answer both these Ends.

---

1. **Seneca:** Lucius Annaeus Seneca (ca. 3 B.C.–A.D. 65), Roman philosopher, dramatist, and statesman.

2. **Tully:** Marcus Tullius Cicero (106–43 B.C.), Roman orator.

3. **phlegmatic and vaporish:** hysterical or hypochondriacal.

Nor is it only where there is a Difference of Sex that I think Youth ought to be upon its Guard:—The Dangers in that Case are too universally allowed to stand in need of any Remonstrances, and yet perhaps are not greater than others which both may happen to fall into among those of their own.—Are not almost all the Extravagancies Parents with so much Grief behold their Children guilty of, owing to ill-chosen Company?—Great is the Privilege of Example, and some are so weak as to think they must do as they see others do.—The Fear of being laughed at has made many a young Gentleman run into Vices to which his Inclination was at first averse; but, alas! by Habitude become more pleasing to him: He has in his Turn too play'd the Tempter's Part, and made it his Glory to seduce others as himself had been seduced.—It is this Love of Company, more than the Diversions mentioned in the Bills,[1] that makes our Ladies run galloping in Troops every Evening to Masquerades, Balls and Assemblies in Winter, and in the Summer to *Vaux-Hall, Ranelagh, Cuper's-Gardens, Mary le Bon, Sadler's-Wells,* both old and new, *Goodman's-Fields,* and twenty other such like Places,[2] which, in this Age of Luxury, serve as Decoys to draw the Thoughtless and Unwary together, and, as it were, prepare the Way for other more vicious Excesses: For there are, and of Condition[3] too, not a few (as I am informed by the *Gnomes* who preside over Midnight Revels)[4] that, going with no other Intention than to partake what seems an innocent Recreation, are prevail'd upon by the Love of Company either to remain in these Houses, or adjourn to some other Place of Entertainment till the sweet Harbinger of Day, *Aurora,*[5] wakes, and blushes to behold the Order of Nature thus perverted; nor then perhaps would separate, did not wearied Limbs, heavy languid Eyes, and *dirty Linnen* remind them of repairing to their re-

---

1. **Bills:** posters, advertisements.

2. **such like Places:** places of public amusement: amusement parks, public gardens, concert halls.

3. **Condition:** high social rank.

4. **Midnight Revels:** Fashionable men and women stayed very late at night at amusement parks, masquerades, and other entertainments.

5. **Aurora:** goddess of the dawn.

spective Habitation, where having lain a while, they rise, they dress, and go again in quest of new Company and new Amusements.

Heaven forbid, and I am far from suggesting that to run such Lengths as these should be common to all who hate Retirement and Reflection: Fortune is sometimes kinder than our Endeavours merit, and by not throwing any Temptations in our way, renders our Carelesness of no worse Consequence than being deprived of those solid Pleasures which flow from a Consciousness of having behaved according to the Dictates of Honour and Reason.

But suppose we make some Allowances to a few of the very Young and Gay, especially the Beautiful and High-born, who, by a mistaken Fondness in their Parents, from the Moment they were capable of understanding what was said to them, heard nothing but Flattery, and are made to believe they came into the World for no other Purpose than to be adored and indulged, what can we say for those who had a different Education, and are of riper Years?—How little Excuse is there for a gadding Matron,[1] or for a Woman who ought to have the Care of a House and a Family at Heart!—How odd a Figure does the Mother of five or six Children make at one of these nocturnal Rambles; and how ridiculous is it for a Person in any Trade or Avocation, to be, or affect to be, above the Thought of all Œconomy, and make one in every Party of Pleasure that presents itself?—Yet such as these are no Prodigies.[2]—All kinds of Regulation and Management require some small Reflection and Recess from Company, and these are two Things so terrible to some People, that they will rather suffer every thing to be ruined than endure the Fatigue of Thought.

*   *   *

To know ourselves, is agreed by all to be the most useful Learning; the first Lessons, therefore, given us ought to be on that Subject.— The Parents or Governors of Children can never answer to themselves a Neglect in this Point—Youth should be try'd and sifted,[3] and when

---

1. **gadding Matron:** married woman who runs about indulging in fashionable pleasures.

2. **Prodigies:** miracles, remarkable occurrences.

3. **sifted:** closely scrutinized.

the favourite Propensity is once found out, it will be easy either to eradicate or improve it, according as it tends to Vice or Virtue.

I must confess, that where there is a kind of heavy Stupidity, or what they call too much Mercury in the Disposition,[1] the one requires a great deal of Art to enliven, and the other no less to fix;[2] and as they are direct Contraries, so contrary Methods should be made use of.— But this is a Duty which ought not to be dispens'd with on account of its Difficulty, nor is perhaps so hard a Matter as it seems, if we consider, that to give Spirit and Vivacity to the Dull, nothing but chearful Objects should be presented; and to the too Wild and Giddy, those of the most serious and affecting Nature.

Where an Excess of Gaiety and the Love of Pleasure is predominant, the Mind should be early season'd with the Knowledge of the many Disappointments, Disasters, and Calamities which are the Portion of the greatest Part of Mankind.—Pity for the Woes of others, and the Certainty, that no Condition or Degree can assure itself with being defended from the Frowns of Fate, will give a more serious Turn to our Ideas, and serve very much to abate that Impetuosity which arises from a too great Redundancy of Fire or Air[3] in Persons of that Disposition.

Few are so happy as to be compos'd of equal Elements,[4] therefore, what is deficient in the Constitution ought to be supplied by Judgment.—The *Earthy* Stupid, and the *Watry* Phlegmatic, are to be rais'd by Exercise, Music, Dancing, and all sprightly Amusements; as the *Fiery* Choleric,[5] and the *Airy* Giddy, are to be temper'd with their Contraries.

But, as I have already taken Notice, this Method, tho' it must not be omitted by the *Tutors,* will fail of Success, if not seconded by the Endeavours of the *Pupils,* when left to the Management of themselves; but where there is a good Foundation laid by those who have had the

---

1. **Mercury in the Disposition:** volatility, sprightliness.

2. **fix:** stabilize.

3. **Fire or Air:** According to ancient chemistry, earth, air, fire, and water were the four elements composing all matter.

4. **equal Elements:** an equal balance of the four component elements.

5. **Choleric:** irascible, angry; a condition early thought to result from an excess of bile or choler.

Care of instructing us in our Youth, it will be intirely our own Fault, if we afterward fall into any very gross Irregularities.

Reflection, therefore, and Recollection are as necessary for the Mind as Food is for the Body; a little Examination into the Affections of the Heart can be of no Prejudice to the most melancholly Constitution, and will be of infinite Service to the too sanguine.[1]—The Unhappy may, possibly, by indulging Thought, hit on some lucky Stratagem for the Relief of his Misfortunes, and the Happy may be infinitely more so by contemplating on his Condition.

So great a Pleasure do many People find in retiring sometimes into themselves, that they would not be denied that Privilege for any other Enjoyment whatsoever.

I once knew a Gentleman who had a Wife of whom he was infinitely fond, and whose Society he preferr'd to all others in the World, at those Times when he was disposed for Conversation;—yet if she offer'd to disturb his Meditations, would grow quite peevish with her.—So valuable to him was the Freedom of his Thoughts that he could not bear an Interruption, even tho' he knew it to be a Proof of Love from her who was by so much the dearest Part of himself.—I remember I was one Day at his House, when his Lady thinking he had been too long alone, had, with a gentle Force, dragg'd him from his Closet.[2]—I wonder'd to see him more than ordinarily grave, and on enquiring into the Cause, was answer'd by him in these Terms. "This dear Creature," said he, "robs me of half the Pleasure of her Love, by not permitting me to contemplate on the Blessings I possess in her."

How then happens it, that such Numbers deny themselves the greatest Satisfaction a reasonable Being can enjoy, and which is also of such high Importance in every Accident in Life, that without it we have no Power either to attain any Good, or defend ourselves from any Evil!

But some People are so ignorant as to imagine, or so wicked as to insinuate, that those who think much, and are Lovers of Solitude, seclude themselves, not from the World, but with a View of doing

---

1. **sanguine:** hopeful, as a result of a predominance of blood in the constitution.

2. **Closet:** small private room.

some Mischief to it.—According to the Stations they are in, they are judg'd capable of ruminating on greater or lesser Evils to Mankind. They will have a sedentary Statesman to be plotting Treason either against his Prince or Country.—A Steward studying new Methods to enlarge his Bills.—A Tradesman to impose upon his Customers, and so on from the highest to the lowest Degree.

A Few Examples have, alas, but too much authoriz'd this Opinion. We have seen great *Thinkers* who have thought only to aggrandize themselves on the Ruins of those they pretended to serve.—Great *Professors* who have spar'd no Pains to gain Confidence, for no other Purpose than to betray.—Great *Advocates* for *Liberty* only to enslave, and great *Preachers* up of *Justice* only to purchase Security for the worst of Criminals.

So gross an Abuse of the Faculty of Thinking is indeed, turning the Arms of Heaven against itself, and forcing that sacred Reason, which was given us for a Guide to *Virtue,* to accompany us in the Paths of *Vice.*—To think to such Purposes, I must confess, is infinitely worse than not to think at all, because the one tends to injure and oppress Mankind in general, the other is for the most part hurtful only to the Persons themselves.

Hypocrisy is detestable both to God and Man;—we are told from an unerring Mouth, that those found guilty of it "shall have the lowest Place in Hell,"[1] and sure on Earth they merit the most contemptible Treatment from their Fellow Creatures.—When once the Mask of Benevolence and Sincerity is pluck'd off from the Face of the seeming Angel, and the grim treacherous Fiend appears in his native Ugliness, by so much the more as our Admiration before was of him, will be our Abhorrence of him afterwards.—We shall hate and fly him, as we once lov'd and follow'd him.—Everybody will be ready to catch up a Stone to throw at him, and no Opportunities of insulting him will be omitted.

* * *

---

1. **Place in Hell:** perhaps a reference to Matt. 23:33, where Christ, characterizing hypocrites as "a generation of vipers," asks, "How can ye escape the damnation of hell?"

FROM BOOK V

Did not Reasons of State, which the *Spectator* must not presume to fathom, engage us at present in a War with *France,* I should advise to send a young Lady, too much bigotted to any one Pleasure into that polite Country, where she would find so vast a Variety, as would give a quite different Turn to her Temper, and make her despise all that before seem'd so enchanting to her.

I foresee that many, on reading this Paragraph, will be astonish'd, and cry out, that by following this Counsel she would lose all Relish for the Delights her own Country affords, only to become more fond of those of another!—This Objection at first may appear plausible enough, but when considered, will be found of no Weight; for besides the Remembrance of those dear Friends she has left behind, there is something of a natural Partiality in us all, to the Place which gave us Birth, which would make her, in a short Time, wish to return; so that of Consequence, she would be much sooner cured of this immoderate Love of Pleasure, than by enjoying it in a Place where nothing is absent to her Wishes.

There are also two Reasons which render the indulging one's self in all, or any particular Kind of Diversion less prejudicial in *France* than it frequently proves in *England:*—The First, because whatever Time is spent in them is so far from being wholly lost, that it is rather an Improvement, than a Diminution of the Education we have before receiv'd, as every Body must allow that knows any Thing of the Customs of that Nation:—The Arrival of a foreign Lady is no sooner known than she is invited to partake of all their Entertainments:— She immediately enters into Balls, Assemblies, Masquerades, and a continual Round of Pleasure in the Palaces of Princes, and Houses of Persons of the first Quality, where she is treated with the utmost Elegance and Delicacy, and hears nothing of those Impertinences and loose Ribaldry, she is liable to be persecuted with, in those mix'd Companies at our mercenary Places of Resort; where all, without Distinction, are admitted for their Money.—A Woman of Honour ought to tremble to think what Creatures may join in Conversation with her in some of our public Rendezvouz, who will not fail afterwards to boast of an Acquaintance with her, and take notice of her as such, if they happen to see her in any other Place.—Few of our *English* Beaus have the Discretion a *French* Gentleman had, who being in the Gallery at an Opera in *Paris,* and sitting near a fine Lady, who, by being dress'd, as he thought, a little too gay for that Part of the House, he took for a *Fille de joy,*[1] and accosted with all the Freedoms used to Women of that Character:—She gave herself no Pains to undeceive him, but evaded suffering him to attend her home, as he expected to have done: Some Days after happening to see her going into Court, attended by a great Number of Pages and Footmen, he ask'd a Person who stood near, who that Lady was, and was answer'd, Madame *de Charleroy* one of the Princesses of the Blood.[2] Ashamed of his former Behaviour to her he was sculking away as fast as he could, but her penetrating Eyes immediately discover'd her *would-have-been* Gallant, and making him be call'd back:—"What, Monsieur," said she, ironically, "is the Lady you entertain'd with so much Freedom at the Opera a few Nights since, not worth a single Salute?"—"O Madam," returned he, with an admirable Presence of Mind, "in Paradise[3] we were on an Equality; but now I know the Respect due to Madame de Charleroy." On which she laugh'd, and own'd the Blame was wholly her own, for indulging a Frolick, which carried her to a Place where she could so little be expected to be found.

Had this Transaction happened at any of our public Diversions, it is possible the Lady need not have been at the Trouble to have the Gentleman call'd back; he would have made her a low Bow to shew his Breeding, and never rested till he had gone through all the Coffee-Houses in Town, and entertain'd the Company with his Intimacy with a certain great Lady, whom, if he did not directly name, he would take Care to describe in such a manner as every one should know.

I appeal to our Ladies themselves, if they have not sometimes been put to the Blush, by being claim'd as Acquaintance by Persons of both Sexes who they have happened to join with in those promiscuous

---

1. **Fille de joy:** prostitute; literally, "daughter of joy."

2. **Madame de Charleroy . . . Blood:** Madame de Charleroy is probably fictitious; at any rate, she is not listed in the French peerage. A princess of the blood is one related to the king.

3. **Paradise:** [Haywood's note] A By-Word they have in Paris for the Galleries, as we say, Among the Gods.

Assemblies; and by whom it is unbecoming of their Characters even to be mention'd.

The other Reason I promis'd to give why the partaking in all Kinds of Diversions in *France* is not attended with the same ill Consequences as in *England,* is this.—The innocent Freedoms allowed in our Sex, give no Encouragement to those of the other to expect such as are not so; it being, without all Question, a Place of the greatest Gaiety, least Scandal, and least room for it, of any in the World:—The Gentlemen there address, present, and treat, with no other View than to shew their own Gallantry; and the Ladies receive all the Marks of Respect that can be paid them, as the Privilege of their Sex, and not as Proofs of any particular Attachment.

I am sorry to say that in *England,* Ladies even of the first Quality[1] are treated with very great Indifference, except by those Men who have a Design upon them; and as for Women of inferior Condition, tho' possess'd of the most extraordinary Talents of Mind or Body, they may shew themselves, as much as they please, in all public Places, without being able to make themselves be taken notice of, if they allow no Hope of one Day purchasing Distinction at too dear a Rate.

On the whole, therefore, as Vanity, and the Desire of Admiration, are the chief Motives which induce our very young Ladies to these continual Rambles, *France* is the only Place where they may find their Inclinations gratified to its full Extent, without Danger to their Virtue, or Prejudice to their Reputation.

But as the Enmity at present between the two Nations, renders such an Excursion impracticable, my Correspondent might send Miss *Biddy,* under the Care of some Relation, or other prudent Person, if her Affairs permit her not to go herself, to *Bath, Tunbridge,* or *Scarborough;*[2] in fine, to any Place where she might be entertain'd with something, that should render her forgetful of what she now so much delights in.

It would be extremely fortunate for her, if, while her Passion for the Pleasures of *Ranelagh*[3] are in their Zenith, one of her Kindred or

---

1. **first Quality:** highest social rank.

2. **Bath, Tunbridge, or Scarborough:** resort towns. Bath and Tunbridge provided warm springs for bathing; Scarborough was a beach resort.

3. **Ranelagh:** an amusement center in Chelsea, a borough of London, much frequented by fashionable young women.

Intimates should happen to marry, and go down into the Country to celebrate their Nuptials:—To accompany the new-join'd happy Pair, and be Witness of the rural Sports, invented for their Welcome, by the innocent Country People, would perhaps be a Scene too novel not to have some Charms for her:—The Woods, the Fields, the Groves, the sweetly purling Streams, the Horn, the Halloo of the Huntsmen, and the chearful ruddy Countenance of those that pursue the Chace, afford also a pleasing Variety of Amusement.

By Ways like these, I fancy she might be cheated, as it were, into a Taste more suited to make her happy, and brought to a reasonable Way of Thinking, without seeming to endeavour it.

This is indeed a Crisis which calls for the utmost Precaution in a Parent: I am told by Persons, who are always consulted on every Occasion that relates to Pleasure, that a Subscription is intended, some say actually on Foot, for *Ridottos* and *Masquerades*[1] at *Ranelagh* next Winter; and if so, our young Ladies will probably live there all Night as well as all Day:—Whether Mr. *Heidegger*[2] will have Interest[3] enough to prevent this Invasion of his Province, I know not; but if it should go on, one may venture to pronounce, without being any great Conjurer,[4] that those nocturnal Rambles will be found of more dangerous Consequence at *Chelsea,* than they have proved at the *Hay-Market.*

I communicated this Piece of Intelligence to a young Lady, who at present passes the greatest Part of her Time at *Ranelagh,* and never in my Life did I see a Creature so transported:[5]—Her Eyes sparkled, her Lips quivered, all her Frame was in Agitation, through Eagerness to know something farther of this important Affair; and when I mention'd the Apprehensions I had, that if such a Design should take Place, it might be prejudicial to the Health of those, who should venture themselves, in the Damps of Winter Nights, in a Place so near

---

1. **Ridottos and Masquerades:** fashionable forms of entertainment. Ridottos offered musical performances and dancing; masquerades were masked balls at which members of different social classes mingled in disguise.

2. **Mr. Heidegger:** John James Heidegger (1659?–1749) managed Italian opera at the Haymarket Theatre in London and supervised masquerades and ridottos there.

3. **Interest:** influence.

4. **Conjurer:** fortune teller.

5. **transported:** ecstatic.

the Water: "O, Madam," cry'd she, "one cannot catch Cold at Ranelagh:"—I could not forbear, after this, giving her some broad Hints of other Inconveniences, which might probably attend being so far from Home, at Hours that might encourage Attempts, no way agreeable to the Modesty of our Sex; on which she only said, "Lord, Madam, how you talk!"—And all my Admonitions had no other Effect than to make her shorten her Visit; no doubt, to impart the Discourse we had together to some of her Acquaintance, and to ridicule my want of Taste.

She has one Motive, as I have been told by the Men, which, notwithstanding, she would be very unwilling to acknowledge, for her prefering Masquerades to all other public Diversions; which is, that she never had a handsome Thing said to her out of a Vizard:[1]— Nature, 'tis certain, has not been over curious[2] in the Formation of her Features, and that cruel Enemy to Beauty, the Small-Pox, has rendered them yet less delicate; but with the Help of new Stays[3] once a Month, and strait Lacing,[4] she has a tolerable Shape; but then her Neck suffers for it, and confesses, in Scarlet Blushes, the Constraint put upon her Waste:[5]—This Misfortune, however, she conceals under a Handkerchief or Pelerine,[6] and high Tucker,[7] and never trips it in the Walks without some Share of Admiration from those who follow and are not nimble enough to overtake her.

A Masquerade may, therefore, well be the Delight of her Heart, where the advantageous Part of her only is revealed; yet, tho' she cannot be insensible of what is amiable in herself, and what the contrary, as she looks so often in her Glass,[8] she was weak enough last Winter to lay herself open to a Rebuff at the Masquerade, which occasion'd a good deal of Raillery[9] among those who heard of it.

---

1. **Vizard:** mask.

2. **curious:** careful.

3. **Stays:** corsets.

4. **strait Lacing:** tight lacing of the corset.

5. **Waste:** waist.

6. **Pelerine:** a kind of cape.

7. **Tucker:** a piece of lace worn around the top of the bodice.

8. **Glass:** mirror, looking glass.

9. **Raillery:** joking, teasing.

To display all her Perfections in the best Light she could, she as-sumed the Habit of a *Diana,*[1] a Green Velvet Jacket, fring'd with Silver, made so strait,[2] that, as I heard, her Chamber-Maid sprained both her Thumbs with buckling it on, very much added to her natural Slenderness:—A Silver Crescent glitter'd on her Head, which had no other Covering than her Hair, of which indeed she has a great deal, and well coloured, braided with Rows of Pearl and Flowers inter-spersed; the Vizard on, it must be own'd she made a very compleat[3] Figure, and attracted the Eyes of a good Part of the Assembly who were there that Night.

But that which flattered her Ambition most was that the great *Im-perio*[4] took notice of her, and imagining that a real *Venus* might be hid under the fictitious *Diana,* order'd a Nobleman who stood near him to go to her, and prevail with her to come to the Beaufet[5] and unmask.—He, who was not unaccustomed to such Employments, readily flew to execute his Commission, and after having brought her to the highest pitch of Vanity by the most extravagant Compliments, to crown all, let her know who it was that sent him, and on what Errand:—Charm'd as she was with the Praises he gave her, it was some Time before she yielded to do as he desired; but at last, all her Res-olution was subdued by the Reflection that she ought not to refuse any Thing to *Imperio,* and she suffered herself to be conducted by him to the Beaufet, near which *Imperio* stood, and presented her with a Glass of Wine with his own Hand, accompanied with many Compli-ments; both which she received with a low Obeysance, and at the same time pluck'd off her Mask.

But fatal was this Complaisance to all her Hopes:—*Imperio* started back, and above the Necessity of concealing the Disappointment of his Expectations:—" 'Twill not do, my Lord," said he to the Noble-man, " 'Twill not do, and I am sorry I gave you so much Trouble."

---

1. **Habit of a Diana:** costume intended to represent her as Diana, goddess of chastity and of hunting.

2. **strait:** tight.

3. **compleat:** perfect.

4. **Imperio:** a fictitious name suggesting high rank and power.

5. **Beaufet:** buffet table.

Several of the Company, whom this Adventure had drawn to that Part of the Room, saw her Face before she could be quick enough to replace her Mask; and a much greater Number heard the Words *Imperio* spoke, as he turn'd from her, so that the whole Time she stayed afterwards she was saluted with nothing but " 'Twill not do," and a loud Laugh.

Had she been Mistress of Resolution enough to have resisted the Importunities of the Emissary Lord, and the Commands of *Imperio*, she would doubtless have heard many Praises of the charming *Diana* repeated afterwards in Company; whereas now the Mystery was revealed, and the real *Diana* known, her greatest Intimates could not forbear laughing at the Mortification she had receiv'd; and on any little Dispute with any of them, the Way they took to be reveng'd was to cry, " 'Twill not do."

Much more lovely Women than the Person I have been speaking of, have sometimes met with little Indignities and Slights, which their Pride could ill sustain; and, indeed, how should it be otherwise, the Men are so censorious, that they look on all those of our Sex, who appear too much at these public Places, as setting themselves up for Sale, and, therefore, taking the Privilege of Buyers, measure us with their Eyes from Head to Foot; and as the most perfect Beauty may not have Charms for all who gaze upon her in this scrutinous Manner, few there are, if any, who have not found some who will pass by her with a contemptuous Toss, no less significant than the most rude Words could be.

O wherefore then will not Women endeavour to attain those Talents which are sure of commanding Respect!—No Form so faultless, but the enquiring Eyes of wanton and ungenerous Men may find a Blemish in. But she who has not the least Pretence to Beauty, has it in her Power, would she but once be prevail'd upon to exert it, to awe the boldest, or most affectedly nice[1] Libertine into Submissions, and force him to confess her worthy of a serious Attachment:—If even by Indigence of Circumstances, or the unjust Parsimony some Parents are guilty of, she is denied the Means of cultivating her Genius, and mak-

---

1. **nice:** discriminating.

ing herself Mistress of those expensive Accomplishments, which might render her, what we call, a shining Figure in the World, Innocence and Modesty are still her own, they were born with her, they will cost nothing to preserve, and, without the Aid of any other Charm, will be a sure Defence from all Insults.

Modesty is the Characteristick of our Sex; it is indeed the Mother of all those Graces for which we can merit either Love or Esteem:—Sweetness of Behaviour, Meekness, Courtesy, Charity in judging others, and avoiding all that will not stand the Test of Examination in ourselves, flow from it:—It is the Fountain Head, as well as the Guardian of our Chastity and Honour, and when it is once thrown off, every other Virtue grows weak, and by Degrees, is in Danger of being wholly lost:—She who is possess'd of it can be guilty of no Crime, but she who forfeits it is liable to fall into all.

How far it is is consistent with that decent Reserve, or even that Softness so becoming in Womankind, I leave any one to judge who has been Witness in what Manner some Ladies come into public Assemblies:—They do not walk but straddle; and sometimes run with a Kind of a Frisk and Jump;—throw their enormous Hoops[1] almost in the Faces of those who pass by them;—stretch out their Necks, and roll their Eyes from Side to Side, impatient to take the whole Company at one View; and if they happen to see any one dress'd less exactly, according to the Mode, than themselves, presently cry out,—"Antiquity to Perfection!—A Picture of the last Age!"—Then burst into a Laugh, loud enough to be heard at two or three Furlongs[2] distant:—Happy if they can put the unfortunate Object of their Ridicule out of Countenance:—Can such a Behaviour pass upon the World for Modesty, Good-Manners, or Good-Nature?

I do not pretend to say that all the Ladies who give themselves an Air of Boldness, meerly because it is the Fashion, are guilty of any Thing which may arraign[3] their Chastity: Many may be innocent in

---

1. **Hoops:** from their hoop skirts, stiffened with circles of bone to expand the skirts' circumference.

2. **Furlongs:** A furlong is 220 yards.

3. **arraign:** indict, accuse.

Fact who are not so in Shew; but are they not then greatly cruel to themselves to assume the Appearance of Vices they are free from!— Some are placed so high as to have their Actions above the Reach of Scandal; and others, by their avowed Manner of Life, render themselves below it; but it is to those I speak who have Reputations to lose, and who are not altogether so independent, as not to have it their Interest to be thought well of by the World.

Far be it from me to debar my Sex from going to those public Diversions, which, at present, make so much Noise in Town:—None of them but may be enjoyed without Prejudice, provided they are frequented in a reasonable Manner, and behaved at with Decency:— It is the immoderate Use, or rather the Abuse of any Thing, which renders the partaking it a Fault:—What is more agreeable than Freedom in Conversation, yet when it extends to Levity and Wantonness, what more contemptible and odious!—Some Pleasure is doubtless necessary to the Human System; taken in Moderation it envigorates both Mind and Body, but indulg'd to Excess is equally pernicious:—In fine, it ought never to break in upon those Hours which, with greater Propriety, might be devoted to Business in Persons of *Maturity;* and to *Improvement* in the *younger* Sort.

Time, always precious, can never be more so than in our early Years: —The first Ideas make the strongest and most lasting Impression:— While the Genius is free, and unclogg'd with any of the Cares of Life, and the Soul acts through the Organs of the Body, uninterrupted with any Passions, Diseases, or Disasters, then it is that we should endeavour to lay in a Stock of Knowledge for our whole Lives:—To acquire those Accomplishments which alone deserve, and will certainly attract Respect, and to establish solid Principles of Virtue, which hereafter growing up into Practice, will conduce to the Happiness of all about us, as well as of ourselves.

This Crisis, if once neglected, can never be retrieved, and will sooner or later be attended with severe Repentance:—How melancholly a Thing must it be for a Lady to hear others, who have better husbanded[1] the inestimable Moments, extoll'd for Perfections she is con-

---

1. **husbanded:** conserved.

scious she might have excell'd in, had she not rashly, and inadvertently let slip the golden Opportunity!

Nor are the Hours employed in Pleasure all that are lost by it, especially when it happens to be of that Sort which takes us much out of our own Houses:—The Idea of it is apt to render us indolent in our Affairs, even the little Time we are at Home;—where the Heart is the Thoughts will continually be when the Body is absent;—the darling Topic engrosses too much of the Mind, and occasions an Inattention to every Thing but itself: It is not, therefore, greatly to be wondered at, that young Ladies, who cannot be expected to have that Solidity which Experience only teaches, should seem so careless of improving Time, when we see very many of those who have been married Years, neglect their Husbands, Children, and Families, to run galloping after every new Entertainment that is exhibited.

But, as there is great room to fear the present Age is too far lost in Luxury and Indolence to listen to any Remonstrance, I would fain perswade the very young Ladies to act so as to render the next more promising.

As Marriage is a Thing which they will one Day think of, and a good Husband is both a natural and laudable Wish, who would not endeavour to render herself deserving the lasting Affection of a Man of Sense:—Such a one who, as Mr. *Rowe* elegantly expresses it, will be always

> Pleas'd to be happy, as she's pleas'd to bless,
> And conscious of her Worth, can never love her less.[2]

So many young Charmers are continually springing up, and the Men grow so excessively delicate in their Taste, that Beauty, in their Eyes, seems to have lost all its Bloom at Sixteen or Seventeen; and how great a Stab must it be to the Vanity of a Woman, who, at Five and Twenty, finds herself either not married at all, or to a Husband who regards her no otherwise than as a withered Rose; for so it will

---

1. **Pleas'd . . . less:** quotation unidentified.

ever be, whatever the Ladies may flatter themselves with, where there
is no Tye more strong, than meerly personal Perfection, to bind the
naturally roving and inconstant Heart:—Convinced by sad Experience
of this Truth, in vain she looks back upon her mispent Days;—in
vain, with Heart-felt Tears, regrets the Time she has lavished in Trifles
unworthy of her;—in vain essays to attone for past Follies by a quite
contrary Behaviour;—all she can do is now too late;—with her, alas!
The Sun of Hope, of Admiration, of Flattery and Pleasure, is set forever, and the dark Gloom of cold Neglect and loath'd Obscurity,
envelopes all her future Life.

*   *   *

FROM BOOK VI

There is one Quality, which has somewhat so heavenly in it, that
by so much the more we are possess'd of it, by so much the more we
draw nearer to the Great Author of Nature.—Of all the *Virtues*, it is
that which finds its Reward within itself, and at the same time most
endears us to Society; attoning for almost every other Deficiency.—
Of all the *Beauties*, it is that which attracts the most lasting Admiration, gives the greatest Charm to every thing we say or do, and renders
us amiable in every Station, and thro' every Stage of Life.

Yet is it no more than what is in the Power of every one, with the
Help of a very little Application, to attain.—It is, indeed, no other
than an Affability of Manners and Behaviour, or what is vulgarly call'd
Good-Nature; but then it must be permanent, sincere, not assum'd or
affected, but flowing from a real Benevolence of Mind, which takes
Delight in contributing all it can to the Welfare of others.

It was always my Opinion, that *Good-Sense* will make *Good-nature,*
because it shews us what is our true Interest and Happiness; and whatever some People say to the contrary, I never can believe a Person can
be possess'd of the one, without some Share of the other. A man may,
indeed, be an excellent *Mathematician, Philosopher, Theologist, Lawyer,*
or *Poet,* have Learning, Memory, Fancy, Ingenuity to a superlative

Degree, yet if in his Deportment there be any Tincture of Arrogance, Peevishness, Moroseness, Sullenness, or any of those Indications by which *Ill-Nature* may be known, I will not allow him to have a clear and strong judgment.—When any extraordinary Endowment makes him treat with Contempt or Impatience the Ideas of those who are less learned, or have less bright Capacities, it shews his own to be clouded; and whatever Sparkles may sometimes issue forth, there is still a dark and uninform'd Corner in his Soul, which hinders him from being the perfect Great Man.

Good-Nature is *Religion* too, in the highest Meaning of the Word; because it will not suffer us to do by any one what we would not willingly have done to ourselves: And tho' I am far from thinking that all those who have not this happy Disposition of Mind are wicked, yet this I venture to affirm that those who are really possess'd of it, never can be so.

A Person may be a strict Observer of the Ten Commandments, yet do a great deal of Mischief in the World: One may despise all mean and base Actions, and have in the utmost Abhorrence the more capital Offences, yet by a teazing or a contemptuous Behaviour drive, as it were, those about one to be guilty even of the worst, and so become the Author, tho' not the Actor of the Crime.

A certain Noble Person, who in his Time was look'd upon as the Arbiter of Wit, found among the many Pieces which were every Day laid on his Toylet[1] for his Inspection, one which had been left by a nameless Author, with a Letter, most humbly requesting his Lordship's Judgment on the Performance:—This, it seems, was a Dramatic Poem entitled *Mariamne,*[2] and whether it was wrote with that Skill and Energy a Story so affecting as that of the *Jewish Princess* merited, or whether it only seem'd to fall short by any Ill-humour the illustrious Reader might happen to be in at that Time, is uncertain; but he was so little satisfy'd with the Piece, that he had no sooner look'd it over,

---

1. **Toylet:** dressing table.

2. **Mariamne:** one of King Herod's wives, whom he had murdered after believing false accusations against her. She was the subject of a seventeenth-century play by Elizabeth Cary and of a tragedy by Elijah Fenton written about 1723.

than taking up his Pen hastily, he wrote on the Outside, and just under the Title these Lines:

> Poet, whoe'er thou art, God d——n thee,
> Go hang thyself, and burn thy *Mariamne.*

This was all the Answer he vouchsafed to give, and on the Gentleman's calling some Days after, was accordingly deliver'd to him by the *Valet de Chambre.*[1]

The Fondness which most young Authors have for their first Performance made him impatient to see how his had been receiv'd; but the Shock was so great on finding the cruel Sentence pass'd upon him, that he executed it immediately, condemning to the Flames his Play, and his Neck to a Halter made of his own Garters.[2]—Nobody can suppose the Noble Lord either intended or desired so dismal an Effect of the Severity he had used to one altogether unknown to him, and who possibly might be a Man of some Merit, tho' he did not happen to be an excellent Poet: It was, however, a Piece of Ill-Nature, which those who are full of take all Opportunities to vent, and I mention it only to shew what fatal Consequences the Derision of Persons on whom we depend may possibly produce.

It looks indeed as if this poor Poet wanted[3] both Spirit and Presence of Mind; for had he been Master of either, he might easily have retorted on the Peer, and oblig'd him in his Turn to take Shame to himself; since I think there could not well be greater Improprieties in the Play, than in the Judgment he pass'd upon it; as any one will see who considers his Lordship's bidding him "hang himself," and afterwards adding, "burn his *Mariamne,*" the second Part of which Injunction was impossible to be perform'd after the fulfilling of the former.—This therefore was, with all Submission to the Memory of so great a Man, a Solecism[6] in Phrase, which the very Trials at the *Old-Bailey*[7] might have instructed any one to avoid.

---

1. **Valet de Chambre:** a gentleman's personal attendant.

2. **Neck . . . Garters:** i.e., he hanged himself, using his garters to make a noose.

3. **wanted:** lacked.

4. **Solecism:** blunder, mistake.

5. **Old-Bailey:** the criminal court of London.

The cruel Lines were however wrote instantaneously, and doubtless, as I before observ'd, to gratify a Spleen,[8] which in that Moment got the better of all other Considerations: But I appeal to all the World, and would to his Lordship's own cooler Thoughts, were he living, if it had not been a greater Proof of his Understanding, as well as of that Good-Manners and Good-Will we all owe to one another, if he had testify'd his Disapprobation of the Piece, modestly submitted to his Censure, with less Abruptness:—Nay, it could not have been in the least derogatory to his Dignity, had he condescended to point out in which Particulars he had swerved from the Rules of Poetry, and even advis'd him what Emendations he might make in that Performance, and how he might avoid falling into the like Errors in any future Attempt.

It is certainly a Fiend-like Disposition to be pleased with giving Pain; yet, how have I seen some People exult and triumph in their Power of doing it! and the more Disquiet they are capable of spreading, the more considerable they imagine themselves.—Ridiculous Infatuation of ill-judging Pride!—Does not a Wasp, or even a common Fly buzzing about one's Ears, inflict a temporary Uneasiness? Not the most insignificant Reptile[1] that the Air or Earth affords, but has the Power of being vexatious to us for a while, and is the Rival of the Ill-natur'd, who by being such but vainly boasts of a superior Reason.

Persons of this Temperament diffuse a Gloom where'er they come: No sooner they appear, than Conversation is at a stand, Mirth is check'd, and every one present seems to have catch'd some Share of the Infection: Whereas, on the contrary, the Sight of one who is known to have *Good-Nature,* invigorates like the Sun, inspires a Chearfulness where it before was wanting, and heightens what it finds.

Whoever reflects on any two Persons in whom this Contrast in Humour is visible, will naturally shun the one, and court the Society of the other, even tho' they have no Concern with either: But where there is any kind of Dependance, or a Necessity of living with, or being much with one of them, the Influence must be felt in proportion to the good or bad Qualities of whichever it happens to be.

---

1. **Spleen:** fit of anger or ill humor.

2. **Reptile:** creeping or crawling creature.

A Sweetness of Disposition is what every one wishes to find in those they are oblig'd to live with, and it is the more endearing according to the Authority of the Person's Station: When the Heads of a Family are in Amity with each other, and behave with Gentleness and Humanity to all beneath them, how perfect is the Harmony that reigns throughout! If there happen to be any dogged or ill-natur'd Persons among them, they will either conceal or endeavour to rectify their Humours by the Example of their Superiors; and a chearful and ready Application to their several Duties renders all Things easy, softens the Asperity of cross Accidents, and gives a double Relish to Prosperity.

But when those, whose Province it is to govern, shew a Dissatisfaction with each other, and receive with Imperiousness and Peevishness the Services done by their Inferiors, how unhappy does it make all about them! A general Discontent runs through the whole: The Commands of such People are obey'd with Reluctance; they may be fear'd, but they cannot be truly loved; and their very Children are capable of paying them no more than an exterior Duty. But most terrible of all is it for either him or her who, by Nature mild and gentle, shares the Bed of one of a contrary Disposition; when, instead of fond Endearments, they find themselves accosted with Testimonies of Disgust, or such as may very well be taken for it; when, instead of soft Repose, they have only Slumbers broken by distracting Dreams, the Effects of waking Quarrels; when, instead of those amicable Consultations which the Affairs of two People whose Interests are one demands, they are treated with either sullen Silence, Reproaches, or equally provoking unreasonable Contradictions:—What Words can paint the Misery of such a forc'd Enduring!

Still worse is it where two Persons equally harsh and unsociable happen to be united in Marriage.—Where ill Conditions clash, and both seem to vye which shall create the most Disquiet to all related or belonging to them, as well as to each other, they form an Epitome of Hell where'er they come, and well may be compar'd to the tormenting Fiends, who capable of feeling no Rest, no Comfort in their own Bosoms, deny it, as much as in them lies, to all besides.

There are two Sources from whence what is called *Ill-Nature* proceeds; the one, is from the Seeds of Tyranny in the Soul; the other, only from Habit or Accidents: The former is hardly ever to be eradicated; fair Means will but sooth, and serve rather to confirm than abate the impetuous Propensity; and rough Measures, tho' never so strenuously pursued, will scarce be able to subdue it; but the latter may easily be removed by one's own Reason and Reflection, without any other Assistance.

I have known several Instances where Persons who on a strict Examination into themselves finding a Tendency to fall into some one or other of those many different Modes, in which *Ill-Nature* appears, have by the Strength of Resolution been able to throw them off; and by keeping a constant Guard over all their Words and Actions, even in the minutest Matters, so restrain'd all turbulent Emotions from breaking out, that they have in Time entirely subsided, and never after return'd.

This is a Task which methinks all People, be they of what Condition or Degree soever, ought to impose upon themselves: Religion, Morality, and even common Policy require it of them; and whatever Difficulties they find, or Pains they take while making the Essay,[1] I am well assur'd both will be much more than compensated for in the Accomplishment.

In order to enable us to do this with the more Ease, we should consider who are the Objects on whom we have the Power of discharging our Ill-Humours:—Are they not such as Fate has in some measure subjected to us? for it is not our Superiors, or those of equal Circumstances with ourselves, will brook ungentle Treatment, and few there are who tempt the Consequences. We should therefore reflect that Old-Age, Infancy, the Poor, the Sick, in fine, whatever is helpless of itself, and stands in need of Tenderness, has an indisputable Claim to it; and as it is only over such we dare assume the Privilege of insulting, how truly mean, base, and ungenerous, as well as wicked, it is, to make use of the Means our happier Stars[2] have given us, to add to the Affliction of those whom it is certainly our Duty to console.

In fact, there would be no such thing as Calamity in the World, did every Member of this great Body behave with any tolerable Degree of *Good-Nature* and *Humanity* to the others. *Good-Nature* is the Ce-

---

1. **Essay:** attempt.

2. **Stars:** imagined as controllers of individual fates.

ment of Love and Friendship, the Bandage of Society, the rich Man's Pleasure, and the poor Man's Refuge.—Peace, Harmony, and Joy reign where it subsists, and all is Discord and Confusion where it is banish'd.

But as all other Vices, so a Sourness of Humour is also more unbecoming in Women than in Men: A Virago,[1] how much soever she may be blown up with Self-Conceit, to imagine that to domineer, and rail, and bounce,[2] denotes her a Person of Wit and Œconomy,[3] is as despicable a Character as any I know; and is deservedly shunn'd and hated by the more gentle of her own Sex, and ridicul'd and laugh'd at by all in general of the other.

Softness and Affability should go Hand in Hand with Modesty, and where the former are entirely wanting, one may very well suspect some Deficiency in the latter. But as a Depravity of Manners shews itself in various Shapes, the sullen and the thwarting Disposition is often as perplexing as the assuming and violent: Unhappy are all who contract any Intimacy with a Woman of either of these Tempers; but greatly to be pitied is the Husband, the Child, and the Servant of such a Wife, a Mother, and a Mistress.[4]

I have often thought it strange that some Ladies, who think no Expence of Time or Money too much for any thing they are told will afford either Addition or Support to their personal Charms, should by an ill Disposition of Mind destroy what all the Arts they can make use of never can repair. *Ill-Nature* is a greater Enemy to Beauty than the Small-Pox ever was; it gives a disagreeable Depth to all the Lines of the Face; it sinks the Cheeks; throws a disagreeable Deadness or a fiery Redness into the Eye, according as the Malady proceeds from an Excess of Phlegm or Choler;[5] it swells the Lip, fades the Complexion, contracts the Brow, and brings on a Decay before the Time: Sure if

---

1. **Virago:** manlike woman, female warrior.

2. **bounce:** bluster, hector.

3. **Œconomy:** economy (i.e., a good household manager).

4. **Mistress:** i.e., of servants.

5. **Phlegm or Choler:** An excess of phlegm (like choler, one of the four humours) was thought to cause sluggishness; an excess of choler caused irascibility.

they who plume themselves chiefly on their Attractions would consider this, it would occasion a prodigious Alteration in the Behaviour of many of them!

Some few there are, indeed, to whom Nature has been so prodigal of her Favours, that it is not even in their own Power to lessen the magnetick Force[1] of their Charms; and these may maintain their Dominion over their Lovers, and perhaps seem faultless for a Time, but when once Marriage has, as the Poet says, debased the imperious Mistress into Wife, all that Blaze of Beauty, which lately was beheld with Awe and Admiration, becomes familiar to the Husband's Eye;—the Lustre of it dazzles him no longer, and he distinguishes the Errors which before he was incapable of imagining were hid under it. He then perhaps discovers Pride, Vanity, Self-Sufficiency, a Contempt of every thing beside herself, and all the Follies, ascribed to the weakest of her Sex, peep out thro' that Form his Passion had once made him look upon as all Perfection. Amazed and angry with the Deception it had put upon him, he attempts to reform and bring the Charmer back to what he lately thought her,—perswades,—remonstrates,—threatens;—all alas too often proves in vain:—Incorrigible, and determin'd to persist, she accuses his too great Penetration, reproaches in her Turn; mutual Indifference occasions mutual Slights, they end one Quarrel but to begin another, and their whole future Lives are sure to be one continued Series of Discord.

This is so common a Case, that I am surprized and grieved to find any Married-Woman can expect to maintain an Authority with, much less over her Husband, but by such Arms as are allow'd alone prevalent in our Sex.—When a Woman unwomanizes herself, renounces the Softness of her Nature, and idly boasts of having it in her Power to conquer, Man has a Right to exert his Strength, and shew her the Vanity of her Attempt.—Complaisance, Tenderness and Fidelity will always have Charms for a Man of Understanding, but rough Measures will never get the better of any thing but a Fool.

To this it may be alledg'd, that it is frequently the Lot of a Woman of true Sense to be join'd to a Man of mean Capacity, and so refractory

---

1. **magnetick Force:** power to attract.

in his Humour, that tho' she does all in her Power to please him, yet he is dissatisfy'd with her Behaviour, and it would be too meanly submissive in her to continue any Marks of Tenderness to a Person so altogether unworthy of them. I grant, that a Wife thus circumstanced is very unhappy, but must think she would but render herself more so by struggling with her Chain: The veryest[1] Coxcomb of them all is sensible of a Husband's Power, and frequently exerts it the more as he has less Reason to do so: For her own Peace, therefore, she ought to do nothing that may stir up his Ill-Humour, and if all is ineffectual, bear with him as much as possible.

I know very well that this is a Doctrine will sound but harshly in the Ears of most Wives; but I appeal to any of those who have made the Trial, whether they ever found any thing was gained by Robustness.[2]

In fine, there are no Provocations, no Circumstances in Life, that I can allow to be a sufficient Excuse for *Ill-Nature:* On some Occasions it is neither unjust nor impolitick to resent being treated with it; but we should never return it in the same manner, since there are many other Ways to shew we are sensible of an Affront, without imitating that which we complain of when offer'd to ourselves.

Much less ought we, when at any time we imagine ourselves hardly dealt with by those, where Duty, Interest, or any other Consideration, obliges us to submit to without any Shew of Resentment, to vent the inward Discontent it may occasion in us on others who have no way contributed to aggrieve us: That were to punish the Innocent for the sake of the Guilty: Yet I am sorry to observe it is but too frequently practiced by Persons of both Sexes, and of all Ages and Degrees.[3]

How often have I seen People, after having met with some Matter of Disquiet abroad, come home and revenge themselves on all they find in their way!—Wife, Children, Servants, down to the favourite Dog, feel the Effects of an Ill-Humour, which the poor Creatures have

---

1. **veryest:** truest.

2. **Robustness:** roughness, rudeness.

3. **Degrees:** social ranks.

been so far from doing any thing to excite, that they even know not the Meaning of.

Nay, there are some so far gone in this Folly, that it extends even to Things inanimate and insensible of the Ill-usage they sustain; as many a shatter'd Set of China, Glasses, Tables, Chairs, and other Utensils, are a Proof.—What monstrous Stupidity is this! What can a Bystander think of the Understanding of any one who acts in this mad Manner!

Nor do the bad Effects of *Ill-Nature* always stop here. If he who receives the first Offence revenges it on another, that Person may perhaps fall on a third by the same Motive; he on a fourth, and so on, *ad infinitum;*[1] so that not one but many Families suffer for the Misbehaviour of a single Person.

Many are the Pretences which those asham'd of such Exploits will make after being guilty of them:—They will tell you, that they are troubled with the overflowing of the Gall,[2] that they have the Vapours,[3] the Spleen,[4] or Lowness of Spirits, which being Distempers of the Body, they can no more help acting in the Manner they do, when the Fit is on them, than a Man in a high Fever can help raving. 'Tis true, indeed, that these are Distempers of the Body; but when we consider how great an Influence the *Mind* has over the *Body*, I believe we shall be forced to acknowledge, that in rectifying the Errors of the *one*, we shall in a great measure prevent not only these but many kinds of Disorders in the *other*.

What Numbers have pined themselves into Consumptions[5] by immoderate Grief!—How dreadful a Ravage has furious Passion occasioned among the Human Specie, under the Names of Fevers, Pleurisies, Convulsions!—It is notorious, and no Physician will deny it,

---

1. **ad infinitum:** endlessly.

2. **Gall:** a liver secretion; thought to cause bitterness.

3. **Vapours:** hypochondria or hysteria; thought to be caused by exhalations from the stomach.

4. **Spleen:** melancholy or morose feelings; considered to be produced by the spleen, a gland near the stomach.

5. **Consumptions:** tuberculosis.

that the violent Agitations of the *Mind* have made more *Suicides* than Poyson, Sword, or Halter.[1]

Well then may our Ill-Conditions create a continual Restlessness within, disturb the Motion of the Animal Spirits, and bring on the Disorders abovementioned; so that the Excuses made on this Score serve rather to exaggerate than alleviate the Fault.

I do not say that the *Mind* has in *all Constitutions* so much the Direction of the *Body*, as to render it sickly or healthy, and prolong or shorten Life *meerly* by its own Operation; but I will venture to affirm, that in *some* it has, and that there are *none* but feel its Effects in a more or less Degree.

I am very sensible there are Diseases which we inherit from our Parents, others that are contracted in our Infancy, and that after we arrive at Maturity too much Sleep or Over-watching,[2] violent Colds or excessive Heats, unwholesome Food, bad Air, too vehement or too little Exercise, and a thousand other Accidents, in which the *Mind* has no Part, may breed Distempers in the *Body,* and hasten Dissolution; but even then, according to the good or bad Affections of the *Mind,* they are greatly moderated, or render'd more virulent.

This is so plain and obvious a Maxim, that it stands in need of no Examples to illustrate the Truth of it; yet I cannot forbear making mention of one which fill'd all who had the Opportunity of knowing it with Admiration.

A Person, with whom I am intimately acquainted, labour'd under a severe Indisposition of more than seven Years Duration: Often have I seen the Struggles between Life and Death: Often have the Animal[3] Functions been at a stand, and seem'd to cease for ever:—Yet did she at the last get the better of this Rack of Nature, recover'd her so long-lost Health and Strength, and those who had taken of her, as they had all the Reason in the World to imagine, their last farewell, now behold her in more perfect Ease than many of them are themselves.—

---

1. **Halter:** noose.

2. **Over-watching:** watching too long or too late; i.e., an excess of wakefulness.

3. **Animal:** physical.

The Cure was wonderful, and the more so as not accomplish'd by the Power of *Medicine,* as the Physicians themselves unanimously agreed; but merely by her own consummate Patience, constant Chearfulness, and steady Fortitude in the midst of all the Agonies she sustain'd.— To add to her Distemper, and at the same time to her Glory in surmounting them, she had also many secret Woes to combat with, the least of which was sufficient to have overwhelm'd a Mind not resolved to be above all Things in this World, and entirely resign'd to the Will of the Supreme Being.

For this one Instance of true Heroism and Magnanimity, I cou'd produce a great Number of others of a different Nature.—Few, if any Families have been without one or more Persons in it, who by their Carelessness in restraining those inordinate Emotions, to which the Mind is so liable, have brought some fearful Ailment in the Body, and then with an equal Meanness have sunk under it.

*   *   *

FROM BOOK VIII

To the FEMALE SPECTATOR.

MADAM,

As I look upon you to be a Person who knows the World perfectly well, and has the Happiness of your own Sex very much at Heart, I wonder you have never yet thought fit to throw out some Admonitions concerning the immoderate Use of Tea; which however innocent it may seem to those that practise it, is a kind of Debauchery no less expensive, and perhaps even more pernicious in its Consequences, than those which the Men, who are not professed Rakes,[1] are generally accused of.

---

1. **Rakes:** libertines.

This, at first Sight, may be looked upon as too bold an Assertion, but, on a nearer Examination, I am perswaded will be found no more than reasonable, and will undertake to prove that the Tea-Table, as manag'd in some Families, costs more to support than would maintain two Children at Nurse.[1]—Yet is this by much the least Part of the Evil;—it is the utter Destruction of all Œconomy,—the Bane of good Housewifry,—and the Source of Idleness, by engrossing those Hours which ought to be employed in an honest and prudent Endeavour to add to, or preserve what Fortune, or former Industry has bestowed.— Were the Folly of wasting Time and Money in this manner confined only to the Great, who have enough of both to spare, it would not so much call for public Reproof; but all Degrees[2] of Women are infected with it, and a Wife now looks upon her Tea-Chest, Table, and its Implements, to be as much her Right by Marriage as her Wedding-Ring.

Tho' you cannot, Madam, be insensible that the trading Part of the Nation must suffer greatly on this score, especially those who keep Shops, I beg you will give me Leave to mention some few Particulars of the Hardships we Husbands of that Class are obliged to bear.

The first Thing the too genteel Wife does after opening her Eyes in the Morning, is to ring the Bell for her Maid, and ask if the Tea Kettle boils.—If any Accident has happened to delay this important Affair, the House is sure to eccho with Reproaches; but if there is no Disappointment in the Case, the Petticoats and Bed-Gown[3] are hastily thrown over the Shoulders, Madam repairs to her easy Chair, sits down before her Table in Querpo[4] with all her Equipage[5] about her, and sips, and pauses, and then sips again, while the Maid attends assiduous to replenish, as often as call'd for, the drain'd Vehicle of that precious Liquor.

---

1. **at Nurse:** in the care of a wetnurse.

2. **Degrees:** ranks.

3. **Bed-Gown:** bathrobe, dressing gown.

4. **in Querpo:** without being properly dressed.

5. **Equipage:** equipment.

An Hour is the least can be allowed to Breakfast, after which the Maid carries all the Utensils down to the Kitchen, and sits down to the Remains of the Tea (or it is probable some fresh she has found Opportunity to purloin) with the same State as her Mistress, takes as much time, and would think herself highly injur'd should any one call her away, or attempt to interrupt her in it: So that, between both, the whole Morning is elapsed, and it is as much as the poor Husband can do to get a Bit of Dinner ready by two or three o'Clock.

Dinner above and below[1] is no sooner over, than the Tea-Table must be again set forth:—Some friendly Neighbour comes in to chat away an Hour:—Two are no Company, and the Maid being very busy in cutting Bread and Butter, one 'Prentice[2] is called out of the Shop to run this Way and fetch Mrs. Such-a-one, and another that Way to fetch Mrs. Such-a-one, so that the Husband must be his own Man,[3] and if two Customers chance to come at the same Time, he frequently loses one for want of Hands to serve them.

It often happens, that when the Tea-drinking Company have almost finished their Regale,[4] and the Table is going to be removed, a fresh Visitor arrives, who must have fresh Tea made for her; after her another, who is always treated with the same Compliment; a third, perhaps a fourth, or more, till the Room is quite full, and the Entertainment prolonged a considerable Time after the Candles are lighted, when the Days are of a moderate Length.

This is sufficient to shew the Loss of Time both as to the Mistress and Servants, and how much the Regularity of the Tea-Table occasions a Want of Regularity in every Thing beside; but, Madam, there is yet another, and more mischievous Effect attends the Drinking too much of this *Indian* Herb.[5]

---

1. **below:** belowstairs, among the servants.
2. **'Prentice:** apprentice.
3. **Man:** helper.
4. **Regale:** entertainment, feast.
5. **Indian Herb:** tea, which was imported from India.

What I mean is too notorious a Fact not to be easily guessed at; but lest it should be misconstrued by any of your Readers, I shall venture to explain it.

Tea, whether of the *Green* or *Bohea*[1] kind, when taken to Excess, occasions a Dejection of Spirits and Flatulency, which lays the Drinkers of it under a kind of Necessity of having recourse to more animating Liquors.—The most temperate and sober of the Sex find themselves obliged to drink Wine pretty freely after it: None of them now-a-days pretend to entertain with the one without the other; and the Bottle and Glass are as sure an Appendix to the Tea-Table as the Slop-Bason.[2]

Happy are those who can content themselves with a Refreshment, which, tho' not to be had in any Perfection in *England,* is yet infinitely less destructive to the human System than some others too frequently substituted in its Place, when it is found too weak to answer the End proposed by taking it.

Brandy, Rum, and other Spirituous[3] Liquors, being of a more exhillerating Nature, at least for the present, are become a usual Supplement to Tea, and, I am sorry to say, by their frequent Use grow so familiar to the Palate, that their intoxicating Qualities are no longer formidable, and the Vapours, Cholic, a bad Digestion, or some other Complaint, serves as an Excuse for drinking them in a more plentiful degree, than the best Constitution can for any length of Time support.

Hence ensue innumerable Maladies, Doctor's Fees, Apothecary's Bills, *Bath, Tunbridge*, the *Spa*,[4] and all that can destroy the wretched Husband's Peace, or impoverish him in his Fortune.

The more is his Affection for a Wife who takes so little Care of his Interest and Happiness, and of her own Health and Reputation, the more will his Affliction be; and the less will she be able to forgive

---

1. **Bohea:** a fine black tea.

2. **Slop-Bason:** for used tea leaves.

3. **Spirituous:** alcoholic.

4. **Bath . . . Spa:** fashionable resorts where visitors could indulge in baths in natural warm springs, thought to have medicinal value.

herself, when brought by a too late and sad Experience to a right way of Thinking.

That you will therefore use your Endeavours that so great an Enemy to the Felicity of the meaner sort of People may be banished from their Houses, is the unanimous Desire of all Husbands, and most humbly petition'd for by him who is,

With the greatest Admiration of your Writings,
MADAM,
Your most humble, and
Fryday-Street,   *Most obedient Servant,*
Nov. 2, 1744.   JOHN CAREFUL.

I dare say one Half of my Readers will expect me to be very angry at this Declamation against an Amusement my Sex are generally so fond of; but it is the firm Resolution of our Club to maintain strict Impartiality in these Lucubrations; and were any of us ever so deeply affected by the Satire,[1] (which thank Heaven we are not) we should, notwithstanding, allow it to be just.

There cannot certainly be a Subject more tickling to the Spleen[2] of the Ill-natur'd, or afford more Matter of Concern to the Gentle and Compassionate, than the Affectation of some Tradesmen's Wives in the Article Mr. *Careful* complains of; and, it must be own'd, he has done it in so Picturesque a manner, that it is impossible to read him without imagining one sees the ridiculous Behaviour he describes.

No Woman, who is conscious of being guilty of it, can, in my Opinion, behold herself thus delineated without a Confusion, which must occasion a thorough Reformation.

Tea is, however, in itself a very harmless Herb, and an Infusion of it in boiling Water agrees with most Constitutions, when taken moderately; but then, it must be confess'd, we have Plants of our own

---

1. **the Satire:** the attack conveyed by John Careful's fictional narrative.

2. **Spleen:** morose feelings.

Growth no less pleasing to the Palate, and more effectual for all the Purposes which furnish an Excuse for the Afternoon's Regale.

This is a Truth allowed by all, even by those from whom we purchase Tea at so dear a Rate; but alas! the Passion we have for Exotics discovers itself but in too many Instances, and we neglect the Use of what we have within ourselves for the same Reason as some Men do their Wives, only because they are their own.

The three Objections which Mr. *Careful* makes, or indeed that any body can make against the Tea-Table, are *First,* The Loss of Time and Hindrance to Business;—*Secondly,* The Expence;—and, *Lastly,* The Consequences, often arising from it, *Dram-drinking*[1] and *Ill-health.*.

To the *first* it may be answered, that were *Tea* to be entirely banished, and *Baum,*[2] Sage, Mint, or any other *English* Herb substituted in its Place, and used in the same manner, the Effect would be the same as to that Point, because the one would engross the Hours as well as the other.—Nor does the *second* carry any great Weight, the Expence of Tea itself, exclusive of those other Apurtenances, which would be equally necessary with any other Herb is an Indulgence, which, where there is any thing of a Competency, might be allowed the Wife without Prejudice to the Circumstances of her Husband.— But the *third* is not so easily got over: This is what indeed renders the Use of *Indian* Tea, above all other, pernicious. None, I believe, that drink it constantly twice a Day, but have experienced the ill Effects it has on the Constitution:—They feel a sinking of the Heart, a kind of inward Horror, which is no ways to be removed but by that dangerous Remedy Mr. *Careful* mentions, and which, in Time, proves worse than the Disease itself.

It is therefore to be wished, that People of all Ranks would endeavour to wean themselves from it; and I have the more room to hope it will be so, because Persons of Quality,[3] whose Example made it first the Mode, begin every Day to take less and less Pleasure in the

---

1. **Dram-drinking:** drinking hard liquor.
2. **Baum:** balm, a common herb.
3. **Quality:** high rank.

Tea-Table.—As it gain'd not, however, Estimation all at once, we cannot expect it should entirely lose its Credit all at once; and those who suffer by the Use of it, may comfort themselves in the Assurance my spectatorial Observation gives them, that it is already very much declined.

I cannot conclude this Subject without repeating what was said to me some Years ago by a certain Lady with whom I was intimately acquainted:—She was one of the greatest Devotees to the Tea-Table I ever knew:—*Bohea* and Bread and Butter was her chief Sustenance, and the Society of those who loved it as well as she did, her only Amusement.—An Accident, not material to mention, separated us for a considerable Time; but on the first Visit I made her afterward, was very much surpriz'd to find she had left off *Bohea,* and would drink only *Green,* which I thought more prejudicial to her Constitution than the other, she being extremely lean, and inclining to a Consumption.—Having expressed my Sentiments to her on this Head, "I am sensible," replied she, she, "that it is very bad for me:—I have had continual Pains in my Stomach ever since I drank it, and cannot enjoy one Hour's sound Sleep in a whole Night:—Yet what can I do?—I had rather endure all this than have my Brain disordered, and I assure you, if I had continued the Use of *Bohea* but a very little longer, I should have been mad."

These Words, delivered in the most grave and solemn Accents, made me not only then, but ever since, as often as I think on them, smile within myself at the Infatuation of making the drinking Tea of some kind or other of such Importance, that there is no such thing as quitting it, and to chuse that sort which will do us the least Mischief, is all we have to consider.

As these Monthly Essays are published with a View of *improving* the *Morals,* not *complimenting* the *Frailties* of my Sex, those who remember that *Excesses* in all Things are blameable, will not think what I have said too severe.

In fine, nothing ought to be indulged till it becomes so far habitual, that we cannot leave it off without Difficulty, when we find it any way prejudicial or inconvenient.

The Snuff-Box[1] and Smelling-Bottle[2] are pretty Trinkets in a Lady's Pocket, and are frequently necessary to supply a Pause in Conversation, and on some other Occasions; but whatever Virtues they are possess'd of, they are all lost by a too constant and familiar Use, and nothing can be more pernicious to the Brain, or render one more ridiculous in Company, than to have either of them perpetually in one's Hand.

I know a Lady who never sits down to Dinner without her Snuff-Box by her Plate, and another that cannot sleep without her Bottle of *Sal Volatile*[3] under her Pillow;—but I shall reserve expatiating on the Folly and Misfortune of this Bigotry of Custom till some other Time, lest the fair Author of the following Letter should think herself neglected.

To the FEMALE SPECTATOR.
Dear Female Sage,

I have a vast Opinion of your Wit; and you may be convinced of it by my asking your Advice;—a Compliment, I assure you, I never paid to my own Mother, or any Soul besides yourself.—You must know that, among about half an hundred who make their Addresses to me, there are three who flatter themselves with Hopes of Success; and indeed with some Reason, for I have given to each of them all the Encouragement could be expected from a Woman of Honour:— But I will give you their Characters, and the different Sentiments they have inspired me with, that you may be the better able to judge which of them I ought to make Choice of for a Partner for Life.

The first is a tall graceful Man, of an honourable Family, has a large Estate, and offers me a Jointure[4] beyond what my Fortune, tho' it is very considerable, could demand: He is besides addicted to no kind of Vice, and has the Reputation of a more than common Understand-

---

1. **Snuff-Box:** small ornamental box containing snuff, a form of tobacco that eighteenth-century men and women introduced into their nostrils to make themselves sneeze.

2. **Smelling-Bottle:** ornamental bottle containing smelling salts.

3. **Sal-Volatile:** an aromatic solution used as a restorative in fainting fits.

4. **Jointure:** marriage settlement providing for the wife's income in the event of her husband's death.

ing; but, with all these good Qualities, there is somewhat in him that displeases me:—He ought, methinks, whenever we are alone together, to entertain me with nothing but his Passion; but, instead of that, he often talks to me on Subjects which he may easily perceive are not agreeable to my Humour, and are indeed too serious to suit with the Years of either of us, he being no more than three and twenty, and I but seventeen.—We were a Week ago to visit a Relation of mine whose House has a Prospect[1] of the Sea, and happening to look out of one of the Windows while we waited for my Cousin's coming down, how do you think he diverted me? Why with some grave Reflections on that uncertain Element,—the unhappy Fate of brave Admiral *Balchen,*[2]—and the Loss the Navy and whole Nation had of him;— as if I had anything to do with the Admiral, the Navy, or the Nation: Would it not have better become him, since he must needs talk of the Sea, to have compared me to the *Venus*[3] rising out of it, or to the charming *Hero,* for whose sake *Leander* swam the *Hellespont.*[4]

I could give you a thousand such odd Instances of his Behaviour; and tho' I am convinced that he loves me, because he has rejected several Proposals of more advantagious Matches in the precarious Hopes of obtaining me, yet he is such a strange Creature that he never once told me that he could not live without me, or swore, that if he could not have me, he would have nobody.—But I have said enough about him, and will now go on to the second.

He is what you may call a Lover indeed:—He follows me wherever I go:—My Shadow, or the Dial to the Sun, is not more constant:— Then he is sure to approve of all I say and do; and I frequently both act and speak what my own Reason tells me is absurd, merely to try

---

1. **Prospect:** view.

2. **Balchen:** Sir John Balchen (1670–1744), who went down with his ship in the English Channel.

3. **Venus:** Roman goddess of love and beauty. According to myth, she was born out of the foam of the sea.

4. **Hero . . . Hellespont:** In Greek mythology, Hero, a virgin priestess of Aphrodite in the Turkish town of Sestos, was loved by Leander, who lived in Abydos, an ancient town in Asia Minor on the other side of the Strait of Hellespont. He drowned in an attempt to swim across the strait between them, and she subsequently committed suicide.

how he will relish it:—But the poor Creature seems to have no Will but mine, and on my Conscience I believe, were I to bid him cut off his right Hand, he would not hesitate to obey me.—When I but smile upon him, he is all Extasy; and if I frown, his Countenance becomes so meagre, that you would think he had been sick a Week.—I have been two or three times about to give him his final Answer, but was obliged to retract my Words to prevent his running himself through the Body.—In short, the Passion the Man has for me makes him quite silly, and the greatest Objection I have against marrying him, is, that his excessive Fondness would render us the Jest of our Acquaintance.— As to the rest, he has a very good Estate,[1] a Person[2] agreeable enough, a fine gilt Berlin,[3] and the most beautiful String of Horses, except his Majesty's, that ever I saw in my Life.

The third is gay, witty, genteel, handsome as an Angel, and dresses to a charm:—He is intimate with all the great World, knows all their Intrigues, and relates them in the most agreeable manner:—Then he has a delightful Voice, a tolerable Skill in Music, and has all the new Tunes the Moment they come from the Composer.—In fine, there is no one Perfection we Women admire in the Sex, that he does not possess in an infinite Degree.—We never are in the Mall,[4] at the Play, Opera, Assembly, or any public Place, but all Eyes are fixed upon him, and then turned on me with a kind of malicious Leer, for engrossing so pretty a Fellow to myself.—Such a Lover, you will own, might be flattering enough to the Vanity of any Woman; and I cannot say but it highly diverts and pleases me, to observe the little Artifices some, even among my own Acquaintance, put in Practice in hopes of gaining him from me.

But yet in spite of all these engaging Qualities in him, in spite of the Gratification it gives my Pride to see myself triumphant over all who wish to be my Rivals, my Reason tells me he deserves less of my Affection than either of those I have been describing, not only because his Estate is less, but because he seems to make too great a Merit of

---

1. **Estate:** inherited money and property.
2. **Person:** personal appearance.
3. **Berlin:** four-wheeled covered carriage.
4. **Mall:** a fashionable promenade in St. James's Park, London.

preferring me to the rest of my Sex:—He is always telling me of the great Offers daily made to him;—of the Invitations given him by one celebrated Beauty, and the kind Glances he receives from another; and tho' he always closes these Speeches with vowing it is not in the Power of any Thing to come in Competition with me, yet he seems, on the whole, to take more Pains to convince me how much he is beloved, than how much he loves; and this makes me conclude him to be what the World calls *a Man too full of himself.*

This is as exact a Picture as I can give you of my three Lovers, and I do not doubt but you are impatient to know which of them it is my Heart is most inclined to favour.—I will tell you then, with the utmost Sincerity, that they have all their Places, and I am, as it were, divided among them.—The first has my Esteem,—the second my Pity,—and the third my Love:—But yet I have not so much *Esteem* for the first, as should occasion me to despise either of the others I should make Choice of; not so much *Pity* to the second, as to engage me to allow any Favours prejudicial to whoever should be my Husband; nor so much *Love* for the last, as not to be able to withdraw it, if once I bestow my Person on a different Object.

As I am entirely at my own Disposal,[1] I would fain make such a Choice as should be approved on by the World, and afford the greatest Prospect of Happiness to myself.—You being a Person who can be no way prejudiced in favour of any Pretenders to me, are best capable of advising me in so important an Affair, and, I flatter myself, will take the Trouble of giving me such Reasons for whatever Part you take, as will determine me to be wholly guided by your Opinion, and enable me to put an End to the long Suspence the above-mention'd Gentlemen have languished in, as well as the fluctuating Condition of my own Mind.

A speedy and cordial Compliance with this Request, will lay under the greatest Obligation her who is,

Dear Creature,
Your constant Reader,
And humble Servant,.
BELLAMONTE.

Pall-Mall
Nov. 7, 1744.

---

1. **at my own Disposal:** as to marriage: she can make her own choice.

There is no Stage nor Rank in Life, that is not attended with some Portion of Disquiet of one kind or other, and I do not doubt but this young Lady feels little less in the Uncertainty which of her Lovers it will best become her to make Choice of, than the most passionate of them does in the Fears of being rejected. However, if she is really as ready to take Advice as the *Female Spectator* is to give it, the best in our Power shall be done to set her right.

It must be confessed she is no less just than discerning in dividing the present Affections of her Soul.—The first of her Admirers demands all the Esteem she can bestow.—The second, if sincere, is indeed a pity-moving Character.—And the fine Person and Accomplishments of the third, if really such as she imagines them to be, may claim some Share of Inclination. But as all these favourable Sentiments must at last center in one, and Esteem, Pity, and Admiration blend to compose a perfect Tenderness, it would be well for her to consider that the *two last* of themselves, without more solid Merits to attract the *former,* can form but a short-liv'd and unsubstantial Passion.—*Love* is not deserving to be called Love, when not accompanied by *Friendship,* and Friendship can only be founded on *Esteem.*—He therefore who is found worthy of *that,* has a just Title to the *other* also, if no Disparity of Age, Birth, Fortune, or a disagreeable Form, forbids the soft Impulse, and forces Nature to oppose Reason.

By this, I dare say, *Bellamonte* expects I will decree for her first Lover, as she acknowledges none of the Impediments I have mentioned can be alledged against him; and if her extreme Youth will permit her to think with that Seriousness the Matter requires, I am sure she has a sufficient Fund of good Sense to know that Things are not always what they seem.—A very little Observation will serve to inform her that the most dying Lover is frequently far removed from the most affectionate Husband; and also, that a Man who values himself upon his *personal* Excellencies, has often been too careless of his *mental* Part, to be convinced within himself that Admiration ought only to be the Reward of *acquir'd Virtues,* not of such *casual Perfections* as a handsome Face, well-turn'd Limbs, or an agreeable Voice, which a thousand Accidents may deprive him of, and consequently convert the Love he so much plumes himself upon, into an adequate Contempt.

If her first-mention'd Lover does not on every Occasion fall into Despair, and threaten to lay violent Hands on his own Life, as the second does, it shews he has less of the Froth of Love, but does not denote he is not more full of the permanent and valuable Part; on the contrary, his Passion evaporates not in Words:—The Spirit remains entire[1] within his Breast, and it is scarce to be doubted will last as long as Life.

But because she seems to have an equal Share of Good-Nature as of Wit, I would have her be under no Apprehensions that any thing fatal will ensue on her refusing the second Lover; the Deaths threatened by a Man of his Cast, are as fictitious as the Darts and Flames of his pretended Deity;[2] and we often see those of them who prosecute their Aim with the greatest Vigour, bear a Disappointment with the most Indifference. Much less would I have her imagine, that in preferring him to the others, she should be certain of retaining the same Power over his Will and Actions after Marriage as he now flatters her with.—Many Women have been deceived by this Shew[3] of Obsequiousness in those who have afterward become their Tyrants, not remembering what the Poet says:

> The humblest Lover, when he lowest lies,
> But kneels to conquer, and but falls to rise,[4]

But as mere Pity and Compassion is all our *Bellamonte* bestows on this whining *Strephon,*[5] I am under no great Concern for her on his Account: He may whistle out his Lamentations to the Fields and Groves, or what is every whit as likely, if not much more so, carry them to the Feet of some less obdurate Fair, without her breaking her Peace for his Relief.—I wish I could say the handsome, talking, rat-

---

1. **Entire:** unimpaired, fully realized.

2. **pretended Deity:** Cupid, the Roman god of love.

3. **Shew:** show.

4. **The humblest Lover . . . rise:** quotation unidentified.

5. **Strephon:** a generic name for a shepherd in pastoral poetry—often a lovelorn shepherd.

tling, singing Gentleman had no more Danger in him.—The Heart is a busy, fluttering, impudent Thing: It will not lye still when one bids it, nor are its Dictates to be silenced by Reason, or guided by the Head; and if the *Beau*[1] by his Dress, Address, or any other Charm, has got an Entrance there, I am very much afraid poor *Esteem* will come off a Loser in spite of all can be urged by the *Female Spectator*.

I therefore sincerely wish it may be as she says;—that the Inclination she confesses for him may not have been so firmly establish'd, but that she may be able easily to withdraw it; for to deal freely with her, there is no one Part of his Character which seems to promise her any lasting Happiness.

However, the better to enable her to gain this Conquest over herself, I will give her some small Sketches of those Scenes which I may venture to affirm there is more than a Probability she must make an Actor in, after prevailed upon to enter into a Marriage with this modern *Narcissus*.[2]

A Week or ten Days passed over, for no more will I allow to the *Douceurs*[3] of such a Union, the Bridegroom rises, says "Good Morrow, Madam," perhaps bestows a faint Kiss, repairs to his Dressing Room, passes the whole Morning at his Toilet,[4] then throws himself into his Chariot, goes to the Mall, imagines every fine Woman regrets his being married, and puts on all her Charms to supplant his Bride in his Affection:—Returns Home about three;—walks backward and forward in the Room humming over some dull Tune, and viewing himself in the Glass every Turn he takes.—*Bellamonte* looks on him all this while with wishing Eyes, says a thousand tender Things;—He still sings on, makes no Answer.—Dinner is served up:—She offers to help him,[5] he coldly thanks her; and tho' she begins ever so many Subjects for Conversation, he enters into none, nor interrupts his Meal with

---

1. **Beau:** fop, dandy.

2. **Narcissus:** in Greek mythology, a beautiful youth who fell in love with his own reflection in a pool and pined away as a result.

3. **Douceurs:** sweetnesses.

4. **Toilet:** the process of getting dressed.

5. **to help him:** to serve him food.

any thing farther than an "Aye, Madam," or a "No, Madam":—If, by Chance, he says a civil Thing, the Sound discovers[1] it to be forced from him rather by the Laws of good Breeding, than those of Love, and he looks another Way all the time he speaks.—She has too much Penetration not to discover the Change:—She weeps in secret, and her inward Griefs at length break forth in gentle Reproaches: This he thinks unreasonable, and replies to with as much Peevishness as he dare, for fear of distorting the Muscles of his Face; but she is sure to meet, as often as she seems dissatisfied with his Behaviour, this or the like Rebuff: "—Gad, Madam, you are the most ungrateful Woman in the World:—You ought to be highly contented that I made you my Wife, in prejudice to so many fine young Creatures, who, it is well known, were dying for me."

This is all her *Resentment* will be able to effect; and if she endeavours to work by *Fondness* on his Indifference, tells him she is never happy but in his Company, and begs him to take a little Tour with her among their Relations and Friends, or to pass an Evening with her at some public Place or other she may happen to think on, he will be ready to cry, "—Laird,[2] Madam, how silly you are!—Don't you know that the most ridiculous Spectacle in Nature is a Man in Company with his Wife?"

If *Bellamonte* can submit to this Treatment, let her indulge her Inclination; but I am apt to imagine what I have said will make her turn her Eyes into the World, where she will find a sufficient Number of Instances to prove this Truth, that a Man who admires himself, can never sincerely admire any thing beside.

I would also beg her to reflect that Marriage is a kind of Precipice, which, when once leap'd, there is no Possibility of reclimbing;—and wary ought the Person who stands upon it to be, lest, instead of a delightful Valley enamel'd with Flowers, blooming with perpetual Sweets, she plunges not into one where Thorns and Briars are only shadowed over with a few gaudy Tulips and tall Sun-Flowers, that yield no Savour, and fade upon the Touch.

---

1. **discovers:** reveals.
2. **Laird:** lord.

But to quit Allegory: The Gentleman first described appears to me to have in him all the Qualifications that can make a Woman of Merit, such as I believe *Bellamonte* to be, truly happy in a Husband; and is so far from coming into any Degree of Competition with his two Rivals, that in balancing between them she has been guilty of an Injustice to him, which she can no way repair but by giving herself speedily to him, and thereby putting a final Period to the Hopes and Pretentions of every other Suitor.—I dare almost answer for him, that when the Esteem she now feels for him shall be converted into a more warm and tender Passion, she will have no Occasion to lament the Want of an adequate Return:—Honour, Good Sense, Gratitude and Duty will serve as Oil to feed the Flame of conjugal Affection, and the Hymeneal Torch[1] burn with its first Brightness to the End of Life.

I have dwelt the longer on this Subject, as I am compelled by a secret Simpathy to take a more than ordinary Interest in the Fate of this unknown Lady; and also as it is probable there may be many into whose Hands these Pages may fall, who may equally stand in need of that Advice she alone has vouchsafed to ask.

*   *   *

FROM BOOK X

Tho' my late celebrated Brother,[2] and many other Authors, have given the World their various Opinions concerning *Jealousy,* I fancy it will not be impertinent to add something to what has been already said on a Subject which has, and will forever continue to create the most terrible Disorder that can befal Mankind; not only because whatever may serve as a Preservative against it cannot be too often repeated, but also because, I think, with all due Deference to those who have hitherto treated on it, that they have not been so copious as might

---

1. **Hymeneal Torch:** emblem of marriage (associated with Hymen, Greek god of marriage).

2. **Brother:** the Spectator, presiding persona of the periodical published by Joseph Addison and Richard Steele (see Introduction).

have been expected, and that the greatest Part of them have done it more Honour than it deserves.

What I mean by doing it more Honour than it deserves, is, that they speak of it only as the Effect of a too ardent Love and Admiration of the Object; whereas, tho' this may sometimes be the Case, is far from being always so; and, I believe, we shall find no Difficulty to prove, that the Origin of it may more often be deduc'd from the very *worst* instead of the *noblest* Passion of the Soul:—It may, indeed, with great Propriety, be call'd the *Bane* of Love; but whenever it is found the *Offspring,* it can only be of a base and degenerate Inclination, not of that pure and refined Passion which is alone worthy of the Name of Love.

This certainly can be denied by none who allow that true Love is founded on that Esteem which the Opinion we have of the good Qualities of the Object excites in us; and, I believe, few Examples can be produc'd of the real and unfeign'd Permanence of the one, when the other wholly ceases to exist.

I believe I shall be easily understood to mean that Affection which is between Persons who are either already married, or engag'd to be so to each other by mutual Assurances of a lasting Tenderness.

For as to that Timidity which is the natural Companion of Love in its Infancy, and before it receives Encouragement necessary to strengthen Hope, it proceeds only from a Diffidence of our own Merits, not from a Distrust of the beloved Object, and can, with no degree of Propriety, be term'd *Jealousy.*

As it is therefore only after being possess'd of all we had to wish, or having been flatter'd with a Belief we should infallibly be so, that those distracting Ideas, which constitute Jealousy, can find any Entrance in the Brain; I think it sufficiently justifies my Assertion, that this mischievous Passion discovers rather the meanest Opinion of the Object than a too vehement Admiration, unless suspecting a Person guilty of Perjury, Inconstancy, and the most shocking and worst kind of Deceit, can be call'd so.

There are People in the World who know not how to support[1] Prosperity, and when arrived at the End they long have labour'd under,

---

1. **support:** endure.

find in themselves something which will not suffer them to be at quiet;
—they have attained all,—they have no more to wish, and, like the
Macedonian Conqueror,[1] are vex'd they have nothing farther to oppose
them:—This Restlessness of Mind puts them on reflecting[2] how, and
by what means they may possibly be deprived of what they have acquired, and whatever is *possible,* they soon present to themselves as
highly *probable* too; and by degrees bring up into a downright *Certainty* of happening.

Fancy is a creative Faculty, and when agitated by Fear, can work
Wonders:—It forms Apparitions, and then shews them as real Substances;—it turns what is, into what is not, and converts nothing into
something;—it levels the Mountain, and exalts the Vale;[3]—it unites
the greatest Contraries, and divides the firmest and most cemented
Bodies;—in a word, it either makes or overthrows whenever it pleases,
destroys the Order of all Things, and performs what Nature has not
the Power to do.

> When Reason sleeps, our mimic Fancy wakes,
> Supplies her Part, and wild Ideas takes,
> From Words and Things ill-suited and misjoin'd,
> The Anarchy of Thought, and Chaos of the Mind.[4]

Thus by an Impatience of Temper, and the Force of Imagination,
are many misled to ruin their own Peace, and that of the Person they
pretend to love; yet is this the least unpardonable Source from which
Jealousy proceeds, because it may, as the Poet says, be taken

> For the high Pulse of Passion in a Fever![5]

---

1. **Macedonian Conqueror:** Alexander the Great (356–323 B.C.), king of Macedon, an ancient country on the Balkan peninsula, who regretted that he had no more worlds to conquer.

2. **puts them on reflecting:** causes them to reflect.

3. **exalts the Vale:** raises up the valley.

4. **When Reason . . . Mind:** John Dryden, *The State of Innocence* 3.2.5–8.

5. **For the high Pulse . . . Fever:** quotation unidentified.

And if the Faults of Love by Love are to be justified, those who are rendered uneasy on this Score may the more readily excuse the Effects, in consideration of the Cause.

But what have they to alledge in Vindication of the Discontent they occasion, in whom

> No Sign of Love remains,
> But that which sick Men have of Life, their Pains![1]

Many there are, Heaven knows, too many of such, whom a moderate Share of Observation may point out:—There are those who, without being capable of feeling one tender Emotion, or having any true Regard even for the Person of him or her to whom they happen to be join'd, have discovered a Jealousy, which has rendered all within the reach of its Effects, extremely miserable.

This is, indeed, so common a Case, unnatural as it may seem, that I dare answer there is not one into whose Hands the *Female Spectator* may fall, that have not some time or other in their Lives had an Acquaintance with Families where it has happen'd; but following the received Maxim, that Jealousy is the Effect of Love, have rather pity'd than condemn'd the Extravagancies they may have seen occasioned by it.

But well may a disinterested Person judge in this Manner, when those most concern'd, and best able to discover the Truth, have frequently been deceived; and when treated in the most cruel and injurious Manner have submitted to it with a secret Satisfaction, and even plumed[2] themselves upon the Force of a Passion, which they imagin'd excited only by an Excess of Inclination.

This kind of Infatuation puts me in Mind of a Story I have heard of the *Russian* Women, who, they say, look on Blows as the greatest Proof of Affection their Husbands can bestow upon them; and if they are not well beaten, once a Day at least, will run to their Friends and complain of the Injustice they are treated with.—Whether there is any

---

1. **No Sign . . . Pains:** quotation unidentified.
2. **plumed:** preened, congratulated.

Truth in this I will not pretend[1] to say, having never yet employed any *Silph*[2] in the Examination; but according to the Delicacy of my Country-Women in other Respects, it appears full as odd to me, that any of them can be pleased with such Words and Actions as may justly be look'd upon in *England* equally injurious with Blows in the Territories of *Russia*.

But as Vanity, and a high Opinion of Self-Merit, sometimes renders one Party easy and contented, nay, as I before observed, even delighted with Reproaches and ill Usage; so is it Pride, and an over-bearing Arrogance in the other, which will not suffer them to endure the least innocent Civility to be paid to any but themselves:—The Person to whom they have vouchsafed to give their Hand must not dare to think of any thing but pleasing them;—no Merit but their own must be taken Notice of;—they must forgo all Complaisance, all Decency, and be rude and savage to every one beside;—a Smile, a Courtesy, is a Crime deserving the most opprobrious Reflections, and they must behave in such a manner, as to deserve the Hatred and Contempt of all the rest of the World, to engage a tolerable Regard from this over tenacious Partner for Life.

Another Humour there is also which very much prevails in some People, and that is, to avoid being thought weak and incapable of diving to the Bottom of Things, they affect to find out Mysteries in every thing;—they construe into Meanings the most insignificant Trifles;—their Eyes, their Ears are perpetually upon the Watch, and interpret the very humming over a Tune, and even the Gait of the suspected Person, as Indications of some latent Plot to delude their Penetration.

Thus by endeavouring to be wiser than their Neighbours, they become the veryest[3] Fools in Nature; and while they imagine every Body stands in awe of their Discernment, are the Jest and Ridicule of as many as have any Acquaintance with them.

---

1. **pretend:** presume.

2. **Silph:** The sylphs were mythical beings who inhabited air and were said to watch over the welfare of women.

3. **veryest:** truest.

I must confess these over-cunning People are, of all others, most my Aversion, and certainly must be the most troublesome to have any Concern with.—I once knew a Gentleman of this Cast, who had a very agreeable, and I dare answer, a very virtuous Woman for his Wife; but the poor Soul could not keep a Thread-Paper[1] without his examining into it:—If a Servant happen'd to come into the Room, and whisper'd her on any domestic Affair, she must immediately repeat the Words that had been spoke; yet this was not thought sufficient to be certain of not being imposed upon; he would go immediately out of the Room, call for the Servant, and oblige her or him, whichever it were, to tell him on what Occasion that Whisper had been; and if every Word did not exactly agree with the Report his Wife had made, he presently concludes there was some Design on Foot between them, to the Prejudice of his Honour, for the Prevention of which the Servant was that Instant discharg'd, and his Wife confin'd to her Chamber:—Nobody could ever knock at the Door without his running to the Window, then half way down Stairs, list'ning to what was said: If too low a Voice deprived him of the desir'd Intelligence,[2] he would go into the Hall, and oblige the Person, whoever it was, to relate the whole Purport[3] of their Errand in his Presence:—In fine, it is impossible for any Family to suffer greater Persecutions than what his did, through this Peculiarity of Temper, for in other Things he behav'd well enough.

There are still a third Sort, industrious to torment themselves and all about them:—Conscious of former Crimes, they judge the Virtue of others by the Standard of their own; and imagine nobody has the Power of resisting a Temptation to which themselves have yielded:—These are not to be satisfied by any Means that can be put in Practice; —tho' Locks and Bars secure the Body, still will they believe the Mind is roving, and be jealous of Intention:—The more is said, and the greater Care is taken to eradicate these Apprehensions, the deeper Root

---

1. **Thread-Paper:** a strip of paper folded so as to contain different skeins of thread; something, therefore, of very little value.

2. **Intelligence:** information.

3. **Purport:** meaning.

they take;—all is look'd upon as Hypocrisy and Dissimulation, and resented as an Aggravation of the Crime, and an Affront to their Understanding.

After all, what but *Pride* in the *Women,* and a *too nice Sense* of *Honour* in the *Men,* occasions most of the Jealousies we hear of!—Love inspires a noble Confidence, both gives and takes all decent Liberties, sets every Action in the fairest Light, nor will believe itself imposed upon but by Conviction.

How great an Injustice is it therefore to this Passion to annex to it another of so pernicious a kind:—A late noble Poet has, in my Judgment, excellently describ'd the Nature and Happiness of a virtuous Love in these Words:

> Love, the most gen'rous Passion of the Mind,
> The softest Refuge Innocence can find:
> The safe Director of unguided Youth,
> Fraught with kind Wishes, and secur'd by Truth.
> The Cordial Drop Heav'n in our Cup has thrown,
> To make the nauseous Draught of Life go down:
> On which one only Blessing God might raise,
> In Lands of *Atheists,* Subsidies of Praise:
> For none did e'er so dull and stupid prove,
> But felt a God, and bless'd his Power in Love.[1]

Nobody will deny that this illustrious Author was perfectly acquainted with Human Nature, and all the Passions incident to it, nor that Mr. *Congreve*[2] was less so, who having occasion to mention Jealousy, has these Words:

> Vile Doubts and Fears to Jealousy will turn;
> The hottest Hell in which a Heart can burn.[3]

---

1. **Love, the most gen'rous . . . Power in Love:** John Wilmot, Earl of Rochester, "A Letter from Artemiza in the Town to Chloe in the Country," ll. 40–49.

2. **Mr. Congreve:** William Congreve (1670–1729), Restoration dramatist.

3. **Vile Doubts . . . burn:** William Congreve, "To Cynthia, Weeping and Not Speaking," ll. 69–70.

Had this judicious Gentleman thought that Jealousy was any Consequence of Love, he would doubtless have said,

A Love too fierce to Jealousy will turn:

Whereas he says, "Vile Doubts and Fears, &c."—Which, I think, plainly indicates he means a mean Distrust, a Restlessness of Nature, and an unsatisfied Disposition, are the chief Materials on which Jealousy is built.

But we need not quote Authorities, nor ransack Texts, to prove a Truth, which, whoever takes Reason for their Guide, may easily explore on any Examination into their own Hearts.

For my Part, tho' I should be extremely sorry for the Sake of those happy few whom *Love* has join'd in Marriage, that *Jealousy* were a kind of Appendix to that Passion, yet I should be equally rejoic'd to find wherever there is *Jealousy* there were some *Love,* in consideration of Millions who have all the Bitters of the *One* without any Mixture of the Sweets of the *Other.*

Aurelia had lived to the Age of Twenty-six, had known all the Gaities of Life, some say was not unacquainted with the Gallantries of it, taken in the worst Sense of the Word:—She then married with *Lucilius,* because it was for her Interest and Reputation to do so, but without feeling for him the least Spark of tender Inclination; yet had he not been two Months her Husband before she became excessively jealous of him;—any little Civility he paid to our Sex, tho' before her Face, gave her the Vapours;[1] but to be told he visited any Woman of what Condition soever, threw her into Fits:—A Pinch of Snuff offered by him to a Cousin-German[2] one Day occasion'd a Quarrel between them, which she would by no means make up till he had sworn never to speak to that Lady more:—She sent Spies after him to watch wherever he went, and if inform'd he was at any Place she did not happen to approve of his frequenting, work'd herself up into such

---

1. **Vapours:** hysteria, hypochondria.

2. **Cousin-German:** first cousin.

Agonies as terminated into real or feign'd Convulsions, which he was sure to bear his Part of at his Return.

Fatiguing as such a Life must necessarily be for a Time, he bore it with a Temper which surpriz'd all who knew him;—humoured her tender Foibles, as he term'd them, to make her easy; debarr'd himself of every thing which he thought would give her the least Subject for Discontent; and imputing all she did to the Excess of her Love for him, not to seem ungrateful to it, counterfeited a Tenderness for her which his Heart had never avowed; for, in effect, there was as small a Share of Inclination on the *one* as on the *other* Side.

The Matter[1] was this:—An Uncle of *Aurelia's* had in it his Power to be extremely serviceable to *Lucilius* in a Post he enjoyed under him and the old Gentleman thinking it necessary his Neice should have the Sanction of Marriage to cover some Liberties which, to him, seem'd not becoming in a Virgin State, took upon him to make the Match between them.—The Thing was no sooner proposed than agreed to by both, as conformable to their several[2] Interests; so that all the Protestations they made each other, during the small Space of Courtship, were of a Piece with those they continued after Marriage, unfelt by themselves, and equally untouching to those they were address'd.

It was therefore wholly owing to the Good-Nature of *Lucilius* that he submitted to obey whatever was dictated by the preposterous Jealousy of his Wife, as that Jealousy had indeed no other Source than what he least imputed it to, an Extravagance of Pride and Vanity, to shew the World she had Charms which could render a Husband even more obsequious than a Lover.

As she found her Account[3] in treating him in this Manner, she would doubtless have persisted in it, but how long his Patience and Philosophy would have enabled him to sustain it is altogether uncertain;—an Accident happened which put an End to their mutual Dis-

---

1. **Matter:** situation.

2. **several:** individual.

3. **found her Account:** served her own interest.

simulation, and shewed those sublime Scenes of dying Love between them to be no more than Farce and Buffoonry.

It was a Custom with *Lucilius* to rise early, and walk an Hour or two before Breakfast, in the Park, into which their House had a Back-Door:—In one of those Mornings he took it into his Head to call on a Friend who lived in the Neighbourhood, for which Reason he made a Circuit, and return'd Home by the Street-Way;—He was within three or four yards of his own Door, when he saw the Footman, that waited on his Wife, come out of the House reading the Superscription of a Letter he had in his Hand, and which, on the first Glimpse he had of his Master, he put hastily into his Pocket.

Lucilius either saw, or imagin'd he saw, a strange Confusion in the Fellow's Face; and tho' Jealousy was a Passion he was wholly unacquainted with, yet there was a secret something, which he knew not how to account for, at that Instant push'd him on to inform himself to whom that Letter was directed:—In order to do this, without being taken notice of by any Persons who might possibly be at their Windows, he stepp'd into a narrow Passage, which led into another Street, and having beckoned the Man to come to him, commanded him to deliver the Letter he had seen in his Hand:—The Fellow durst not refuse, and *Lucilius* was no less amaz'd than shock'd to find it his Wife's Hand, and directed to one of the most dissolute and notorious Libertines,[1] tho' a Man of Quality, in Town:—As that was not a proper Place to examine the Contents, he made the Fellow follow him into an adjacent Tavern, where he hastily broke the Seal, and found it contain'd these Lines.

To the Agreeable Miramount.
SIR,

I have considered on your Request, and my Pity has at last prevail'd upon me to grant it;—all Things indeed seem favourable to your Wishes, *Lucilius* is engag'd for this Evening with Company, who, I

---

1. **Libertines:** men (usually) of loose morals.

know, will keep him late; but as I am under some Apprehensions of being known at the Place mention'd in your's, desire our Rendezvous may be at the Bagnio[1] in *Long-Acre,*[2] where you may depend I shall come to you about Six:—Yet, dear *Miramount,* be assured, that nothing less than the Preservation of a Life so valuable to the World as yours is, should make me injure a Husband who adores me to Distraction.—I rely on your Honour as to an inviolable Secrecy, and every thing else that can render me perfectly happy in being

Your's,
AURELIA.

Had *Lucilius* really loved, how wretched must such a Discovery of her Levity, Perfidy and Deceit have made him!—All indifferent as he was to her Charms, the Consideration of his own Honour was too dear to him not to take all possible Methods to put it out of her Power to sacrifice it.

After giving some Moments to Reflection, he examined the Fellow as to what he knew of his Lady's Acquaintance with *Miramount,* when and where it had began, and how long there had been a Correspondence between them.

These Enquiries were enforc'd by such terrible Menaces, mingled with Assurances of Protection and Rewards if he reveal'd the whole Truth, that a Person of more Resolution and Courage than could be expected in one of his Station, would have been won to answer every thing demanded of him.

He inform'd *Lucilius,* that he believed his Lady first saw the Gentleman in Question at the House of *Clelia,* where she frequently went to play at Cards;—and this, to the best of his Remembrance, was about three Weeks past; that they afterwards had met, either by Chance or Appointment, in the Mall,[3] and that he had carry'd no more than one

---

1. **Bagnio:** a bordello; also used as a place of assignation.

2. **Long-Acre:** a slightly disreputable section of London, although not far from the fashionable environs of St. James's Park.

3. **Mall:** fashionable promenade in St. James's Park.

Letter to him, in answer, as he supposed, to one she had received from him; that when she delivered to him the foregoing, and that which his Honour had now intercepted, she had given him Money, and the strictest Charge never to mention that there was any Intercourse[1] between her and *Miramount;* and promised him, if he were found faithful in this Affair, he should be taken out of Livery[2] and handsomely provided for.

Lucilius listen'd to all with Agitations which it is easy for any one to conceive, but recovering himself as soon as he could, he call'd for Pen and Paper, and imitating his Wife's Hand tolerably well, he copy'd her Letter Word for Word, only chang'd the Place of Assignation, from the *Bagnio* in *Long-Acre,* to the *Swan*[3] at *Chelsea,*[4] and having seal'd it, order'd the Fellow to carry that to *Miramount,* and bring what Answer he should send to him, who would wait his Return at the Tavern where they now were.

The Footman had now no Inducement to be insincere to his Master, for as the Affair was discover'd he had nothing to expect from *Miramount* in case he should let him know what had happen'd, but was sure to suffer all that the Rage of *Lucilius* could inflict on him if he were found to have acted contrary to the Orders he had given him.

The Answer which *Miramount* return'd was such as might be expected, full of Acknowledgments and Protestations of an everlasting Constancy and Love.—This *Lucilius* put into his Pocket, and bid the Man tell his Lady that her Lover had a great deal of Company with him, and could have no Opportunity to write without being taken Notice of, but that she might be sure of his obeying her with the utmost Punctuality.

Lucilius then went Home, breakfasted as usual with his Lady, and so well conceal'd his Discontent, that she had no Cause to suspect any thing of what had happen'd: He staid with her however as short a

---

1. **Intercourse:** social communication.

2. **Livery:** the distinctive clothing of a servant. Aurelia has promised to promote this particular servant to a higher station in life.

3. **Swan:** an inn.

4. **Chelsea:** a western borough of London.

Time as possible;—he dress'd, and having soon determin'd within himself what Course to take, went directly to her Uncle, and acquainted him with the Discovery he had made, and produc'd the Letter *Aurelia* had wrote to *Miramount,* with his Answer to it.

'Tis hard to say, whether the old Gentleman's Surprize or Rage was most predominant; he was truly a worthy honest Person, and tho' he had thought his Neice's Conduct not altogether so prudent as he could have wish'd before Marriage, yet he never suspected she would have gone such Lengths after being a Wife:—He was for going with *Lucilius,* and joining with him in those Reproaches her Guilt thus plainly proved might justify; but this injur'd Husband would by no Means consent to that:—He thought all they could say would have less Force, and the Shock of being detected lose half its Force, if not given her at the very Place where she intended to perpetrate her Crime:—He therefore proposed that they should go together to the *Bagnio* somewhat before the Hour in which she had promised *Miramount* to come, and when expecting to be received with open Arms by a fond Lover, she should be saluted with the Frowns and Upbraidings of a wronged Husband and incensed Parent.

This the Uncle agreed to, and after Dinner was over at Home *Lucilius* perform'd his last Act of Dissimulation towards his Wife by embracing her in the most seeming tender Manner, when he took Leave of her, in order to go, as she imagined, to those Friends, with whom, as she had wrote to *Miramount,* he had promised to pass that Evening; she behaved to him with no less Softness, and conjured him not to leave her too long alone, but to return as soon as he could possibly disengage himself with Decency.

How wretched, how contemptible a Figure did she now make in his Eyes! But he conceal'd the Disdain of his Heart under a fervent Kiss, feeling however a kind of gloomy Satisfaction in his Mind at the Thoughts that now there would be an End of all Constraint, and he should no more be under the Necessity of feigning Ardors to which his Nature had ever been repugnant.

Both, tho' from very different Motives, were impatient enough for the appointed Hour; which being arrived, and the Uncle and Husband waiting her Approach, the Clock had but just struck when a Hackney-

Chair[1] brought the too punctual Fair into the Entry, whence she was shewed up Stairs by a Waiter who had Orders what to do:—How she was confounded, when tripping gaily into the Room she found who were there to receive her, any one may judge.

All her natural Assurance, of which few Women had a greater Share, was too little to enable her to bear up against a Sight more dreadful, more alarming to her guilty Mind than had a Messenger from the other World appear'd to admonish her of her Crime.

In the first Emotions of her Fright she was about to run out of the Room, and with one Jump had got as far as the Door, when *Lucilius* took hold of her Arm and oblig'd her to come back,—"Tho' Madam," said he with the most stabbing Sneer, "the agreeable *Miramount* is not here, and you are disappointed of the Entertainment you expected, such as a Husband and an Uncle, who have both of them a due Sense of your Merit, can afford, you may be sure to find."

She made no Answer to these Words, but threw herself into a Chair with a Look that shewed an inward Rancour, and would have made her pass with any one who had been present and unacquainted with her Crime rather for the Person injur'd than the guilty one; so true is this Sentiment of the Poet:

> Forgiveness to the Injur'd does belong,
> But they ne'er pardon who have done the wrong.[2]

But however the Greatness of her Spirit might have supported her against the Reproaches of a Husband, those her Uncle loaded her with, and the Sight of her own Letter wholly subdued her; and finding there was no Evasion nor Possibility either of denying or excusing what she had done, she fell on her Knees, and with a Shower of undissembled Tears, confess'd her Fault, and begg'd to be forgiven.

After having endeavoured to make her sensible of her Fault, they acquainted her with the Resolution they had mutually agreed to pursue, which was, that in consideration of her Family no public Noise

---

1. **Hackney-Chair:** hired sedan chair.

2. **Forgiveness . . . wrong:** John Dryden, *The Conquest of Granada,* part 2, 1.2.

should be made of it; but that to prevent her taking any future Steps to the Prejudice of her Reputation, and consequently to the Honour of her Husband, she must pass some time with an old Relation who lived at a great Distance from *London,* nor hope to return till she had given evident Proofs of her Conversion:—This her Uncle told her it would become her not only to consent to, but also to go with a Chearfulness which should make every Body think it an Act of Choice.

It was to no Purpose she entreated, in the most submissive Terms, a Remission of a Sentence she acknowledg'd she had but too justly incur'd:—In vain she made the most solemn Vows and passionate Imprecations never to be guilty of any future Miscarriage in Conduct; *Lucilius* was inexorable to all, nor did her Uncle attempt to render him more pliable:—She was that Night carefully watch'd, and early the next Morning sent down into the Country with a Person, whose Integrity her Husband could confide in, to attend her, and at the same time to keep a strict Eye over her Behaviour.

It must be confess'd, that the Precautions taken to keep this Affair a Secret were perfectly prudent; for as the Crime of *Aurelia* had been only in Intention, the Law would not have allowed of a Divorce,[1] yet that Intention was sufficient to have rendered both of them the Subject of Ridicule; nor indeed was there any Possibility of their living together in any Harmony after such a Discovery, even tho' there had been a Certainty of her becoming a real Penitent.

Whether she were so or not Heaven only can determine; but I am inform'd, that she had not been many Weeks in that Retirement to which she was banish'd, before the Grief and Shame either of being guilty, or of having been detected in it, threw her into a violent Fever, of which she died, and left *Lucilius* no inconsolable Widower.

The Truth of this Affair had however remain'd a Secret, had her Lover been endu'd with the same Discretion as her Husband; but that vain Man finding she came not to the *Swan* as he expected, and on sending the next Day to her House being told she was gone into the Country, made him not doubt but that some Accident had discover'd

---

1. **Law . . . Divorce:** because there was no proof of actual adultery, which would be necessary for a legal divorce.

their Correspondence to *Lucilius,* and that he had taken this Method to prevent their Meeting; on which, partly instigated by Revenge against the *Husband,* and partly by the Vanity of being thought to be too well[1] with the *Wife,* he made a Jest, among his Companions, of the *Jealousy* of the *One* and the *Levity* of the *Other,* and even scrupled not to expose the Letters of that unfortunate Lady as a Proof of what he said.

He had so little Circumspection as to whom he talk'd in this Manner, that it soon reach'd the Ears of *Lucilius,* who, unable to endure with Patience this Aggravation of the Insult offer'd to his Honour, sent him a Challenge, which the other was too gallant a Man not to accept:—They met and fought, both were very much hurt, especially *Miramount,* whose Wounds at first were reckon'd dangerous, but he recover'd of them as well as *Lucilius,* and had Honour enough, after he did so, to confess himself every way the Aggressor, and ask Pardon for the Injury he had intended him, as well as for his foolish boasting of it afterwards:—As all this happened before the Death of *Aurelia,* 'tis possible she might, some way or other, be inform'd of it, and that might be one great Means of hastening on her Fate.—She was a Woman of Understanding, and being such, and in a Place where she had no Enchantments to lull asleep Reflection, could not be without a lively Sense of that Shame she had brought on herself and Family; for, as Mr. *Waller*[2] elegantly expresses it,

> Our Passions gone, and Reason in the Throne,
> Amaz'd we see the Mischiefs we have done.
> After a Tempest, when the Winds are laid,
> The calm Sea wonders at the Wrecks it made.[3]

But it is not to my present Purpose to make any farther Comments on this Story, than as it proves the Assertion for which I related it, that there may be a great deal of Jealousy without one Spark of Love:

---

1. **well:** well-acquainted, intimate.

2. **Mr. Waller:** Edmund Waller (1606–1687), lyric poet.

3. **Our Passions . . . Wrecks it made:** quotation unidentified.

—Happy had it been for *Aurelia* had she known the one as well as the other; for tho' the former of these Passions might have been troublesome to her Husband, yet the latter would have secured him from receiving any Injustice from her, or Outrage from the World, and sav'd herself from falling into the Infamy she did.

It is, doubtless, a very melancholly Thing when a Woman of real Virtue, and who has a tender Affection for the Man to whom she is married, either has, or imagines she has, any justifiable Cause to suspect he returns not the Love she bears him with an equal Degree of Warmth; but much more so when she fears he transfers those Ardors, to which she has an undoubted Right, to any other Object: Yet, excuseable as Jealousy may seem in such a Circumstance, it is to be wish'd, that every Wife would endeavour to discourage rather than listen to any Reports made her from Abroad,[1] that might tend to increase those Suspicions her too tender Passion may suggest:—To arm herself against any Insinuations of that Kind, either from her own Heart, or the Malice, Folly, or mistaken Zeal of those she converses with; I would wish her to do Justice to herself, and consider, that if even it were certain that her Husband gave a loose to an inordinate and temporary Pleasure, her Mortification would be but momentary, and terminate to her Advantage:—He would, when once the hurry of a fleeting Passion was over, consider the Merits of a Woman of Virtue, and who had Love enough for him not only to forgive, but overlook those Failings which every Man has not always the Power to avoid falling into.

He that most loves Company finds a Pleasure in a comfortable Recess from it, at sometimes, with his Wife and Family; but if he meets with Reproaches there, how justly soever he may deserve them, thinks the Dignity of his Nature affronted, and flies out again, and perhaps in Revenge runs into worse Evils than those for which he was before upbraided:—I know not if there can be a more lively Picture how little Force Female Arguments can have on a transgressing Husband, than is given us by Mr. *Dryden,* in his Play of *Aurenzebe,* where he puts into the Emperor's Mouth these Words:

---

1. **Abroad:** outside the home.

What can be sweeter than our native Home!
Thither for Ease and soft Repose we come:
Home is the sacred Refuge of our Life,
Secured from all Approaches but a Wife:
If thence we fly, the Cause admits no Doubt,
None but an inmate Foe could drive us out:
Clamours our Privacies uneasy make,
Birds leave their Nests disturb'd, and Beasts their Haunts forsake.[1]

 Few Men of any Condition are gross[2] in their Amours, and wherever there is room to hope the *best*, a Wife ought never to harbour Fears of the *worst:*—A thousand Accidents may happen to which Rumour and Imagination may give the Face of Guilt, that in themselves are perfectly innocent, but even when the Appearances are most strong, it is Wisdom to overlook them.

 Besides, there is one Thing which in my Opinion should deter a Woman of Virtue from discovering any Marks of Jealousy, even where the most flagrant Proofs of the roving Inclination of her Husband might, according to some People's way of thinking, be a Justification of it; and that is, because the most abandon'd Prostitutes of the Town, tho' known to make Sale of their Endearments to any Purchaser without Distinction, no sooner find a Man weak enough to treat them in a manner to which their way of Living has no Claim, than they give themselves an Air, on every little Absence, to be extremely jealous;—they have Tears at Command;—can fall into Fits, and sometimes play the *Roxana,*[3] and menace the offending Keeper with a drawn Dagger: —Some Instances we have had where they have carry'd the Matter yet farther, and pierced in reality the Breast that durst refuse Obedience to the most unreasonable or extravagant of their Demands:—A modest Wife should therefore never affect the Virago, and for her own Sake be wary, even when most provok'd, that nothing in her Behaviour should bear the least Resemblance with such Wretches.—I have in a

---

1. **What can be . . . Haunts forsake:** John Dryden, *Aureng-zebe* 2.273–80.

2. **gross:** flagrant, excessive.

3. **Roxana:** wife of Alexander the Great, a stock figure in stage tragedy.

former *Spectator* taken Notice, that it is not by Force our Sex can hope to maintain their Influence over the Men, and I again repeat it as the most infallible Maxim, that whenever we would truly conquer we must seem to yield.

To be jealous without a Cause, is such an Injury to the suspected Person as requires the utmost Affection and Good-Nature to forgive; because it wounds them in the two most tender Parts, their Reputation and Peace of Mind; lays them under Restraints the most irksome to Human Nature, or in a manner obliges them to Measures which are the Destruction of all Harmony.

Those few therefore who truly love, are in Possession of the Object of their Wishes, and yet suffer this poisonous Passion to disturb the Tranquility of their Lives, may be compar'd to Misers that pine amidst their Stores, and are incapable of enjoying a present Plenty through the Fears of future Want.

That Desire of prying into every thing a Husband does, and even into his very Thoughts, appears to me rather a childish Fondness than a noble generous Passion; and tho' it may be pleasing enough to a Man in the first Months of his Marriage, will afterwards grow tiresome and insipid to him, as well as render both of them ridiculous to others.

We may depend on this, that the most innocent Persons in the World, in some Humours, or unguarded Moments, may happen to say or do something which might not be altogether pleasing to us to be inform'd of:—How mad a Thing then is it to seek out Occasions of Disquiet! Yet this too many Women are ingenious in doing, and afterwards no less industrious in throwing fresh Matter on the Mole-hill they have discovered, till they raise it to a Mountain:—Trifles perhaps too light to retain any Place in the Husband's Memory, and no sooner over than forgotten, or if of Consequence enough to be remember'd by him, are thought on with Remorse, are reviv'd by Reproaches, and made seem less faulty than they are, by the Wife's attempting to represent them as more so.

Nor is this all: Upbraidings when most just, if too often repeated, lose their Force, and he to whom they are given becomes harden'd; but if wantonly thrown out, and to gratify a spleenatick or naturally suspicious Temper, without any solid Foundation, they are intolerable to him, make him grow peevish, perverse, and not seldom drive him to be in effect guilty of that which, without being guilty, he daily receives the Punishment of.

On the whole then, since Jealousy is the worst Rack the Heart that harbours it can possibly sustain, is it not better to cease those Enquiries which can never give us a perfect Satisfaction, and as there is no proving what has no Existence may be as lasting as our Lives; or if which should chance to end in a Certainty of what is so dreadful to us in the Apprehension, must confirm us for ever miserable!

Many a Man has been guilty of an Error, and on Reflection sincerely repented of it, and become a more endearing Husband than before; for it is by the Tribunal in our own Bosoms we alone are justify'd or condemn'd;—all Efforts from without are ineffectual to convince us we have done amiss, if Conscience does not take a Part in the Accusation; and as Human Nature is averse to all Compulsion, especially from those we think have no Authority over us, as in the Case of Husband and Wife, the Pride of Contradiction has perhaps, more often than Inclination, occasion'd that to happen which otherwise might have never been.

I have been sorry to observe, that even among my own Sex, where an Error of this Kind is less excusable than in the other, Revenge for having been unjustly suspected, join'd with the Pride of being able to disappoint all the Precautions of a jealous Husband, has sometimes been too strong for that Virtue, which, without these additional Excitements, might never have been subdued.

Sabina was educated in the strictest Principles of Virtue, and in a Family where she saw nothing but Examples of it before her Eyes; and *Manilius,* to whom she was married very young, received the sincerest Congratulations of his Friends for having obtained a Lady who, they thought, could not but render him extremely happy; and there is no doubt but her Behaviour had every way answered the most sanguine of their Expectations, had not his own imprudent Carriage to her, in that respect I have been speaking of, perverted in her those generous Sentiments she receiv'd from Nature and from Precept.

When one would bring a Person of a Spirit off from any Propensity, which either is, or we think a Fault, the greatest Care ought to be

taken that they may not imagine we take a Pleasure in opposing them;
—we ought rather to make them believe it is with the utmost Grief
of Heart we cannot find in ourselves the Power of approving what
they do, and endeavour to *win* them by *Endearments,* not attempt to
controul them by *Authority.*

Manilius had been a Man of Pleasure, always professed an Aversion
to Marriage, and nothing but the extremest Passion could have made
him change his Resolution;—he was fifteen Years older than *Sabina*
when she became his Wife, and the Conciousness of this Disparity,
join'd with the too great Success he had formerly met with in his
Amours, rendered him less confident than was consistent with his
Peace of Mind of the Virtue of this young Lady:—It had always been
a Maxim with him that all Women were to be won, and that a Husband should never be too secure; and this made him, even from the
first, keep a watchful Eye over all her Actions, Words, and Looks.

As she was perfectly innocent, she was ignorant of Circumspection;
nor ever had once a Thought of restraining herself from any of those
Liberties she saw others take:—It was enough for her she did no ill,
and was alas too thoughtless what Pretences Ill-Nature might form to
judge by Appearances:—She fell soon after her Marriage into Acquaintance, which took a greater Latitude than she had been accustomed to
see while in her Virgin State; but they were People of Condition,[1] and
Reputation too, and therefore she made no Scruple of doing as they
did:—She went frequently to the Public Diversions of the Town,—
and made one at most of the Assemblies;[2]—Cards sometimes engross'd
a good Part of the Night; yet did she not think all this an Error,
because she perceiv'd it was the Fashion:—Her Youth might easily
have excused the inadvertent Steps she took, since they were far from
being guilty ones in reality, or in the Opinion of any other than
Manilius; and had he in gentle Terms reminded her, that the less she
were seen at any of those Places, the more it would redound to her
Praise; and in the lieu of those dangerous Amusements prepared others

---

1. **Condition:** high rank.

2. **Assemblies:** evening gatherings where the principal entertainments were conversation and
gallantry.

to entertain the Sprightliness of her Humour, it would doubtless have been no difficult Task to have rendered her Conduct by degrees such as he most desired it should be.

But instead of taking proper Measures to sooth her from those Pleasures, so enchanting to our early Years of Life,—he received her with Frowns whenever she happened to stay more late Abroad than he approv'd of; and at length finding that was not effectual, plainly told her, that if she desired to live well with him, she must not only keep better Hours, but also entirely refrain all Conversation with some particular Persons of both Sexes, whom he nam'd to her.

The abrupt Manner in which he laid this Injunction was more disobliging to her than the Injunction itself, unjust and cruel as it seem'd;—she knew not how to support such an assuming and majesterial Behaviour from a Man who, but a few Months past, had seem'd to have no Will but her's, nor could conceive any Reason why the Name of Husband should convert the Slave into the Tyrant:—Her good Sense, as well as the Precepts that had been given her on her Marriage, made her know the Man had a Superiority over his Wife, but then she never imagined he was to exert it where nothing of an essential Wrong was done, and in such Trifles as these *Manilius* took upon him to condemn:—She saw that all the Ladies of her Acquaintance allowed themselves greater Liberties after they became Wives than they were permited to do before, and stung to the quick at this arbitrary Proceeding, reply'd to him, that he was extremely in the wrong to marry a Person whom he did not think capable of governing herself without his Direction;—that while she could answer to herself what she did, nor gave the World any Reason to call her Conduct in question, she did not look on herself under any Obligation to incur the Ridicule of as many as knew her, and live like a Recluse, meerly to humour the Caprice of any one Person, even tho' it were a Husband.

This resolute Answer, which was also accompanied with a Look and Tone of Voice denoting the Displeasure she was in, made him repent he had not testify'd his Dislike of her Behaviour with somewhat less Austerity;—he excused it however as well as he could, but as he stuck to his Point, and insisted on her keeping only such Company as should be approved by him, all he could say was far from abating her Discontent, and the Affection she had for him too weak to hinder her from conceiving a Spite that made her take a Pleasure in contradicting him.

In fine, his Remonstrances had so ill an Effect, that instead of complying with the least of his Desires she acted in every thing the very reverse:—He interpreted all she did in the worst Sense, and never Man was more uneasy.

Those who knew the very Soul of *Sabina* aver, that it was impossible for any one to be more free from all guilty Inclinations; and tho', it must be own'd, she gave, more than became a Woman of strict Honour, into all the Gaities of Life, yet they will have it, that she did so more in Revenge to her Husband, and to shew both him and the World that she disdain'd any Proofs of Submission to a Will which she thought too arbitrary, than to any vicious Propensity in herself.

'Tis certain, indeed, that his Proceeding contributed a great deal towards bringing on the Misfortune he so much dreaded; because it not only by degrees destroy'd all the Respect and Tenderness she had for him, and render'd him weak and contemptible in her Eyes, but also gave Encouragement to Addresses, which no Man of Sense will make to a Woman who lives in Harmony with her Husband.

She was yet too young not to be pleased with Adoration, and being entertain'd Abroad with those tender Declarations which *Manilius,* tho' he still lov'd her to Distraction, was too sullen and discontented to flatter her with at Home:—His Presence and his House grew every Day more disagreeable, and she was never easy but when in other Company.

When a Woman once comes to be pleased with hearing fine Things said to her, she is in great Danger of being too much pleased with him that says them; and as I would have all Husbands take Warning by *Manilius,* not to urge or exasperate a Wife too much, so I would have all Wives beware how on any little Discontent at Home they seek a Consolation Abroad:—There are always sly Seducers, who, like the Serpent in *Eden,* are on the Watch to betray Innocence; these no sooner find any Dissatisfaction between the wedded Pair, than they improve[1] it by a thousand subtle Insinuations, till they have entirely stole into the Heart, and usurp'd the Place of him who is the lawful, and ought to be the sole Lord thereof.

But to return:—Among the many who took Advantage of the Disagreement between *Sabina* and her Husband, there was one whose Person and Address gave a double Weight to the Arguments he made use of in order to widen the Breach;—she found a secret yielding in her Heart to all he said, and wishing to be totally convinced, easily became so:—*Manilius* long indifferent became disagreeable, and at length hateful;—the Thoughts of living with him grew insupportable, and on Perswasion of him who was the present Object of her softer Inclinations, she one Night pack'd up all her Jewels, and the richest of her Cloaths, and quitted forever his House and Presence:— To avoid all Prosecutions, her Lover prevail'd on her to go with him to *Boulogne* in *France,* where, changing their Names, they eluded all Enquiry.

Manilius raved like a Madman, spared no Expence, of Pains or Money, to find the Place of her Retreat, or who it was that had seduced her; but all his Efforts were fruitless, 'till the Person, at whom his Revenge was levell'd, was no more.

Sabina enjoy'd but a very short Time the Pleasures of her guilty Flame;—her Lover fell into a Fever and dyed at *Boulogne* in less than two Months after her Elopement:—Those Friends who were trusted with the Affair, in order to remit Money for the Expences of these self-exil'd Pair, and inform them how Matters went, now thought themselves no longer under any Obligations of Secrecy, and made no Scruple of divulging all that had been reposed in them, so that too late for the Gratification of the only Passion now remaining in him, that of Revenge, he heard by whom he had been injur'd.

As for *Sabina,* the Sight of Death, and that of one so fatally dear to her, brought her to a more just way of Reason than she had for some time past accustom'd herself; and resolving to abandon the

---

1. **improve:** intensify.

World, its destructive Pleasures, its Follies, and the Shame which sooner or later overtakes all those who yield to its Allurements, she entered into a Monastery, where she still lives a Pensioner,[1] but with the same Strictness as those who are profess'd Nuns and have taken the Veil.

These were the sad Consequences of a Jealousy, which most People will cry arose from an Excess of Love, but I still take upon me to maintain the contrary:—*Manilius* loved *Sabina* 'tis certain, yet was it not his Love, but the ill Opinion he had of Womenkind in general, which put him on those mistaken Measures to secure her to himself.

For my Part, I cannot help thinking but that this unfortunate Lady has a great Plea for Compassion; for tho' no ill Usage of what kind soever from a Husband can excuse us from revenging it in the Manner she did, yet when one considers the Frailty of Human Nature, and how prevalent, especially in our Sex, is that false Pride which prompts us to return Injury for Injury; we may justly say, that it is Pity a Mind of itself not disposed to ill, should receive any Provocations to be so.

Sabina, indeed, was bred up in the utmost Abhorrence of Vice; those who had the Care of her Education told her what she must do in order to acquire the Love and Esteem of this World, and the Happiness promised to the Virtuous in the other; but then they indulg'd her in all the modish Amusements of the present Age, and suffered her to lavish on them too much of that Time which ought to have been employ'd in improving her Understanding;—in fine, she was train'd up in the Ways young Ladies in *England* ordinarily are; her Relations following the common Opinion, that to sing, dance, play on the Spinet,[2] and work at her Needle,[3] are Accomplishments sufficient for a Woman:—*Wit* she had enough, but was never taught that to accustom herself to Reflection was necessary to ripen that *Wit* into *Wisdom;* and every one knows, that the *One* without the *Other,* like a Ship with too much Ballast, is liable to sink with its own Weight.

---

1. **Pensioner:** boarder.

2. **Spinet:** an early form of the harpsichord.

3. **work at her Needle:** doing embroidery, needlepoint, and other decorative forms of needlework.

We were beginning to lament the Misfortunes our Sex frequently fall into through the Want of those Improvements we are, doubless, capable of, when a Letter, left for us at our Publisher's, was brought in, which happening to be on that Subject, cannot any where be more properly inserted than in this Place.

To the FEMALE SPECTATOR.
LADIES,

Permit me to thank you for the kind and generous Task you have undertaken in endeavouring to improve the Minds and Manners of our unthinking Sex:—It is the noblest Act of Charity you could exercise in an Age like ours, where the Sense of Good and Evil is almost extinguish'd, and People desire to appear more vicious than they really are, that so they may be less unfashionable: This Humour, which is too prevalent in the Female Sex, is the true Occasion of the many Evils and Dangers to which they are daily exposed:—No wonder the Men of Sense disregard us! and the Dissolute triumph over that Virtue they ought to protect!

Yet, I think, it would be cruel to charge the Ladies with all the Errors they commit; it is most commonly the Fault of a wrong Education, which makes them frequently do amiss, while they think they not only act innocently but uprightly;—it is therefore only the Men, and the Men of Understanding too, who, in effect, merit the Blame of this, and are answerable for all the Misconduct we are guilty of:—Why do they call us *silly Women,* and not endeavour to make us otherwise?—God and Nature has endued them with Means, and *Custom* has established them in the Power of rendering our Minds such as they ought to be;—how highly ungenerous is it then to give us a wrong turn, and then despise us for it!

The *Mahometans,* indeed, enslave their Women, but then they teach them to believe their Inferiority will extend to Eternity;[1] but our Case is even worse than this, for while we live in a free Country, and are

---

1. **Inferiority . . . Eternity:** because of the Islamic view of Paradise as a place of sensual enjoyment, where beautiful women will be at the disposal of men.

assured from our excellent *Christian* Principles that we are capable of those refined Pleasures which last to Immortality, our Minds, our better Parts, are wholly left uncultivated, and, like a rich Soil neglected, bring forth nothing but noxious Weeds.

There is, undoubtedly, no Sexes in Souls, and we are as able to receive and practise the Impressions, not only of Virtue and Religion, but also of those Sciences which the Men engross to themselves, as they can be:—Surely our Bodies were not form'd by the great Creator out of the finest Mould, that our Souls might be neglected like the coarsest of the Clay!

O! would too imperious, and too tenacious Man, be so just to the World as to be more careful of the Education of those Females to whom they are Parents or Guardians!—Would they convince them in their Infancy that Dress and Shew are not the Essentials of a fine Lady, and that true Beauty is seated in the Mind; how soon should we see our Sex retrieve the many Virtues which false Taste has bury'd in Oblivion!—Strange Infatuation! to refuse us what would so much contribute to their own Felicity!—Would not themselves reap the Benefit of our Amendment? Should we not be more obedient Daughters, more faithful Wives, more tender Mothers, more sincere Friends, and more valuable in every other Station of Life?

But, I find, I have let my Pen run a much greater Length than I at first intended:—If I have said any thing worthy your Notice, or what you think the Truth of the Case, I hope you will mention this Subject in some of your future Essays; or if you find I have any way err'd in my Judgment, to set me right will be the greatest Favour you can confer on,

LADIES,
Your constant Reader,
And humble Servant,
CLEORA.

Hampton-Court,
Jan. 12, 1744–5.

After thanking this Lady for the Favour of her obliging Letter, we think it our Duty to congratulate her on being one of those happy

Few who have been blest with that Sort of Education which she so pathetically laments the Want of in the greatest Part of our Sex.

Those Men are certainly guilty of a great deal of Injustice who think, that all the Learning becoming in a Woman is confined to the Management of her Family; that is, to give Orders concerning the Table, take care of her Children in their Infancy, and observe that her Servants do not neglect their Business:—All this no doubt is very necessary, but would it not be better if she performs those Duties more through Principle than Custom? and will she be less punctual[1] in her Observance of them, after she becomes a Wife, for being perfectly convinced, before she is so, of the Reasonableness of them, and why they are expected from her?

Many Women have not been inspired with the least Notion of even those Requisites[2] in a Wife, and when they become so, continue the same loitering, lolloping,[3] idle Creatures they were before; and then the Men are ready enough to condemn those who had the Care of their Education.

Terrible is it, indeed, for the Husband, especially if he be a Tradesman, or Gentleman of small Estate, who marries with a Woman of this Stamp, whatever Fortune she brings will immediately run out, and 'tis well if all his own does not follow:—Even Persons of the highest Rank in Life will suffer greatly both in their Circumstances and Peace of Mind, when she, who ought to be the Mistress of the Family,[4] lives in it like a Stranger, and perhaps knows no more of what those about her do than an Alien.[5]

But supposing her an excellent Œconomist, in every Respect what the World calls a notable Woman,[6] methinks the Husband would be

---

1. **punctual:** exact.

2. **Requisites:** requirements; the "Duties" that have just been specified.

3. **lolloping:** sprawling, lounging. The *O.E.D.* cites this sentence of Haywood's to illustrate the usage of the word.

4. **Mistress of the Family:** woman with authority over the servants.

5. **Alien:** foreigner.

6. **notable Woman:** good household manager. This meaning developed from the more general sense of notable as "worthy"; a notable man, at this period, was one particularly industrious at business.

yet infinitely happier were she endued with other good Qualities as well as a perfect Understanding in Houshold Affairs:—The Governess of a Family, or what is commonly call'd Houskeeper, provided she be honest and careful, might discharge this Trust as well as a Wife; but there is, doubtless, somewhat more to be expected by a Man from that Woman whom the Ceremony of Marriage has made Part of himself:[1]—She is, or ought to be, if qualified for it, the Repository of his dearest Secrets, the Moderator of his fiercer Passions, the Softner of his most anxious Cares, and the constantly chearful and entertaining Companion of his more unbended Moments.

To be all this she must be endued with a consummate Prudence, a perfect Eveness of Temper, an unshaken Fortitude, a gentle affable Behaviour, and a sprightly Wit:—The Foundation of these Virtues must be indeed in Nature, but Nature may be perverted by ill Customs, or, if not so, still want many Embellishments from Education; without which, however valuable in itself, it would appear rude and barbarous to others, and lose more than half the Effect it ought to have.

The younger *Dryden*'s Translation of that admirable Satire of *Juvenal*[2] has these Words:

> Children, like tender Oziers, take the Bow,
> And as they first are fashion'd always grow:
> For what we learn in Youth, to that alone,
> In Age we are by second Nature prone.[3]

How much therefore does it behove those who have the Care of Youth, to mould their tender Minds to that Shape which will best become those Stations in Life they may be expected to fill.

---

1. **Ceremony . . . himself:** because man and wife are "one flesh." As St. Paul puts it, "So ought men to love their wives as their own bodies. He that loveth his wife loveth himself" (Eph. 5:28).

2. **Juvenal:** Decimus Junius Juvenalis (first–second century A.D.), Roman satiric poet.

3. **Children . . . prone:** John Dryden, trans., "The Fourteenth Satire of Juvenal," ll. 50–51, 96–97.

Our Sex, from their very Infancy, are encourag'd to dress and fondle their Babies;[1] a Custom not improper, because it gives an early Idea of that Care and Tenderness we ought to shew those real Babes to whom we may happen to be Mothers: But I am apt to think, that without this Prepossession, Nature would inform us what was owing from us to those whom we have given Being:—The very Look and innocent Crys of those little Images of ourselves would be more pre- vailing than any Rules could be:—This the meerest Savages who live without Precept, and are utterly ignorant of all moral Virtues, may inform us;—nay, for Conviction in this Point, we may descend yet lower, and only observe the tender Care which the Beasts of the Field and the Fowls of the Air take of their young ones.

To be good *Mothers,* therefore, tho' a Duty incumbent on all who are so, requires fewer Lessons than to be good *Wives:*—We all groan under the Curse entail'd upon us for the Transgression of *Eve.*

Thy Desire shall be to thy Husband, and he shall rule over thee.[2]

But we are not taught enough how to lighten this Burthen, and render ourselves such as would make him asham'd to exert that Au- thority, he thinks he has a Right to, over us.

Were that Time which is taken up in instructing us in Accomplish- ments, which, however taking[3] at first Sight, conduce little to our essential Happiness, employ'd in studying the Rules of Wisdom, in well informing us what we are, and what we ought to be, it would doubtless inspire those, to whom we should happen to be united, with a Reverence which would not permit them to treat us with that Light- ness and Contempt, which, tho' some of us may justly enough incur, often drives not only such, but the most innocent of us, to Extrava- gancies that render ourselves, and those concern'd with us equally mis- erable.

---

1. **Babies:** dolls.
2. **Thy Desire . . . thee:** Gen. 3:16.
3. **taking:** captivating, attractive.

Why then, as *Cleora* says, do the Men, who are and will be the sole Arbitrators in this Case, refuse us all Opportunities of enlarging our Minds, and improving those Talents we have received from God and Nature; and which, if put in our Power to exert in a proper Manner, would make no less their own Happiness than our Glory?

They cry, of what use can Learning be to us, when Custom, and the Modesty of our Sex, forbids us to speak in public Places?—'Tis true that it would not befit us to go into the Pulpit, nor harangue at the Bar; but this is a weak and trifling Argument against our being qualify'd for either, since all *Men* who are so were never intended for the Service of the Church, nor put on the long Robe;[1] and by the same Rule therefore the Sons as well as Daughters of good Families should be bred up in Ignorance.

Knowledge is a light Burthen, and, I believe, no one was ever the worse for being skilled in a great many Things, tho' he might never have occasion for any of them.

But of all Kinds of Learning the Study of Philosophy[2] is certainly the most pleasant and profitable:—It corrects all the vicious Humours of the Mind, and inspires the noblest Virtues;—it enlarges our Understanding;—it brings us acquainted with ourselves, and with every thing that is in Nature; and the more we arrive at a Proficiency in it, the more happy and the more worthy we are.—Mr. *Prior* tells us,

> On its best Steps each Age and Sex may rise,
> 'Tis like the Ladder in the Patriarch's Dream,
> Its Foot on Earth, its Height beyond the Skies.[3]

Many Examples have there been of Ladies who have attained to very great Perfection in this sublime and useful Science; and doubtless the Number had been greatly increased but for the Discouragement our Sex meets with, when we aim at any thing beyond the Needle.

---

1. **the long Robe:** of the lawyer.

2. **Philosophy:** natural science.

3. **On its best . . . beyond the Skies:** Matthew Prior, "To Dr Sherlock, on his Practical Discourse Concerning Death," ll. 33–35.

The World would infallibly be more happy than it is, were Women more knowing than they generally are; and very well worth the while of those who have the Interest of the Female Part of their Family at Heart, to instruct them early in some of the most necessary Rudiments of Philosophy:—All those little Follies now ascrib'd to us, and which, indeed, we but too much incur the Censure of, would then vanish, and the Dignity of Human Nature shine forth in us, I will venture to say, with, at least, as much Splendor as in the other Sex.

All that Restlessness of Temper we are accused of, that perpetual Inclination for gadding from Place to Place;—those Vapours, those Disquiets we often feel meerly for want of some material Cause of Disquiet, would be no more, when once the Mind was employ'd in the pleasing Enquiries of Philosophy;—a Search that well rewards the Pains we take in it, were we even to make no considerable Progress; because even the most minute Discovery affords Matter for Reflection and Admiration.

Whether our Speculations extend to the greatest and most tremendous Objects, or pry into the smallest Works of the Creation, new Scenes of Wonder every Moment open to our Eyes; and as Love and Reverence to the Deity is by every one allowed to be the Ground-Work of all Virtues and Religion, it is, methinks, no less impolitick than unjust to deny us the Means of becoming more good as well as more wise.

From the Brute Creation we may learn Industry, Patience, Tenderness, and a thousand Qualities, which tho' the Human Soul possesses in an infinitely larger Degree, yet the Observation how exercis'd by Creatures of inferior Specie, will oblige us to look into ourselves, and blush at the Remembrance, that for want of Reflection we have sometimes forgot what we are, and perhaps acted beneath those very Animals we despise, and think on as no more than the Dust from which they sprung.

It is certainly a very great Misfortune as well as a Fault in us, that we are apt to have Pride enough to value ourselves highly on the Dignity of our Nature, but yet have not enough to act up in any Measure to it:—This is, methinks, paying too great a Regard to Names, and neglecting Essentials.

The Men in this respect are, indeed, as much to blame as we, nay, much more so, those at least of a liberal Education, who having those Advantages of Learning, which are deny'd to us, behave as tho' they had never been instructed in any thing but how to indulge the Senses in the most elegant Manner.

The Women, at worst, could but act as many of the Men do who are refused no Improvements;—they ought, therefore, to make Tryal of us, and not grudge the Expence of Books and Masters to the one Sex any more than to the other.

If, by the Texture of the Brain, as some pretend to alledge, we are less capable of deep Meditations, and have a Multiplicity of volatile Ideas, which, continually wandering, naturally prevent our fixing on any one Thing; the more Care should be taken to improve such as may be of Service, and suppress those that have a contrary Tendency.

That this is possible to be done, I believe, those who reason most strongly this way, and pretend to understand the Mechanism of our Formation best, will not deny.

But I agree no farther than in Supposition to this Common-Place Argument, made use of by the Enemies of our Sex:—The Delicacy of those numerous Filaments which contain, and separate from each other what are call'd the Seats of Invention, Memory, and Judgment, may not, for any thing they can prove to the contrary, render them less strong; but as I am not Anatomist enough to know whether there is really any such Difference or not between the Male and Female Brain, I will not pretend to reason on this Point.

I have an Opinion of my own, which, being approv'd of by *Mira* and *Euphrosine,* I will venture to declare, tho' our noble Widow laughs at us all for it.—It is this:

The Vivacity of our Ideas,—the Quickness of our Apprehensions, and those ready Turns which most Women, much more than Men, have on any sudden Exigence, seem to me to proceed from a greater Redundance of the animal Spirits;[1] and if they sometimes appear too confus'd and huddled, as it were, together, it is but like a Crowd of

---

1. **animal Spirits:** nervous energy; the source of physical sensation and movement.

Mob round the Stage of a Mountebank,[1] where all endeavouring to be foremost, obstruct the Passage of each other.

If this should happen to be the Case, as I shall always believe 'till convinced, by very good Reasons, of the contrary, it is easy to check the too great Velocity of these Particles, by laying down one great Point, into which, as to a Center, they might all direct their Course.

The most subtil Spirits may be fixed[2] by that Sovereign Chymist, solid Reflection:—*Thought* will give them a due Weight, and prevent their Evaporation; but then the Subject must be delightful as well as serious, or the Mind may be in Danger of an opposite Extreme, and from being too giddy, become irrecoverably mop'd.[3]

Philosophy is, therefore, the Toil which can never tire the Person engag'd in it;—all its Ways are strewed with Roses, and the farther you go, the more enchanting Objects appear before you, and invite you on.

That this Science is not too abstruse for our Sex to arrive at a great Perfection in, none can presume to deny; because many known Examples, both in ancient and modern Times, prove the Certainty of it.

Who has not heard of the fam'd *Hypatia,*[4] who read Lectures of Philosophy in the Public Schools in *Alexandria,* and of whose Eloquence and Wisdom, St. *Cyril,* then Bishop of that Place, stood so much in Awe, that finding it impossible to bring her over to his Opinion in Matters of Religion, he never rested till he had found Means to take away her Life:—An Action for which he has been severely reproach'd by after and less bigotted Ages.

Many others acquired an equal Share of Reputation with this fair *Greek,* but there is no need of searching Antiquity for that which the present age gives any unquestionable Proof of in the celebrated Donna *Lawra,*[5] who has not only disputed with, but also confuted the most

---

1. **Mountebank:** an itinerant seller of quack medicines who typically entertained his audience by juggling, tricks, and jokes.

2. **fixed:** stabilized.

3. **mop'd:** dejected.

4. **Hypatia:** (d. 415), a Neoplatonic philosopher in Alexandria, Greece, renowned for her beauty, learning, and eloquence.

5. **Donna Lawra:** probably Laura Bassi, an eighteenth-century Italian scientist who was Professor of Anatomy at the University of Bologna. I owe this identification to Anita Guerrini and Saba Bahar.

learned Doctors in *Italy,* in those Points on which they happen'd to differ from her.

Some Branches of the Mathematicks are also very agreeable and improving Amusements for young Ladies, particular *Geography,* in which they may travel the World over, be acquainted with all its Parts, and find new Matter to adore the Infinite Wisdom,[1] which presiding over and throughout such a Diversity of contrary Climes, suits every one so as to be most pleasing and convenient to the Inhabitants.

History must not be omitted, as it cannot fail engaging the Mind to Attention, and affording the strongest Precept by Example:—The Rise and Fall of Monarchies;—the Fate of Princes, the Sources from which their good or ill Fortune may be deduc'd;—the various Events which the Struggles for Liberty against arbitrary Power have produc'd, and the wonderful Effects which the Heroism of particular Persons has obtained, both to curb Oppression in the Tyrant, and Sedition in the Subject, affords an ample Field for Contemplation, and at the same time too much Pleasure to leave room for any Amusements of a low and trifling Nature.

These are what I would have the serious Employments of a young Lady's Mind:—Music, Dancing, and the reading of Poetry and Novels may sometimes come in by way of Relaxation, but ought not to be too much indulg'd.

But any Study, any Amusement, should be suited to the Genius[2] and Capacity of the Person to whom it's prescrib'd:—I only mention these as worthy Employments of the Mind; there are others which perhaps may be equally so, and are to be adhered to, or rejected, according to the Judgments of those who have the Government[3] of Youth.

All I insist on, and all I believe that *Cleora,* or any other Well wisher to our Sex, and through us to the Happiness of Mankind in general, can desire, is, that the Talents with which we are born may not be stifled by a wrong Education.

---

1. **new ... Wisdom:** new cause for worship (i.e., awe at the wonders of God's creation).

2. **Genius:** natural gifts.

3. **Government:** direction.

I cannot, however, take leave of this Subject without answering one Objection which I have heard made against Learning in our Sex, which is, that the politer Studies take us off from those that are more necessary, tho' less ornamental.

I believe many well-meaning People may be deceived into this Opinion, which, notwithstanding, is very unjust:—Those Improvements which I have mention'd, sublime as they are, will never be of Prejudice to our attending to those lower Occupations of Life, which are not to be dispensed with except in those of the great World.— They will rather, by making a Woman more sensible than she could otherwise be, of what is either her Duty, or becoming in her to do, that she will be doubly industrious and careful, not to give any Excuse for Reproaches, either from her own Conscience, or the Tongues of those who would suffer by her Transgression.

In a word, it is entirely owing to a narrow Education that we either give our Husbands room to find fault with our Conduct, or that we have Leisure to pry too scrutinously into theirs:—Happy would it be for both, were this almost sole Cause of all our Errors once reform'd; and I am not without some Glimmerings of Hope that it will one Day be so.

The Ladies themselves, methinks, begin to seem sensible of the Injustice which has long been done them, and find a Vacuum in their Minds, which, to fill up, they, of their own accord, invented the way of sticking little Pictures on Cabinets, Screens, Dressing-Tables, and other little Pieces of Chamber-Furniture, and then varnishing them over so as to look like one Piece of Painting; and they now have got into the Art of turning Ivory into whatever Utensils they fancy:— There is no doubt but a Pair of Globes will make a better Figure in their Anti-Chambers[1] than the Vice and Wheel;[2] but great Revolutions are not to be expected at once, and if they once take it in their Heads to prefer Works of Ingenuity, tho' in the most trifling Matters, to

---

1. **Anti-Chambers:** antechambers, waiting rooms.

2. **Vice and Wheel:** vise, for holding wood in the process of working it; wheel, for turning ivory or clay.

Dress, Gaming and rambling Abroad, they will, it is to be hop'd, proceed to more noble and elevated Studies.

If the married Ladies of Distinction begin the Change, and bring Learning into Fashion, the younger will never cease solliciting their Parents and Guardians for the Means of following it, and every Toilet[1] in the Kingdom be loaded with Materials for beautifying the Mind more than the Face of its Owner.

The Objection, therefore, that I have heard made by some Men, that Learning would make us too assuming,[2] is weak and unjust in itself, because there is nothing would so much cure us of those Vanities we are accused of, as Knowledge.

A beautiful well dress'd Lady, who is acquainted with no other Merit than Appearance, never looks in her Glass without thinking all the Adoration can be paid to her, is too small a Tribute to her Charms; and even those of our Sex, who seem most plain in the Eyes of other People, never fail to see something in themselves worthy of attracting the most tender Homage.

It is meerly want of Consideration, and the living, as most of us do, in a blind Ignorance of what we truly are, or what we ought reasonably to expect from the World, that gives us that Pride, for which those, who to our Faces treat us with the greatest Respect, laugh at, and despise us for behind our Backs.

It has ever been agreed, by Men of the best Understanding, that the farther they go in the wonderful Researches of Nature, the more abash'd and humble they are:—They see the unfathomable Depth before them, and with it the Insufficiency of human Penetration:— The little they are able to discover convinces them that there are Things still out of their reach, and even beyond their Comprehension; and while it raises their Ideas of the Almighty Wisdom, puts an entire Check to all vain Imaginations of their own.

O but, say they, Learning puts the Sexes too much on an Equality, it would destroy that implicit Obedience which it is necessary the

---

1. **Toilet:** dressing table.

2. **assuming:** presumptuous.

Women should pay to our Commands:—If once they have the Capacity of arguing with us, where would be our Authority!

Now will I appeal to any impartial Reader, even among the Men, if this very Reason for keeping us in Subjection does not betray an Arrogance and Pride in themselves, yet less excusable than that which they seem so fearful of our assuming.

I will also undertake to prove, not only by my own Observation but by that of every Person who has taken any Pains to examine the World, that those Women have always been the most domineering, whose Talents have received the least Improvement from Education.

It may happen, indeed, that some might grow overbearing on such Advantages, for there are Tempers too turbulent for any Bounds to restrain; but I will at the same time maintain, that they would have been still worse if kept in Ignorance that to be so was a Fault:—Nature will always be the same, and she who is prone to Pride and Vanity will give Testimonies of it, even tho' she has no one Perfection either of Mind or Body to serve as a Pretence.

But, as of two Evils the least is to be chosen, is it not better, therefore, for any Man who has the Misfortune to have a termagant[1] or imperious Wife, that when People speak of her Behaviour they should say, "She is a Woman of an admirable Understanding and great Learning, she only knows her own Merit too well;" than to hear them cry, "What a vain, idle, ignorant, prating[2] Creature she is?"—I dare answer, there is not a Husband in all *Great Britain* that would not be glad to hear the *first* rather than the *last* Character[3] given of the Woman to whom he is united.

This, however, is certain, that Knowledge can make the Bad no worse, and would make the Good much better than they could be without it.

If, therefore, the Parents of a young Lady thrust her out into the World unfinish'd, as I may venture to call it, when no Care is taken

---

1. **termagant:** overbearing, nagging.

2. **prating:** chattering.

3. **Character:** character sketch, characterization.

of her better Part, it would not, methinks, be unbecoming in her Husband to supply that Deficiency:—She would receive Instruction from his Mouth with double Pleasure, and it must certainly be an infinite Satisfaction to him to perceive the Improvement his fair Pupil daily made under his Tuition:[1]—Nothing in my Opinion could more endear them to each other, nor be a greater Proof of their mutual Affection. *Milton*[2] most elegantly expresses such a Circumstance in the Eighth Book of his *Paradise Lost,* where *Raphael*[3] being in Conversation with *Adam* on Matters then above the Comprehension of *Eve,* she withdrew that she might afterwards hear it from her Husband.

> —By his Countenance seem'd
> Ent'ring on studious Thoughts abstruse; which *Eve*
> Perceiving where she sat retired in sight,
> With Lowliness Majestic from her Seat,
> And Grace, that won who saw to wish her stay,
> Rose, and went forth among her Fruits and Flowers,
> To visit how they prosper'd, bud and bloom,
> Her Nursery; they at her coming sprung,
> And touch'd by her fair Tendance gladlier grew,
> Yet went she not, as not with such Discourse
> Delighted, or not capable her Ear
> Of what was high:—Such Pleasure she reserv'd
> *Adam* relating, she sole Auditress;
> Her *Husband* the Relator she prefer'd
> Before the *Angel,* and of him to ask
> Chose rather: He, she knew, would intermix
> Grateful Digressions, and solve high Disputes
> With conjugal Caresses; from his Lip,
> Not Words alone pleas'd her.—O when meet now
> Such Pairs, in Love and mutual Honour join'd![4]

---

1. **Tuition:** instruction.

2. **Milton:** John Milton (1608–1674), epic and lyric poet.

3. **Raphael:** archangel sent, according to Milton's account, to instruct Adam about the universe and humankind's place in it.

4. **By his Countenance . . . Honour join'd:** John Milton, *Paradise Lost* 8.39–58.

And again, speaking of the Delights they found in each other's Conversation;

> For while I sit with thee I seem in Heaven,
> And sweeter thy Discourse is to my Ear
> Than Fruits of Palm-Trees (pleasantest to Thirst
> And Hunger both from Labour) at the Hour
> Of sweet Repast: They satiate, and soon fill
> Tho' pleasant; but thy Words with Grace Divine
> Imbued, bring to their Sweetness no Satiety.[1]

Where there is that Union of Hearts as well as Hands, which can alone answer the Ends for which Marriage was first instituted, the Husband in finding his Precepts effectual and delightful must feel no less Rapture in himself, and Increase of Love for the dear Authoress of it, than the same incomparable Poet, just now quoted, ascribes to the great Father of Mankind,[2] when speaking of *Eve* he defines the Passion he has for her, and the Motives of it in these Terms:

> —It is not
> Neither her outside Form so fair, nor ought
> In Procreation common to all Kinds,
> (Tho' higher of the Genial Bed by far,
> And with mysterious Reverence I deem)
> So much delights me, as those graceful Acts,
> Those thousand Decencies that daily flow
> From all her Words and Actions, mix'd with Love
> And sweet Compliance, which declares unfeign'd
> Union of Mind, or in us both one Soul;
> Harmony to behold in wedded Pair.[3]

Methinks it would be no Difficulty for two People who love each other as they ought, and some such there doubtless are, to practise

---

1. **For while . . . no Satiety:** *Paradise Lost* 8.210–16.

2. **Father of Mankind:** Adam.

3. **It is not . . . wedded Pair:** *Paradise Lost* 8.596–605 (slightly altered).

over a little of the Behaviour of our first Parents[1] in their State of Innocence:—'Tis true, they would incur a good deal of Ridicule from the more gay and noisy World on first attempting such a thing, but that would wear off in time by their Perseverance; and the Benefits accruing from it to all belonging to them, as well as to themselves, would become so demonstrative, as might, perhaps, induce the most Thoughtless to make tryal of such a way of Life.

But all this, I doubt,[2] will be look'd upon as visionary,[3] and my Readers will cry, that my Business, as a *Spectator,* is to report such Things as I see, and am convinced of the Truth of, not present them with Ideas of my own Formation, and which, as the World now is, can never be reduc'd to Practice:—To which I beg leave to reply, that the Impossibility lies only in the *Will;*—much may be done by a steady Resolution,—without it, nothing.

I do not, indeed, flatter myself with living to see my Counsel in this Point make any great Impression; the Mode is against me, and those who may approve the most of what I say will yet be asham'd to confess it.

*   *   *

FROM   BOOK   XIII

There is a Lust in Man no Charm can tame,
Of loudly publishing his Neighbour's Shame:
On Eagles Wings immortal Scandals fly,
While virtuous Actions are but born and dye.

HARV. JUV.[4]

---

1. **first Parents:** Adam and Eve. The phrase is from *Paradise Lost* 4.6.

2. **doubt:** suspect.

3. **visionary:** fanciful.

4. **There is . . . born and dye:** Stephen Harvey, trans., "The Ninth Satire of Juvenal," ll. 193–96.

Nothing more plainly shews a weak and degenerate Mind, than taking a Delight in whispering about every idle Story we are told, to the Prejudice of our Neighbours: This is a Fault charged more generally on our Sex than the other; and, I am sorry to say, with but too much Justice. Some will have it, that this unlucky Propensity in us proceeds from a greater Share of Envy and Malice in our Natures; others, less severe, ascribe it meerly to a Want of something else wherewith to employ ourselves. This latter is certainly the most true, because we often find Women, who in no other Respect can be accused of Ill-nature, yet take a prodigious Pleasure in reporting every little Scandal they hear, even tho' it be of Persons whom they have neither any Quarrel against, nor can any way be supposed to envy.

But this Motive, tho' less criminal, is equally shameful; and ought to make every Woman blush, when about to repeat the little Affairs of Persons with whom she has no manner of Concern, to think she finds an Incapacity in herself of attending to those of her own, and which, it is not to be doubted, stand in sufficient need of Regulation.

I have seen a fine Lady, who has been sunk, as it were, in Lassitude, half dying with the Vapours, and in such a Lethargy, both of Mind and Body, that it seem'd painful to her even to drawl out a Word, or lift up a Finger; yet this Insensible to all Things else, has no sooner heard of some new Intrigue, no Matter whether true or false, or between Persons of her Acquaintance, or those she only knew the Names of, than all the Lustre has return'd into her Eyes, Smiles have dimpled her Cheeks, and she has immediately started up, called in a Hurry to be dress'd, ordered her Coach, and almost killed a Pair of Horses in galloping round the Town with this Intelligence.

So great is the Vanity some People have of being thought to be the first in hearing any Piece of News, that to it they will sacrifice all Considerations whatever, or rather Consideration is itself absorb'd in this ridiculous Ambition:—An Ambition did I call it?—Of what?—Of being a Tale-bearer!—A Gossip!—A Lover of raking into Filth!—Shameful Character even for the lowest bred, much more so for a Woman of Quality and Condition:—None, I believe, will be willing to acknowledge it their own, but too many give substantial Proofs that it is so.

I will have the Charity to suppose that some are even ignorant themselves, that they have this Vice in their Composition; but then I must beg Leave to ask them why they are so?—Has an Examination into one's own Heart never been recommended? Nay, has it not been often enjoin'd as the first and greatest Study of our Lives?—Is it not a Study which the meanest, as well as the highest Rank of People have it in their Power to attend to? and is it not equally necessary to both?—All have not a Stock of Good-nature to enable them to treat their Fellow-Creatures with that Tenderness required of us both by Divine and Human Institutions; we ought therefore to supply that Deficiency by *Principle,* which can only flow from Reason and Recollection.

Whenever we hear any invidious Reflections cast upon a Person, is it too much Trouble for us just to think that there may be a Possibility of their being false, or supposing them too true, that it is none of our Business to censure or condemn their Faults, even in our own Breasts, much less to give the Liberty to others to do so by favouring the Scandal by our Report?

Cruel in us is it to insult the Weaknesses of Human Nature, but most base and unjust to accuse where there is no real Matter for Accusation, as is very often the Case:—Those who are fond of Intelligence of this kind, should, whenever they hear any, put this Question to their Judgement, "May not these People tell me this on purpose to amuse me, and because they think it pleases me?"—Of this there is more than a Probability; many a fair Reputation has been blasted, meerly by the Folly I have mentioned, of having something new to say, or through a mean Design in the Reporters, of ingratiating themselves with some Person, who, to his or her Shame, was known to delight in Scandal.

Would every one resolve to give no Ear to Informations of this Nature, how soon they would drop!—It is by Encouragement that Stories, derogatory to the Honour of the Persons mention'd, gather Strength; and in my Opinion, those who give Attention to them are equally culpable with the Relators.—What then must it be to repeat them? to take Pleasure in sounding the Trumpet of Infamy, and exulting[1] that fallen Virtue, we should rather commiserate, and use our

---

1. **Exulting:** exulting over.

best Endeavours to retrieve?—O there are no Words to paint a Disposition so barbarous, so inconsistent with the Character of Womanhood!

There are some who are possess'd of a Notion, false and absurd as it is, that the Destruction of other People's Reputation is the building up of their own;—that whatever good Qualities they have, or would be thought to have, will be rendered more conspicuous by throwing a Shade over those of every Body else: But this is so far from answering the Purpose aim'd at by it, that it often gives the Hearers a Suspicion that the Woman, who is so fond of expatiating on the Faults and Follies of her Neighbour, does it only with a View of drawing off any Attention to her own; nor are they always mistaken who judge in this Manner of Detraction.

But supposing the Subject of our Ridicule be ever so just, that the Errors we condemn are so obvious, that there is not the least room to doubt of them, are not we certain, alas, that such Errors will infallibly draw on the guilty Head a Train of Misfortunes, which ought rather to excite our Pity than our Mirth?

Besides, tho' we may be acquainted with the Fault, we seldom can be so with the Circumstances, by which the Person has been perhaps, ensnared into it; and it often happens, that while we are railing at them for it, a secret Conviction may have reach'd their Hearts; they may judge themselves with the same Severity we do, and resolve to attone for their past Behavior by the greatest Regularity of future Conduct: How inhuman is it then to expose such a one, and, 'tis ten to one, disappoint all their good Intentions by so doing; since nothing is more common, than when a Woman finds her Reputation is entirely ruin'd by the Discovery of one Fault, she makes no Scruple to commit more, as she cannot suffer more than she has already done!—All Sense of Shame grows dead within her, and she thinks she has nothing to do but go on in Defiance of the World, and despise the Censures she had it not in her Power to silence.

In fine,[1] there is no Circumstance whatever which can justify one Person in villifying the Character of another; and as I believe it is more often done through a certain Wantonness of the Tongue, than any

---

1. **In fine:** in short.

propense Malice in the Mind, I would have every one, who find in themselves an Inclination that way, to keep in Memory *Shakespear's* Reflection upon it.

> Good Name in Man or Woman,
> Is the immediate jewel of our Souls:
> Who steals my Purse, steals Trash: 'tis something, nothing,
> 'Twas mine, 'tis his; and has been Slave to thousands.
> But he that filches from me my good Name,
> Robs me of that which not enriches him,
> And makes me poor indeed.[1]

Curiosity is the Parent of this Vice; if we were not eager to pry into the Affairs of others it would be impossible for us to know so much of them as we do:—The Passion for finding out Secrets is, in reality, so predominant in most of us, that it requires a very great Fund of good Sense and Consideration to enable us to subdue it: Yet if we remember how severe the Men are upon our Sex on Account of this Weakness, we should not, methinks, grudge taking a little Pains to shew it is in our Power to divest ourselves of it.

Will the Knowledge of what other People do make us wiser or happier?—"Yes," some will answer, "we may profit by taking Example by the good Œconomy of some, and take Warning by the Mistakes of others, not to fall into the same."

This Argument might be of some Weight, indeed, were there no written Examples of both for our Direction; but, thank Heaven, they are numerous, and of the first Sort, are to be found much easier in History than in present Observation: In an Age where Vice and Folly shine with so much Lustre, the Virtuous and the Wise chuse to sit in the Shade rather than expose themselves to the Influence of too warm a Sun; their Actions, therefore, must be less conspicuous, and consequently can serve as a Pattern but to a few; and as for others, if the Monitor within our own Bosom fails to admonish us we are doing wrong, no Examples from without will have sufficient Efficacy to prevent us from falling into the very Errors we condemn in others.

---

1. **Good Name . . . poor indeed:** William Shakespeare, *Othello* 3.3.160–66.

Curiosity, therefore, on this Score has a very slender Excuse, and they who make it but deceive themselves; nor have we any real Motive for being solicitous in our Enquiries after Things no way relating to us, but to gratify that idle Vanity of reporting them, and attain the Reputation of being one whom nothing can escape.

The Men too, however they may condemn it in us, are not altogether free from this Foible;—especially those among them who affect to be great Politicians:—Some, if they happen to get a Secret, can neither eat nor sleep till they have communicated it to as many as they know; and those who pass for more wise and prudent, tho' they declare it not in Words, cannot help, on any Talk of the Affair, giving significant Shrugs, Nods, Winks, Smiles, and a thousand Indications, that they know more than they think proper to speak:—How do Men of this Cast haunt the *Levees*[1] of the Great, the Lobby,[2] the Court of Requests, think they read Meanings in the Look of every Face they see there, and if they chance to hear a Word *en passent,*[3] compliment their own Penetration with having discovered Wonders from a single Sentence; then run from Coffee-House to Coffee-House, and with a solemn Countenance, whisper the imaginary Secret, from one to another quite round the Room.

But these Male-Gossips have been sufficiently exposed already, and I should not have made any mention of them, but to take off some Part of the Edge of that Raillery they are so ready to treat our Sex with on this Occasion.

The best way, however, is for us to give them no Pretence for it; and I think nothing can be less difficult, if we would once seriously set about it, and reflect how much we lay ourselves open to Censure while we are exposing others:—How natural it is for People to return in kind an Injury of this Sort, and that if even they should be less severe than we in Reason can expect, yet we are certain of incurring the Character of a malicious Person from as many as hear us.

'Tis strange, methinks, that this wide World, and all the various Scenes which the Hand of the Creator has so bounteously scatter'd

---

1. **Levees:** receptions.

2. **Lobby:** entrance hall to the House of Commons, which was open to the public.

3. **en passent:** in passing.

through the whole, can afford no Matter of Conversation to an intelligent Being, without having Recourse to degrading the most exquisite and perfect of his Works, at least of all that Nature presents us with beneath the Moon, or that we are able to discover with mortal Eyes.

The *Turks* maintain that Women have no Souls, and there are not wanting some among *Christians* who lean to that Opinion: How mean is it, therefore, in us to give any Room for Arguments so unworthy and disgraceful to ourselves, by behaving as if we were incapable of Thought and Reflection, which are, indeed, the Essence of the Soul?

The Use of Speech was given us to communicate such Things, as Reason and Judgement supply us with from the Storehouse of the Mind, for the mutual Improvement of each other: Let us not then convert this noble Benefit to Purposes so contrary to the Intention of the Giver:—Let not the Tongue, instead of displaying Talents not inferior to the other Sex, be employ'd in lessening the Dignity of our Species by Defamation and Evil-speaking.—What Faults we find among ourselves, it is certainly our Business to conceal, and palliate as much as possible; the Men are but too quick-sighted to our Prejudice, and while they call us Angels, are ready enough to think us of the Number of the fallen Ones.

But, as I have before observed, the Number of those who thro' Envy and Malice make, or repeat scandalous Stories, is small in Comparison with those who do it meerly because they find it pleases others, or for the Want of any thing else to say; it obliges me to return to my old Argument, of the Necessity there is for us to have a little Retrospect into ourselves, and never to *speak* any more than to *do,* any thing of Moment without having well deliberated on what may be the Consequence.

The slightest Aspersion, or even an ambiguous Hint, thrown out before Persons who may make a cruel Advantage of it, is liable to be improv'd into the blackest Tale, and frequently has been so to the utter Ruin both of Character and Fortune:—The Sails of ill Report are swell'd by every Breath of Hate, Detraction, and Envy; even vain Surmises help to waft the envenom'd Loading, 'till it reaches Belief, where most it will be fatal, poisoning all Love, all Tenderness, all Respect, between the dearest Friends or Relations.

What irreconcilable Jars¹ has sometimes one rash Word occasioned, what unhappy Differences have arose, what endless Jealousies have been excited, only to gratify the Spleen or inconsiderate Folly of those who make or find some Matter that will bear an ill Constriction!

What says the old Poet *Brome*² on this Occasion:

> O Reputation, darling Pride of Honour!
> Bright fleeting Glare! thou Idol of an Hour!
> How in an Instant is thy Lustre tarnish'd!
> Not Innocence itself has Power to shield thee
> From the black Steam Detraction issues forth:
> Soil'd by each Breath of Folly; Words unmeant
> To reach thy crystal Sphere, oft darken it,
> Enveloping in misty Vapours, Virtue's Crown:
> Rend'ing thy Title dubious, if not false,
> To Eyes of Clay which see not through the Clouds.³

In another Place this Author pursues the same Theme, though with different Thoughts and Expression.

> Good Name, thou tender Bud of early Spring!
> How wouldst thou flourish, how shoot forth thy Blossoms,
> Did no keen Blasts shrivel thy op'ning Sweets!
> But e'er thy Summer comes, how often blighted
> By cruel Winds, and an inclement Season!
> All that should charm the World, bring Praise to thee,
> Driven back into thy Self,—thy Self alone,
> Conscious of what thou art; and Man unblest
> With thy expected Fruits.⁴

---

1. **Jars:** quarrels.

2. **Brome:** Alexander Brome (1620–1666) a minor poet. The lines Haywood quotes do not appear in the twentieth-century collected edition of Brome's poetry, edited by Roman R. Dubinski (Toronto: Univ. of Toronto Press, 1982).

3. **O Reputation . . . through the Clouds:** quotation unidentified.

4. **Good Name . . . expected Fruits:** quotation unidentified.

I cannot help here quoting another Poet, who very emphatically complains of the Severity of the World in Point of Fame.

> How vain is Virtue, which directs our Ways
> Through certain *Dangers* to uncertain *Praise:*
> Barren and airy Name! Thee Fortune flys,
> With thy lean Train the Pious and the Wise.
> Heav'n takes thee at thy Word without Regard,
> And lets thee poorly be thy own Reward.[1]

But it is altogether needless to bring Authorities to prove how inestimable a Jewel Reputation is, and how manifold a Wickedness and Cruelty all Attempts to deprive us of it have ever been accounted:—The most common Capacity sees into it;—the Thing speaks for itself, and Nature and Fellow-feeling convince us above Argument.

Why do we then so wantonly sport with the most serious Thing in Life?—A Thing, in which consists the greatest Happiness or Misery of the Person concern'd?—What Shadow of an Excuse is there for prejudicing another, in a Matter which can afford no manner of Benefit to ourselves; but on the contrary, renders us obnoxious to all civil and reasonable Society?

Were this Error only to be found where there is a Defect in the Understanding, it would not so much excite our Wonder; but I am troubled to say, that there are Persons of the best Sense, in other Respects, who suffer themselves to fall into it, through the Instigation of some favourite Passion, not sufficiently restrain'd by those who had the Care of them in their early Years, and which they are afterwards too proud, or too indolent, to make any Efforts to combat with.

The Mischiefs occasion'd by a Tongue delighting in Scandal, are too well known to stand in need of my repeating any Examples; yet I cannot forbear giving my Readers a very recent one, which has something in it more than ordinary particular.

---

1. **How vain . . . Reward:** quotation unidentified.

Fillamour and *Zimene* were look'd upon as a very happy and agreeable Pair; they had been married about three or four Months, and there seem'd not the least Abatement of their first Bridal Fondness, when *Ariana,* one of those gay inconsiderate Ladies I have been describing, came to visit *Zimene,* big with a Secret she had just discovered.

Some busy Body, it seems, had inform'd her that *Sophronia,* a great Pretender to Virtue, had a private Rendezvous with a young Gentleman, at a certain House where Masquerade Habits[1] are sold, or hired out occasionally:—That they met twice every Week there, had always a fine Collation,[2] and never parted till late at Night.

Ariana assured *Zimene* that her Intelligence was undoubted:—That *Sophronia,* as much a Prude as she was, had certainly an Intrigue, and concluded with saying, it would be a charming Thing if they could find out the Person who made a Conquest of that Heart, which pretended to be so impregnable.

Zimene was no less curious, and they presently began to contrive together what Means would be most likely to succeed; at length they pitched upon one which indeed carry'd with it a good deal of Probability, and, in reality, answer'd the End proposed by it.

Ariana, as least known in that Part of the Town where the Assignation[3] was kept, went and took a Lodging in the House, as for a Friend of her's, who was expected very shortly in Town: After having made the Agreement, she call'd two or three Times in a Day, under the Pretence of seeing every thing in order;—the extravagant Rent that was to be paid excused the continual Trouble she gave the People; but to render it less so, she treated them whenever she came with Tea, Wine, and Sweetmeats:[4]—At last, she perceiv'd they appear'd in somewhat an unusual Hurry; great running up and down Stairs was heard, and she found that Fires were lighted in the Apartment over that she

---

1. **Habits:** costumes.
2. **Collation:** light meal.
3. **Assignation:** tryst, arranged meeting of lovers.
4. **Sweetmeats:** candied or crystallized fruit.

had taken:—She seemed, however, not to observe any thing of this, but stepp'd privately out, and sent her Footman, who was always in waiting at the End of the Street, to let *Zimene* know that she found the lovers were expected.

The other rejoiced at receiving the Summons, and exulted within herself at the Opportunity she should have of retorting on *Sophronia* some bitter Jests she had formerly pass'd on her.

In fine, she came muffled up, as if just arriv'd in Town, and excused her having no Servants with her, under the Pretence that she had left them with her Baggage, which she said was not expected 'till two or three Days after.

The People of the House gave themselves no Trouble to consider the Probability of all this; they doubted not but whatever was the Motive of her coming to lodge with them, it would turn to their Advantage in the end; and, perhaps, were not without some Conjecture that one, or both these Ladies had their Favourites to meet as well as *Sophronia.*

The two fair Spies, however, having order'd that Supper should not be got ready for them 'till Ten o'Clock, shut themselves into their Apartment, as tho' *Zimene* wanted to take some Repose till that Time after the Fatigue of her Journey; but, indeed, to prevent any Suspicion of their Design, which might have made those whom they came to observe more cautious.

Being left to themselves, *Ariana* put out the Lights, and having opened one of the Windows in the Dining-Room very softly, watched there to see who came in, while *Zimene* took her Post at the Bed-Chamber Door, which opening just against the Staircase, she could, with all the Ease in the World, see through the Key-hole every one who passed either up or down.

It was not long before *Ariana* perceived a Chair[1] with the Curtains close drawn stop at the Door, and come into the Entry, and *Zimene* plainly saw the Face of *Sophronia* by the Light that hung on the Stair-Case:—Both were now satisfy'd that the Intelligence *Ariana* had receiv'd was true, and were not a little impatient for the Arrival of the

---

1. **Chair:** sedan chair; a closed vehicle seating one person, borne on poles by two carriers.

happy Gentleman, which would compleat the Discovery, and enable them to spread the Story, with all its Circumstances, through the Town.

A few Minutes put an end to their Suspense, which, however uneasy such a Situation may be in some Cases, was a Heaven to that Distraction, which in this, the cruel Certainty produced in one of them.

Ariana having seen a second Chair come in, with the same Privacy as the former, quitted the Window, and ran to the Peeping-place *Zimene* had all this Time occupy'd, which, however, was large enough for them both to see through.

But, good Heaven! the Consternation they were in when *Fillamour* (for it was he) appear'd!—The Wife could scarce believe her Eyes, and turning to *Ariana,* cry'd, "Who is it?—It cannot be my Husband!—Dear Creature, ease me of my Torture, and convince me I am mistaken."

"I wish I could," reply'd *Ariana,* almost as much amazed, "but the Person we saw pass, is too surely the perfidious *Fillamour!*"

One cannot be very certain whether this Lady was really so much troubled at the Injustice done to her Friend as this Expression seemed to signify; People of her Disposition being glad of any thing to afford Matter of Conversation, even tho' it were to the Prejudice of those they most pretend to esteem.

I will not say, this was directly the Case with *Ariana,* but instead of reasoning with *Zimene,* and perswading her to Moderation in so stabbing a Circumstance, she omitted nothing that she thought would exaggerate the Crime of her Husband, and consequently heighten her Indignation against him:—Nay, she was even for having her apply to a Justice of the Peace, and exposing *Sophronia* by those Methods, which the lowest and most abject People take to revenge themselves, when injured in the Manner it was plain she was.

But tho' the other had too much good Sense to come into any such Measures, as only serve to make Diversion for the Rabble, yet she had not a sufficient Share to enable her to bear her Wrongs with that Patience which was necessary to make *Fillamour* ashamed of what he had done:—She no sooner found that Supper was carry'd up, than

she follow'd the Person quick enough to prevent the Door being shut;
—she flew at *Sophronia,* attempted to tear her Hair and Head-clothes,
and would certainly have treated her pretty severely, had not *Fillamour,*
confounded as he was, stepp'd between with these Words:—"No,
Madam," cry'd he, "whatever may be your Imaginations, or whatever
Appearances may seem to be against me, I cannot suffer you to be
guilty of a Rudeness which I am sure your cooler Thoughts would
condemn."

He was about to add something more, when she, turning from her
Rival, pluck'd off his Wig and threw it into the Fire,—"Monster!
Villain!" said she, "every thing is justify'd by Injuries like mine."

She spit at him;—she stamp'd upon the Floor, and behaved in all
her Words and Actions like a Woman utterly deprived of Reason:—
Sophronia in the mean time was so overcome with Shame, Apprehension, and, perhaps, Remorse, that she fell into a Swoon:—*Fillamour*
seeing her in that Condition, could be restrained by no Considerations
from running to support her; which Action aggravating the Fury *Zimene* before was in, she snatch'd his Sword which lay in the Window,
and had doubtless committed some Deed of Desperation on one or
both of them, if *Ariana,* who had follow'd her up Stairs, had not
catch'd hold of her Arm.

The confused Noise among them soon brought up the People of
the House, who easily perceiving the Occasion of it, got *Sophronia* out
of the Room; after which the Husband and Wife continued a Dispute,
in which the latter had the better in every thing.

Fillamour, at first, would fain[1] have perswaded her that he came not
to meet *Sophronia* on his own Account, but on that of a Friend; who
having an honorable Passion for her, and by an unforeseen Accident
was prevented that Evening from coming himself, and had intreated
him to make his Excuse.—But this was a Pretense too shallow to
deceive *Zimene,* and was besides contradicted by *Ariana,* who told him
that he could not come in that private Manner twice every Week on
the Score of a third Person.

---

1. **fain:** gladly, by preference.

In fine, no Subterfuge serving his Purpose, he at last threw off all Evasion, exerted the Husband,[1] and threw the Blame of every thing on *Zimene:*—He told her, though without the least Foundation in Truth, that he had always perceived her of an inquisitive jealous Nature, and that whatever had happened between him and the Lady in question was only out of a Principle of Revenge, adding, that when a Wife gave herself up to Jealousy, and shewed a Want of Confidence, there could be no Abuse of it, nor any Obligation on the Husband to put the least Restraint upon his Pleasures.

This Reflection, as it well might, because both cruel and unjust, heightened the Agitations she before was in to such a Degree, as it is scarce possible to conceive, much less to give any Description of:—If his attempting to evade her Accusations, and cover his Falshood, was provoking to her good Sense, his avowing his Crime was much more so to her Pride; as the Poet says,

> Rage has no Bounds in slighted Womankind.[2]

But he stayed not long to see the Effects of it, and flung out of the Room, leaving her to act as she thought fit in the Affair.

The Woman of the House fearing some ill Consequences to herself from this Adventure, spared neither Oaths nor Imprecations to make *Zimene* believe she was wholly innocent:—That she knew not but the Gentleman and Lady were Man and Wife:—That they had told her they were privately married, but on the Account of Relations were obliged to conceal it.

Zimene little regarded all she said on this Score; and as there was a Possibility of its being true, offer'd not to contradict it: *Ariana* went home with her, and lay with her that Night, for she was resolved to sleep no more by the Side of a Man, who had not only wronged her in the most tender Point, but, as she imagin'd, had added Insult to Deceit, by taking so little Pains to alleviate his Transgression, or obtain

---

1. **the Husband:** the power of a husband.
2. **Rage . . . Womankind:** quotation unidentified.

Forgiveness:—"He has never once vouchsafed to ask my Pardon," cry'd she, in the utmost Agony of Spirit;—"he despises,—sets my just Rage at nothing, and I hate him for that, even more than for his Falshood."

It is to be supposed she suffered *Ariana* to take but little Repose that Night, too small a Punishment, indeed, for that inquisitive talking Humour which had occasioned all this Confusion: All the Hours till Morning were employ'd in consulting in what Manner would best become *Zimene* to behave in so unhappy a Circumstance; at last it was agreed, that she should quit her Husband's House, and retire to that of an Uncle, who had been her Guardian; and accordingly she pack'd up all her Jewels, Dressing-Plate,[1] and Cloaths, and with *Ariana,* her Woman, and one Footman, went away very early:—Before her Departure she called for *Fillamour*'s Valet *de Chambre,*[2] and bad him tell his Master, that she left his House forever, to be govern'd by the Lady to whom he had given his Heart.

Whatever Anxieties the offended Wife endur'd, it is easy to believe the transgressing Husband had his Share: His Intrigue with *Sophronia* was of a long Date;—the Vehemence of his Passion for her was worn off even before his Marriage, and he wish'd for nothing more than an Abatement of her's, that he might break off with Decency;—but whenever he gave the most distant Hint of the Inconveniences attending a Continuation of their Acquaintance, she fell into such Agonies as he had too much Compassion for her to be able to endure the Sight of:—She protested that when the dreadful Moment of parting them should arrive it should be the last of Life, and talk'd of nothing but Poison or Dagger: This kind of Behaviour it was that had alone obliged him to make a Shew of some Remains of Attachment to her, and now to be detected in his Fault, to be catch'd without any Possibility of Defence, fill'd him with the most extreme Vexation a Heart could be oppress'd with; but then the Violence, the Outrage with which *Zimene* behaved on the Occasion, alarm'd his Pride, and

---

1. **Dressing-Plate:** silver-plated objects for the dressing table.
2. **Valet de Chambre:** personal attendant.

as a *Man,* much more, as a *Husband,* he thought himself above yielding to any thing imposed on him in that arbitrary Fashion.

Unhappy *Zimene!* how great a Pity was it that she could not command her Temper:—Softness would have easily accomplished what Rage could never bring about; and as much as *Fillamour* condemn'd himself for the Injury he had done her, he yet more condemn'd her for the Manner in which she resented it.

On being told she was gone, and the Message she had left for him, he was, indeed, very much shocked on Account of her Friends,[1] and what the World, whom he doubted not but would be acquainted with the whole of the Affair, would say of him; but he found nothing of those tender Emotions for being deprived of her Society, as he would certainly have done, had she borne the Detection of his Fault with more Gentleness and Moderation.

The whole Transaction, as he imagined it would be, soon became the Talk of the Town:—*Zimene* was loud in her Reproaches on his Infidelity:—He, in Excuse for what he had done, exclaimed with equal Virulence against her ill Temper, which, he pretended, had driven him to seek Ease Abroad:—Both now hated each other with more Passion than they had ever lov'd:—In vain the Kindred[2] on both Sides endeavour'd to make up the Matter;—they were equally irreconcilable,— and rendered the more so by an unhappy Punctilio[3] in both their Tempers:—*Zimene,* knowing herself the injured Person, thought the least Attonement he ought to have made was the Acknowledgment of his Transgression;—a solemn Promise of repeating it no more, and an Entreaty of Pardon for what was past.—*Fillamour* on the other hand, tho' conscious of his Crime, look'd on the Means she took to publish it as an Offence he ought as little to forgive; the bitter Expressions her Rage threw out against him seem'd to him yet more inexcuseable than the Occasion he had given her for them; and made him imagine, or at least gave him a Pretence for doing so, that there were Seeds of Ill-

---

1. **Friends:** relatives.
2. **Kindred:** relatives.
3. **Punctilio:** scrupulous attentiveness to small points of conduct.

nature in her Soul, which would have some time or other broke out, though he had done nothing to deserve them.

In fine, none of them wanted Matter to harden them against each other, nor could they be brought to agree in any one thing but an Article of Separation,[1] which was accordingly drawn up; after which *Zimene* retired into the Country where she still lives; and *Fillamour* accepted of a Commission in the Army, meerly to avoid the Discourses which he could not help hearing in Town, in all Company on this Affair.

As for *Sophronia* she went directly to *Dunkirk,* and entered herself a Pensioner in a Monastery, not being able to shew her Face any more in a Place where she had been detected of a Fault she had so severely censured in others.

Whether *Ariana* has been enough concern'd at the Distraction her inquisitive Temper occasioned, to make use of any Efforts to restrain it for the future, I will not pretend to say; but I hope it will be a Warning to others, neither to busy themselves with Affairs in which they have no Concern, nor be too fond of reporting what Chance may discover to them.

The Behaviour of *Zimene* also may shew our Sex how little is to be got by Violence, and a too haughty Resentment:—Patience, and a silent enduring an Infringement on those Rights which Marriage gives us over the Heart and Person of a Husband, is a Lesson, which, I confess, is difficult to practise; yet, if well observed, seldom fails of bringing on a sure Reward.—I have more than once, in the Course of these Speculations, recommended Softness as the most prevailing, as well as most becoming Arms we have to combat with; and which, even in the most provoking Circumstances ought never to be thrown aside.

*   *   *

---

1. **Article of Separation:** legal arrangement for living apart; providing for the wife's financial support.

FROM BOOK XIV

Whether these Monthly Essays answer the great End proposed by them, of conducing in some Measure to that Rectification of Manners which this Age stands in so much need of, we cannot yet be able to determine; but of this we are certain, by the Letters we receive, that Wit, and the Love of Virtue are not altogether banish'd the Realm: The following, as well as many we already have had the Pleasure of transmitting to the Public, is a Proof of it.

To the FEMALE SPECTATOR.
MADAM,

As I perceive you intersperse your moral Reflections with such Adventures as promise either Instruction or Entertainment to your Readers, I take the Liberty of enclosing a little Narrative, which I can answer is a recent Transaction, and the Truth of it known to a great many others as well as myself.

I shall make no Apology for any Blunders in Stile, having drawn up[1] as well as I could, and leave the Correction and Amendment to your more elegant and judicious Pen, which I am well convinced can smooth the harshest Expression, and extract even Gold from the coarsest Metal.—I am, with the most perfect Admiration and good Wishes for your Undertaking,

MADAM,
Your very humble Servant,
And Subscriber,
ELISMONDA.

Kensington
April 16, 1745

The *LADY'S REVENGE.*

Among the Number of those gay Gallants who pride themselves on being distinguish'd at all public Places, none had more Reason to boast of the modish[2] Accomplishments than *Ziphranes:* He sung, danc'd,

---

1. **drawn up:** composed.

2. **modish:** fashionable.

dress'd well;—had the Knack of setting off, to the best Advantage, his Family, his Fortune, and his Person:—Knew how to trace his Ancestors long before the Conquest;[1] to discover some particular Perfection in every Acre of his Land, to give all his Limbs and Features such Gestures as his Glass[2] inform'd him would be most becoming:—In fine,[3] he was what we Women call a mighty pretty Fellow: For as the Poet too justly says of us,

> Our thoughtless Sex is caught by outward Form
> And empty Noise, and loves itself in Man.[4]

As he either found or thought himself admir'd by all the Ladies he conversed with, he in Return seem'd to admire them all:—Many Friendships were broke, and great Animosities have arose on the Score of this *Almanzor*[5] in Love, who triumph'd wherever he came, without giving any of the fair Contenders for his Heart leave to think she had the Power of entirely subduing it:—If one seem'd to have the Advantage over him Today, she was sure of yielding it Tomorrow to some other Beauty, who again lost it in her Turn:—Nay, sometimes in the same Hour he would press one Lady by the Hand, whisper a soft thing in the Ear of another, look dying on a third, and present a Love Sonnet of his own composing to a fourth.

In this Manner did he divide his Favours till he became acquainted with *Barsina,* a Lady of a good Fortune and very agreeable Person:— She lived mostly in the Country, and when she was in Town kept but little Company, and seldom appear'd in any public Place:—She was, indeed, more reserved than any one I ever knew of her Age and Circumstances, and tho' she had an Infinity of Wit, chose rather to be thought to have none, than to expose it by speaking more than she

---

1. **Conquest:** the Norman Conquest of 1066.

2. **Glass:** looking glass, mirror.

3. **In fine:** in short.

4. **Our thoughtless . . . Man:** quotation unidentified.

5. **Almanzor:** hero of John Dryden's tragedy, *The Conquest of Granada* (1670, 1671).

thought consistent with that Modesty, which she set the higher Value upon, as she saw others value it so little.

It was, perhaps, as much owing to this Character of Reserve as to any other Perfection in her, tho' few Women can boast of greater, that made the Conquest of her Heart more flattering to the Vanity of *Ziphranes,* than any he had yet gain'd:—But be that as it may, he approach'd her with a different kind of Homage to what he had ever paid to any other Woman; and not only gave her that Proof of his serious Attachment, but also a much greater, which was this: He entirely gave over[1] his Gallantries[2] to every former Object of them, and confined his Addresses to her alone, to the Astonishment of all his Acquaintance, who spoke of it as a Prodigy,[3] and cry'd, "Who would have believ'd it—Ziphranes is grown constant!"[4]

This Change in his Behaviour, join'd with a secret liking of his Person,[5] and the Sanction of a near Relation's Perswasion, who had introduced him to her, and thought they would be a proper Match for one another, engag'd her to receive him in quality[6] of a Lover; tho' long it was before he could prevail on her to acknowledge she did so through any other Motive than meerly in Compliance with the Request of a Person so nearly allied to her.

To make Trial of his Perseverance, she pretended Business call'd her into the Country; he begg'd Leave to accompany her, but that not being permitted, he follow'd to her Retirement, took Lodgings as near her as he could, and visited her every Day, renewing the Declarations he had made in Town, nor would return till she had fixed the Day for coming also.

As she came in the Stage-Coach, she could not prevent him from doing so too, if she had been affected enough to attempt it: Yet could

---

1. **gave over:** ended.
2. **Gallantries:** flirtations.
3. **Prodigy:** miracle, remarkable occurrence.
4. **constant:** faithful.
5. **Person:** personal appearance.
6. **quality:** the role.

not all his Assiduity, his Vows, his Protestations, meet any farther Reward than the bare Acceptance of them.

By Degrees, however, he gain'd further on her, and got the better of that cruel Caution which had given him so much Trouble; and she at last confess'd, that she thought him worthy of every thing a Woman of Honour could bestow.

With what Rapture he express'd himself at hearing these long wish'd-for Words any one may judge, by the Pains he had taken to induce her to speak them.—He had now nothing to do but to press for the Confirmation of his Happiness, and in the most tender Terms beseech'd her to settle a Day for that Purpose; to which she blushing answer'd, he must depend for that on the Gentleman who first brought[1] them acquainted, and had always been so much his Friend.

This he seem'd very well satisfy'd with, as she doubted not but he would, and as she knew the Person she mention'd had greatly promoted the Interest of his Love; and she now began to set herself to think seriously on Marriage, as of a State she should soon enter into.— Some Days, however, pass'd over without her hearing any thing of the Matter, than that *Ziphranes* told her, that he had been to wait on[2] her Cousin, but had not the good Fortune to meet with him at home.

Prepossessed as she was in favour of this Lover, it seem'd a little strange to her, that the Vehemence of the Passion he profess'd, should not influence him to watch Night and Day for the Sight of a Person to whom she had refer'd the Grant of what he had seemed so ardently to desire:—Besides, she very well knew there could have been no Difficulty in finding him, had the other attempted it in good earnest; and this, with the Imagination that she observed somewhat of a less Tenderness than usual in his Looks and Behaviour to her, fill'd her with very perplexing Agitations.

A week was hardly elaps'd, since she made him that soft Concession above recited, when he sent to acquaint[3] her, he was extremely indisposed with a Cold, and could not have the Pleasure of waiting on her.

---

1. **brought:** made.
2. **wait on:** call on.
3. **acquaint:** inform.

This Message, and the Manner in which it was deliver'd, heighten'd her Suspicions, that she had deceiv'd herself in an Opinion either of his Love or Honour:—"I am betray'd," cry'd she in a good deal of Agony of Spirit, "it is owing to the Coldness of his own Heart, not any the Inclemency of the Season has inflicted on him, that he absents himself."

She kept her Vexation conceal'd however, and tho' her Relation had visited her several Times since she had seen *Ziphranes,* she never once mentioned any thing concerning him, till that Gentleman one Day, in a gay Humour, said to her, "Well, Cousin, how thrive my Friend's Hopes?—When are we to see you a Bride?" On which, before she was aware, she cry'd, "I am not the proper Person to be ask'd that Question:—What does *Ziphranes* say?"

"I cannot expect that Confidence from him, which you so near a Relation deny," answer'd he; "but indeed I wanted to talk a little seriously to you on that Head:—I am afraid there is some Bruleê[1] between you, for I have met him two or three Times, and he rather seems to shun than court my Company."

To hear he was abroad[2] at the Time he had pretended Sickness, and that he had seen the very Person to whom she had consign'd the disposing of herself,[3] without speaking any thing to him of the Affair, was sufficient to have opened the Eyes of a Woman of much less Penetration and Judgment than she was:—She was at once convinced of his Falshood and Ingratitude, and the Indignation of having been so basely imposed upon was about to shew itself, by telling the whole Story to her Cousin, when some Ladies that Instant coming in to visit her prevented it.

No Opportunity offering that Night to disburthen the inward Agony she was inflam'd with, by reason her Cousin went away before the rest of the Company took Leave, she pass'd the Hours till Morning in a Situation more easy to be conceiv'd than describ'd.

---

1. **Bruleê:** quarrel.

2. **abroad:** in circulation, in public.

3. **disposing of herself:** in marriage. She had given her relative the authority to decide the arrangements for her marriage.

She would have given the World, had she been Mistress of it, to have been able to have assign'd, some Reason for so sudden a Change in a Person, whose Love and Constancy she had as many Testimonies of as were in the Power of Man to give:—The more she reflected on his past and present Behaviour, the more she was confounded; and how far soever he had insinuated himself into her Heart, she suffered yet more from her Astonishment than she did from her abused Affection.

The Greatness of her Spirit, as well as her natural Modesty and Reserve, would not permit her either to write, or send[1] to know the Meaning of his Absence; and her Cousin not happening to come again, she had none on whose Discretion she could enough rely to make a Confidant of in an Affair, which she look'd upon as so shameful to herself; and endur'd for three Days longer a Suspence more painful than the Certainty which the fourth produced had the Power of inflicting.

As soon as she rung her Bell[2] in the Morning, her Maid brought a Letter which she told her was left for her very early, by a Servant belonging to *Ziphranes*.—"*Ziphranes,*" cry'd *Barsina*, with a Hurry of Spirits which that Moment she had not Command enough over herself to be able either to repel or to conceal,—"What is it he can say?"

To BARSINA.
MADAM,

Since I had last the Honour of waiting on you, a Proposal of Marriage was made to me, which I found very much to my Convenience to accept; and I did so the rather, as I knew there was too little Love on your Side to render it any Disappointment:—I thought myself obliged to acquaint you with it before you heard it from any other Hand;[3] and wish you as happy with some more deserving Man as I

---

1. **send:** send a messenger.
2. **rung her Bell:** to summon her maid.
3. **from . . . Hand:** by written communication from someone else.

hope this Morning will make me:—I shall always continue to think of you with the greatest Respect, and am,

MADAM,
Your most humble,
And most obedient Servant.
ZIPHRANES.

What she felt on reading this Letter any Woman who, without Love, has the least Pride or Sense of Resentment may judge; but as *Barsina* had certainly once a very great Share of Regard for this perfidious Prophaner of the most ardent Vows and Protestations, her Affliction must be violent indeed, at the first News of his Inconstancy.

But whatever it was, with her usual Prudence, she confin'd it to her own Breast, and tho' that Day, and several succeeding ones, she heard of nothing but *Ziphranes*'s Marriage, and the Wonder every one express'd at the Suddenness of it, as well as that it was to any other than herself; yet did she so well stifle all the Emotions of her Soul, that none could perceive she was the least disturb'd at it.

His ungenerous Behaviour had doubtless turn'd her Heart entirely against him:—She soon grew to despise him much more than ever she had loved; but then the Thought how much she had been deceiv'd in him, and that he had it in his Power to boast that he had made an Impression on her, gave her the most poignant Anguish.

In fine, all the Passion she now had for him was Revenge, and by what Method she should inflict a Punishment, in some measure proportionable to his Crime, took up her whole Thoughts; and at last having hit on one to her Mind,[1] was not long before she accomplish'd it.

She knew he was accustomed to walk every Day in the Park, and being informed that since his Marriage he continued to do so, she made it her Business to throw herself in his Way; and meeting him according to her Wish, accompany'd only with an old Gentleman, who did not seem to be a Person of any very great Consequence,[2] she

---

1. **to her Mind:** that suited her.

2. **Consequence:** importance.

went directly up to him, and told him she desir'd to speak with him, on which the other immediately took Leave.

Ziphranes was so confounded[1] at the Sight of her, that he was scarce able to return the Salutation she gave him with the Complaisance of a Gentleman; which she perceiving, to add to his Mortification, told him she did so, but added with a great deal of seeming Gaiety, that he had no Reason to be under any manner of Concern; for tho' his quitting her for another was extremely cruel, he had it in his Power to attone, and it was for that End she came to seek him.

All this, which he could not but look on as Raillery,[2] was very surprizing to him from a Woman of her serious and reserved Temper:[3]—And his Confusion both at that, and meeting her, was still so great, that he could not answer it in kind as he would have done, had he been more Master of himself, and it was but with a stammering Voice he at last drawled out, that he should rejoice to oblige her in any thing he could.

What a Force has conscious Guilt!—How mean, how cowardly does a base Action render one!—He who found it easy to commit the Crime, trembled at the Reproaches it deserv'd:—*Barsina* felt a gloomy Satisfaction in her Mind at the Pain he was in, but that was little to what her Resentment demanded; and it was necessary to ease his present Disquiets, in order to have it in her Power to inflict on him others of a more terrible Nature.

She therefore assumed as much Softness in her Eyes and Voice, as a Person not accustomed to Dissimulation could possibly put on, and with a half Sigh, "Well, *Ziphranes,* I accuse you not," said she; "Love I know is an involuntary Passion, and besides I have heard say there is a Fate in Marriage which is not to be withstood:—I only think the long Acquaintance we had together ought not to have been so abruptly broke off:—I might have expected you would have taken one tender Leave of me at least!"

---

1. **confounded:** confused, discomfited.

2. **Raillery:** joking, teasing.

3. **Temper:** temperament.

He was beginning to make some pitiful Excuse or other for his Behaviour in this Point, but she would not suffer[1] him to go on:—"Say nothing of it," interrupted she, "what is done is past Recall; but if you would have me think you ever meant me fair,[2] or that all the Vows you made were but to ensnare and triumph over my artless Innocence, you must comply with the Request I now make you, which is to let me see you once more at my Lodgings:—You may depend on hearing no Upbraidings:—I desire no nore than to take a last Farewel, and if you gratify me in this, which I know you will think, and I confess, is but a Whim, I give you my solemn Promise never more to trouble you."

Such an Invitation, and deliver'd in this Manner from a Mouth, whom he had Reason to believe would have been filled with Expressions of a vastly different Sort, might very well amaze him:—He thought her Behaviour, as indeed it was, a little out of Nature,[3] and quite the reverse of that Reserve and perfect Modesty she had formerly treated him with; but to whatever Source this Change in her was owing, he could not be so unpolite as to refuse what she desir'd of him, and it was agreed between them that he should breakfast with her the next Morning.

Accordingly he came; she received him with great Civility, but somewhat more serious and more like herself than the Day before:—Chocolate was served up, and the Maid attending while they breakfasted, *Barsina* entertain'd him only with Discourses on ordinary Affairs.—When they had done, she order'd a Bottle of *Cyprus* Wine to be set upon the Table, and made a Sign to her Servant to leave the Room.

Now being alone together she fill'd out two Glasses, and presented one to *Ziphranes,* but he desir'd to be excused, telling her he never drank any Sort of Wine in a Morning.—"You must break through that Custom for once," said she smiling; "and to engage you to do

---

1. **suffer:** allow.

2. **meant me fair:** meant to treat me justly.

3. **out of Nature:** unnatural.

so, as well as to shew I have not the least Animosity to the Lady who has supplanted me in your Affections, the Toast shall be Health and Happiness to your Bride. This, sure, you will not offer to refuse."

With these Words she put the Glass a second Time into his Hand, "Well, Madam," answer'd he, "it would not become me to disobey you, since you so much insist upon it:—I will do myself the Honour to pledge[1] you."

She then drank the above-mention'd Health, and he having drain'd his Glass to the same, "Now I am satisfy'd," cry'd she, "tho' my cruel Stars[2] deny'd me the Pleasure of living with you, we shall die together, at least:—I drank my happy Rival's Health sincerely, and may she enjoy long Life, and many prosperous Days, if she can do so without *Ziphranes,* but for a little, a very little longer shall she triumph with him over the forsaken *Barsina.*"

"What is it you mean, Madam!" said he hastily. "That you have drank your Bane,"[3] answer'd she: "The Wine I gave you, and partook of myself, was mix'd with the most deadly Poyson, nor is it in the Power of Art[4] to save the Life of either of us."

"You would not do so sure!" cry'd he: "What could I do but die," reply'd she, "when your Inconstancy had made Life a Burthen not to be borne? and to have dy'd without you would have been mean and poor, unworthy of my Love or my Revenge:—Now both are gratify'd."

'Tis a Question whether these last Words reach'd his Ears, for before she had quite given over[5] speaking, he started up and ran out of the Room like a Man distracted,[6] uttering a Volley of Curses on her, and on himself, as he went down the Stairs.

What Effect the Draught had on *Barsina,* and what kind of Reflections enter'd her Head, when left to think seriously on what she had

---

1. **pledge:** drink with (in response to a request).

2. **Stars:** fate.

3. **Bane:** death, destruction.

4. **Art:** skill.

5. **given over:** stopped.

6. **distracted:** crazed.

done, the Reader shall hereafter be inform'd at full; but we must now follow *Ziphranes,* who had not the least Inclination to die, and see how he behav'd in a Situation so terrible to him.

The Moment he got within his own Doors he sent for a Physician, told him he had swallowed Poyson, and that he had Reason to fear it was of the most mortal[1] Kind; tho' by whom administer'd, and for what Cause, he kept a Secret, not to alarm his Wife.—Oyl was the first Thing judged necessary, great Quantities of which he took; but nothing appearing but what any Stomach thus agitated might disgorge, more powerful Emetics were prescrib'd; but even these had no other Effect than to throw him into fainting Fits:—Yet low[2] and weak as he was, he continually cry'd out, "Have I yet evacuated the Poyson?" and being answer'd in the Negative, told the Doctor and Apothecary that they were ignorant Fellows, and he would have others sent for.

It was in vain, the one assured him that there was not in the whole *Materia Medica*[3] a more efficacious Medicine than what he had prescrib'd; or that the other alledg'd, his Shop afforded the very best Drugs in Town; he still called out for better Advice, and accordingly two others of the same Faculty were sent for.

These said that it was possible the Poyson might be lodg'd in some of the *secretory Passages,* and therefore the former Prescription, which could reach no farther than the *Primæ Viæ*[4] wanted its due Effect:— That there was a Necessity for the whole *Viscera* to be cleansed;—that every *Gland* must be deterg'd;[5]— all the Meanders of the *Mesentery*[6] penetrated;—not a Fibre, or Membrane, even to the Capillary Vessels, but must suffer an Evacuation;—and the whole Mass of Nervous Fluid also rarify'd; and that after all this was over, he must go through a Course of Alternatives, which should pass with the *Chile*[7] into the

---

1. **mortal:** fatal.

2. **low:** weak, lacking vitality.

3. **Materia Medica:** the remedial substances used in the practice of medicine.

4. **Primae Viae:** primary passages.

5. **deterg'd:** cleaned.

6. **Mesentery:** intestinal membranes.

7. **Chile:** usually *chyle:* lymph that is milky from emulsified fats.

subclavian[1] Vein, in order to purify the Blood and abrade the Points of any sharp or viscous[2] Particles which the Poyson might have thrown into it, and were not to be eradicated by any other Methods.

This, and a great deal more learned Cant, which it was impossible for any one not practised in Physick[3] either to understand or remember, our Patient listened to wtih the utmost Attention, and looking on this second Doctor as an *Esculapius,*[4] told him, he rely'd upon the great Judgment he found he was Master of, and put himself wholly under his Direction.

Glisters,[5] Cathartics, and Diaphoretics[6] in abundance were now prescrib'd, all which *Ziphranes* readily submitted to, and went through their different Operations with a consummate Resignation, till, to avoid Death, he was brought even to the Gates of it; and when reduced to such a Condition as not to be able to move a Finger, or speak articulately, it was thought proper, in order not to lose so good a Patient, that some Intermission of his Tortures should be permitted, and in their room[7] Balsamic Cordials,[8] and all manner of Restoratives administer'd.

As Youth, and a good Consitution help'd him to sustain the Asperity[9] of the first Medicines, so it also greatly added to the Efficacy of these latter ones, and he was in a few Days able to sit up in Bed, and take nourishing Food, pretty frequently, tho' in small Quantities.

The Fears of his own Death dissipated, he began to have a Curiosity to know what was become of *Barsina,* and accordingly sent privately to enquire after her in the Neighbourhood where she lived.

The Person charged with this Trust, brought him Word that she was dead, and had been buried in a very private Manner about three

---

1. **subclavian:** located under the clavicle or collarbone.
2. **viscous:** slow-moving.
3. **Physick:** medicine.
4. **Esculapius:** legendary Greek physician and god of medicine.
5. **Glisters:** or clysters: medicines injected into the rectum.
6. **Diaphoretics:** medicines that increase perspiration.
7. **in their room:** in place of them.
8. **Balsamic Cordials:** soothing medicines.
9. **Asperity:** harshness.

Weeks past; and that some of those he had questioned concerning her, spoke, as if 'twas whisper'd she had been guilty of her own Death; but as to that they could not be positive, tho' they were so as to her Decease; and that they saw her Coffin put into a Hearse and Six[1] at five o'Clock the very next Morning after they heard of her Death, attended by one Mourning Coach with only her Maid in it and that it was supposed they carry'd her out of Town.

This Intelligence[2] made him hug himself for the Precautions he had taken, to which alone he thought he owed the Preservation of his own Life; but then at the same time he shudder'd at the Reflection of the Danger he had escaped.

He did not, however, enjoy any Calm of Mind but for a short while, a Friend of his who came to visit him unluckily happened to mention Doctor *Mead*'s Treatise on Poysons, which maintaining that there was a Possibility for the Venom to lurk in some Parts of the Body, for many Years after it was thought to be entirely expell'd, and then break out with a Fierceness which no Art could subdue, the poor unhappy *Ziphranes* presently imagined that might be his Case, and could not be at rest till he had again consulted his Physician.

Few People chuse to argue against their own Interest; *Ziphranes* had been too liberal of his Fees for the Doctor to offer any thing in Opposition to this Tenet; but on the contrary favour'd it obliquely by asking him if he did not sometimes feel little Twitches in his Head, his Back, or about his Heart? Which he answering with great Concern that he did (as indeed it was impossible he should not, after the violent Operations he had undergone) "Alas! Alas!" cry'd the Empyric,[3] shaking his Head, "these are bad Symptoms:—You must have more Physic: —I am afraid indeed the Venom is not quite expunged." And then run on a long Discourse on the Nature and Subtilty of some Poysons, till he had terrify'd his Patient almost out of his Senses.

Whether the same Medicines as were before prescrib'd, or others of a different Kind were now administer'd, I will not pretend[4] to say; but

---

1. **Hearse and Six:** hearse drawn by six horses.

2. **Intelligence:** news.

3. **Empyric:** a doctor relying on experience alone.

4. **pretend:** presume.

whatever they were, they brought him into such a Condition that his Life was despair'd of; and the Doctor was obliged indeed to have recourse to all his Art to save him.

But not to be too tedious in so disagreeable a Part of my Story, I shall only say, that Fate had not yet decreed to call him hence:—He once more recovered, and seemed to want[1] only Change of Air to re-establish his former Health.

As he was thought too weak to travel so far as his own Country Seat,[2] which was near a hundred Miles from *London,* Lodgings were hired for him at a little Village call'd *Casehaughton,* the Air of which was judged extremely proper for his Condition by his Doctor, as being neither thick nor too pure for one so much weaken'd as he had been.

He soon experienced the good Effect of it, or of having entirely left off even the most palatable Compositions of the Apothecary's Shops:— And in a few Days was able to walk about the Gardens, every Morning bringing him an Increase of Strength, of Appetite, and Spirits.

In fine, he grew in a very small Time so perfectly well, that he was beginning to think of returning home, when an odd and surprizing Accident happened to throw both his Mind and Body into fresh Dis-orders, equal, at least, I may say, to any he had before experienced.

He was indulging the pleasing Meditations of his Recovery, one Evening, in a fine Lane at a little Distance from the Village, when as he was walking on he saw a Lady dress'd all in white, leaning over a Gate that opened into some Fields belonging to a Gentleman in that Part of the Country:—He thought nothing of this Adventure, but pass'd forward, when being advanc'd within twenty or thirty Paces of the Gate he imagin'd he beheld the Figure of *Barsina,* her Shape, her Stature, her Face, the very She in every Part.—He started back and stopp'd, all Horror and Amazement; but unwilling to be deceiv'd by Similitude, summon'd up all his Courage, and still look'd attentively, till the Object of his Terror turned full upon him, which before it had not, and crying out *Ziphranes!* immediately vanish'd from his Sight, or rather his Sight forsook his Optics, for he fell into a Swoon

---

1. **want:** lack, need.

2. **Seat:** estate.

the Instant he heard his Name pronounced, and by a Voice so exactly the same with that of *Barsina,* that he was certain it could proceed from no other than her Ghost.

Unluckily for him he had gone out this Evening entirely alone, which since his Illness he had never done before; and had not the Diligence of one of his Servants, who fearing, as the Night was drawing on, the Air might be prejudicial to him, made him come in search of him, he had probably lain in that Condition till some worse Accident had befallen him.

The Fellow seeing him prostrate and motionless, at first thought him dead, but rubbing his Temples, and partly raising him, perceiv'd his Mistake, and with much ado brought him to himself; the first Words he spoke seem'd strangely incoherent, for he talk'd of nothing but Ghosts and Death, and said it was not his Fault that she killed herself:—Recollecting his Senses, however, by Degrees, he ceased these Exclamations, but ask'd his Man if he had seen nothing, to which he answering that he had not; "No," cry'd *Ziphranes* wildly again, " 'tis only myself that both alive and dead must be persecuted by her."

He was at last perswaded to go to his Lodgings where he immediately went to Bed, but made his Servant sit in the Room near his Bedside, who was amaz'd to find that instead of sleeping he talk'd all Night to himself in so odd a Manner, that the other believ'd him delirious, as indeed he was; the Fright he had sustain'd had thrown him into a high Fever, and the next Morning the Physician was sent for once more.

In his Ravings he discovered to every Body that came near him all that had pass'd between *Barsina* and himself, and how not content with attempting to poyson, her Spirit had appear'd and call'd to him: —Nay, so strongly did the Remembrance of what he had seen work on his distemper'd Mind, that he frequently imagin'd he heard her Voice crying out to him, *Ziphranes!*

In this unhappy Situation let us leave him for a while, and return to the Authoress of it, the injured, but well reveng'd *Barsina.*

After she found herself forsaken for another, at a Time when she thought herself most secured of her Lover's Affections, she bewail'd not the Loss with Tears, but bent her whole Thoughts on gratifying

her Resentment for the Affront:—To this end she affected to appear
so passive, neither upbraiding his Infidelity, nor discovering[1] any Surprize at it, till she prevail'd with him, as I have already related, to come
to her Lodgings, when she indeed frightened him to some Purpose.
The Wine she gave him was just as it came from the Merchant, un-
mix'd with any poisonous Drugs, but as she judg'd it happen'd:—
Conscious he deserved all the Vengeance she could inflict on him, he
easily believed she had in reality done as she said, and the Terrors he
was in, which he in vain strove to conceal under a Shew of Rage, as
he went from her, gave the highest Satisfaction.

She made her Kinsman and her Maid privy to the Plot she had laid,
and between them they found Means to get Intelligence how he behav'd, and the cruel Operations he submitted to in order to get rid of
the supposed Poison, all which gave her a Diversion beyond what can
be express'd.

Not thinking him yet sufficiently punish'd, she order'd it to be given
out[2] she was dead, and to strengthen the Report, caus'd a Coffin to
be carry'd from the House she lived in, attended by her Maid.—The
Reader knows already the Effect this Stratagem produced, therefore it
would be impertinent to make a Repetition.

To prevent all Possibility of his being undeceiv'd, she retired to a
Place where she was not at all known, and happen'd to be near that
very Village where *Ziphranes* went for the Recovery of his Health.

Chance in the very Choice of her Situation assisted her in Revenge,
when she was beginning to grow weary of prosecuting it any farther:—
As she admitted no Company but her Cousin, who had provided that
Recess for her, and sometimes came down to visit her, she frequently
walk'd about the Fields belonging to the House without any Body
with her; and as if every thing concurr'd to favour the undesign'd
Deception, she happen'd to have a white loose *Robe de Chamber*[3] on,
when in one of those little Excursions she saw, and was seen by her

---

1. **discovering:** revealing.
2. **given out:** announced.
3. **Robe de Chamber:** dressing gown.

perfidious Lover: As she had not heard he was so near a Neighbour, the unexpected Sight of him made her shriek out *"Ziphranes,"* without any Design of renewing his Terrors; nor did she immediately know the Effect it had upon him, for she flew back into the House with all the Speed she could, not caring to run the Hazard of what Treatment she might receive from him in a solitary Place, by way of Retort for the Plagues she had given him.

The next Day, however, afforded her sufficient Matter to have gratify'd her Spleen,[1] had any remain'd in her against a Man, now too much her *Contempt* to be any longer the Object of her *Hate:*—Every one's Mouth was full of the News, that a Gentleman had seen a Spirit over the Gate by the Lane, and that he was run mad upon it.

Impossible was it for her to refrain being merry at the first Part of this Intelligence; but mean and base as he was, she could not avoid affording him some Share of Pity as to the last:—She resolv'd, however, not to give herself any farther Trouble concerning him, and having gratify'd the just Resentment she had against him, even more than she had expected to do, returned to Town, and appear'd with all her former Serenity and Good- humour.

Tho', as I have already observed, she never kept a great deal of Company, she was yet seen by enough to have it known every where that she was alive.

The whole Transaction afterwards got Wind,[2] 'till it was in the Mouth of all their Acquaintance: Those who loved *Barsina* highly approved of the Method she took to punish his Inconstancy, and even the Friends of *Ziphranes* could not condemn it.

It was some Time before he could be brought to believe what he was told from every Quarter, and even when his Fever left him, and he grew perfectly restored, as to his Bodily Health, yet still his Mind continued in a very disturb'd Situation; and after being with great Difficulty convinced of the Truth, the Raillery he found himself treated with wherever he came, on the Subject of poisoning, and

---

1. **Spleen:** anger.
2. **got Wind:** became known.

having seen a Spirit, so much soured his Temper, that from being that gay, polite, entertaining Companion I at first describ'd him, he is now one of the most morose ill-natur'd Men in the World.

Disregarded by his Wife, ridiculed by his Acquaintance, and uneasy in himself, he lives an Example of that Vengeance which Heaven seldom fails to take on Perjury and Ingratitude; and even *Barsina,* tho' the Instrument of inflicting it, almost pities his Condition, and confesses the Consequences of her Stratagem, are more severe than she either wish'd or intended.

I heartily wish, however, that all Women who have been abandoned and betrayed by Men, either through a determin'd Baseness, or Caprice of Nature, would assume the Spirit she did, and rather contrive some Means to render the ungrateful Lover the Object of Contempt, than themselves, by giving way to a fruitless Grief, which few will commiserate, and which greatly adds to the Triumph of the more happy Rival, if she can be call'd happy, whose Felicity consists in the Possession of a Heart that has once been false, and consequently can never be depended upon.

This Story, for which *Elismonda* has the very sincere Thanks of all the Members of our little Society, gave us a double Pleasure in the reading, not only for the agreeable Manner in which it is related, but also, as we were before acquainted with some Part of it from common Report, we were glad to be inform'd in the Particulars of so extraordinary an Adventure, by a Person, who, it is easy to be seen, is well acquainted with even the most minute of them.

The Force of Imagination has employed the Pens of many learned Authors; and indeed there cannot be a Subject more worthy the Consideration of a philosophic Genius, as it is common to every one, and makes a great Part of our Happiness or Misery:—It not only enhances all our Pains and Pleasures, but is of that prolific Nature as to produce, from one single Hint, a thousand and ten thousand subsequent Ideas: —It also imposes upon our Senses, or to speak more properly, renders them subservient to its own creative Faculty, so as to make us call them in for Witnesses to Things that never were; and we really believe we hear, see, or touch what is most remote from us, and oftentimes what is not, nor cannot be in Nature.

It is not therefore to be wondered at, that the Plot contrived, and so artfully executed by *Barsina,* had such an Effect on *Ziphranes:* A Man of more solid Judgment than his Character denotes, might have been deceiv'd, by the same Means, into the Horrors he testify'd; and also having once receiv'd them, suffered[1] their Dissipation with as much Difficulty.

In this respect the *Body* discovers a more quick Sensation than the *Mind:*—After enduring any exquisite Torture, such as the Stone,[2] Gout, Sciatica, and many other Persecutors of the Human System, the Moment as the Fit is over how does the afflicted Person cry out, in a Transport of Joy, *That he is eased! That he is in Heaven!* and soon loses the Memory of his former Pains:—Whereas those Agonies that have once invaded the *Mind* are hard to be erased, and when one is even convinced that the Cause of them is entirely vanish'd, they still leave a heavy Languor on the Spirits, which continues for a long Time, and sometimes is never wholly dispersed.

The Reason of this is plain; the *Body* being endued only with sensative Faculties can suffer no longer than it *feels,* but the *Mind,* of which *Memory* is a Part, cannot be wholly at rest, till *Reason,* which, tho' *sure,* is *slow* in its Operation, exerts its Power to chace all dark Ideas thence. As old *Massenger*[3] says:

> My Memory, too faithful to its Trust,
> Brings my past Woes forever present to me.[4]

Indeed, when we have once got the better of that Mellancholly which past Ills have left behind, and begin to grow thankful for recovered Peace, we then are doubly happy, and enjoy the present Blessings with a much higher Relish; as after a long Famine every thing is a Delicate.[5]

---

1. **suffered:** endured.

2. **Stone:** kidney stones.

3. **Massenger:** Philip Massinger (1583–1640), dramatist who wrote both comedies and tragedies and may have collaborated with Shakespeare.

4. **My Memory . . . present to me:** quotation unidentified.

5. **Delicate:** delicacy.

But this can only be when the Misfortunes we have sustain'd have not been brought upon us by any base Action of our own, and we have rather suffered through the Faults of others than ourselves; then, and never but then, we look back with Pleasure on the Tempests we have escap'd, give all due Praises to protecting Heaven, and laudably exult in our own good Fortune.

As for *Ziphranes,* he can indulge no such pleasing Meditations, and I do not think it at all strange, either that he should so easily believe his Condition as bad, or even worse, than it was represented to him, or that he was so hard to be convinced that the Danger was over, even when those about him found it their Interest he should be so.

In fine, wherever there is *Guilt* there will be *Fear:*—We naturally *expect* what we are conscious we *deserve:*—So true are *Dryden*'s Words:

Fear ever argues a degen'rate Mind.[1]

It must be own'd *Barsina* acted her Part admirably well; yet still the first Scene of this Tragi-Comedy was only her's;[2]—the rest was performed by his own Apprehensions, which gave Scope to the Physicians to exert their Talents for making the most they could of him.

In ordinary Distempers,[3] indeed, nothing is more frequent than for People to take a Load of Drugs, improperly called Medicines, till they destroy that Life they are endeavouring to preserve; but in the Case of Poison the common Opinion is, that it must be *immediately* expell'd, or *not at all;* and doubtless to give him one sudden Shock was all the Lady intended by her Stratagem, or could have expected from it; it succeeded, however, in a Manner which made not only his Guilt, but the Meaness and Cowardice of his Mind exposed, so as to render him an Object of public Contempt; and had he even fallen a Sacrifice to the Force of his own Imaginations and the Practices of his Physicians, I cannot look on *Barsina,* but the Crime he was guilty of, as

---

1. **Fear . . . Mind:** John Dryden, trans., Virgil, *Aeneis* 4. 17.

2. **only her's:** i.e., only the first scene was hers.

3. **Distempers:** diseases.

the primary Occasion of his Death; to which, as she did not design it, she could not have been more than a guiltless accessory.

I am glad, notwithstanding, for her Sake, that it happened otherwise, because had he dy'd in reality, I know not but there might have been People malicious and cruel enough to have suggested that the Wine she gave him was actually poisoned, and that she had secured herself by taking an Antidote, from any Effect the partaking it with him would otherwise have produced.

Had no worse ensued than barely the spreading about Insinuations of this Sort, it would have been a Circumstance very disagreeable to a Woman of that Character we find her in all respects so tenacious of preserving.

I also believe, tho' *Elismonda* has been silent on that Head, that she would have repented, even to a Degree of Affliction, what she had done, had the short Punishment she intended him proved of that fatal Consequence it was so near accomplishing.

It therefore must be acknowledg'd that this Adventure adds one demonstrative Proof to the Numbers which are every Day produced, how ready we are to judge of every Action by its Success:—From the greatest down to the most minute Affair, the Praise or Blame depends on the Event:[1]—Heaven and Fate, which alone sees the secret Springs of every Heart, and either forwards or controuls our Purposes, can alone determine how far they are laudable, or the contrary.

Hudibras, in his whimsical Way, gives us a very just Idea of the Mistakes the World is guilty of on this Account.

> Success, the Mark no mortal Wit,
> Or surest Hand can always hit:
> For whatsoe'er we perpetrate,
> We do but row, we're steer'd by Fate,
> Which in Success oft' disinherits,
> For spurious Causes, noblest Merits;
> Great Actions are not always true Sons
> Of great and mighty Resolutions:

---

1. **Event:** outcome.

> Nor do the very best bring forth
> Events still equal to their Worth,
> But sometimes fail, and in their stead,
> Fortune and Cowardice succeed.[1]

We therefore join to congratulate the amiable *Barsina,* for an Event which so abundantly answer'd[2] all her Purposes, and at the same time secured her Reputation from Censure.

I doubt not, having mentioned the great Force of Imagination, but my Readers will expect I should say something on so copious a Subject, and endeavour at least to display what an Infinity of *Happiness* or *Misery* we are capable of receiving by it; to the end[3] that every one, by the the Strength of Reason and Reflection, might either indulge or correct it, so as to procure the *one*, and avoid falling into the *other State.*

But besides, that this has been so frequently and so well treated on by other Hands,[4] that it is scarce possible to add any thing new; every one who is possess'd of common Understanding must know enough of his own Temper as to be sensible[5] whether it inclines him most to *pleasing* or to *melancholly* Images; in fine, whether *Hope* or *Fear* be the most prevailing Passion in him; and this Knowledge, without the Help of any Rules or Precepts, will make him, unless he is very much his own Enemy indeed, use his utmost Efforts to *cherish* the *one*, and *dissipate*[6] the *other.*

It is certain, that on any Menace of immediate Death, the Soul catches the Alarm; those Apprehensions which Nature has implanted in every one of us, in a more or less Degree, on the Score of Dissolution, puts all our Faculties in a Hurry, and we have not then the Power of exerting our Reason in such a Manner as is necessary for

---

1. **Success . . . Cowardice succeed:** Samuel Butler, *Hudibras* 1.1.871–82.

2. **answer'd:** served.

3. **to the end:** with the purpose.

4. **other Hands:** other writers.

5. **sensible:** aware.

6. **dissipate:** make vanish.

the dreadful Occasion:—It is Religion, and an absolute Resignation to the Divine Will, which can alone support us under that Shock:—I shall therefore conclude with the Words of *Horace,* as translated by the late Lord *Roscomon.*

> Virtue, dear Friend, needs no Defence,
> Our surest Guard is *Innocence;*
> None knew till *Guilt* created *Fear,*
> What Darts, or poison'd Arrows were.[1]

The Letter signed *Philo-Naturæ* came Yesterday to our Publisher; we have just read it, and think ourselves obliged to thank the ingenious Author for the Favour he does us in that useful Essay, more especially as he promises to continue a Correspondence with us on a Topic which, in his agreeable Manner of treating, cannot fail being of general Service.

End of the FOURTEENTH BOOK.

* * *

FROM BOOK XV

That there is no Account to be given for *Taste,* is a Maxim we hear commonly repeated; and that it is so seldom disputed is because we see such Variety of odd Whims take Place, each of which are, by its Followers, supported with Vehemence: But this will be found of no Weight with any one who takes the Pains to distinguish between that *Taste* which is guided by the *Senses,* and that which is purely the Effect of the *Mind.*—In our Food, in our Apparel, our Equipages,[2] the build-

---

1. **Virtue . . . Arrows were:** "The Twenty-Second Ode of the First Book of Horace," ll. 1–4, trans. Wentworth Dillon, Fourth Earl of Roscommon.

2. **Equipages:** carriages.

ing or furnishing our Houses, there is doubtless a *true* and *false* Taste; nor is it always that the most shewy and expensive merit the greatest Approbation: But all these are of small Moment[1] when put in Competition with other more essential Matters, which are equally in our Choice; for tho' better Judges may find Fault with our Inelegance in these Particulars, yet we shall not be the less virtuous, nor worse Members of Society, for being mistaken in any or all of them.

But it is not so with that kind of *Taste,* which flows from Thought and Reflection: By this we judge of others, and are judged ourselves; by this we merit the Esteem or Censure of the World. The Character of a *fine Taste* stands in need of no Addition;—it implies whatever is great and valuable, and a *bad* one every thing that is mean and contemptible.

Many there are who flatter themselves with being possessed of this amiable Talent in the most refined Degree, and such, generally speaking, know the least of it of any People:—They imagine they are eminently displaying it, while in Fact they are only following the Dictates of some irregular Propensity and Caprice.—It is almost impossible to cure those who have gone on for a long Time in this Course of Self-deception, because of the Repugnance they have to be convinced they have ever been in the wrong.

How much, therefore, does it behove all who are entrusted with the Government[2] of Youth, to take the greatest Care in forming the yet docile and tractable Mind in this important Point!—In effect, nothing can be called a *true Taste,* that is not regulated by *Reason,* and which does not incline us to what will render us *better* and *wiser:* For, indeed, these two Qualities are inseparable; to be *good* is to be *wise,* in the most just Sense of the Word, and if we are *wise* we cannot fail of being *good.*

They certainly argue extremely wrong, who maintain that there are some Tempers[3] so morose, so rugged, and perverse, even from their

---

1. **Moment:** importance.
2. **Government:** guidance.
3. **Tempers:** temperaments.

very Infancy, that all Efforts to render them obliging, soft, or pliable, are entirely thrown away: It was always my Opinion, that even the most disagreeable behaved Person in the World was not so by Nature; and I find every Day fresh Reasons to confirm me in it. It is only ill Habits contracted in our Youth, which, not sufficiently check'd by those who have the Power, become rooted in us, and make as it were a Part of our very Soul.

But an early Knowledge of ourselves, and of the World, will prevent any ill Humours from getting the better of us; and, as we rise towards Maturity, produce that distinguishing Power in us which we express by the Name of *true Taste:* Without being tolerably versed in the first, we shall never be able to attain to any degree of Perfection in the latter:—Our Understanding will be but wavering at best, perhaps, be led astray:—We shall be liable either to be dazzled with the Lustre of our own Talents, so far as to be regardless of the Merit of others; or, depending too much on the first Impression we may happen to take, be rendered partial and unjust; frequently condemning what is right, and applauding what ought to be censured:—It is from this *false Taste* are derived those little Affectations in Behaviour,—those over Delicacies, which make us fancy every thing offensive:—From this proceeds the running into such Extremes in our liking, or disliking, whatever is presented to us; and hence it is that so many Fopperies are espoused, while all that would contribute to our own Happiness, as well as that of others, is in a manner totally neglected.

There is undoubtedly a great deal of Pity owing to those whose Parents have either by a mistaken Indulgence, or a Want of knowing better themselves, humoured them in Follies they ought rather to have corrected: Such, as I have already said, it is scarce possible for Precept or Example to reform. The Change, if it comes at all, must come wholly from themselves; and it is little to be expected, that a Person, who has been taught to think whatever she does is becoming, will take the Trouble to examine whether the Applause she is flattered with is really her Due.

A long Habitude of any favourite Passion, Manner, or Custom, requires the utmost Exertion of one's Reason to throw off; the Reproofs

we have from Abroad,[1] only serve to teize,[2] and sometimes harden us:
—How often have I heard a Person, when admonish'd in the most
friendly and candid Manner of some gross Solecism in Behaviour, cry
out, "For Heaven's Sake, don't preach to me! It is my Nature, and I
can't help it."

It is this that frequently deters those who have a right to put a
Check on our Inclinations from making any Attempts that way:—
They will tell you they cannot approve of such or such Things in the
Person they have under their Care;—that they are sorry to see them
so untractable, but that there is no more a Possibility of changing the
Temper than the Features of the Face, or the Make of the Body; and
this Excuse for an Indolence, which is unpardonable, gives a kind of
Sanction to half the Errors we daily see committed.

But I must take the Liberty to answer, that tho' there is no con-
verting what is really deformed, either by Nature or long Custom,
which is in effect the same Thing, into perfect Beauty, yet if the *Mind*
were attended to with the same Care as is the *Body,* it might be
brought nearer to what is lovely:—Those who are the least anxious
about their personal Charms, can find means to purify their Complexions, to take out Pimples, Freckles, and Morphew[3] from the Skin:
—Their Glasses[4] instruct them how to add Softness to their Eyes, and
Graces to their Smiles, the Taylor's Art reforms the Shape; and the
Dancing-Master the Motions of the whole Frame:[5]—And will not
Reason and Reflection enable us to erase whatever is a Blemish in the
Mind?—Surely they will:—They have it in their Power, and it is only
a firm Resolution to call them to our Aid, and to be wholly guided
by them, that is wanting to render us worthy of that Character, which
we all are ambitious of attaining, though for the most part we pursue
it by very wrong Methods.

---

1. **Abroad:** outside the household.
2. **teize:** tease.
3. **Morphew:** a skin eruption.
4. **Glasses:** looking glasses, mirrors.
5. **Frame:** body.

There are three Things in which our *good* or *bad Taste* are chiefly discoverable; and these are,

Ist, IN the Judgment we give of whatever is submitted to it.
2dly, IN the Distribution and Manner of conferring Favours.
3dly, IN the Choice we make of our Amusements, Diversions, and Employments.

As to the first;—A *true Taste* will never take any thing upon the Credit[1] of others:—It will examine for itself, judge according as it finds, and continue firm to its first Sentence; whereas the *false,* is wholly govern'd by Prejudice, will cry up or depreciate whatever is the Mode,[2] and as often as that changes, change also.

The *One* is timid, and slow in censuring what it cannot approve;—The *Other* is decisive, imperious, and takes Pleasure in condemning.

The *One* will never transport us beyond our Sphere, but rather deter us from interfering in Matters where we have no Concern.—The *Other* is assuming,[3] and pretends a right to know, and to regulate the Affairs of every one.

The *One* is polite, modest, affable and gentle: The *Other* haughty, tenacious, over-bearing and disdainful.

The *One* affects to know rather *less* than it does; the *Other* infinitely more.

The second Distinction between the *true* and the *false Taste* is not so generally obvious as the former:—Gratitude and Self-Interest will make those who reap any Advantage from our Good-Will, full of Praises on our *distinguishing Capacity;* and those who are not admitted to our Confidence, partake not of our Bounties, or any other Testimony of Favour, will, perhaps, with equal Injustice, rail[4] at our *Partiality:*—It is only such, therefore, as are entirely disinterested, that can judge of us in this Particular, and to do it with any Certainty, the

---

1. **Credit:** authority.
2. **Mode:** fashion.
3. **assuming:** making high claims for oneself.
4. **rail:** scold, complain.

Character of the Person *obliged,* as well as that of the *Obliger,* must be examined.

A *fine Taste* is quick in discerning Merit, whereever it is concealed; is industrious in rendering it conspicuous, and its Professor happy:— The *gross Taste* seeks nothing but its own Adulation:—The Flatterer, the Sycophant, the Time-server,[1] without Birth, Parts,[2] Integrity, or any one worthy Quality, is, by a Patron of this worthy Turn of Mind, caressed, protected, and frequently promoted even to ridiculous Heights.—Heaven knows we can look but into few Places without being convinced of this:—O, how can Persons of Condition,[3] who have it so largely in their Power to cherish Wit and Virtue, and discourage Vice and Folly, pretend to any Degree of *true Taste,* while they suffer the *One* to languish in Obscurity, perhaps in all the Miseries that Penury and cold Neglect can inflict; and at the same time reward the *Other* with Smiles and Benefactions!—How many Wretches do we see have a Seat at the Tables, and in the Coaches of those, whose Stables or Kitchens, they are, by Birth, Education, and Behaviour, much more qualified to serve in.

I know the general Excuse is, that Creatures, such as I have described, are only entertained in order to make Diversion for the rest of the Company:—If you ask a Nobleman, or a Lady of Quality,[4] how they can suffer any thing so unworthy in their Presence, they will presently answer,—"Why to make me laugh:"—And this serves as a sufficient Pretence, because in former Times, not only Kings, but great Men, had their Jesters or Buffoons, who were permitted to say or do almost any thing; but then our modern Lovers of laughing forget that those Jesters were always Men of Wit, and made use of the Privilege allowed them to *reprove* as well as to *divert* their Patrons; a Thing that at present wou'd not be at all relished.

History is full of many notable Admonitions given by these Jesters, which had oftentimes more Effect on those they were intended to

---

1. **Time-server:** one who shapes his views to conform with those in favor at the moment.

2. **Parts:** personal attributes, especially intellectual gifts.

3. **Condition:** high rank.

4. **Quality:** high rank.

reform, than the most serious Advice coming from any other Quarter.—Our inimitable *Shakespear,* who was perfectly well versed in the Humour of the Age he lived in, and also in many past, before he had a Being, in most of his Plays introduced a Clown or Buffoon, who, under the Shew[1] of Simplicity, spoke the boldest and the wittiest Things of any Person in the Drama.

But whether this be the Motive which influences some of our great Pretenders to *fine Taste,* in the Choice of their Companions, I appeal to common Observation.

Nor is it only in great Things that the *true good Taste* displays itself; —the meanest Acts of Charity we do are so many Testimonies of it: A Person may be liberal, even to Profusion, but if he makes no Distinction in his Bounties he cannot be said to be possessed of it:— *Reason* and *Judgment* should direct *Compassion,* not only on whom to bestow what we have to give, but also to bestow it so as to be of real Service to the unhappy Object:—Abandoned Infancy, decrepid Age, the Sick, and the Prisoner, have all an indisputable Claim to Pity and Relief.—These will be the first Care of a Person of *true Taste,* and such a one of what Rank soever, will not be above examining into the Calamities of the imploring Wretch, and endeavour to suit the Benefaction to the Condition. To throw Money among a Crowd that hover about our Doors, without any Regard who picks it up, in my Opinion, has somewhat of Ostentation in it; and though it may be said, that Heaven bestows its Sunshine and its refreshing Dews on all alike, yet as the most wealthy, here below, has not the same inexhaustible Fund, *true Charity* and *true Taste* oblige us to be more particular.

The *Manner* also in which we confer Favours of any kind, whether great or small, is a plain Indication either of our *good* or *bad Taste;* and this, I may say, is one of the principal Tests, at least, if we allow *Good-Nature* and *good Breeding* to be some of the Requisites of a *good Taste,* as certainly they are:—One may do a very essential Kindness to a Friend, yet do it so as to make him repine at the Necessity of being

---

1. **Shew:** appearance.

obliged:—And one may order[1] it so, that the smallest Concession in his Behalf, shall be esteem'd by him as an infinite Favour.—There is a peculiar Softness in *true Taste,* which, notwithstanding, loses no Part of its Dignity, that enhances the Value of every thing we do, doubles the Price of every Grant, and renders our very Refusals pleasing.

I am very well aware, that by many of my Readers this will be thought going too far, and that according to my Definition of a *good Taste,* it is morally impossible for any one to be possessed of it: But this is an Argument which the third Proposition I laid down will immediately confute, and it may easily be shewn, that the Choice of our Amusements, Recreations, and Employments is not only a Proof of having a *good Taste,* but will also enable those to acquire it who have it not by Nature.

Wherever we see a Person lavish away Time in Trifles, and fond only of such Amusements as can be no way improving to the Mind, we may be certain that such a one has not a Taste for any thing more elegant, and also that he never will; because by the very indulging those low and gross Ideas, he puts it out of the Power of the Thinking-Faculty to exert itself, and Reason, by Degrees, loses its native Force:—The Mind, as well as the Body, will grow weak and feeble without proper Exercise, and become no more than the Grave of its own Perfections.

But as great an Enemy as *Indolence* is to our spirituous[2] Part, *Activity* in Things *unfit* is yet much more so:—To be vehement in supporting any Prejudices, whether imbib'd in our Infancy, or adopted by us in Maturity, it matters not;—or, on the contrary, to have no settled Opinion of our own, but to be continually fluctuating, and espousing the last we hear of others.—To be transported with every new Caprice, and incessantly hurrying from one Folly to another, soon confounds the best Understanding, and makes a kind of Chaos in the Mind.

But they who can once resolve to employ themselves in such a manner as becomes a Person of *fine Taste,* however repugnant they

---

1. **order:** arrange.
2. **spirituous:** spiritual.

may be at first, will, by Degrees, be brought insensibly[1] to have it in reality.

It is one very great Step towards acquiring a *good Taste,* to be sensible[2] of our Deficiencies that way; it will at least prevent us from doing those Things which would discover us to have one eminently *bad.*—It is therefore the Business of every one to examine their own Hearts:—By this means they may know how to conceal, if not rectify those Propensities which are opposite to Reason. But I again repeat it as my firm Opinion, that whoever has Fortitude enough to forbear putting into Action a vicious Inclination for any time, will at last be able to conquer that Inclination, and become virtuous out of Choice as well as Principle.

But as ill Customs are so difficult to be worn off, and it must cost the Person who endeavours, by the Force of Reflection, to get the better of them, many a severe Pang before the Work can be accomplished; it is the utmost Cruelty in Parents and Governors,[3] to neglect accustoming us betimes to love and revere those Things, which it will become us to practise in our riper Years.

Curiosity is the first and most natural Passion of the Human Soul: We begin no sooner to think than we discover an Eagerness of Knowledge, and on the Direction and well Management of this, depends, in a great measure, the Praises we hereafter may deserve:—If therefore a wrong Turn be given to it, if we are allowed only to pry into such Things as had better to be forever unknown to us, it is no wonder that we should be devoted to Vanity and Trifles our whole Lives.

If we become early Connoisseurs in the Mode,[4] can make smart Remarks on the Dress of every one we see at the Ball, the Court, the Opera, or any other public Place, take so much Delight in hearing and reporting every little Accident that happens in Families we are acquainted with,—how much more Pleasure should we find in examining the various and beautiful Habits with which Nature cloaths those Plants and

---

1. **insensibly:** imperceptibly.

2. **sensible:** aware.

3. **Governors:** tutors.

4. **Mode:** fashion.

Flowers which adorn our Gardens, and in making ourselves acquainted with those great and wonderful Events which History presents us with, and the yet more surprizing Adventures, Dangers, Escapes, and Hardships which Books of Voyages and Travels afford.

These are Entertainments which we may partake while in our Hanging-Sleeves;[1] and though we should run them over never so cursorily, as Children are apt to do, they would still prepare the Mind for more solid Reflections afterwards; they could not fail of enlarging the Ideas, informing the Understanding, and above all, of inspiring in us a Love and Reverence for the great Author, Director, and sole Disposer of every thing in Nature.

By beginning to pass our Time in this manner, we shall prevent all those unruly and disorderly Passions from getting the better of us, which afterward cost so much labour to suppress, and are of such ill Consequence if indulg'd.

We shall become acquainted with the World before we have any thing to do with it, and know how to regulate our Conduct so as neither to give Offence to others, nor be in Danger of receiving any ourselves.

We shall be enabled to prize every thing according to its real Value, and be entirely free from all Prejudice and partial Attachments.

In fine,[2] we shall be possessed of all those useful and agreeable Talents, which in their Assemblage compose what may justly be called the *true fine Taste;* for though many People are so unhappy as to degenerate from a religious Education, and put in Practise the Reverse of every thing they have been taught; yet I am apt to believe it is because the Precepts of Piety and Virtue have been inculcated in a rough and undelicate Manner:—It is not every one has the Art of rendering Instruction pleasing; besides, as Youth is naturally head-strong, and submits to Constraint but with Pain, it seldom retains what is imposed upon it, those Rules are sure therefore to make the deepest Impression which are not laid down to us as such, but disguised under the Shew of Amusements and Recreation:—It is only

---

1. **Hanging-Sleeves:** loose open sleeves worn by children.
2. **In fine:** in short.

then we love them, and pursue with Eagerness what otherwise we should hate and avoid, as much as possible, the Thought of.

I am very certain the most profitable Parts of Learning may be attained by such Means as would afford us as much Delight, while in the Study of them, as Honour in the Acquisition.

But I shall postpone what I have to say farther on this Head, in order to oblige my Readers with that ingenious Letter which my last gave the Promise of, and which our Society takes a particular Pleasure in publishing; as it agrees so exactly with our own Sentiments, and is what we would wish to say ourselves upon the same Occasion.

To the FEMALE SPECTATOR.
MADAM,

As it is very evident those Monthly Essays, with which you oblige the Public, are calculated for no other End than the Improvement of the Morals and Manners of an Age which stands in the utmost need of so agreeable a Monitor; I flatter myself you will pardon my offering you a small Hint, whereby they may be rendered yet more effectual for the Accomplishment of so laudable an Undertaking.

Your Predecessor, the never too much admir'd *Spectator,* used frequently to adapt his Lucubrations[1] to the Season of the Year; and I am of the Opinion his Thought in it was extremely just, because we are much more sensibly[2] affected with what is said on Things which are that Moment present to us, than we can be with any thing *past,* or *to come.*

London, Madam, is now growing a perfect Wilderness:—The Play,—the Opera,—the Masquerade and Ball, no longer attract the Attention of the gay and polite World:—Scenes pencilled by Heaven's own Hand begin, in this beauteous Month, to be displayed, and every one hastens to partake the Charms of a rural Life.

Those hurrying Pleasures that so lately seemed to monopolize our Time, and every busy Care, from which the Greatest are not wholly

---

1. **Lucubrations:** studies and the products of study.

2. **sensibly:** acutely.

exempt, left all behind, what Advantages might not the Mind receive amidst that Variety of Amusements the Country affords, did we contemplate Nature as we ought! But if we cursorily pass them over, and enjoy, without Attention, the rich Regale prepared for every Sense, we deprive ourselves of the greatest, noblest, Satisfaction, and contradict the Purpose of the all-beneficent Bestower.

It is not enough that we behold those Fields, Meadows, and Pastures, which but a few Months past appear'd a dreary Waste, now plentifully stored with Food for Man and Beast:—Those Gardens so lately destitute of every Ornament, save only here and there a solitary *Yew,* perhaps, or *Cypress,* that stood nodding over the naked Plots, now clad in Colours which no Art can imitate, and even surpassing the celestial Bow;[1]—nor that we smell the Odours of ten thousand different Flowers gently wafted to us by the ambient Air;—nor that the Taste is gratified with the luscious Strawberry, the blushing Cherry, the refreshing Sallad, and all those early Products of the useful Olitory:[2] —Nor that our ravished Ears are from every Grove saluted with Notes more melodious than those of *Handel* or *Bononcini,*[3] though warbled through the Throat of *Farinelli* or *Curzoni:*[4]—Nor even is it enough that we have Gratitude to acknowledge and be thankful for the Blessings which every where surround us:—There is still a Something wanting to render our Felicity compleat, a Something which is not in the Gift of Heaven, because we are furnished with the Means of enjoying it in ourselves, and therefore depends wholly on ourselves.

You will easily conceive, Madam, I mean the Study of *Natural Philosophy;*[5] but, though Contemplation on any thing may be called a Study in a more or less Degree, I would not be thought to recommend to the Ladies (for whose Use I take your Lucubrations to be chiefly intended) that severe and abstruse Part which would rob them of any

---

1. **celestial Bow:** rainbow.

2. **Olitory:** kitchen garden.

3. **Handel or Bononcini:** George Frederick Handel (1685–1759), born in Germany, became a British citizen and composed in England his famous oratorios. Giovanni Bononcini (1670–1749), an Italian, wrote operas for English audiences.

4. **Farinelli or Curzoni:** famous Italian singers in London.

5. **Natural Philosophy:** natural science.

Portion of their Gaity:—On the contrary, I would not advise them to fill their Heads with the Propositions of an *Aldrovandus,*[1] a *Malbranche,*[2] or a *Newton:*[3]—The Ideas of those great Men are not suited to every Capacity;—they require a Depth of Learning, a Strength of Judgment, and a Length of Time, to be ranged[4] and digested so as to render them either pleasing or beneficial.

Not that I presume to deny, but that there are some Ladies every way qualified for the most arduous Labour of the Brain; but then I shall find little Forgiveness from my own Sex to persuade those Enliveners of Society to any thing which would deprive us of their Company for any long Time.

No, no, I am not so great an Enemy to myself:—What I mean by the Study of Natural Philosophy, is only so much as Nature herself teaches, and every one's Curiosity, if indulged, would excite a Desire to be instructed in.

Methinks, I would not have them, when the uncommon Beauty of any Plant strikes the Eye, content themselves with admiring its superficial Perfections, but pass from thence to the Reflection with what wonderful Fertility it is endowed, and what Numbers in another Season will be produced from its prolific and Self-generating Seed:—Even the most common, which springs beneath their Feet as they are walking, has in it some particular Vertue, which it would not be unbecoming them to be acquainted with; if they do not all contribute immediately to our Nourishment, or to the Cure of those Diseases to which Mankind is incident, they at least serve for Subsistence to many Animals, and even Insects to whom we owe a great deal.

We cannot walk or throw our Eyes Abroad without seeing ten thousand and ten thousand living Creatures, all curious[5] in their Kind, all created for our Use, and which no less testify the Almighty Wisdom and Goodness than the greatest and most noble of his Works.

---

1. **Aldrovandus:** Ulysse Aldrovandi (1522–1607), celebrated Italian naturalist.

2. **Malbranche:** Nicholas Malebranche (1638–1715), French Cartesian philosopher.

3. **Newton:** Sir Isaac Newton (1642–1727), English physicist, mathematician, and philosopher.

4. **ranged:** organized.

5. **curious:** made with art.

Even those Worms which appear most despicable in our Eyes, if examin'd into, will excite our Admiration:—To see how in those little Creatures Bodies are cased in Bodies:—How, when one Form grows withered and decayed, the happy Insect has another in Reserve, and, shaking off the old, appears again in all the Freshness and Vigour of Youth:—What would a certain Lady, often taken Notice of in your Essays, and many other antiquated Beauties, give, they had the same Power?

Can there be a more agreeable Amusement, than to observe how those flying Insects, which are most pleasing to the Eye, spring from such as but a few Days past crawled upon the Earth?—We admire the Beauty of the gaudy Butterfly, but reflect not how it rises from the grovelling Caterpillar, nor how that Worm, after having changed its Skin several Times, takes a different Shape, assumes Wings painted in that gorgeous Manner, and skims over the Tops of those tall Trees, whose Branches he before ascended but with Difficulty and Length of Time.

There is something extremely curious[1] and well worthy Observation in the Death and Resurrection of these Insects:—If you put one of them into a Box with small Holes at the Top to let in Air, and take care to supply them with Leaves proper for their Sustenance, you will perceive that after a certain Time they will cease to eat, and begin to build themselves a Kind of Sepulchre; as there are various Sorts of Caterpillars, they have various Ways of making this Inclosure, but all in general compleat it by a certain Glue out of their own Bowels, which, by their Manner of spinning and winding it round their Bodies, becomes a hard Consistence, and the Head, Paws, and hairy Skin, being work'd into it, form a Kind of Shell, which incloses the Embryo of the Butterfly; this Shell is by the Learned called a *Crysalis,* it lies wholly inanimate the whole Winter, and in the Beginning of Summer bursts at one End and discovers the Butterfly, which, having fluttered about and enjoyed itself for a Season, lays its Eggs for the Produce of a new Generation of Caterpillars.

This, the Ladies who keep Silk-worms, which are indeed of the same Nature, though more useful and beautiful, are no Strangers to:—They

---

1. **curious:** remarkable.

will tell you those pretty Creatures, from whose Bowels so much Finery is derived, after having finished their Work, erect themselves little Tombs, such as I have mentioned, and then revive in Butterflies in order to propagate their Species.

But all those Curiosities, which are discoverable by the naked Eye, are infinitely short of those beyond it:—*Nature* has not given to our Sight the Power of discerning the Wonders of the minute Creation:—*Art,* therefore, must supply that Deficiency:—There are *Microscopes* which will shew us such magnificent Apparel, and such delicate Trimming about the smallest Insects, as would disgrace the Splendour of a Birth-day:[1]—Several of them are adorned with Crowns upon their Heads, have their Wings fringed with Colours of the most lively Dye, and their Coats embroidered with Purple and with Gold.—Even the common Fly, black as it is, is not without its Beauties, whether you consider the Structure of its Frame, the curious Glazing of its transparent Wings, or the Workmanship round the Edges of them:—But, above all, the Eyes deserve Attention:—They are like two Half-Moons encompassing the Head, both which are full of an infinite Number of small Eyes, which at once penetrate above, below, on each Side, and behind, thereby fully gratifying the Curiosity of the Creature, if that Term may be allowed to Insects, and enabling it to defend itself from any threatening Danger.

The Glasses[2] which afford us so much Satisfaction are as portable as a Snuff-Box, and I am surprized the Ladies do not make more Use of them in the little Excursions they make in the Fields, Meadows, and Gardens.

There is, indeed, no Part of this Terrestrial Globe, but what affords an infinite Variety of living Creatures, which, though not regarded, or even not discernible as we pass by, or, perhaps, tread over them, would very much enlarge our Understanding, as well as give a present agreeable Amusement, if viewed distinctly through one of those Magnifiers.

Every Body has Heard of the *Ant;* its Œconomy, its Industry, and its wonderful Foresight, has employed the Pens of many learned Authors; I am therefore surprized that such Numbers of People can tram-

---

1. **Birth-day:** the King's birthday, annually celebrated with elaborate court ceremony.
2. **Glasses:** magnifying glasses.

ple over the little Mounds they with indefatigable Labour throw up in the Earth, without a Desire of examining how and by what Means they are enabled to effect it, and for what Purposes they take all this Pains.

Man, when he would erect or pluck down a Building,—when he would furrow or make plain[1] the Earth, or, in fine, do any thing for his Pleasure, Convenience, or Defence, is supplied by Art with Tools and Instruments proper to the Design he undertakes; but the *Ant* is indebted to Nature alone for all the Help it enjoys:—These Creatures are incased in a Coat perfectly resembling that of Mail, and by this are defended from any Hurt their tender Bodies would receive from a too great Weight of Earth falling in upon them;—they have Claws which they can extend whenever they please, and withal so sharp, that they will fasten into any thing;—they have two Horns before, and as many behind, and these serve as Ears to give them Intelligence of every thing;—they have little Trunks or Proboscis's, which penetrate into the hardest Earth, and a Kind of Saw to each Leg, that by constant Working enlarges the Cavity; and, as several Thousands work together, they soon build themselves subterraneous Mansions, into which they run on the Appearance of any Danger, and make the Repository of their Winter Stores; here also they lay their Eggs, breed up their Young, and take Repose after their long Fatigues.

Their Sagacity, as well as the Order they preserve in every thing, is thus finely expressed by Mr. *Dryden* in his Translation of *Virgil:*

> Thus in Battalia march embodied Ants,
> Fearful of Winter and of future Wants;
> T'invade the Corn and to their Cells convey
> The plunder'd Forage of their yellow Prey.
> The sable Troops, along the narrow Tracks,
> Scarce bear the weighty Burthen on their Backs:
> Some set their Shoulders to the pond'rous Grain,
> Some guard the Spoil, some lash the lagging Train:
> All ply their different Tasks, and equal Toil sustain.[2]

---

1. **plain:** level.

2. **Thus in Battalia . . . Toil sustain:** John Dryden, trans., Virgil, *Aeneis* 4.582–90.

All the ancient Poets were full of the Virtues of these little Insects. *Horace,* as *english'd* by our Famous *Cowley,*[1] says of them:

> The little Drudge does trot about and sweat,
> Nor will he strait devour all he can get;
> But in his temperate Mouth carries it Home:
> A Stock for Winter which he knows must come.[2]

But if the Ants with so much Justice claim our Admiration, what shall we think of the Bees?—Those who have been curious enough to prepare for them a Glass Hive will tell you such Wonders of their Œconomy, Order and Policy as might render them Patterns for the best regulated Government.

We could not, indeed, do better than to become their Imitators, since what we call Instinct in them is, in Fact, the immediate Direction of Divine Providence, which impels them with a resistless Force to do all those Things which are necessary for the common Good of their whole Community, as well as that of each particular Individual:—It has furnished them with Arms offensive and defensive; it has given them Bags to contain and carry Home the Food they labour for, and also for that poisonous Juice which they so easily dart out on their Assailants; but then they never exercise that Power without being first attacked.

On Man the Almighty Wisdom has bestowed Reason, "that Sovereign Power," as the Poet says, "of knowing Right from Wrong;"[3] but, when we find it is in Danger of being led astray by the Influence of ill Passions, as it too often is, let us have Recourse to the *Bees,* and reflect that it is our Duty, and befits the Dignity of our Nature, to do those Things by our own Choice which they do by an unavoidable Impulse:—Ambition, Lust, and Avarice, those Fiends that persecute and lay waste half the Human Species, pervert the beauteous Order of Nature, and render all her Works a Chaos, would then be banish'd

---

1. **Cowley:** Abraham Cowley (1618–1667), poet and essayist.

2. **The little Drudge . . . must come:** Abraham Cowley, "I'dmire, Maecenas, how it comes to pass," ll. 37–40.

3. **that Sovereign . . . Wrong:** quotation unidentified.

from among us, and this great Hive, the World, enjoy the same Tranquility we behold in each Repository of those happy Insects.

But I forget that it is to your Female Readers I address myself, none of whom I can suspect of being the Authors of any of those Mischiefs which happen in the World; except those few whose Lot it is to become Sovereign Princesses;—then indeed it is not to be greatly wondered at if they throw off all Womanhood, despise the Softness of their Sex, can behold whole Provinces depopulated, and, for the Sake of that false Glory, which is too often the Appendix of Royalty, rejoice and fatten in the Blood of slaughter'd Millions.—Such was *Semiramis*,[1] Descendant of the first Tyrant and Oppressor of the Earth, *Nimrod:*[2]—Such was *Thomyris* of *Scythia*,[3] and such, I grieve to say, may even in this Age be found: Yet all of the Fair Sex who have worn Crowns have not been so:—*England* can boast of two glorious Princesses who preferred the Works of Mercy to the Charms of Conquest: —*Elizabeth*,[4] of immortal Memory, had the happy Art of rendering herself formidable to her Enemies without Bloodshed; and her late Majesty Queen *Anne*[5] rejoiced more in putting an End to a long, though successful War, than ever she did in all the Victories gain'd by her Arms.

You will pardon this short Digression, Madam, which a sudden Thought, which came I know not how into my Head, enforced from me, and led me into Subject very foreign to my Purpose:—I was going to observe, that though there are but few Ladies who, I may suppose, can have any Occasion to regulate their Passions by the Example of the moderate *Bees;* yet those who are Lovers of Œconomy and Temperance will certainly be pleased to perceive the Occupation of these

1. **Semiramis:** in Assyrian mythology, an early queen of Assyria.

2. **Nimrod:** legendary figure who appears in the Bible as a mighty hunter; said to come from Assyria.

3. **Thomyris of Scythia:** Tomyris, Queen of Scythia; her army defeated and killed Cyrus when he attempted to annex her kingdom.

4. **Elizabeth:** Elizabeth I (1533–1603), Queen of England 1558–1603, during whose reign the English navy conquered Spain and England achieved commercial and military supremacy.

5. **Queen Anne:** (1665–1714), under whose reign (1702–14) the War of Spanish Succession was brought to an end after eleven years.

Animals, delightful, though toilsome to themselves, and so full of Utility to us.

Their Magazines[1] of Wax and Honey ought, and I think cannot but interest us in Favour of those from whom we receive such Benefits, and at the same time inspire us with the most exalted Love, Reverence, and Gratitude to the Divine Goodness which created us so many Slaves, and which also feeds, cloaths and instructs them to work for us, and for us alone, while we sit at Ease, and enjoy the Fruit of their Labours without Care and without Expence.

The Contemplation therefore on the Works of Nature affords not only a most pleasing Amusement, but it is the best Lesson of Instruction we can read, whether it be applied to the Improvement of our Divine or Moral Virtues.

It also furnishes Matter for agreeable Conversation, especially for the Ladies, who cannot always be furnished with Discourse on the Article of Dress, or the Repetition of what fine Things have been said to them by their Admirers; but here they never can want Matter:[2]— New Subjects of Astonishment will every Day, every Hour start up before them, and those of the greatest Volubility will much sooner want Words than Occasions to make Use of them.

As Ladies frequently walk out in the Country in little Troops, if every one of them would take with her a Magnifying Glass, what a pretty Emulation there would be among them, to make fresh Discoveries?—They would doubtless perceive Animals which are not to be found in the most accurate Volumes of Natural Philosophy; and the *Royal Society*[3] might be indebted to every fair *Columbus* for a new World of Beings to employ their Speculations.

To have their Names set down on this Occasion, in the Memoirs and Transactions of that learned Body, would be gratifying a laudable Ambition, and a far greater Addition to their Charms than the Reputation of having been the first in the Mode, or even of being the

---

1. **Magazines:** stores.

2. **Matter:** material.

3. **Royal Society:** founded in London in 1662 to provide a forum for discussion of scientific issues.

Inventress of the most becoming and best fancied Trimming or Embroidery, that ever engrossed the Attention of her own Sex, or the Admiration of ours.

All this Pleasure, this Honour, this even deathless Fame, may be acquir'd without the least Trouble or Study:—We need but *look* to be *informed* of all that Books can teach us of this Part of Natural Philosophy ; and it must, for that Reason, be extremely proper for such of the Fair, who are too volatile to have Patience to go through those tedious Volumes, which are requisite for the understanding all other Sciences.

In this, one Summer is sufficient to make them perfect Mistresses, and furnish a Stock of beautiful Ideas for their whole Lives:—Not but when we once have entertain'd a Desire of Knowledge, and been in any Measure gratified in that Desire, it rests not there, but extends itself in Proportion to the Objects that excite it.

Whoever, therefore, has a true Taste for the Researches I have been speaking of, will never cease their Enquiries, because the Theme is boundless, and they will still wish to fathom it: So that, whenever the chearing Spring begins to call the latent Sap forth from the Roots of Vegetables, and kindles the hidden Embryo dormant in its Cell into new Life, the fair Philosopher will be eager to survey the Resurrection, and see what Form will now display itself; and whether the seeming Death, both Plants and Insects have passed through, have wrought any Transformation in either:—In the former she will find no more than a Renovation of that State she saw them in before; but in almost every Species of the second she will find amazing Transformations:—And how lively an Idea this gives of something yet more demanding Consideration,[1] it is easy to conceive.

That, however, I will not take upon me to mention, for fear of rendering the Subject too grave; but of itself it will occur, and prove, to a Demonstration, that the Study of *Nature* is the Study of *Divinity.*—None, versed in the *One,* I am confident, will act contrary to

---

1. **something . . . Consideration:** the resurrection and transfiguration of the body after death.

the Principles of the *Other,* and that all your fair Readers will make the Experiment is the Wish of,

MADAM,

A sincere Admirer of your Productions,

And consequently your most devoted,

Inner-Temple,   *Faithful, humble Servant,*

April 27, 1745.   PHILO-NATURÆ.

P.S. Madam, if you think this is worthy of a Place in your next Essay, or that it will be agreeable to your Readers, I shall hereafter send you some loose Thoughts, as they may happen to occur to me, either on the same Subject, or any other that I shall think will be acceptable to you, or useful to the Public.

I believe there are none into whose Hands this Piece may fall, but will readily join with us in allowing it to be extremely just:—Our Sex, in particular, are infinitely obliged to the ingenious Author, and I flatter myself there are a great many will testify the Sense they have of this Advice by putting it in Practise:—He may, at least, assure himself of this, that our little Society, who have agreed to pass a few Days at a Country Seat, belonging to our President, the excellent *Mira,* will not go unfurnished with Microscopes, and other proper Glasses, in order to make those Inspections he recommends.

At our Return, or as soon as Leisure permits, we shall be glad to find the Performance of his Promise; since Admonitions, delivered in that polite and elegant Manner, he is so perfect a Master of, cannot fail of making all the Impression they are intended for.

It must certainly be confessed, that there is nothing more entertaining, or more profitable to the Mind, than the Study of Natural Philosophy, or that is with so little Difficulty attained.

We may be enabled by it to entertain ourselves with the most agreeable Ideas, and to entertain others so as to render our Conversation valuable to all who enjoy it:—We shall be led insensibly into the highest Notions of the Dignity of Human Nature, and all Coldness, all Indifference, for that supreme and omnipotent Power, who gave Being to such innumerable Creatures for our Use, be intirely banished from our Hearts.

In fine, a sincere and ardent Love of God would be conveyed to us through our Admiration of his Works, and the Benefit we receive by them; and wherever that is once truly established, it is impossible for Vice to take any deep Root:—*Swerve* we may from Virtue, the best have done it, but can never *wholly deviate:*—Though we stumble, we shall not fall, at least beyond the Power of rising:—The Vision, with which we were near being intoxicated, will vanish, and we shall cry out with *Solomon,*

<blockquote>All is Vanity and Vexation of Spirit.[1]</blockquote>

So great is the Emolument and innate Satisfaction in passing one's Time in those Employments *Philo-Naturæ* recommends, and in some others, which I shall hereafter mention, that I am pretty confident there are scarce any so lost in Vanities, but, if they would prevail on themselves to make Trial of the Change, would never more relapse into those absurd and ridiculous Follies, which at present too much engross their Hours.

The Love of Reading, like the Love of Virtue, is so laudable, that few are hardy enough to avow their Disgust to it.—I know Ladies who, though they never had Patience to go through a single Page of any thing, except an Opera or Oratorio, have always a Book of some Estimation in the World lying near them, which, on hearing any Company coming into the Room, they will immediately snatch up, as though their Thoughts had been engaged on the Contents of that, when, perhaps, they had only been taken up in contriving some new Ornament for their Dress, or debating within themselves which of the various Assemblies,[2] they frequented, should have the Honour of their Company that Night.

---

1. **All . . . Spirit:** Eccl. 1:14.

2. **Assemblies:** social gatherings where the entertainment might include music, conversation, and dancing.

None, indeed, but those who accustom themselves to Reading, can conceive the Pleasure which some Sort of Books are capable of affording:—A young Lady, whose Head is full of the gay Objects of the World, is too apt to imagine, it is losing more Time than she has to spare to make Trial of this Amusement; but in that Case I would have her make her Woman[1] read to her, while she is dressing, or at such Hours when, after being hurried and fatigued with Diversions, a Kind of Indolence falls upon her, and she grows peevish, and in a Kind of Anxiety for something new to kill the tedious Time.

In those Moments, if she have a Person about her of Discretion enough, to make Choice of some interesting Part of History, it will insensibly engage her Attention:—She will grow fond of Knowledge in those Things which are truly worth knowing, and the very Novelty at first endear that to her, which a more perfect Understanding of its Value afterward will make her unable to neglect.

What I mean, when I say some interesting Part of History, is the Relation of some Event which may be most interesting to the Person who is to hear it; as there is scarce any Circumstance or Character in modern Life, that has not its Parallel in Antiquity, I would have her begin with what affords Examples of such Events as there is a Possibility may happen to herself, or those Persons for whom she has the most tender Concern:—By this her noblest Passions will be awaked;— she will forget every thing beside;—she will rejoice, or weep, according as the different Accidents excite;—her whole Soul will take a new Turn, and become all Generosity and Gentleness.

This is going a great Way toward acquiring that *fine Taste* which is so much talked of, and so little understood; but the Way to be possessed intirely of it is not to stop here.

When the Mind is once prepared by these, other Kinds of Reading will become no less agreeable:—The Person, who is happily a Convert to that improving and most delightful Amusement, will always find some Excitement to continue it:—She will never hear Mention made of any great Author, but she will have a Desire to examine his Works,

---

1. **Woman:** personal servant.

in order to know if they do Justice to his Merit, or have over-rated it:
—When she hears of any notable Transaction in the Field[1] or Cabinet,[2] she will be impatient to look over the Annals of past Times, to find if the present really excel all that have gone before, or whether it be, as the Wise-Man before quoted says, that, in Fact,

There is nothing new under the Sun.[3]

Neither will she be content with knowing that such and such Things were done; she must also pry into the Motives by which they were brought about, and as far as is in her Power inform herself whether they were such as deserved Praise, or the contrary:—And by this Means she will be enabled to judge of Affairs, not by their Success, but by the Intentions of those who conducted them.

Not that I would have any one become so devoted to Books as to be lost to their Friends and Acquaintance; two or three Hours every Day employed that Way will be sufficient, provided the Matter we have been reading be well digested;—*that,* our own Reflexions on it, when we happen to be alone, or blending it in any Conversation we fall into, will easily accomplish:—We may read a Multitude of Authors, without being the better, or even remembering one of them, if we do not read with Attention, and a Desire of being instructed; but, if we are once strongly possessed of that Desire, every Trifle we take up will be of some Advantage to us.

However, as it requires a great deal of Judgment to know what we should endeavour to retain, and what is better forgotten than remembered, happy is it for those who make Choice of such Books as lay them under no Necessity of picking the *Wheat* from among the *Tares:*[4]—Of this Kind, after the inspired Writings, are Histories, Voy-

---

1. **Field:** of war.

2. **Cabinet:** private room.

3. **There . . . Sun:** Eccl. 1:9.

4. **Tares:** weeds closely resembling wheat. Haywood is alluding to Jesus's parable (Matt. 13: 24–30) about the necessity of distinguishing between wheat and tares.

ages, Travels, and the Lives of eminent Persons; but even here great Care must be taken to select those Authors on whose Veracity there is most Reason to depend.

Fabulous Accounts of *real* Facts, instead of informing the Mind, are the most dangerous Corrupters of it, and are much worse than *Romances,* because *their* very Titles warn us from giving any Credit to *them;* and the *others* attempt to beguile our Understanding, and too often succeed by the Cloke of *Simplicity* and *Truth.*

Next to Matters of *Faith,* it behoves us not to be imposed on in those Events which *History* relates:—*Fiction* ordinarily wears a more pleasing Garb than *Truth,* as indeed it stands in need of Flourishes which the *other* scorns, and therefore is apt to make a very deep Impression; or, more properly speaking, creates a Prejudice in us, which sometimes shuts our Eyes against Conviction, and we *will not* be convinced, because we *do not care* to be so.

To various People, and under various Circumstances, some particular Parts of History may be most useful; but as to the Ladies, who have no Occasion to make any one their Study, but only to have a general Notion of all, I advise them to cast their Eyes back to the Creation in its Infancy; it will give them an infinite Pleasure to survey the Manners of that Age which justly may be called a golden one:— How, for the Space of Eighteen Hundred Years, Man lived in a perfect Liberty and Independency on each other:[1]—How every Family was then a little separate State, of whom the Father was sole Head, and knew no other Superior.—Then, from those Times of Peace and Plenty, our Thoughts may descend to the Change, which happened in the World soon after the Deluge:[2]—Scarce was it re-peopled, and began to wear the same Face it had done before that tremendous Waste, when Avarice and Ambition, Vices till then unknown, entered the Hearts of this new Race:—All Faith, all Unity, all Brotherly Affection ceased:—The Lust of Power prevailed;—those Arms invented

---

1. **How . . . Other:** Haywood imagines the time of the Old Testament patriarchs as an idyllic Golden Age.

2. **Deluge:** the great flood in the time of Noah.

for their Defence against wild Beasts, with savage Fury, were turned against each other, and made the Instruments of enslaving their Fellow-Creatures.

Nimrod, mentioned by *Philo-Naturæ,* was, indeed the first who, finding himself stronger than his Neighbours, seized on their Territories, and erected himself into a Monarch:—His Example emboldened others to do the same, who also became Kings at the Expence of public Liberty; for, whatever some Writers have taken upon them to assert, it is certain that it was not by Choice that the People submitted to the Yoke of Servitude, but by the Force and Violence of the first Conquerors.

Thus began the famous *Assyrian* Empire, which lasted thirteen Centuries, and fell at last by the Indolence and Luxury which *Sardanapalus*[1] introduced: Three potent Monarchies rose out of the Ruins of this unweildy State, and they again were destroyed and plundered by the *Jews,* by *Alexander* the Great, and by the *Romans:*—To these last all became a Prey, and they were Sovereign Masters of the conquered World, till they fell into the Vices and Effeminacies of those they had subdued, and were themselves undone by their own Victories.

It is not, however, on those remote Ages of the World that I would have the Mind to dwell too much:—A cursory View of them will be sufficient to enable us to make Comparisions, and give Employment for our Judgment.

The lower we go, and approach nearer to our own Times, every thing will be more interesting:—From the Æra I have mentioned down to the present Now, we shall find scarce any thing but amazing Revolutions.[2]—Sure there cannot be a more delightful Subject for Contemplation, than the Rise and Fall of Empires:—From what minute Accidents they arrived at the utmost Pitch of Human Greatness; and by others, seemingly as inconsiderate, sunk, and became in a Manner Provinces to other Nations, who triumphed in their Turn.

---

1. **Sardanapalus:** Assyrian monarch legendarily associated with luxury and self-indulgence; probably from the seventh century B.C.

2. **Revolutions:** changes.

Thus it has ever been, since Ambition in great Men has been ranked among the Number of magnanimous Qualities, and Virtue has been thought to consist in the Acquisition of new Conquests; For, as Mr. *Otway*[1] justly observes,

> Ambition is a Lust that's never quench'd,
> Grows more inflam'd, and madder by Enjoyment.[2]

How wretched a Figure in Life would a Man make, who should be found totally unacquainted with History!—He would, indeed, be unqualified for any Post or Employment of Consequence, and likewise equally so for Conversation; but though Custom, and too little Attention to the Education of our Sex, had rendered this Want in us less contemptible than in them, yet, as we have reasonable Souls as well as they, it would, methinks, be a laudable Pride in us to exert ourselves on this Occasion, and lay hold of every Means to attain what will render us the more conspicuous, as it is the less expected.

Pleasure innate, Applause deserved, and Virtue unaffected, are the sure Rewards of our Researches after Knowledge while on Earth; and nothing can be more certain, than that, the greater Degree of Perfection we arrive at here, the more we shall be capable of relishing those incomprehensible Objects of Joy, which are to be our Portion in another World.

*　　*　　*

A letter has been left for us at our Publisher's from Mrs. *Sarah Oldfashion,* the first Correspondent the *Female Spectator* was favoured with; but we do not think proper to insert this, because the Contents can be of no Manner of Service to the Public.

She reproaches me bitterly for the Advice I gave her to send Miss *Biddy* into the Country,[3] where she fell passionately in Love with the

---

1. **Otway:** Thomas Otway (1652–1685), tragic dramatist.

2. **Ambition . . . Enjoyment:** quotation unidentified.

3. **Advice . . . Country:** in Vol. 1, Bk. V of the *Female Spectator*.

Groom of a neighbouring Gentleman, and has privately married him.—To this I think myself obliged to answer, that she has not followed my Advice, but her own:—Whoever will give themselves the Trouble to turn back to the Fifth Book of the *Female Spectator,* will find I was totally averse to her sending the young Lady into a Place, where she could meet with no Diversions to compensate for the Want of those she left behind.—The good old Gentlewoman confesses also, that, instead of ordering she should be indulg'd in all those innocent Sports a rural Life affords, she gave a strict Charge to the Person who had the Care of her, to keep her continually at Work,[1] and threatened herself with very severe Punishments, if she did not embroider the Hanging of a very large Drawing-Room before the Summer was elapsed.

This was taking a very improper Method, indeed, to make her forget the dear Delights of *Ranelagh,*[2] and the fine Things which doubtless were said her, not only there, but in all other public Places.

Nor can I by any means approve of compelling young Ladies of Fortune to make so much Use of the Needle, as they did in former Days, and some few continue to do:—There are enough whose Necessities oblige them to live wholly by it; and it is a Kind of Robbery to those unhappy Persons to do that ourselves which is their whole Support:—In my Opinion, a Lady of Condition should learn just as much of Cookery and of Work, as to know when she is imposed upon by those she employs in both those necessary Occasions, but no more: —To pass too much of her Time in them may acquire her the Reputation of a *notable*[3] *House-wife,* but not of a Woman of *fine Taste,* or any way qualify her for polite Conversation, or of entertaining herself agreeably when alone.

It always makes me smile, when I hear the Mother of several fine Daughters cry,—"I always keep my Girls at their Needle."—One, perhaps, is working her a Gown, another a Quilt for a Bed, and a

---

1. **Work:** needlework.

2. **Ranelagh:** an amusement center in Chelsea, a borough of London, much frequented by the fashionable.

3. **notable:** capable, industrious.

third engaged to make a whole Dozen of Shirts for her Father:—And then, when she has carried you into the Nursery, and shewn you them all, add, "It is good to keep them out of Idleness, when young People have nothing to do, they naturally wish to do something they ought not."

All this is very true; but then there are certainly Avocations to take up the Mind, which are of a more pleasing as well as more improving Kind:—Such as those I mentioned, and I will appeal to any young Lady, under the above-mentioned Confinement, if she had not rather apply to Reading and Philosophy than to Threading of Needles.

It is not enough, that we are cautious in training up Youth in the Principles of Virtue and Morality, and that we entirely debar them from those dangerous Diversions in Fashion, and which have been the Ruin of so many, in order to make them remember that Education we have given them, and to conduct themselves according to it when they come to be their own Managers; we should endeavour to make them *wise,* and also to render Virtue so pleasing to them, that they could not deviate from it in the least Degree without the utmost Repugnance.

> Children, like tender Osiers, take the Bow,
> And as they first are fashion'd always grow.[1]

It is not encouraging the natural Haughtiness of a young and beautiful Girl, and flattering her with the Opinion that she deserves every Thing, and may command every Thing, that will stem the Torrent of Inclinations, if it once fixes on a Man beneath or unworthy of her; but inspiring her with those just Notions, which will prevent her from giving way at first to any Inclinations unbefitting her Rank and Station in Life:—In fine, it is cultivating her Genius,[2] improving her Understanding, finding such Employments for her as will rectify her Mind, and bring her to that *good Taste,* which will not suffer[3] her to approve

---

1. **Children . . . grow:** John Dryden, trans., "The Fourteenth Satire of Juvenal," ll. 50–51.
2. **Genius:** natural gifts.
3. **suffer:** allow.

of, or be pleased with any Thing that is indecent or unbecoming, even in the most minute, much less in any important Thing.

On this Occasion a Letter, lately come to our Hands, claims a Place: —Not that the Matter it contains is of any great Moment, any farther than it proves, that in the most trifling Things, one can possibly imagine, a *good* or *bad Taste* may be discovered:—We shall therefore for that Reason present our Readers with it.

To the FEMALE SPECTATOR.
Dear Female Moralizer,

You have not a Reader in the World more inclined to wish you well than myself; yet I must tell you, that I am a little angry with you, and so are several others of my Acquaintance, that you confine all your Satire to our Sex, without giving One Fling at the Men, who, I am sure, deserve it as much to the full, if not more than we do.

I defy the most strict Examiner to find any one Folly in us, that they do not abound with in an equal Degree:—If we have our Milleners, Mantua-makers, and Tire-women[1] to take up our Time, have they not their Taylors, Barbers; aye, and their Face-menders[2] too, to engross as much of theirs?—Are there not as many Implements on the Toylet[3] of a Beau,[4] as there can be on one of the greatest Coquet[5] among us?—Does he not take the same Pains to attract, and is as much fond and proud of Admiration?—Are not the Men in general affected with every new Mode, and do they not pursue it with equal Eagerness?—Are there any of the fashionable Diversions (call them as absurd as you will) that they do not lead into by their Example?—If we affect a little of the Rusticity of a Country Maid in our Walk and Motions, do not they shoulder into all public Places with the Air and

---

1. **Milleners . . . Tire-women:** hatmakers, dressmakers, and ladies' maids.

2. **Face-menders:** attendants to apply cosmetics.

3. **Toylet:** dressing table.

4. **Beau:** dandy.

5. **Coquet:** flirt.

Mein of a *German Hussar?*[1]—If we sometimes put on the *Romp,*[2] I am sure they act the Part of the *Russian* to the Life.

I will tell you how I was served the other Day in the Mall:[3]—There were five of us perfectly well dress'd; for my Part I had a new Suit of Cloaths on, I had never wore before, and every body says is the sweetest fancied[4] Thing in the World:—To speak the Truth we took up the whole Breadth of the Walk; unfortunately for me, I happened to be on the outside, when a Creature, who I afterward heard was a *Dettingem* Hero,[5] came hurrying along, with a Sword as long as himself, hanging dangling at his Knee, and pushing roughly by me, his ugly Weapon hitched in the pink'd Trimming of my Petticoat, and tore it in the most rueful Manner imaginable.

I am so happy as not to be enough concern'd for any of that Sex to give myself any Sort of Pain, how ridiculous soever they make themselves:—I only laughed at the *Khevenbuller*[6] Cock of the Hat, so much the Fashion a little Time ago, and the fierce *Arm-a-kembo*[7] Air in a Fellow that would run away at the Sight of a Pot-gun.[8] As the Poet says,

All these Things moved not me.[9]

But as my whole Sex, and myself in particular, have been aggrieved by Swords of this enormous Size, and the Manner in which they are worn, I could not help communicating my Thoughts to you on the

---

1. **Hussar:** officer of a cavalry regiment marked by brilliantly colored, elaborately ornamented uniforms.

2. **put on the Romp:** act like a fun-loving, merry girl.

3. **Mall:** a fashionable London promenade.

4. **fancied:** designed.

5. **Dettingem hero:** one who had fought at the Battle of Dettingen, in which allies led by England had defeated the French in 1743, during the War of Austrian Succession.

6. **Khevenbuller:** unidentified.

7. **Arm-a-kembo:** a pose with the hand on the hip and the elbow turned out; associated with aggression.

8. **Pot-gun:** pop-gun; a child's toy gun that shoots paper wads.

9. **All . . . me:** quotation unidentified.

Occasion, which I beg you will not fail to insert in your next Publication.

If you are really as impartial as you would be thought, you will add something of your own, to make the Men ashamed of appearing in a Country which, thank Heaven, is at present at Peace within itself, as if they were in a Field of Battle, just going upon an Engagement.[1]

A Touch also upon some other of their Follies and Affectations I am very confident will be extreamly agreeable to all your Female Readers, and in a particular Manner oblige her who is,

With the greatest Good Will,
MADAM,
Your humble, and
Most obedient Servant,
LEUCOTHEA.

Pall-Mall,
May 30, 1745.

P.S. Just as I had finished the above, a young Lady came to visit me, and, on my shewing her what I had wrote to you, desired I would hint something about the Men loitering away so many Hours at Coffee-house[2] Windows, meerly to make their Observations, and ridicule every one that passes by; but as this Subject is too copious for a Postscript, and I am too lazy to begin my Letter anew, if you bestow a few Pages on the Folly of such a Behaviour, it will add to the Favour of giving this a Place.—Adieu for this Time, good *Female Spectator,* if any Thing worth your Acceptance falls in my way hereafter, you may depend on hearing from me.

I own myself under an Obligation to the good Wishes of this Correspondent; but must take the Liberty to say she is guilty of some Injustice in her Accusation:—Vanity, Affectation, and all Errors of that Nature are infinitely less excuseable in the Men than in the Woman, as they have so much greater Opportunities than we have of knowing better.

---

1. **upon an Engagement:** to fight a battle.

2. **Coffee-house:** Coffee houses, where men went to converse, drink coffee, read newspapers, and watch passers-by, were extremely popular in London.

If therefore I have directed my Advice in a peculiar Manner to those of my own Sex, it proceeded from two Reasons, First, because, as I am a Woman, I am more interested in their Happiness: And secondly, I had not a sufficient Idea of my own Capacity, to imagine, that any Thing offered by a *Female Censor* would have so much Weight with the Men as is requisite to make that Change in their Conduct and Œconomy, which, I cannot help acknowledging, a great many of them stand in very great need of.

As to the Grievance she complains of, it is a common Observation, that in Time of War the very Boys in the Street get on *Grenadier*[1] Caps, hang wooden Swords by their Sides, and form themselves into little Battalio's:[2]—Why then should she be surprized that Boys of more Years, but not older in their Understanding, should affect to look like Warriors for the Queen of *Hungary,*[3] and equip themselves as much as possible after the Mode of those who fight the Battles of that famous *German* Heroine.[4]

Many have already made a Campaign in her Service, and possibly it is in the Ambition of others to do so, if the War[5] continues, as in all Likelihood it will, and they are now but practising the first Rudiments of Fierceness, as the Curtsy precedes the Dance.

One of the distinguishing Marks of a *bad Taste* in either Sex, is the Affectation of any Virtue without the Attempt to practise it; for it shews that we regard only what we are *thought to be*, not what we *really are:*—A rough boisterous Air is no more a Proof of Courage in a Man, than a demure, prim Look is of Modesty in a Woman.

These long Swords, which give so much Offence to *Leucothea,* might be, perhaps, of great Service at the late Battle of *Fontenoy,*[6] because

---

1. **Grenadier:** The term "grenadier," originally designating soldiers assigned to throw grenades, had by this time come to refer to members of regiments composed of the tallest and finest men in the army. Their uniforms were therefore especially attractive to small boys.

2. **Battalio's:** battalions.

3. **Hungary:** The hussars originated in Hungary; other European countries copied their lavish uniforms.

4. **German Heroine:** Maria Theresa (1717–1780), Queen of Hungary and Archduchess of Austria, was of German birth.

5. **War:** the War of the Austrian Succession (1740–48).

6. **Battle of Fontenoy:** (1745), in which the English were badly defeated by the French.

each would serve his Master for a Crutch upon Occasion; but here, at *London,* in my Opinion, and according to my Notion of Dress, they are not only troublesome to others, but extreamly unbecoming, because unnecessary to those that wear them.

I believe, however, that if the Ladies would retrench a Yard or two of those extended Hoops they now wear, they would be much less liable, not only to the Inconveniences my Correspondent mentions, but also to many other Embarassments one frequently beholds them in when walking the Streets.

How often do the angular Corners of such immense Machines,[1] as we sometimes see, though held up almost to the Arm-pit, catch hold of those little Poles that support the numerous Stalls with which this populace[2] City abounds, and throw down, or at least indanger the whole Fabrick,[3] to the great Damage of the Fruiterer, Fishmonger, Comb and Buckle-Sellers, and others of those small Chapmen.[4]

Many very ugly Accidents of this Kind have lately happened, but I was an Eye-witness from my Window of one, which may serve as a Warning to my Sex, either to take Chair or Coach, or to leave their enormous Hoops at Home, whenever they have any Occasion to go out on a *Monday,* or *Friday,* especially in the Morning.

It was on one of the former of those unhappy Days, that a young Creature, who, I dare answer,[5] had no occasion to leave any one at Home to look after her best Cloaths,[6] came tripping by with one of those Mischief-making Hoops, which spread itself from the Steps of my Door quite to the Posts placed to keep off the Coaches and Carts; a large Flock of Sheep were that Instant driving to the Slaughter-House, and an old Ram, who was the foremost, being put out of his Way by some Accident, ran full-butt into the Foot-way, where his Horns were immediately entangled in the Hoop of this fine Lady, as

---

1. **Machines:** the large whalebone hoops supporting hoop skirts.

2. **populace:** probably a mistake for *populous.*

3. **Fabrick:** structure.

4. **Chapmen:** tradesmen.

5. **answer:** assert.

6. **had no . . . Cloaths:** because she was wearing them.

she was holding it up on one side, as the genteel Fashion is, and indeed the Make of it requires:—In her Fright she let it fall down, which still the more encumbered him, as it fix'd upon his Neck;—she attempted to run, he to disengage himself,—which neither being able to do, she shriek'd, he baa'd, the rest of the Sheep echo'd the Cry, and the Dog, who follow'd the Flock, bark'd, so that altogether made a most hideous Sound:—Down fell the Lady, unable to sustain the forcible Efforts the Ram made to obtain his Liberty;—a Crowd of Mob,[1] who were gathered in an Instant, shouted.—At last the Driver, who was at a good Distance behind, came up, and assisted in setting free his Beast, and raising the Lady; but never was Finery so demolished:—The late[2] Rains had made the Place so excessive dirty, that her Gown and Petticoat, which before were yellow, the Colour so much revered in Hanover,[3] and so much the Mode in *England*, at present, were now most barbarously painted with a filthy Brown:—her Gause[4] Cap half off her Head in the Scuffle, and her *Tete de Mutton*[5] hanging down on one Shoulder. The rude Populace, instead of pitying, insulted her Misfortune, and continued their Shouts till she got into a Chair, and was quite out of Sight.

These are Incidents which, I confess, are beneath the Dignity of a *Female Spectator* to take notice of; but I was led into it by the Complaint of *Leucothea,* and the Earnestness she discovers[6] to have her Letter inserted.

It is not, however, improper to shew how even in such a trivial Thing as Dress, a *good* or *bad Taste* may be discerned, and into what strange Inconveniencies we are liable to fall by the latter.

Of this we may be certain that wherever there is an Impropriety, there is a manifest Want of *good Taste;*—if we survey the Works of the divine Source and Origin of all Excellence, we shall find them full

---

1. **Mob:** the disorderly part of the population.
2. **late:** recent.
3. **Hanover:** in Germany. George III, King of England, belonged to the House of Hanover.
4. **gause:** gauze.
5. **Tete de Mutton:** a fashionable elaborate headdress.
6. **discovers:** reveals.

of an exact Order and Harmony,—no jostling Atoms disturb the Motion of each other,—every Thing above, below, and about us is restrain'd by a perfect Regularity:—Let us all then endeavour to follow Nature as closely as we can, even in the Things which seem least to merit Consideration, as well as in those which are the most allowed to demand it, and I am very sure we shall be in no Danger of incurring the Censure of the World, for having a *bad Taste.*

A great Pacquet of Letters is just now brought to us by our Publisher, of which we yet have only Time to read three;—that from *Eumenes* deserves some Consideration, and if, on weighing more maturely the Affair, we can assure ourselves it will be no ways offensive, it shall have a Place in our next, with some Reflections on the Matter it contains.

As for *Pisistrata*'s Invective (we hope she will pardon the Expression) as it is a Rule with us never to enter into private Scandal, we are surprized she could expect to see a Story of that Kind of propagated by the *Female Spectator.*

Amonia's Remonstrance claims more of our Attention, and that Lady may assure herself, that a proper Notice will be taken of it, provided those others, which we yet have not had the Pleasure of looking over, oblige us not to defer making our proper Acknowledgements till the ensuing Month.

End of the FIFTEENTH BOOK.

*   *   *

FROM BOOK XVI

Being returned from that little Excursion we made into the Country, it was our Design to have presented our Readers with what Observations this dreary Season would permit us to make; but some Letters, contained in that Pacquet mentioned in our last, seem to us of too general Service to be postponed for any Speculations, not so immediately tending to the Rectification of such Errors, as render those, who might be most easy in private Life, miserable in themselves, and troublesome to all about them.

As, therefore, Hints of this Nature are conducive to bring about the main End,[1] for which these Essays are published, our Correspondents may always depend, that on the receiving any such, whatever we had purposed to say of ourselves shall give Place, in order for them to appear.

The first we shall insert is on a Subject, than which scarce any thing occasions more Discourse in the World, or is the Cause of greater Dissention among private Families.

To the ingenious Authors of the FEMALE SPECTATOR.
LADIES,

As it was easy to perceive from the Beginning, that your Works were intended to correct all ill Habits, whether natural or acquired, particularly those which are a Disturbance to Society; I have been impatient for every new Publication of the *Female Spectator,* in Hope it would touch on the ungenerous and cruel Behaviour some of our Sex are guilty of after they become Step-Mothers.

Nothing, in my Opinion, can be more incongruous, than for a Woman to pretend an Affection for her Husband, yet treat his Children with all the Marks of Hatred; yet this is so common a Thing, that we shall scarce find one, whose Father had made a second Venture, without having Reason for Complaint of the sad Alteration in their Fate, even though the Person, who is put in the Place of her that bore them, has all those Qualifications which, in the Eye of the World, may justify the Choice made of her.

It must certainly be a mean[2] Envy of the Dead, or a ridiculous Distrust of the Living, that can make a Wife look with an evil Eye on those Tokens of Tenderness her Husband bestows on the Children he had by a former Marriage; and I am amazed any Man, who perceives

---

1. **End:** purpose.

2. **mean:** debased, despicable.

this Disposition in his Wife, can depend either on her having a sincere Affection for himself, or that she will discharge any Part of the Duty expected from her to those he has put under her Care.

I wonder, therefore, any Woman can be so impolitic as to shew her Ill-nature in this Point, since if the Husband have one Grain of Tenderness to those that owe their Being to him, he cannot but be extremely offended at it:—If Dissimulation can ever be excused, it certainly might in a Circumstance of this kind; since good Usage, though not flowing from the Heart, would render the Persons, who experienced it, easy in their Situation.

But how shocking is it for a young Creature,[1] accustomed to Tenderness, and arrived at sufficient Years to know the Value of that Tenderness, to be, all at once, obliged to submit to the insolent and morose Behaviour of a Person, who was an entire Stranger in the Family till Marriage set her at the Head of it!—A Son, indeed, has less to apprehend, because the Manner of his Education renders him less at Home, and consequently not so much exposed to the Insults of a barbarous Step-Mother; yet does he often suffer in the Want of many Things, by the sly Insinuations and Misrepresentations she makes of his most innocent Actions to perhaps a too believing Father: But a poor Girl, who must be continually under the Eye of a Person, invested with full Power over her, resolved to approve of nothing she does, and takes Delight in finding Fault, is in a Condition truly miserable:—Want of proper Encouragement prevents her making the Progress she might do in those Things she is permitted to be instructed in, and then she is reproached with Stupidity, and an Incapacity of learning, and very often, under this Pretence, all future Means of Improvement are denied to her.

Then as to her Dress; that is sure to be not only such as will be least becoming to her, but also such as will soonest wear out, to give the artful Step-Mother an Opportunity of accusing her of ill Housewifry and Slatterness.[2]

---

1. **Creature:** human being.

2. **Slatterness:** slatternly or slovenly behavior.

It is impossible to enumerate the various Stratagems put in Practise to render a young Creature unhappy:—First, she is represented as unworthy of Regard, and ten to one but afterwards made so in reality by her very Nature being perverted by ill Usage.

But this is a Circumstance which, I dare say, Ladies, you cannot but have frequently observed much more than I can pretend to do, though you have not yet thought fit to make any mention of it.—It is not, however, unbecoming your Consideration, as it is so great a Grievance in private Life, and is sometimes attended with the worst Consequences that can possibly happen in Families.

How many young Ladies, meerly to avoid the Severity and Arrogance of their Mother-in- laws,[1] have thrown themselves into the Arms of Men whose Addresses they would otherwise have despised; and afterwards, finding they had but exchanged one Slavery for another, either broke through the Chain by the most unwarrantable Means, or pined themselves almost to Death under the Weight of it!

Others again, who have had a greater Share of Spirit and Resolution, or, perhaps, were so happy as not to be tempted with any Offers of Delivery from their present Thraldom to go into a worse, have thought themselves not obliged to bear any Insults from a Person whom only a blind Partiality had set over them:—These, returning every Affront given them, and combatting the Authority they refuse to acknowledge, have armed the Tongues of all their Kindred, on the Mother's Side at least, with the sharpest Invectives:—The Family has been divided,—at Enmity with each other, and the House become a perfect *Babel.*[2]

I was once an Eye witness of an Example of this kind, where I went to pass the Summer, at the Country Seat of a Gentleman, whose Family, till his second Marriage, was all Harmony and Concord; but

---

1. **Mother-in-laws:** stepmothers.

2. **Babel:** where Noah's descendants, who originally spoke one language, lost the ability to communicate with one another as a punishment for their presumption in trying to build a tower to heaven. Hence, a situation in which there are many competing unintelligible sounds.

soon after became the Scene of Confusion and Distraction, through the Aversion his Wife immediately conceived against his Children, who being pretty well grown up, repaid in kind every Indignity she treated them with;—This, on her complaining of it, highly incensed the Father; he reproved them with the utmost Severity, which yet not satisfying the Pride of his new Choice, she converted her late Endearments into Reproaches, no less severe on him than them.—The young Family had the Good-Will and Affection of all the neighbouring Gentry, who failed not to remonstrate to him the Injustice of the Step-Mother:—Blind as his Passion at first had rendered him, he began at last to be convinced, and fain would have exerted the Power of a Husband to bring her to more Reason; but he soon found she had too much been accustomed to command, to be easily brought to obey: —She turned a kind of Fury,[1]—made loud Complaints to all her Relations, who espousing her Cause against him and his Children, there ensued such a Civil War of Words, that all disinterested Persons, and who loved Peace, avoided the House.—I, for my Part, left it much sooner than I intended, as I found there was no possibility of being barely civil to one Party without incuring the Resentment of the other; and, indeed, being exposed to such Marks of it, as I did not think myself under any Obligation to bear.

I have since heard most dismal Accounts from that Quarter:—The eldest Son, who had a small Estate left him by his Grandmother, independant of his Father, retired to it; and falling into mean Company, was drawn in to marry a Girl very much beneath him, and of no good Character as to her Conduct:—The second, no more able to endure the perpetual Jars[2] at Home than his Brother had been, came to *London,* where he was perswaded to go into the Army, and fell, with many other brave Men, at the fatal Battle at *Fontenoy.*—One of the Daughters threw herself away on a Fellow that belonged to a Company of strolling Players;[3] another married a man of neither Fortune nor Abilities to acquire any; and a third of a Disposition yet more

---

1. **Fury:** avenging spirit.

2. **Jars:** quarrels.

3. **Players:** actors.

gay, indulged herself, by way of Relaxation from the Domestic Persecutions, in going so often to an Assembly[1] held at a neighbouring Town, that she was seduced by a young Nobleman to quit the Country before the Family did so, and come up to *London* with him, where she soon proved with Child; was afterward abandoned by him, and in that dreadful Condition, ashamed and fearful of having any recourse to her Father or Friends, entered herself for Bread into one of those Houses which are the Shops of Beauty,[2] and was let[3] out for Hire to the best Bidder.

So many Misfortunes happening, one on the Back of another, in his Family, has almost broke the Heart of the old Gentleman, and are rendered the more severe to him, as his Wife lays the Fault of them entirely on his having formerly used[4] his Children with too much Lenity,[5] and he is now thoroughly convinced that the Miscarriages[6] they have been guilty of are wholly owing to the Cruelty of her Behaviour, which drove them from his House and Protection.

Dear Ladies, be so good to insert this in your next Publication, and as I am certain you cannot be without a great Number of Instances of the like Nature, if you would please to add some few of them by way of corroborating the Truth of this, and setting forth the ill Effects of using unkindly the Children of a Husband by a former Marriage, I am of Opinion it would be of great Service towards remedying this general Complaint.

I do assure you, I have been instigated to troubling you with the above by no other Motive than my good Wishes for the Preservation of Peace and Unity in Families, and the same will, I doubt not, have an Effect on yourselves, and influence you to draw your Pen in Defence of those who stand in need of such an Advocate against the

---

1. **Assembly:** social gathering for dancing, music, and conversation.
2. **Shops of Beauty:** brothels.
3. **let:** rented.
4. **used:** treated.
5. **Lenity:** gentleness, softness.
6. **Miscarriages:** misdemeanors, misconduct.

Barbarity of Step- Mothers; in which Confidence I take the Liberty to subscribe myself,

> *With the greatest Respect,*
> LADIES,
> *Your most humble, and*
> *Haymarket, Most obedient Servant,*
> *June 16, 1745.* PHILENIA.

P.S. LADIES, The Hardships I have mentioned are still more cruel when exercised on Infants, who are incapable of making any Sort of Defence for themselves; and that Step-Mother who makes an ill Use of her Power over such helpless Innocence, ought, methinks, to be obnoxious to the World, and shun'd like a Serpent, by all those of her own Sex, who are of a different Disposition, till, ashamed of what she has done, she repairs the past by future Kindness:—But I flatter myself you will not leave this Point untouched, and it would be Folly to anticipate any Meaning you are so infinitely more capable of expressing in Terms proper to reach the Soul.—Adieu, therefore, good Ladies, pardon this additional Intrusion, and believe me, as above,

> *Sincerely Yours, &c. &c.*

　　It is impossible to converse, or indeed to live at all in the World, without being sensible[1] of the Truth *Philenia* has advanced; and every one must own,[2] with her, that there cannot be a more melancholy Circumstance than what she so pathetically describes.—Every Tongue is full of the Barbarity of Step-Mothers; nor is there any Act of Cruelty more universally condemned by the World, or which doubtless in more detestable in the Sight of Heaven, than that we sometimes see practised upon Children, by those Women whose Duty it is to nurture and protect them.

　　Yet ought we not to think that all Step-Mothers are bad because many have been so; nor suffer ourselves to be prejudiced by a Name

---

1. **sensible:** aware.

2. **own:** acknowledge.

without farther Examination: I am very certain it is impossible for a Woman of real Sense and Virtue in other Things, to be guilty of a Failure in this:—I do not say she will feel all that Warmth of Affection for her Husband's Children, by another Wife, as she would do for those born of herself; but she will act by them in the same Manner, and if there should be any Deficiency in the Tenderness she has for them, it will be made up with a double Portion of Care over them:— Conscious of the Apprehensions they may be under on her Score, and how liable to Suspicion is the Character she bears, she will be industrious to remove both the one and the other, and behave in such a Manner, as to make them and the World perceive no Difference between their Way of Life under their *natural Mother* or their *Mother-in-law.*

Thus far Prudence and Good-nature will go; but where there is an extraordinary Tenderness, or what we call the Passion of Love for the Husband, it will carry a Woman yet greater Lengths towards his Children; the being *his* will endear them to her, the same as if she had an equal Part in them herself:—She will have all the Fondness as well as the Care of a Mother for them, and do that by Inclination which she is bound to do by Duty.

How happy must a Man think himself when he finds such a Proof of Affection in the Woman he has made Choice of!—Such Instances are, however, very rarely to be met with, and both Husband and Children ought to be content, when a Step-Mother *acts* in every thing like a Mother, and not too scrutinously enquire into her Heart for the *Sentiments* of one.

But there is one Misfortune which frequently destroys that Union which ought to subsist between Persons thus allied;—which is this:— Children, by a former Venture, are too apt to suspect the Sincerity of any good Office they receive from a Mother-in-law; and this unhappy Delicacy being for the most Part heightened by the foolish Pity of their Acquaintance, makes them receive with Coldness all the Testimonies she gives them of her Love. This occasions a Dissatisfaction in her:—If they in their Hearts accuse her of Hypocrisy, her's reproaches them with Ingratitude:—A mutual Discontent grows up on both Sides, which at length discovers itself in piquant Words and little

Sarcasms:—These by frequent Repetitions become sharper and sharper, till they end in an open and avowed Quarrel, and involve the whole Family in Confusion.

Prejudice and Prepossession misconstrues every thing, and while that remains, it is an Impossibility for the best-meant Actions to be well received; and I am of Opinion, that if we strictly examine into the Origin of most of these Family-Dissentions, we shall find them, in reality, derived from no other Source.

Children are apt, on the first mention of their Father's marrying again, to conceive a Hatred for the Person intended for his Wife:— They run over, in their Minds, all the possible Disadvantages she may occasion to them, and then fix[1] themselves in a Belief, that the worst they can imagine will certainly befal them.

The Woman, on the other hand, thinking it natural for them to be displeased with the Power about to be given her over them, assures herself that they are so, concludes all the Respect they treat her with is enforced, and returns it too often either with a haughty Sullenness, or such an Indifference as makes them see they are suspected by her:— Both Parties being thus prepared for Animosity, they no sooner come together than the Flame breaks out. As Doctor *Garth*[2] justly observes,

> Dissentions, like small Streams, at first begun,
> Scarce seen they rise, but gather as they run:
> So Lines that form their Parallel decline,
> More they advance the more they still disjoin.[3]

In fine,[4] these Sort of Conjunctions can never be rendered happy, without all the Parties concerned in them are endued with a greater Share of Good-Sense and Good-Nature than is ordinarily to be found; for if any one of them happens to be repugnant, the Peace of the other

---

1. **fix:** make firm.

2. **Doctor Garth:** Sir Samuel Garth (1661–1719), well-known London physician and poet.

3. **Dissentions . . . disjoin:** Sir Samuel Garth, *The Dispensary* 3. 200–203.

4. **In fine:** in short.

will infallibly be destroyed, and Contention spread itself through the whole Family by Degrees.

For this Reason, I must confess, I never could approve of second Marriages where there are Children by the first, nor think any of the various Pretences made by those who enter into them, of sufficient Weight to overbalance the almost sure Destruction of their Peace of Mind, if not, as is but too frequently the Case, that also of their Fortune and Reputation in the World.

But all the Inconveniences above-recited are infinitely aggravated when the Step-Mother happens to bring a new Race into the World, to claim an equal Share of the Father's Care and Fondness:—All the Kindred of the first, and present Wife then interest themselves in the Cause of those of their own Blood, and are jealous of every thing he does for the others. How equally soever he may behave himself between them, he will still be accused of Partiality by both Parties; and the World will always look on the Children of the Deceased as Objects of Compassion, and condemn every Indulgence he shews to those he has by their Step-Mother as so many Acts of Injustice.

The poor Lady, guilty or not guilty, will yet be treated with more Severity:—She will be loaded with every thing that Scandal can invent, and have so much to sour her Disposition, as if good before, may in Time render her, in reality, what she is said to be.

For my Part, it has ever been a Matter of the greatest Astonishment to me, that any Woman can have Courage enough to venture on becoming a Mother the first Day of her Marriage:—It would be endless to repeat the many Impediments in her Way to Happiness in such a Station, and if she has the good Fortune to surmount them, it ought to be recorded as a Prodigy.

I say the good Fortune, for I think it easy to be proved from every Day's Observation, that the most benign, affable, and disinterested Behaviour on her Part, will not have its due Reward, either with those of the Family to whom she is joined, or from the Character[1] of the World.

---

1. **Character:** characterization.

I should be sorry, however, to find that any thing I have said should be construed into an Intent to vindicate the Barbarity of such Step-Mothers, who, by their ungenerous Treatment of those committed to their Care, draw a general Odium on all Women who are under the same Circumstances.

On the contrary, I think, with *Philenia,* that they deserve the severest Censure;—that there is not any Crime, not excepting those which incur the heaviest Penalty of the Law, can render the guilty Person more hateful both to God and Man, especially when committed on helpless Infancy:—Those who are arrived at sufficient Years to be sensible how little Right a Step-Mother has to use them ill, can, and will, as it is natural, exert themselves, and return the Insults they receive; but for those little dear Innocents whose Smiles would turn even Fury itself into Mildness, who can only testify their Wants by their Cries; when they, I say, are injured, and injured by the Person who now lies in their Father's Bosom, what Words can paint out, as it merits, the Enormity of the Fact!

That some such Step-Mothers there are I am but too well convinced, and to these all Admonitions would be vain:—Those who are neither sensible of the Duties of their Station, nor of what Religion, nay even common Morality exacts from them, and are divested of that Softness and Commiseration which ought to be the Characteristick of Womanhood, will never be moved with any thing that can be urged by an exterior Monitor.

But how much soever a Woman is to be condemned who uses ill the Children of her Predecessor, I cannot help being of Opinion, that she who puts it in the Power of a Man to treat her own with Inhumanity, is yet more so:—There is something, which to me seems shockingly unnatural, in giving up the dear Pledges of a former Tenderness as a kind of Sacrifice to a second Passion; and I am surprized any Woman who has Children, at least such as are unprovided for, and are not entirely out of the Reach of those Injustices it is in the Power of a Step-Father to inflict, can entertain even a Thought of subjecting them in that Manner.

Every one knows a Wife is but the second Person in the Family:—A Husband is the absolute Head of it;—can act in every thing as he pleases, and though it is a great Misfortune to lose either of our Parents while young, and unable to take Care of ourselves, yet is the Danger much greater when the Place of a Father is fill'd up by a Stranger, than it can be under a Mother in-law:—The Reason is obvious;—the one can do of himself, what the other can only accomplish by the Influence she has over her Husband.

I am very well aware that those of my Readers, of both Sexes, who have ventured on a second Marriage, having Children by the first, will think themselves too severely dealt with in what I have advanced on this Head.[1]—The Mirror that sets our Blemishes before our Eyes is seldom pleasing; but if these Remonstrances may be efficacious enough to remind any one Person of his or her Parental Duty, the *Female Spectator* will be absolved for being the Instrument of giving some little Pain to those conscious of having swerved from it.

It would be judging with too much Ill-nature to imagine, that any Parent, who marries a second Time, foresees the bad Consequences that may arise from such a Venture:—It often is the very Reverse, and they are made to believe, that in quitting their State of Widowhood they shall do a greater Service to their Children than they could do by continuing in it.

As many seeming Reasons may contribute to form such an Appearance of a Change for the better in their Condition, as there are different Circumstances, and Characters in the World; therefore, though one may venture to say, that though all Persons who marry twice (having Children) merit Compassion, yet all are not equally to be condemned.

The greatest Prudence is not always sufficient to keep us from being led astray by those Illusions which play before our Eyes, and bar the Prospect of that Path we ought to take; for though, according to *Cowley*,[2]

> 'Tis our own Wisdom moulds our State:
> Our Faults or Virtues make our Fate.[3]

---

1. **on this Head:** under this heading.
2. **Cowley:** Abraham Cowley (1618–1667), poet and essayist.
3. **'Tis our own . . . Fate:** quotation unidentified.

Yet there are Faults which we sometimes are not able to avoid;—
we are driven, as it were, by an irresistible Impulse into Things which
would excite our Wonder to see others guilty of, and perceive not the
Error in ourselves till we feel the Punishment of it.

A truly tender Parent will, however, keep a continual Guard, not
only on the Senses, but also on their very Thoughts:—They will repulse in the Beginning, even the least Prelude to an Overture for a
second Marriage:—They will shut up all the Avenues of the Soul
against those imaginary Advantages may be offered to it:—They will
be blind and deaf to all the Allurements of Birth, Beauty, Wit, or
Fortune, and place their sole Happiness, their sole Glory, in being
constant to the Memory of their first Love, and the dear Remains of
the deceased Partner of their Joys.

If any one should take it into their Heads to disapprove what I have
said, by producing some particular Instances of second Marriages that
have been fortunate, though there were Children by the first, I shall
give only this Reply;—That a Thing being *possible* does not infer that
it is *probable:*—It would be, I think, the highest Madness to assure
ourselves of being blessed meerly because it is not out of the Power
of Fate to make us so:—It is an Opinion rooted in me, and confirmed
by a long and watchful Observation, that there is no State of Life
which in general is more full of Confusion. The Poet says,

There have been fewer Friends on Earth than Kings.[1]

And I will venture to maintain, (with this Proviso, where there are
Children by the first) that there have been fewer *happy second Marriages*
than *Blazing Stars.*

*   *   *

---

1. **There . . . Kings:** quotation unidentified.

FROM BOOK XVII

We are frequently deceived, by a present Hurry of Passion, so far as not to be sensible[1] what passes in our own Hearts:—Nothing is more common than for us to imagine we hate what in reality is most dear to us.—*Sergius* is a very handsome Man, but of so unaccountable and peevish a Disposition, that though he married *Aranthe,* a celebrated Beauty, meerly for Love, she had not been his Wife two Months before he gave her Cause to think herself the most unhappy Woman breathing:—He, on his Side, was no less discontented; all the Passion she long had felt for him, and which was not at all inferior to that which induced him to make Choice of her, could not enable her to support[2] his Treatment:—She returned his ill Humour with Interest;— there was a fatal Parity in their Tempers, which would suffer neither of them to agree to any thing but what was first proposed by themselves:—Both took a Pleasure in Contradiction;—both were equally impatient under it; each thinking the Right of being obliged was solely in themselves, neither of them would condescend to oblige the other: —*Sergius,* as he was the Husband, thought he ought to be obeyed; and *Aranthe* expected the same Complaisance from him as when he was a Lover; and this mutual Disappointment seemed to have extinguished all manner of Tenderness on both Sides.—Not only the World, which saw the Contentions between them, believe they heartily hated each other, but also they themselves imagined so, and wished, with no less Ardency, that there was a Possibility of breaking the Bands which joined them, than they had formerly done to be united in them.

In fine,[3] their Animosities at length arrived to such a Height, that there were no longer any Rules of Decency observed between them, and the ill Life they past together became so notorious, that the Friends[4] on both Sides thought it much better to separate than continue to distract all about them with continual Clamours.

---

1. **sensible:** aware.

2. **support:** endure.

3. **In fine:** in short.

4. **Friends:** relatives.

The Thing was proposed to each apart from the other, and both testifying their Approbation, *Sergius* consented to allow *Aranthe,* who brought[1] but a very small Fortune, an Annuity out of his Estate for her Support;—and she entered on her Part into an Engagement, for the fulfilling of which, one of her Kindred became Surety, that she should contract no Debts in his Name, nor any other way molest him.

Thus they were parted with all the Form that could be, exclusive of a Divorce, which neither of them had any Pretence to sue for.[2]

For a while they seemed highly satisfied with what they had done, and declared in all Company wherever they came, that the Day which separated them afforded a Joy more exquisite, as well as more reasonable, than they felt on that which had joined them.

Each really thought that the being freed from their late disagreeable Situation, was the greatest Blessing that Heaven, as they were circumstanced, could have bestowed upon them; but how little they knew of themselves in this Particular a short Time evinced.

The Rage and the Disgust which both had imagined they had Reason to conceive against each other, being evaporated by mutual Revilings, and Hatred no longer finding any Fuel to support its Fire, sunk, by degrees, into a Calm, which had the Appearance of Indifference, but, in effect, was far from being so:—Their cooler Thoughts enabling them to reflect on all that had passed between them, those Offences which before seemed of such enormous Size, now lost much of their Magnitude, and still decreased as they the more considered the Provocations which excited them.

Both having Leisure to examine into their own Conduct, each found enough in it to condemn, and consequently to excuse that of the other; and Absence fully convinced them of that, which it is hardly probable they would ever have been sensible of had they continued together.

Good Sense, which neither of them was deficient in, now they had Leisure to exert it, having utterly conquered those little peevish Hu-

---

1. **brought:** to the marriage.

2. **Pretence to sue for:** Adultery was at this time the only ground for divorce, which was difficult to obtain and required parliamentary action. "Pretence" means "pretext."

mours and unruly Passions, which had occasion'd their Disagreement, Memory and Recollection brought the Hours of their first Courtship back:—Every tender Pressure,—every soft Concession,—each fond Desire,—each agonizing Fear, which either had experienced, returned to the respective Breast:—*Sergius* would often cry out to himself, "How charming was then *Aranthe!* Why did I urge her once gentle Nature, and by my Harshness become the Destroyer of a Happiness I would have died to purchase!"—"Why," said *Aranthe* sighing, "did I not consider the Worth, the Honour of my Husband's Soul?—Why did I provoke him to renounce that Love he once had for me!"

In a word, the mutual Tenderness they at first had felt for each other still lived in both their Hearts, though it had seemed dead, and recovering the same Strength and Energy as before, made both now doubly wretched in a too late Repentance; since neither knew the other was possessed of adequate Sentiments, and despaired of ever being a second Time able to inspire.—*Sergius* now knew he loved *Aranthe,* but believed himself the Object of her Hate; and *Aranthe* was too sure she doated on *Sergius,* who, she doubted not, thought on her with Contempt and Detestation.

This Opinion, which indeed seemed reasonable enough, prevented all Attempts on either Side for a Reconciliation: On the contrary, they shunned all Places where there was a likelihood of their meeting, and Chance had not yet befriended them so far as to bring them together without their seeking it.

It indeed was just they should have some Time of Penance for the Follies they had been guilty of; but at last the Hour arrived which was to put a final Period to their Anxieties, and render them much more happy, not only than they could ever expect to be, but also than they would have been, had never any Rupture happened between them.

Self-convicted of their Errors, the Reflection how madly they had thrown away all that could give them any Satisfaction, made both of them extremely melancholy.—*Sergius,* to conceal his from the Observation of the World, passed most of his Time in the Country; and when he was in Town pretended Business kept him from going to any of those gay Diversions he had been used to frequent:—*Aranthe,* taking no longer any Pleasure in the Living, grew fond of conversing among the Dead, and went almost every Day into *Westminster-Abbey,* amusing herself with reading the Inscriptions on the Tombs.

Sergius one Day happened to wander into that famous Repositary of the pompous[1] Dead, and before he was aware, came up close to *Aranthe,* without seeing or being seen of her, till they even jostled as they met; so deeply were both involved in Contemplation:—Each started at the unlooked-for Presence of the other, but had not Power to draw back above two or three Paces though (as they have since confessed) both had it in their Thoughts to do it.

"*Aranthe!*" said *Sergius* in the utmost Confusion:—"*Sergius!*" cried *Aranthe* with a faultering Voice:—No more was said on either Side, but their Eyes were fixed intent upon each other's Face, till *Aranthe,* too weak to support the violent Emotions which that Instant overwhelmed her Soul, was ready to faint, and oblig'd to lean against a Pillar of the Church, near which it was her good Fortune to stand:— *Sergius* observed the Condition she was in, and quite dissolved in Tenderness, flew to her and took her in his Arms:—"O, *Aranthe,*" cried he, "is it possible that the Sight of me has this Effect upon you!"—"O, *Sergius,*" answered she, "we once loved each other!"— "How happy was that Time!" resumed he; and would have said something more if the rising Passion had not choaked the Utterance of his Words; but the tender Grasp, with which he still held her enclosed, was sufficient to inform her how much he regretted that Time she mentioned had ever been interrupted.

Aranthe, far from opposing his Embrace, reclined her Head upon his Breast, and wetted it with Tears:—"O, *Aranthe,*" said *Sergius,* as soon as he had Power to speak, "it was no Fault of thine that parted us:"—"Nor of yours," cried she sighing, "I confess myself the sole Aggressor:"—"That is too much," replied he, "for it was I alone that was to blame."

Some Company, who were coming to see the Tombs, appearing at a Distance, obliged him to quit that endearing Posture, and they adjourned to a more retired Part of the Cathedral, and sat down together

---

1. **pompous:** magnificent, splendid.

on a Stone, where each condemning themselves for what had happened, and entirely absolving the other of all Errors, never was a more perfect Reconciliation.

They went together to the House of *Sergius,* and the unexpected Return of *Aranthe* filled all the Servants with Surprize which they were not able to conceal:—The now happy Pair presently observed it, and remembering with Shame, how much the Family[1] had suffered by their Quarrels, doubted not but they were alarmed at the Apprehensions of being again involved in the same Confusion.

To put an End, therefore, to all their Anxieties on this Score,—"Be not uneasy," said *Sergius;* "I knew not the Value of the Treasure I possessed in this Lady till I had lost it, but it shall now be my Endeavour to attone for all my past Inadvertencies, and, by making her perfectly contented, render all about us so."

"Forbear, my Dear," rejoined *Aranthe,* "to lay those Accusations on yourself which are alone my due:—I was too ignorant of my Happiness, as well as of my Duty; but my future Behaviour shall convince you, our Servants, and all who know us, that I now am truly sensible of my Mistakes."

The next Day *Sergius* ordered a fine Collation[2] to be prepared, to which all the Friends[3] on both Sides were invited, to do Honour to this Reconciliation, which he called his second Nuptials; and both him and *Aranthe* repeated over and over to the Company what they before had avowed in the Presence of their Servants, to the great Satisfaction of every one, as well as to themselves.

Each was now indeed too sincerely sensible wherein they had done amiss, to relapse into their former Errors:—They have ever since taken more Pleasure in condescending to whatever they perceive to be the Inclination of each other, than ever they did in opposing it.

Seldom, however, does one meet with a Catastrophe[4] like this; nor can it ever happen but where there is a very great Fund of Love on

---

1. **Family:** household.

2. **Collation:** feast.

3. **Friends:** relatives.

4. **Catastrophe:** conclusion, resolution.

both Sides: For where the Passion is once totally extinguished, it is scarce possible ever to rekindle it, and we say with *Morat*,[1]

> To Flames once past I cannot backward move;
> Call Yesterday again, and I may love.[2]

The Parting, therefore, of Persons who have been once joined in Marriage, has in it something extremely shocking; and, to add to the other Misfortunes it infallibly brings on, is generally attended with the Loss of Reputation on both Sides:—If they behave with the greatest Circumspection, they will still be suspected to have other Engagements;[3] and, as many in those Circumstances are really but too guilty, those most innocent cannot keep themselves from falling under the like Censure, and all their *Virtue* will be looked upon no more than as a *Vice well hid.*

Since then so many Inconveniences are the sure Effects either of living together in a mutual Disaffection, or of separating entirely, how carefully ought we to examine the Principles, Sentiments, and Humour of the Person we think of marrying, before we enter into a State, which there is no Possibility of changing but by Death, or what, to those who have any Share of Prudence and Sense of Honour, must be worse than Death.

Different Opinions in Religion are, indeed, of all others the least capable of Reconciliation: It is not in Nature for two People, who think each other in the wrong in so material a Point, to agree long together, though they should endeavour to do it ever so strenuously.— The strongest Reason and the best Understanding will hardly be able always to guard against the Prejudice of Education, and those Precepts instilled into us in our early Years of Life; and though all who run the same Risque with that unfortunate Pair, whose Story I related in my last, may, by their being less bigotted, not fall into the like Calamities they did, nor even any thing adequate[4] to those *Amonia* laments, yet

---

1. **Morat:** younger son of the emperor in John Dryden's play, *Aureng-zebe* (1675).

2. **To Flames . . . may love:** *Aureng-zebe* 5. 127–28.

3. **Engagements:** sexual connections.

4. **adequate:** equivalent.

is it almost impossible but Words, at some time or other, will be let drop by one of them, which will give Umbrage to the other on this Account, and be the Cause of Heart-burnings, and secret Murmurs, which cannot fail to embitter all the Felicities of their Union, if not dissolve it quite.

But I shall now take my leave of this Subject:—The Enclosure of my Pacquet affords yet one more Letter, which has a Right to be inserted, as it touches on a Foible too common in both Sexes, but more particularly ascribed to those of my own.

To the FEMALE SPECTATOR.
MADAM,

It is a Maxim with me, that whatever is needless is impertinent, and to make you any Compliments on the Laudableness of your Under-taking, or the judicious and agreeable Manner in which you execute it, would be no more than to tell the World it is Day-light when the Sun shines in his full Meridian Splendor:—Every Body is sensible of, and confesses the Merit of your Writings, and I am but one among the Million of your Admirers.

Beside, or I am very much deceived, I see enough into your Soul to know you will be better pleased even with the smallest Hint that may contribute to the Usefulness of your Work, than with any thing that could be said in Commendation of it.

I may, however, acknowledge, that as in a beautiful Face there is some one Feature which more particularly strikes the Eye, so in your late Essay of the Distinction between *good* and *bad Taste,* there is somewhat that affords superior Pleasure and Improvement.—You there, I think, may be said to have outdone yourself, and I cannot help believing that immerged[1] as we are in Folly and Stupidity, what you have advanced in that Piece will have an Effect on many of your Readers.

Were there to be a perfect Rectification of Taste, it would be im-possible for us to err in any one thing; but though that would be to become Angels before our Time, and cannot be attainable while on

---

1. **immerged:** immersed.

this Side the Grave, yet does it behove every one to come as near it as Human Nature will admit.

Your Sex, Madam, whose beautiful Formation renders you half cherubial from your Birth, have it in your Power to appear altogether so with a very little Care: How great a Pity is it then, when, instead of improving those Charms Heaven has so bounteously endowed you with, you disguise, deform, and very often entirely murder them:—Nay, take more Pains to render yourselves disagreeable, than you have occasion to do to become the most compleat Work of the Creation.

The *Female Spectator* has, indeed, remonstrated, that if half the Assiduity which is paid to the *Person* were employed in embellishing the *Mind,* Women might easily vie with us Men in our most valuable Accomplishments; but I am sorry to observe, that there are Ladies, who, tho' they read with Pleasure what they imagine is a Compliment to their Sex, make no manner of Progress towards their own particular deserving it.

I am very far from accusing the Ladies of any vicious Propensities:—On the contrary, I believe them much more free from any thing can be called so, than we in general are. What I mean is, that they are too apt to mistake what is most becoming in them, and by aiming to *please too much,* make themselves incapable of *pleasing at all.*

It would be endless to repeat the various Artifices of the Toilet;[1] nor can I pretend to be perfectly acquainted with them, having never yet been blessed with a Wife:—All I know is from two Sisters, who are yet both unmarried, and I hope will continue so, while they continue to think the sole Glory of a Woman consists in having fine Things said to her, on those Endowments which can never render a reasonable Man happy, and which in Time will bring her into Contempt, even with with the very Fop who pretends to admire her.

But I descend not so low as to take Notice of the Curling-Irons, the False-Locks, the Eyebrow-shapers, the Pearl-Cosmetick,[2] the *Italian* Red,[3] or any of those injudicially called Face-mending Stratagems,

---

1. **Toilet:** dressing table.

2. **Pearl-Cosmetick:** face powder.

3. **Italian Red:** rouge.

or even of the studied Leer, or the forced Languor, of the Eye, nor of the screwed-up Mouth, or strained Pout of the under Lip, nor of a thousand other unnatural Modes and Gestures of the Body, however ridiculous they who practise them may appear; but it is that kind of Affectation in the Manners, which, more than all I have mentioned, deprives them of that Respect they would otherwise command from our Sex.

What I mean, is when they forget themselves so far as to imagine that which was scarce pardonable in Youth is agreeable in Maturity, or even Old Age.

When I see a Girl of Fourteen or Fifteen, always jumping, laughing, patting the Man who talks to her on the Shoulder, or frisking from him, as if frighted at the Sight of a Person of a contrary Sex, I only think she has Skill enough to know the Difference between them, and am not shocked at her Behaviour: When I find one of Five and Twenty playing the same Tricks, I am ashamed and sorry for her:—But when the Gambol continues to Thirty, Forty, and so on, what can be more preposterous!

A Woman may have her Charms in every Stage of Life, provided she knows how to manage them.—Extreme Youth pleases with its Simplicity:—Maturity excites our Love with Elegance of Conversation; and Old Age commands Respect, with its Advice and chearful Gravity.

In a word, the Sex can never be disagreeable but when Discretion is wanting; and when it is, the most beautiful among them can never retain, for any long Space of Time, either the Love or Esteem of a Man of true Understanding.

I was perswaded, by a Friend of mine, to go with him one Day to visit *Lysetta,* a Lady to whom the World gave no very favourable Character:—They said she was a Widow of between thirty and forty Years of Age, had a Face far from Handsome, and was so very fat, that she might pass more for a *Wapping*[1] Landlady than a Person of Condition; yet that she had the Vanity to pretend to Youth, Beauty,

---

1. **Wapping:** a district in the dock section of London populated by members of the working class.

and good Shape, and was, in effect, one of the greatest Coquets[1] of the Age.

Prejudiced with this Idea, I went without imagining myself in any Danger of becoming her Captive; but never was I so much amazed, as when, instead of the giddy, fluttering old Girl I was made to expect, I found myself received in the politest Manner, by a Lady who, though she seemed about the Years I was informed, had nothing about her of the Decays of Time:—Her Features were not indeed the finest turned I had ever seen, but very regular, and had a certain Sweetness and Composure in them which to me appeared amiable:—Neither was her Bulk so disagreeable as had been represented, because she seemed to take no Pains to constrain it, and her Deportment, the whole Time we staid, such as Malice itself could not accuse of any thing unbecoming her Circumstances in the least respect whatever.

In fine, I thought her such as no Man need be ashamed to make the Mistress of his Heart; and though I cannot say I was downright in Love with her, I verily believe that seeing her a few Times more, such as she then was, would have made me so.

I could not help reproaching my Friend for the Report he had made of this Lady, who, I told him, I could find no way answerable to it; to which he replied, that he had said no worse than what was said by all that knew her, but that he confessed he was a little surprized, for he had never before seen her either look or behave so well, and that he could not imagine what had wrought so great a Change in her for the better.

I took little Notice of what he said, as to that Point, not doubting but she had always been the same, though he pretended the contrary: —Eager, however, to be convinced, I some Time after asked him if he would take me with him again to make her a second Visit:—He readily complied with my Request, and told me, that if she always behaved in the Fashion she did when I was there before, he should think her a very conversable[2] Woman.

---

1. **Coquets:** flirts.

2. **conversable:** easy and pleasant in conversation.

We found her at Home, and my Acquaintance sending up his Name, she ran to receive us at the top of the Stair-case:—"O my dear, Sir John," bawled she out (with a Voice as different from that she spoke in when I saw her first as a Quail-Pipe[1] from a Lute) "I despaired of ever seeing you again:—Why I was *A la mort*[2] when you were here last,—half dead with the Vapours,[3] and so hideously grave that I was enough to fright you."

"You have, however, recovered your Spirits I see," replied Sir *John;* giving a Look at me, who was astonished at the Difference in the same Woman, more than I remember to have ever been in my whole Life.

By this Time we were all got into the Dining-room, but, good God, What a Hoyden![4] What Affectation of Youth!—How did she aim to give a Spring sometimes to one Window, sometimes to another:— Her Legs, indeed would have performed their Office well enough, but her unweildy Hips came waddling after, like two Paniers on the Back of a Mule.

As to the Discourse she entertained us with, I will give you a Part in her very Words.—"Sir *John,* you and your Friend shall Squire me to *Ranelagh*[5] to Night;" but on our saying we were engaged at another Place,—"Hang you," said she, "you should not go with me if you would:—I will send for Mr—: No, now I think on it, I'll have my Lord *M*—: What a Fool I am to forget Sir *Thomas*:—Aye, aye, he shall go with me; it will make his Wife go mad, poor Wretch!" Then closed her fine Speech with a "ha! ha! ha!" loud enough to have set all the Dogs in the Neighbourhood a barking.

From this she run into telling us of a Country Squire, that had hanged himself in his own Barn on seeing her take Snuff out of the Parson's Box,[6] then gave us a Detail of a thousand fine Things she had lately bought;—railed against the War which threatened the Pro-

---

1. **Quail-Pipe:** small whistle.

2. **A la mort:** at the point of death.

3. **Vapours:** depression or hypochondria.

4. **Hoyden:** boisterous girl or woman.

5. **Ranelagh:** amusement park in Chelsea, a borough of London.

6. **Country . . . Box:** Presumably the squire hangs himself from despair over her apparent preference of a rival.

hibition of Cambricks;[1]—wished all the *Papists,*[2] except the Queen of *Hungary,* at the *D—vil;* cried up *Sullivan's* singing at *Ranelagh;*[3] said nothing in *Cock's* last Auction[4] was worth a Groat; repeated two half Stanzas of a Song made on a Lady at *Scarborough* Spaw;[5] and amidst this Medley of Incoherencies interspersed so much of her own Affairs, as to let us know that the Banker, who had most of her Fortune in his Hands, had like to have made a Break,[6] and that the News of his being gone off, had put her into that solemn Humour Sir *John* had found her in at his last Visit.

He could not on her relating this help congratulating her, that she received Intelligence early enough to lodge her Money in more safe Hands:—"Aye," cried she, "it was lucky; I should have been obliged otherwise to have taken up with some Fellow of Quality or another in order to support my Equipage:[7]—Ha,—Would not that have been a mortifying Thing?"—Then turned her Eyes into a half Squint.

But, Madam, had you seen the thousand different Gestures, with which this Inundation of Impertinencies were accompanied, you would, doubtless, have blushed for her; sometimes she would throw herself back in her Chair, and extend her Arms, with two Fists at the end of them, each of which was big enough to fell an Ox; sometimes again they were contracted, and the Shoulders which, indeed Nature had placed pretty near the Ears, were thrust up to meet them quite, in what, I suppose she thought, a genteel Shrug; but the Motion I perceived she most delighted herself in, was displaying her plump and well-jointed Fingers, in continually putting in Order the Curls that

---

1. **Cambricks:** fine white linen fabric imported from Belgium, one of Britain's enemies in the War of the Austrian Succession.

2. **Papists:** Catholics.

3. **Sullivan's singing at Ranelagh:** Daniel Sullivan (d. 1764) was a popular Irish counter-tenor. Musical performances comprised an important part of the entertainment at Ranelagh, a fashionable London amusement park.

4. **Cock's last Auction:** Public auctions of furniture, china, and other household appurtenances were a fashionable form of recreation.

5. **Scarborough Spaw:** a resort in northern England.

6. **made a Break:** gone bankrupt.

7. **Equipage:** carriage and the servants who attend it.

hung down in her Neck, and making them perform the Office of a Comb, in straitening or buckling[1] the Hair at Pleasure.

In fine, such a Lump of Affectation and Impertinence, as she now appeared to me, quite wearied my Patience, and made me pluck Sir *John* by the Sleeve two or three Times, in order to engage him to shorten his Visit, before I could prevail on him to do it;—which, he afterwards owned, was Malice in him, and that he kept me there in order to revenge the little Credit I had given to his Character of this Lady, who, indeed, I was now convinced, merited much more than he had said, or that, in effect, was in the Power of any Words to describe.

From her House we went to a Tavern, where he was extremely merry on me for the Disappointment I had received, and rallied me in a Manner which, I must confess, I truly deserved, for imagining I could discover more of a Woman by being one Hour in her Company, than he, who was a Man that knew the Town as well as myself, could be able to do in an Acquaintance of some Years Duration.

We fell, however, by degrees, into more serious Conversation, and could not forbear lamenting the unhappy Propensity this Woman had to Gaiety, and the little Care she took in distinguishing between what would render her amiable or ridiculous, as it was really in her Power to make herself either the one or the other.

He owned with me, that she was perfectly desirable the first Time I saw her; and I acquiesced as readily with him, that she was on my second Visit the very reverse.

The Misfortunes, which it seems she was apprehensive of falling into, had taken off all that Fierceness and wanton Roll of her Eyes, which I had just now seen in them, and which appears so disagreeable, and given a certain Composedness to all her Features at that Time, which was infinitely becoming; but those Fears once removed, she relapsed again into her former Follies, and became as despicable as ever.

There are, doubtless, good *Female Spectator,* more Women, beside the Lady I have been speaking of, who must be made *miserable* before

---

1. **buckling:** curling.

they can made *happy,* and be brought to think themselves *disagreeable* before they can be thought *handsome* by others.

You may possibly have heard of a young Creature of the Town, known more by the Name of the *Kitten* than by that she derived from her Father:—She was young, extremely slender, and had small and fine proportioned Limbs, and the little Antiques[1] with which she diverted her Customers were becoming enough in one of her Age and Circumstances; but when a Woman of Fortune and Condition, though she be even young and well made, condescends to play the *Kitten,* and ape one of those Wretches, who behave in that Manner only for Bread,[2] they must have more Complaisance[3] for the Sex than I pretend to, that can treat them with any degree of Respect.

How doubly absurd is it, then, when People of an advanced Age and gross[4] Body, give themselves those childish and affected Airs, thereby losing all the Praise of what they *are,* by endeavouring to excite Praise for what they *are not,* nor can ever be!

Had the Lady I have mentioned been in reality deprived of all that we call the Goods of Fortune, she would certainly have been estimable for those which are peculiarly the Gifts of Heaven and Nature, a reasonable Soul and a graceful Person:—While under those Anxieties, she doubtless had the Power of Thought and Reflection, and the too volatile Part of her Constitution being abated, made her look and act as she ought; but the Misfortune was, that these Apprehensions were no sooner removed than she relapsed again into her former Self, and became as giddy, as vain, and as truly contemptible as ever.

But when I sat down to write to the *Female Spectator,* it was not my Intention to dwell on any individual Person; and I know not how I have been led into a Prolixity, on the mention of this Lady, which I am far from being pleased with myself; but as the Picture I have drawn for her may bear a Resemblance of many others, it may go some way towards answering the End I have in View.

---

1. **Antiques:** antics.
2. **Wretches . . . Bread:** whores.
3. **Complaisance:** courtesy.
4. **gross:** stout.

Which is, Madam, to prevail with the Ladies to be as well satisfied with themselves at Fifty as at Fifteen; to convince them that there are Charms, which are not in the Power of the old Gentleman with the Scythe and Hourglass[1] to mow down; and that it is entirely their own Fault if they do not find him in reality more a Friend than an Enemy, since, for one Perfection he deprives them of, they may, if they please, receive a thousand from him.

I am always very much concerned when I see a Lady dejected and miserable in her Mind at the first Approach of a Wrinkle in her Face; and more industrious to conceal the smallest Crease about her Eyes, than she would be to heal the largest Scar in her Reputation: But I am yet more troubled, when conscious of her Age, and the Decays it has brought on, she thinks to hide it from the World by assuming the Airs, Dress, and Behaviour of Youth, and affects to be at Forty what, if she has common Sense, she would have been ashamed to be at Five and Twenty.

Yet this is so reigning a Foible among the Fair, that were they all to wear Vizard- Masks,[2] there would be no Possibility of distinguishing the Beldam[3] from her great Grand-daughter. For my part, I expect nothing more than that, in a little Time, the old Ladies will wear Hanging-sleeve Coats, and Bibs and Aprons, as well as little round-eared Caps and Curls in their Necks.[4]

But as all this proceeds meerly from the Terror of being thought old, I despair of seeing the Ladies act in a more reasonable Manner, till they can reconcile themselves to submit to those different Stages which Nature has allotted, and which they may equally be agreeable in, if they take proper Methods to be so.

I know no Doctrine which would more become you to inculcate into your Fair Readers, nor that would preserve them so effectually against falling into Errors of all kinds: In expectation therefore that

---

1. **old . . . Hourglass:** the personified figure of Time.

2. **Vizard-Masks:** disguising masks.

3. **Beldam:** old woman.

4. **Hanging-sleeve . . . Necks:** the costumes of very young children.

you will vouchsafe this a Place in your next Lucubrations,[1] and add something of your own on the Occasion, I remain, with the most perfect Veneration,

MADAM,

Your most humble, and
Most devoted Servant,

J.M.

It is to be wished, indeed, that the Character this Gentleman has given us, under the Name of *Lysetta* might not be ascribed to a great Number of our Sex; and that the Impartiality the *Female Spectator* has promised to observe, would have permitted us to have stifled, under the Pretence of its being a personal Reflection, a Piece of Satire, which we fear will be looked upon as but too general.

What is there, after all, that is so terrible in being known to have more Years over our Heads than we had twenty Years ago?—Is not the Desire of a long Life natural to us all?—Is it not the Wish of our best Friends, and the Compliment of our politest Acquaintance?—Why then do we murmur at attaining it?—endeavour as much as we can to conceal we have arrived at it, and run back into all the Follies of Youth to cheat the Discernment of those that see us, and give the Lie to Time?

How vain also is the Attempt!—*December*'s Frost might as easily assume the Livery[2] of gaudy *May*, as Fifty look like Fifteen: Yet both Seasons have their Pleasures, and as we provide warm Clothes and Fire to defend us against the Blasts of Winter, so, if we take Care betimes[3] to lay in Stock of Knowledge and Experience, Age will find sufficient in itself to compensate for the Loss of Youth.

The Joys afforded by the one are fleeting, hurrying and sensual; that of the other permanent, solid, and spiritual, says a celebrated *French* Author.[4] And the Truth of his Words I am confident will be confessed

---

1. **Lucubrations:** studies.

2. **Livery:** costume.

3. **betimes:** speedily.

4. **Author:** unidentified.

by all those who, having indulged the Gaieties of Youth, know how to improve the Advantages of riper Years.

The Affectation of appearing younger than we are is certainly the most gross of any we can be guilty of, because it includes in it all those different kinds, which, singly practised, render a Person ridiculous.

But I think our Correspondent in the Character of *Lysetta,* whether real or feigned, has summed up every thing that can be said on this Head, in regard to our Sex, except that *Envy,* which an absurd Ambition of being thought less old than we are, naturally excites in us against all who are younger than ourselves in effect, or that appear so by having more delicate Complexions, or Features, less subject to the Decays of Time.

I must confess I have been an Eye-witness of Instances, which, if I had not been so, would have been incredible to me on the Report of others; wherein this Passion has been carried to such a Height in some Women, as to make them hate even their own Daughters only for being possessessed of that Bloom which themselves had lost.

How cruelly then may we expect such Women will deal with all those of their Acquaintance, less advanced in years!—How many thousand Faults will blackening Envy find or invent to destroy, as much as possible, all the good Opinion the World has of them!—Detraction will lessen the Merit of the most conspicuous Virtues: Defamation misrepresent those of a more doubtful kind, and Malice magnify every little Error to a mountainous Extent.

It is hard to say whether the Folly or the Wickedness of such a Disposition is most predominant:—Sure nothing can be more absurd than to imagine ourselves enriched by our Neighbour's Poverty; nor can any thing be more Fiend-like than to take Pleasure in the Ruin of others.

There requires but a common Share of Understanding, methinks, to shew us, that it is not by the Merit of others, but our own, that we are judged:—Shall I be the more virtuous because another is discovered to be vicious? Will the Defects of other People's Features render my own more lovely?—Wild Imagination! how can any one impose thus upon themselves!

If every one, instead of endeavouring to expose all the Faults of her Acquaintance, and depreciating all their Perfections, would endeavour to regulate her own Conduct and Behaviour, I dare answer,[1] let her Face be never so plain, or her Years ever so much advanced, she will suffer nothing from the World on the Score of her Age and Ugliness: —Every Imperfection of the Person will be swallowed up and lost in observing the Beauty of the Mind and Manners, and all who know will both esteem and love her.—As we used to say of a celebrated Actress, who, with all the Disadvantages of a bad Voice, and worse Person, became the greatest Ornament of the Stage, that "She played away her Face and Voice:" So, whoever acts up to the Character Heaven has placed her in Life, and does not deviate from Reason and from Nature, will have such Attractions in her Behaviour as will entirely take off the Attention from any personal Blemishes or Decays, be they ever so great.

O, that it were possible for my whole Sex to be convinced of this great Truth, and it then never would be said there was an old or an ugly Woman in the World. Our Conversation would be always sought with Eagerness, and no Man would quit our Company but with a Desire to re-enjoy it.

This Reflection is sufficient, one would imagine, to make every Woman take those Methods of pleasing which alone have the Power of doing it:—The Desire of rendering ourselves agreeable to Society is no less laudable than it is natural; but no Woman of Understanding, would wish to receive Applause for those very Things which, she is conscious in herself, rather deserve Censure.—It is only the thoughtless Coquet who is delighted with Praises, which, she may easily perceive, if not too much blinded by her Vanity, are as far from being meant by the Person who speaks them as they are from being just.

But, as ridiculous as little kinds of Affectation are in our Sex, they are yet less supportable in the other.—When a Man, with all the Advantages of a liberal Education, a general Conversation in the World, and who ought to know that his least Merit is a handsome Face, shall tremble at a Pimple, and be alarmed at the very Thought

---

1. **answer:** affirm.

of a Wrinkle, how strangely does he degenerate from the Intent of Nature!

Yet, that such may be seen every Day sauntering in the Park, at Court, at all our great Coffee-Houses,[1] and in most public Places, I believe none of my Readers need be told.

It has often made me smile to myself to hear some Men, who in other Things have a great Share of Understanding, yet are so weak in this, that whenever any Transaction is mentioned that happened in the Time of their Youth, they artfully pretend not to be perfectly acquainted with it, and ask a thousand impertinent Questions, that the Company may believe they had not then attained to a sufficient Age to be capable of remembering any thing concerning it, and think themselves happy if they can, by this Stratagem, drop a few of the Years they have passed over.

In fine, though long Life is a Blessing desired and prayed for by every one, we shall find few willing to acknowledge the Attainment of it; and of all the Gifts that Heaven bestows, this is the least boasted of, though Mr. *Waller*[2] so justly says of the last Years of a long Life,

> The Soul with nobler Resolutions deck'd,
> The Body stooping does herself erect.
> Clouds of Affections from our younger Eyes,
> Conceal that Happiness which Age descries.
> The Mind's dark Cottage, batter'd and decay'd,
> Lets in new Light thro' Chinks that Time has made.
> Stronger by Weakness wiser Men become,
> As they draw near to their eternal Home.[3]

But, however we may reason on this Occasion, that there is somewhat of an Irksomeness to growing old, which few People are wise enough to keep themselves from feeling, and fewer yet have Prudence

---

1. **Coffee-Houses:** where men gathered to talk, read newspapers, and drink coffee.

2. **Mr. Waller:** Edmund Waller (1606–1687), lyric poet.

3. **The Soul . . . Home**: Edmund Waller, "Of the Last Verses in the Book," ll. 3–4, 11–16 (slightly altered).

enough to conceal.—Whether this is implanted in Nature or not, I will not take upon me to determine absolutely; but may venture to give it as my Opinion, that, to what Source soever owing, it may be conquered by a due Reflection on the many solid Advantages which Age bestows, and is wholly our own Fault if we do not enjoy.

I might add too, that the Necessity of submitting to the Laws of Nature should make us endeavour to be easy under a Change which we know all must suffer, if not cut short by an untimely Fate; but Resignation is not a Virtue every one can practise, those only who have the Seeds of true Piety in their Hearts are capable of it, and such stand in no need of Admonitions:—As to others, all that can be urged may be summed up in this short Maxim.

Not to affect the Manners of Youth, and then old Age will neither be burthensome to ourselves, nor displeasing to those about us.

*   *   *

FROM BOOK XIX

As to an Examination into the Nature of those Things which are in the Compass of our Comprehension, and of which we daily receive the Benefit, I think no one can be excused who neglects an Opportunity of making it.

This is, in effect, the most useful Branch of that Study which the worthy *Philo-Naturæ* . . . [1]so strenuously recommends to all Degrees of People in Proportion to their Circumstances and Avocations; for it is not to be supposed that either he, or any who wishes the Good of Mankind, would advise a Person to pass that Time in inspecting the Root of a Vegetable, or the Organs of an Insect, which should be employed in getting Bread for his Family.

Such Speculations, it is certain, best befit those of the great World, or at least such as have Fortunes independent of Business, who have

---

1. **Philo-Naturæ:** whose letter appears in Book XV of the *Female Spectator.*

a Sufficiency of Leisure, and will hardly find a more beneficial Way of filling up their vacant Moments.

Yet, though these happy few have it in their Power to make a greater Progress in learning the Beauties of Nature, there are scarce any who may not find some little Time, if they would be perswaded to lay hold of it, in tracing the Outlines, as one may call them, of her Perfections: —The meanest Artificer allows himself some Holidays in the Year;— he walks the Fields, perhaps has a little Garden himself, and in the smallest Spot of Earth may find enough to afford him some Degree of Improvement and Pleasure.

The Country Dame need not neglect her Dairy, yet be acquainted with the Properties of those Simples[1] which grow about her very Door: —The Beasts themselves instruct us in the Virtues of many Vegetables, by their making Choice of the most proper in any Disease, to which their Kind is incident;[2] and *Hipocrates*[3] himself owed the Discovery of the wonderful Effects of an *Elk*'s Hoof, by perceiving that Creature, when sick, always held his Foot for a long Time close to his Ear.

As most of our worst Disorders spring originally from the Head, this great Philosopher and Physician presently imagined, that the Foot of this Animal might not only be of Service in any Obstruction of the capillary Vessels, but also in others, which in fact are occasioned by the same Cause; and as he knew it could not be of any Prejudice[4] to the Persons on whom he made the Experiment, tried it with a Success, which all succeeding Ages have had Reason to bless him for.

Many other great and valuable Secrets have been found out by an Observation of the Animal Creation:—For Example; the Virtues of the Plantain might, perhaps, have to this Day been unknown to us, had we not seen the Toad, when bloated and almost bursting with its own Venom, crawl to that healing Plant, and immediately regain Ease and recover Vigour.

---

1. **Simples:** medicinal herbs.

2. **incident:** susceptible.

3. **Hipocrates:** Hippocrates (ca. 460–ca. 370 B.C.), a Greek physician considered the father of medicine.

4. **Prejudice:** harm.

But these are Reflections which the gay Part of my Sex, whether old or young, will tell me are not worth their Notice: If they find themselves any way disordered, they have their Physicians to apply to; and have no Occasion to trouble themselves with any thing relating to Medicine.

This I readily grant to be true, as to the higher Class; but for the more inferior Part of Womankind, I think the World will allow that it would be no Diminution to them to know a little of these Matters.

But, however incongruous it may be with the Character of a fine Lady to busy herself about Vegetables, used either in the Kitchen or Distillery,[1] it cannot be so to have a little Concern for those that so much gratify her Smell and Sight;—those which she wears in her own Bosom, and in her Hair, and are her most becoming Ornaments, even amidst the Blaze of Jewels, and the glowing Gold of the richest and best fancied[2] Brocade or Embroidery.

Flowers, and those aromatic Greens with which our Gardens are covered, may be justly called the Regale[3] that Nature presents us with; and sure, of all those innumerable Pleasures she bestows upon us, none can be said to be more exquisite.

The Jonquil, the Rose, the Jessamin, the Orange-Flower, the Auricula, and a thousand others, ravish two of our Senses with their Beauty, and the Fragrancy of their Odour.—Scarce any Person so stupid as not to be charm'd with them.—They are, I think, the universal Taste;—we not only see them in Gardens, but preserved in Pots and *China* Basons in Ladies Chambers; and, when deprived of the Originals by the cold Blasts of Winter, we have them copied in Painting, Japanning,[4] and in Embroidery.

How then can we forbear visiting our Green-Houses sometimes, and observing the Production, the gradual Growth, and the Preservation of those Plants and Flowers, which afford us so much Pleasure!

---

1. **Distillery:** an establishment for making liqueurs or other alcoholic beverages.
2. **fancied:** styled.
3. **Regale:** complimentary present.
4. **Japanning:** decorative lacquer work.

Why should our Gardeners be wiser than ourselves?—Why should we put it in their Power to deceive us, and not be able to detect either their Negligence or Want of Skill in the cultivating a Produce we are so proud of, when brought to Perfection?

What can be more beautiful than an Assemblage of various Flowers, all growing on the same Tree; and, while we delight our Eyes with beholding it, would not our Pleasure be still more elegant in knowing how it comes to pass?

Would it not furnish agreeable Matter for Conversation, both to inform those less knowing than ourselves, and to be able to argue with those as pretend to[1] greater Skill, on the wonderful Progress of the distinct[2] Sap which feeds every different Flower, proceeding from so many Arms of the same Stem?

Among all the Occupations of Gardening, there is none so astonishing as Grafting; and we never can too much admire the Force of that Genial[3] Juice, which, in a small Sprig taken off one Tree and grafted into another, still retains its primitive[4] Nature; and even tho' twenty various Kinds should be inoculated in the same Manner, all of them would preserve their native Purity without the least Confusion, or blending with each other:—So that the Flowers, sent forth by these grafted Scions,[5] no way differ in Colour, Scent, or Figure, from those of their own Species, which grow naturally from one Stem.

Methinks it is a most becoming Amusement, to Persons of my Sex, to sit by while the Gardener is performing so curious[6] an Operation, nor in the least beneath the Dignity of the greatest Lady to assist his Work:—It requires the utmost Gentleness and Delicacy to cut the little Scion exactly to tally with the Cleft made in the Bark of that Stock in which it is intended to be grafted; and also afterwards to close

---

1. **pretend to:** claim.
2. **distinct:** individual.
3. **Genial:** conducive to growth.
4. **primitive:** original.
5. **Scions:** grafts.
6. **curious:** careful, delicate.

and swathe up the Trunk, that no chilling Air or Rain may penetrate, and prevent the Union of the one with the other, till an outer Bark shall grow over and cement them.

I know that there are a great many People who have an Aversion to grafting Scions of different Natures, such as the Apple and the Plumb, the Medlar[1] and the Grape, or the Rose and the Tulip, the Carnation and the Lilly, on the same Tree:—They cry it is an Absurdity,—something of a monstrous Appearance, instead of a pleasing Wonder; and that every different Fruit and Flower looks most agreeable, when supplied from its own Root, as ordained by Nature; any Innovation, or Breaking-in upon, of which, are of all things to be avoided.

But these Objections seem to me as proceeding only from a sour cinical Disposition:—The Trial how far *Art* may be reconciled with *Nature,* is, in my Opinion, perfectly harmless; affords an innocent Amusement; sharpens Invention; and, as to its offending the Eye instead of pleasing it, one may as well say that a Nosegay, or a Bough-Pot,[2] does so, which are always composed of as many different Flowers as the Season will permit.

I wonder People, who talk in this manner, do not condemn Nature herself for bestowing on the Orange-Tree Fruit in its Maturity, quite green, and even in Blossom, all at the same Time; or explode[3] the Plant, and turn it out of their Collections and Gardens, as an Absurdity and a monstrous Appearance.

Or rather, why do these Enemies to Art, in this Point, allow of it in others? Why do they form so many Parterres,[4] Arcades, Trees cut in such Variety of Figures, and Shrubs rounded in such a manner by the Gardener's Scissars, as not to seem they ever had been the Productions of Nature?—Why do they not suffer every thing to grow in that Luxuriancy and Wildness as we see in Forrests, and uncultivated Desarts?—The Order and Regularity of a Garden seems, methinks,

---

1. **Medlar:** a small fruit similar to a crabapple.

2. **Bough-Pot:** flowerpot or bouquet.

3. **explode:** banish.

4. **Parterres:** ornamental formal gardens with paths between the beds.

not to be correspondent with their Notions.—Away with all Terrasses, Cascades, Palisades,[1] Bowers, and those other Arrangements, which make the Difference between the Ground possessed by a Nobleman and that of a Peasant:—Let every thing grow as the Soil and Air directs, and savage Simplicity be the only Beauties of a Rural Scene.

But, supposing we put all this out of the Question, and confine our Speculations intirely to what is merely natural, we shall then never want[2] a vast Sufficiency to entertain us:—The Circulation of that Fluid in Vegetables, which, with a regular and uninterrupted Motion, like the Blood in our own Veins, fills every little Twig with Spiral[3] Vigour, if considered with the least Attention, must excite in us a pleasing Astonishment.

To behold the Progress of a Flower from its Infant Bud, then gradually increasing, and at last opening its long-hid Beauties to our View, and charming us at the same Time with its refreshing Odour, is certainly well worthy our Observation.

But the *Senses,* methinks, ought not to ingross so glorious a Benefit: The *Mind* should certainly come in for a much greater Part, and explore those Wonders in them, which cannot fail of ravishing[4] all its Faculties.

Every Tree of the Forrest, and Herbage of the Field, as well as those nobler Plants which gain Admission into our Gardens, are all crown'd with Flowers, more or less beautiful. These Flowers produce a Seed which perpetuate the Species.—Some Seeds are inclosed in Fruits, others in Chives,[5] which, when the Flower is withered, and in a manner dying, scatter themselves into the Earth, and the next Year revive again in Plants.

To content ourselves with tasting the Relish of those luscious Fruits, which, from Month to Month, are successively presented to us;—to smell the Fragrancy of some Flowers, and to look upon the variegated

---

1. **Palisades:** rows of trees or shrubs forming hedges.

2. **want:** lack.

3. **Spiral:** a botanical term for a kind of vessel in plants.

4. **ravishing:** enchanting, captivating.

5. **Chives:** stamens and pistils.

Beauty of others, is beneath the Dignity of a rational Being. If we go no farther than this, the Birds of the Air, the Beasts of the Field, and even every creeping Insect, enjoys the Charms of Nature in as great Perfection as we do.

Perhaps too, even the meanest Reptile may out-rival us in this Point; for, I think, it is agreed on by the Learned, that the Animal Creation in general have a quicker and more poignant Sensation than is bestowed upon us.

It is in our Reason, and the Power of contemplating on the Blessings we receive, that the chief Happiness of possessing them consists.

It is *that,* more than his outward Form, which distinguishes Man from the rest of sublunary Beings: It is *that* which crowns him Lord of all; and if he wilfully degrades himself, and puts himself on a Level with his Subjects, he is unworthy of the Honour conferred upon his Species, and ungrateful to the Divine Bestower.

Can it be supposed that the Almighty Wisdom gave such a Profusion of Varieties merely to feast the *Senses* of Mankind!—*Senses,* which all the different Religions in the known World, the *Mahometan* not excepted, agree to teach us that we ought not to indulge to an Excess: —No, certainly;—no one who permits himself but a Moment's Consideration, will venture to affirm it.—They were, without all Question, destined for a much nobler and exalted Purpose, to convey Instruction through the Canal[1] of Pleasure;—to inspire us with the highest Ideas Human Nature is capable of conceiving, of that Divine Bounty to which we are indebted for them; to harmonize the Soul, and at the same Time to enable it to pour forth a due Tribute of Praise and Adoration.

How strangely incongruous is it, then, with Reason, or even with Common Sense, to imagine, that all those vast Bodies we see glitter in the Firmament, and even those we do not see, are made wholly to serve us, yet think nothing of those about us, the Benefits of which we have the sole Sovereignty; since we alone enjoy the Whole of what all other Creatures share but their different Parts.

---

1. **Canal:** channel.

Man, if he surveys and reflects as he ought to do, on the innumerable Advantages, Conveniencies, and Pleasures, which, wherever he steps or casts his Eyes, incessantly surround him, has sufficient in this World to gratify his Pride, without arrogantly pretending a Right over those he knows nothing of.

Of this we are certain, that the Good Things of this World are given us for our Use and Contemplation, and to us alone, as alone capable of enjoying them truly.

But I shall now take my Leave of this Subject, which having carried me somewhat beyond my Intentions, I find it impossible to present the Ladies with the *Mirror for true Beauty* till next Month, when they may be certain of its being inserted; with also some other very agreeable Pieces lately come to hand, calculated for general Service, but more Particularly for those of my own Sex.

End of the NINETEENTH BOOK.

*   *   *

FROM BOOK XX

Our Sex are, for the greatest Part, so very fond of seeing their own Pictures, that I am afraid many of them will be disobliged with the *Female Spectator* for having till now withheld from them the *Mirror for True Beauty,* which *Philocletes* was so good as to prepare for them.

But, notwithstanding Curiosity is a Passion impatient for Gratification, I would advise my Sex to moderate it as much as they can, and take the Warning *Philocletes* himself gives in his Letter, which served as a Cover to the Present he makes them, and is equally worthy the Attention of all who wish to find an agreeable Representation of themselves, in a Glass,[1] which has nothing of the Properties of those they have been accustomed to look in.

---

1. **Glass:** mirror.

To the FEMALE SPECTATOR.
MADAM,

I shall make no manner of Apology for troubling you with the inclosed, because it is evident by all those Writings with which you have obliged the Public, that you have the Honour and Welfare of your Sex too much at Heart to be offended with anych thing that can possibly tend to their Profit, Pleasure, or Emolument.

To lend, therefore, what helping Hand I can to so laudable an Endeavour, I take the Liberty to present them, by your Canal,[1] with *A Mirror for true Beauty,* which to those who are really possessed of so inestimable a Blessing, cannot but afford an adequate Satisfaction.

But, as I would be sorry to give Pain to any, even of those least deserving Respect, I would have all who are conscious of any secret Blemish, beware how they look into it, lest, instead of meeting with an agreeable Object, they should see something which should make them start back with Horror and Amazement.

It is not a Set of fine turned Features, a Complexion for Whiteness out-dazling the new fallen Snow, or Cheeks of a more beautiful Tincture than the Damask Rose:—It is not the Coral Lip, or Eyes that equal the Stars in Brightness, that can assure the curious Fair she will find herself in this Mirror such as she appears in others.

All these, and every other unspeakable Grace on which the Sex most pride themselves, are insufficient to compleat the *true Beauty,* which it is absolutely necessary to be possessed of, in order to find *here* such a Reflection as those who consult it would desire.

Nothing is in fact *true Beauty,* but what is universally allowed to be such;—what is every Man's Taste, and enforces Love and Admiration from all who behold it:—Now *Beauty,* taken in the common Acceptation of the Word, never can be so, because there are almost as many different Opinions concerning the Requisites for that Character, as there are different Fancies to be charmed by it.

---

1. **Canal:** channel.

Our famous *English Pindar,*[1] than whom no Man that ever lived was a greater Admirer of it, discovers, however, with the most admirable Propriety and Justice, the Impossibility of fixing[2] a Standard for deciding what is, and what is not Beauty.

> Beauty, thou wild fantastick Ape,
> Which dost in every Country change thy Shape;
> Here black, there brown, here tawney and there white:
> Who hast no certain What nor Where,
> But variest still, and dost thyself declare
> Inconstant, as thy She-Professors are.[3]

Dryden also has two excellent Lines to the same Purpose, in his Poem of *Palamon* and *Arcite.*

> The Cause of Love can never be assign'd,
> 'Tis in no Face but in the Lover's Mind.[4]

They must therefore be possessed of that kind of Beauty which hits every Inclination, who can view themselves in this Mirror with any Satisfaction.

Yet let not those least flattered by the World be afraid of looking into it, perhaps they will find Charms they have never before considered the Value of; and though they will not be vain on the Discovery, an innate Pleasure, which no Words can represent, will be the Consequence of it.

Let not then Small Pox, Sickness, Old Age, or any other of those Infirmities the Sex stand in so much fear of, deter any one from seeing her Resemblance in the Mirror I now set before them; for I am very well assured, that those who expect to find the fewest Perfections in themselves, will, on looking seriously into it, confess the Picture truly

---

1. **English Pindar:** Abraham Cowley (1618–1667), poet who adapted the form of the Greek Pindaric ode to English verse.

2. **fixing:** setting.

3. **Beauty . . . She-Professors are:** Abraham Cowley, "Beauty," ll. 1–3, 7–10.

4. **The Cause . . . Mind:** quotation unidentified.

amiable; and be easily reconciled to Nature, for having bestowed on them Graces, infinitely superior to any she may have happened to deny them, be the Deficiency ever so glaring, or may have rendered them never so contemptible in the Eyes of the ill-judging.

My Mirror has also this peculiar Property:—It is not like other Glasses daubed on one Side with Quicksilver,[1] but clear, transparent as Innocence and Truth:—It not only shews the Person who looks into it herself, such as she is in reality; but displays impartially every Charm or Imperfection to those who stand on the other Side, and even at a very great Distance from her.

Even in an Age when the Fair Sex seem to study nothing so much as to destroy that *true Beauty* they received from the Hands of their all beneficient Creator, I hope there will be found among the Number of your Readers some who may fearless appear before this all betraying Glass:—At least I might depend upon it, could I but as easily assure myself, that what the *Female Spectator* has taken the Pains to remonstrate[2] to them, had had its due Weight.

But be that as it may, it is the Duty of all those who wish well to the most lovely Part of the Creation, to neglect nothing that may add to their Charms.

It is on this Occasion, Madam, I am proud to enter into your Labours, and am, with the most unfeigned Respect, and Veneration,

Yours, and your worthy Companions,
Very much devoted,
Sept. 16, 1745,   *and faithful Servant,*
Cavendish-square.   PHILOCLETES.

A Mirror for True Beauty

Most humbly presented to those, who, on due Examination of themselves, think proper to look into it, by their

Most humble Servant and sincere Admirer,
PHILOCLETES.

---

1. **Quicksilver:** mercury; used as a backing for mirrors.
2. **remonstrate:** demonstrate.

Approach, ye charming few!—ye happy! Select whose interior
Beauty shines through your outward Form, adding new Graces to what
Nature gave; approach and see your lovely Portraitures faithfully displayed:—Behold Perfections in yourselves which is not in the Power
of the Painter's Art to copy, nor the most passionate and eloquent of
your Lovers to describe.

And first, ye spotless Virgins, who having never known a married
State, are equally ignorant of all tumultuous Desires, all Impatience
for entering into it:—You, who consider the Difference of Sexes no
farther than to take Care to behave in such a Manner, as not to
encourage any Presumption in the one, or provoke the Malice of the
other:—You, who despise the gay Fopperies of the Times, and find it
sufficient to appear once at each Place of present Resort,[1] to be able
to shun them all for ever after:—You, who free from Pride, Affectation, Vanity and Ill-nature, divide your Hours between Acts of Duty
and innocent Recreation,—fearless draw near, and behold the angelic
Sweetness that dwells on every Feature;—see how the unblemished
Mind shines through the Eyes, diffusing Chearfulness to all around,
and making a kind of Heaven wherever you come.

Next in *true Beauty,* ye chaste Wives draw near!—You, whose pure
Hearts never entertained one wandering Wish:—You, whose Inclinations, in all Respects in Life, have still[2] gone Hand in Hand, if not
prevented[3] the Will of him on whom Heaven has bestowed you:[4]—
You, to whom all Mankind, besides him you have sworn to love, are
but so many Pictures:—You, whose Œconomy and prudential Care
enables you to appear so as to make your Fortune seem double to
what it is, yet whose Hospitality renders all easy who come near you:—
You, who know how to repay the Endearments of the most tender
Husband with ample Interest; and you, in whom the greatest Provocations of an ill and cruel one cannot excite even the most distant
Thought of injuring his Interest, Honour, or Reputation:—You, who

---

1. **of present Resort:** to which (fashionable) people at present go.
2. **still:** always.
3. **prevented:** anticipated.
4. **him . . . you:** your husband.

either by your Wisdom, and reserved Behaviour, have avoided every thing that can be called Temptation; or by your firm Adherence to Virtue, have known how to testify a decent Abhorrence of them, in all Circumstances and in all Events:—Ye, glorious Patterns of Connubial Fidelity, may approach and view the awful[1] Dignity that sits enthroned upon your Brows, and sheds a Lustre over all your Persons, at once commanding Love from all good Men, and Admiration even from the worst.

Last, but not least in Fame, ye venerable Tribe of widowed Matrons! You, who have past with Honour your two first Stages of Life, and support the third with a becoming Fortitude and Patience, behold in me your graceful Aspects:—You, over whose unvariable Affection Death has no Power:—You, in whose faithful Hearts your Husband still survives: You, who continue wedded to the Memory of your first Love, and fly all second Offers, though accompanied with Titles, Wealth, and every gilded Prospect, so enchanting to the less constant of your Sex:—You, whose happy Offspring feel not a Father's Loss in the rich Blessings of maternal Care and doubled Tenderness:—You, whose Example, and whose sage Advice preserves the Innocent, and reclaims the Guilty:—You, whose *candid Praises* give new Strength to *Virtue,* and whose *mild Reproofs* make *Vice* abhorrent of itself:—You, who know how to temper Gravity with Chearfulness, and to dress all, even the strictest *Duties* of a *Woman* and a *Christian* in the Garb of *Pleasure:*—You, who answer[2] the Character the wisest of Men gives of a virtuous Woman, *That her own Works shall praise her in the Gates:*[3] That Praise will not only be yours, but you will see yourselves in this Mirror, and be seen by others through it with Charms which will well compensate for those which either you have been denied by Nature, or which Time may have deprived you of: There will be something of an unspeakable Majesty, whether you look, or speak, or move, creating Esteem in every Beholder's Heart; and you, and those of the

---

1. **awful:** awe-inspiring.

2. **answer:** act in conformity with.

3. **That . . . Gates:** Prov. 31:31.

preceding Classes, will appear such as our admirable *Milton* describes the Mother of Mankind, while in her State of Innocence:

> Grace was in all her Steps, Heav'n in her Eyes!
> In all her Motions Dignity and Love.[1]

These are the *true Beauties* which alone can see themselves with any Pleasure; for as for those who have forsaken *Wisdom* and followed *Folly,* who have devoted themselves to midnight Masquerades,[2] immoderate Gaming,[3] forgot the Duties of their Sex and Place, and are in any respect the Reverse of such as I have described, they must not be angry with the Mirror, if it presents them with Deformities they little expected:—If, instead of blooming Graces, and an attractive Air in their Complexion and Features, they find Wrinkles which no *Cosmetick* or *Italian Fucus*[4] can fill up:—Dimness and sinking in the Eyes, Contortions in the whole Face, such as no studied Arts can rectify, or bring back to their primitive Harmony:—Let, therefore, those fly hence, lest the too terrifying Representation should drive them into Frenzy; at least let them take this Caution, to approach with Fearfulness, and by Degrees: Even that may serve to render their Blemishes less hideous than they would seem on a Surprize, and as they grow more sensible[5] of themselves, those Blemishes would doubtless, if not quite wear off, become not so conspicuous as before.

We think ourselves obliged, in the Name of the whole Sex, to thank *Philoctetes,* for the amiable Pictures he has given us of what is *true*

---

1. **Grace . . . Love:** *Paradise Lost* 8. 488–89.

2. **Masquerades:** masked balls, popular at this time and considered dangerous because they allowed the mixing of social classes as well as various kinds of sexual threat.

3. **Gaming:** gambling.

4. **Fucus:** a wash or coloring for the face.

5. **sensible:** aware.

Beauty in Womankind, through the three material[1] Circumstances in Life, and in which, indeed, all the others also are included.

For this Reason it is utterly impossible to add any thing on a Subject, which in the most brief and concise Manner he has given the fullest Idea of, and which to expatiate upon, would be not only needless, but instead of giving any Lustre, would rather serve to take from that it has received from his more masterly Genius, and render it more languid, and consequently less effectual.

But, methinks, I hear some of our modish fine Ladies cry out,—"What does the Man mean?—Does he think the Qualifications he sets down would get any of us one more Lover in our Train?—Would they not rather render us the Jest of all the pretty Fellows[2] in Town?"—Others again, of a yet somewhat more ferocious Disposition, will say, "That if a Woman must answer in every Point to the Character he gives of *true Beauty,* there would be no such Thing to be found among the Sex."

As to the first, it would be altogether in vain to make them any Answer, since it would doubtless be treated with the same Contempt as the Mirror itself; but as to the others, I would beg them to reflect, that it is in the Power of every Woman to be possessed of that *true Beauty* which *Philoctetes* has delineated, and it is only the Libertine Part of the other Sex who ought to make a Question of it.

It is true, that all have not an equal Share of the Perfections of the *Mind,* any more than of the *Body,* but all may endeavour to improve those they have; and that very Attempt would make them appear not altogether deformed, even in *Philoclete*'s Mirror.

But I have already, in a former *Spectator,*[3] taken Notice, that if we took but half the Care of embellishing our intellectual Part as we do of setting off our Persons, both would appear to much more Advantage.

Whether any Remonstrances of mine, or others who are Well-wishers to the Sex, have been able to work the Effect they aimed at,

---

1. **material:** important.

2. **pretty Fellows:** fine fellows, fops.

3. **in a former Spectator:** in *The Female Spectator,* Bk. X.

is uncertain; we ought not, however, to give over,[1] because a Moment may bring about what whole Ages in vain have toiled for; and sometimes a slight Word, which perhaps when spoken was unheeded, has afterwards recoiled upon the Memory, and made an Impression on the Mind beyond what the most elaborate Treatises had done.

While therefore I am convinced within myself, that what I am doing is not only intended, but also may possibly make any of my Readers either better or wiser, I shall easily absolve myself for being less entertaining than many of them may desire or expect from me.

It has, notwithstanding, been hithero the Care of the *Female Spectator* to mingle Pleasure with Instruction, and we are far from discontinuing the same Measures, though it must be confessed we have of late pursued Subjects of a more serious Nature, than those with which we at first set out.

*   *   *

FROM BOOK XXI

Among the various kinds of Errors into which Human Nature is liable to fall, there are some, which People of a true Understanding are perfectly sensible[2] of in themselves, yet either wanting[3] a Strength of Resolution to break through what by long Custom is become habitual, or by being of too indolent a Temper to endeavour an Alteration, still persist to act in Contradiction to the Dictates of even their own Reason and Judgment.

What we call Prejudice, or Prepossession, is certainly that which stands foremost in the Rank of Frailties:—It is the great Ring-Leader of almost all the Mistakes we are guilty of, whether in the Sentiments of our Hearts, or the Conduct of our Actions.

---

1. **give over:** stop.
2. **sensible:** aware.
3. **wanting:** lacking.

As Milk is the first Aliment[1] of the Body, so Prejudice is the first Thing given to the Mind to feed upon:—No sooner does the Thinking Faculty begin to shew itself, than Prejudice mingles with it, and spoils its Operations.—Whatever we are then either taught, or happen of ourselves to like or dislike, we, for the most part, continue to like or dislike to our Life's End; so difficult is it to eradicate in Age that Tendency we have inbibed in Youth.

It is this fatal Propensity which binds, as it were, our Reason in Chains, and will not suffer it to look Abroad,[2] or exert any of its Powers:—Hence are our Conceptions bounded; our Notions meanly[3] narrow;—our Ideas, for the most part, unjust; and our Judgement shamefully led astray.

The brightest Rays of Truth in vain shine out upon us, when Prejudice has shut our Eyes against it:—We are rendered by it wholly incapable of examining any thing, and take all upon Trust that it presents to us.

This not only makes us liable to be guilty of Injustice, Ill-nature, and Ill-manners to others, but also insensible[4] of what is owing to ourselves: We run with all our Might from a real and substantial Good, and court a Phantom, a Name, a Nothing:—We mistake Infamy for Renown, and Ruin for Advantage:—In fine,[5] wherever a strong Prejudice prevails, all is sure to go amiss.

What I would be understood to mean by the Word *Prejudice,* is not that Liking or Disliking, which naturally arises on the Sight of any new Object presented to us.—As for Example, one may happen to fall into the Company of two Persons equally deserving, and equally Strangers to us, and with neither of whom we either have or expect to have the least Concern; yet shall we have, in spite of us, and without being able to give any Reason for it, greater good Wishes for the one than the other.—But this is occasioned by that Simpathy and Antip-

---

1. **Aliment:** nourishment.
2. **Abroad:** outside itself.
3. **meanly:** debasedly.
4. **insensible:** unaware.
5. **In fine:** in short.

athy, which, I think it is very plain, Nature has implanted in all created Beings whatsoever.

This, therefore, is what we call Fancy, and far different from that Prejudice I am speaking of, and which, indeed, enters chiefly through the Ears:—When our Notions of Persons and Things, which of ourselves we know nothing of, are guided, and our Approbation or Disapprobation of them excited meerly by what we are told of them, and which afterwards we can never be convinced is unjust, and persevere in an Opinion, which no Proofs of Merit, or Demerit, can change; then it is that we may be said to be governed by that settled Prepossession so dangerous to the World, and to our own Characters, Interest, and Happiness; for the other is light, volatile, and of little Consequence.

A very learned Author calls this unhappy Impulse "The Jaundice of the Mind,"[1] and I think there cannot be a more just Comparison; for, as the Poet says,

> As all seems yellow to the jaundic'd Eye,[2]

So one may truly add,

> All takes from Prejudice's Taint its Dye.

Could we once divest ourselves of the Prepossessions we have received,—forget all the Stories we have been told, and examine all Things with the unbiassed Eye of Reason, how widely different from what they at present seem, would most of them be found!

I am very sensible, that this is a Task extremely difficult, because the greatest Mistake of all that Prejudice makes us guilty of is, that of mistaking that Enemy to Reason for Reason:—We look on its Dictates as the Dictates of Truth, and think we should sin against both *Reason*

---

1. **The Jaundice of the Mind:** Alexander Pennecuik, "Stream from Helicon" (1720), l. 420, actually uses the phrase to describe conscience.

2. **As all . . . Eye:** Alexander Pope, *An Essay on Criticism*, l. 561.

and *Truth* if we were not strenuous in adhering to what we imagine is right.

We are all of us too apt to imagine we know ourselves, when, in fact, there is nothing in the whole World to which we are greater Strangers:—Hard as it is to be perfectly acquainted with the Heart of a Person we converse with, we can yet form by his Actions, his Word, or even his Looks, a more true Judgment of it than of our own.

And how, indeed, should it be otherwise! Prejudice begets Passion, and Passion infallibly blinds our Eyes, and shuts our Ears against every thing that offers to contradict it.

That Passion especially which is excited this way, is infinitely of the worst Sort, because all others, be they never so headstrong and tenacious for a Time, will at length grow cool, and by Degrees subside; but Prejudice keeps the Fire of Obstinancy eternally alive, and still finding fresh Fewel for its Support, renders it rather more strong, than any way diminished, or less fierce by Age.

Yet, blind as we are to this Error in ourselves, how quick-sighted are we to discover, and how ready to laugh at it in other People! Applauding our own Strength of Reason, and vain of a superior Sense of Things, a Person who is prejudiced, though he should happen to be on the Side of Truth, is the perpetual Subject of our Ridicule; and often it proves, that he who thinks himself most free from it, is in reality, more guilty than the very Man he condemns for it.

To be plain, the World is wholly governed by Prejudice, and I think it scarce possible to find any one Person, whose better Judgement is not in a more or less degree, perverted by it.

How vain then, and impertinent, will some of my Readers say are any Annimadversions on it! Why any Pains taken to decry and rail against an Emotion, which is inherent to our Nature, and therefore not to be avoided!

To which I beg Leave to answer, that it is only inherent to our Nature, as Custom, which, indeed, is second Nature, has made it so; but not born with us, nor are we subjected to it by any Laws of Fatality.

It is only to the first Impressions the Soul receives, that those indelible Marks of Partiality I have mentioned, and which we see every where, are entirely owing: The unhappy Tendency, is not, therefore, properly speaking, *our own,* but infused into us by *others;* and though, notwithstanding it afterwards becomes so powerful as to put into Subjection all those nobler Faculties, which are, indeed, the Gift of Heaven, yet is it still but the *Depravity* of Human Nature, not Nature itself.

Parents, who are possessed with a strong Opinion of any thing themselves, are sure to instil it into the Minds of their Children, and so render Prejudice hereditary: Whereas, if the young Mind were left to itself, Reason would have room to operate;—we should examine before we judged, and not condemn, or applaud, but as the Cause deserved.

Whoever is entrusted with the Care of Youth, as Parents are by *Nature,* and Governors,[1] Tutors, and Preceptors by *Commission* from them, should, methinks, endeavour rather to calm than excite any violent Emotions in their Pupils:—They should convince them that nothing but *Virtue* was truly worthy of an Ardency of Love or Ambition, and that *Vice* alone ought to be held in Abhorrence.

This would be a laudable Prejudice!—A Prejudice which would go Hand in Hand with Reason, and secure to us that Peace and Happipiness which all other Prejudices are sure to destroy.

What sad Effects have not many Kingdoms experienced by the hereditary Prejudice between two powerful Families; who have hated each other meerly because their Forefathers did so? As for Example; the *Guelphs* and *Gibelines*[2] of Italy;—the *Marius* and *Metelli*[3] of old *Rome*; and the Barons Wars[4] of *England.*

National Prejudices are yet more dangerous, and indeed much more ridiculous:—What can be a greater Absurdity than for one whole People to hate another, only for being born in a different Climate, and

---

1. **Governors:** tutors.

2. **Guelphs and Gibelines:** late-medieval political opponents whose conflict originated in Germany in the twelfth century but continued in Italy for almost three centuries more.

3. **Marius and Metelli:** Roman families of the first century B.C. whose struggle against one another continued for two generations.

4. **Barons Wars:** (1263–67) a struggle between King Henry III and a group of barons headed by Simon de Montfort over how much power should be accorded to the nobility.

which they are taught to believe, inspires them with some Sentiments or Inclinations oppugnant[1] to their own, though, perhaps, all this may be without Foundation.

Whoever, therefore, by his Example or Precept, labours to keep these foolish Animosities alive, in my Opinion deserves little Thanks from the World, either for his Wit, or Good-Will to Mankind: And as wise and great a Man as the late Earl of *Rochester*[2] was in other Things, in this he testified a Partiality unworthy of his Character.

In his Poem on *Nothing*, which, it must be confessed, is a Masterpiece, and wants[3] nothing but Justice in some of the Allusions to be esteemed, not only the best he ever wrote, but even superior to all others of the Kind, he has these Lines:

> *French* Truth, *Dutch* Prowess, *British* Policy,
> *Hibernian*[4] Learning, *Scotch* Civility,
> *Spaniards* Dispatch, *Danes* Wit, are chiefly seen in thee.[5]

Now these Reflections, however just as to the general, are certainly the contrary as to Particulars:—I never can believe, that meerly being born in this or that Kingdom has any Influence over the Disposition of the Natives:—It is certainly a very narrow way of judging.—In spite of the little Faith there is to be given to *French* Promises, or even Treaties, I cannot be so uncharitable as to believe there is no sincere and honest People among that populous Nation; much less can I be brought to think, that every Man born in *Holland* would prefer Ease to Glory:—The *British* Policy may indeed sometimes have been said to nod, but then it has awaked, and roused itself again, to the Confusion of all those who thought to take Advantage of its Supineness.— As to the Learning of *Hibernia,* many of her Sons have given evident

---

1. **oppugnant:** antagonistic.

2. **Earl of Rochester:** John Wilmot, second Earl of Rochester (1647–1680). An accomplished poet, he was noted as a libertine and rarely considered "wise and great."

3. **wants:** lacks, needs.

4. **Hibernian:** Irish.

5. **French . . . in thee:** "Upon Nothing," ll. 46–48.

Proofs that Blunders are not entailed upon that Nation any more than others.—Then as to the *Scots,* none can dispute a Possibility of their equalling in Politeness any Nation in the World, who remembers the late Dukes of *Argyle* and *Hamilton,* or has the Honour of knowing his Grace of *Buccleugh,* the Earl of *Marchmont,*[1] and many others now living Ornaments of their Country, and the Delight of all who see them, and who have no need of being named to be distinguished.— The *Spaniards,* it must be confessed, move slow for the most part, yet there have been Instances of their being more alert.—Nor ought we to suppose the *Danes* are all insipid Clods, because our Libraries give no Proofs to the contrary.

But were what this noble Lord has here advanced strictly true, yet as it helps to preserve National Prejudice, and consequently National Ridicule, he had much better have employed that prodigious Talent he was a Master of another way.

Many others beside his Lordship have, with less Abilities, and more Ill-nature, done all in their Power to divide *England* against itself, and render County and County obnoxious to each other.—The Stage, which was designed the School of Morality, and by mingling Pleasure with Improvement, to harmonize the Mind, and inspire Amity among Men, has, in some Theatrical Representations, been most shamefully prostituted to Ends, the very reverse, and not only Gentlemen who happen to live out of *London,* but the most eminent Citizens who live within the Sound of *Bow* Bell,[2] made a public Ridicule: A Country 'Squire and an Alderman[3] of *London* are sure to be the Characters to excite Laughter:—Our modern Writers are more polite than *Shakespear, Johnson,*[4] and their Cotemporaries,[5] who always made the Fools in their Plays Court-Parasites, or at least Jesters, but the City and Country are now the only Places from which a Buffoon is to be picked.

---

1. **Dukes . . . Marchmont:** members of the English and Scottish nobility distinguished for their military and/or diplomatic and political service to their countries.

2. **Bow Bell:** in the church of St. Mary-le-Bow in mid-London. It is a tradition that only a person born within the sound of this bell is a true Londoner.

3. **Alderman:** chief officer of a London ward.

4. **Johnson:** Ben Jonson (1572–1637), dramatist and lyric poet.

5. **Cotemporaries:** contemporaries.

The Sarcasms vented here and elsewhere have often a Poignancy in them, which cannot but be resented by those who have Understanding enough to perceive when they are affronted, and sometimes occasion Heart-burnings[1] against those who encourage, and seem to be pleased with the Ridicule; which are no way agreeable to that Cordiality and Good-will which ought to subsist between every Community of a Nation, in order to render the Whole a truly happy People.

All this, and innumerable other Ills, are the Effects of that Prejudice I mean; but I was led into a Reflection on it by a late Instance, which, though in private Life, deserves the Attention of the Public, as it may be a Warning against instilling into Youth Principles which are not to be erased in Maturity.

A Gentleman, who had acquired a considerable Fortune in the Mercantile Way,[2] left at his Decease a Son of about twelve Years of Age, and a Daughter of five: As the Mother was dead some Time before, the one was continued at *Westminster* School, by the Persons appointed for his Guardians, and the other committed to the Care of a Sister of her Mother's.

This good Lady was extremely fond of her young Charge, and, as she grew up, neglected nothing that might render her perfectly accomplished:—The Means allowed her for Improvement were not thrown away; she had a very good Capacity, and took such Pleasure in learning whatever she was taught, that the Progress she made was infinitely beyond the Expectations of those appointed for her Instructors.

To add to this, her Person[3] was very lovely; Nature had bestowed on her a thousand Charms, and without being what one may call an exquisite Beauty, there was something in her yet more agreeable, and more formed to attract, than we often find in those who are accounted so.

Being such as I have described, it is not to be wondered at that there were many who thought her worthy of their serious Addresses; but though she began early to have Admirers, she seemed utterly in-

---

1. **Heart-burnings:** distress.

2. **in the Mercantile Way:** by activity as a merchant.

3. **Person:** personal appearance.

sensible of any tender Emotions, and all the fine Things said, and wrote to her, had no other Effect than to give her Diversion.

Her Brother, after having perfected himself in every thing that was thought necessary for his Education at Home, was sent Abroad to make himself acquainted with the Customs and Manners of other Countries; and after having passed some Time in *France,* and seen all *Italy,* returned a very accomplished and compleat Gentleman.

Sabina, for so I shall call this young Lady, was but between the Years of nineteen and twenty when he came back to *England:*—As they had not seen each other for above[1] four Years, each found so many new Embellishments in the other, as rendered both extremely satisfied; few Brothers and Sisters ever loved with a more sincere Affection, or would have gone greater Lengths to oblige each other.

They were always proud of being seen together,—in the *Mall,*[2] or at any Place of public Resort, they were constant Companions:—They had been one Night at the Opera, when, as he was seeing her safe Home, as was always his Custom, he said laughing to her, "I believe, Sister, you have made a Conquest to Night;—I perceived a certain Friend of mine in the Pit,[3] who seemed more engrossed by you than any thing on the Stage."—"I should be sorry," answered she, in the same gay Tone, "that any Friend of yours should have so bad a Taste as to let any thing draw off his Attention from those delightful Sounds we have been hearing."

"O," resumed he, "Musick is an Incentive to Love, and as he did not hear that of your Voice, he might not lose what issued from the *Orchestra,* by having his Eyes fixed upon your Charms, which they really were so strongly, during the whole Entertainment, that I am sure you must have taken Notice of it yourself, if you would confess the Truth."

"It is so common," said she, "for those in the Pit to stare into the Boxes, that I should have found nothing particular in what you tell

---

1. **above:** more than.

2. **Mall:** fashionable promenade in St. James's Park.

3. **Pit:** the part of the theater auditorium that is on the floor (as opposed to balconies and boxes).

me, had I really observed it, which I assure you, without any Affectation, I did not."

On this he rallied[1] her a little on pretending to be absolutely free from the Vanity, which the Men will have it is so inherent to our Sex, that none of us are without some Share; which she returned, with equal Pleasantry, on the Foibles of the other;[2] and this Kind of Chitchat brought them to her Door, where he took Leave of her, being engaged to sup with some Gentlemen at a Tavern; and she went in, and it is likely thought no more of what had passed between them.

It is possible also, that the young Gentleman himself had not been much in earnest in what he said, but if he was not at that Time, he certainly was very much so afterward.

The Friend he had mentioned to his Sister happened to be one of the Company with whom he had engaged that Night.—He was a Gentleman of fine Parts[3] and Education, had a very graceful Person, and was in Possession of a large Estate in the Principality of *Wales,* of which he was a Native, and descended from an antient and worthy Family.

This Gentleman, whose real Name I beg leave to conceal under that of *Luellin,* was, in effect, very much charmed with *Sabina,* and not knowing who she was, told her Brother he was an extreme happy Man, to have the Pleasure of entertaining in so free a Manner, as he perceived he did, the finest Woman in the World.

To which the other replied in Terms which made him know the young Person he had so good an Opinion of was his Sister; and what he said being confirmed by another of the Company, who was also at the Opera, and had seen *Sabina* before, *Luellin* resumed that Gaiety which was natural to him, but had been a little interupted, while he knew not but in the Person of an intimate Friend he might find an Impediment to those Desires, which young as they were had already made a very great Progress in his Heart.

---

1. **rallied:** teased.

2. **the other:** the other sex.

3. **Parts:** intellectual qualities.

He made no farther Discovery[1] of them that Night, however, but early the next Morning went in search of the Brother of his Adorable; and having found him, after a very short Prelude acquainted him, that the Business he came upon was Love; that though he had seen his charming Sister but once, he had for her all the Passion a Man could be possessed of:—That his Life would henceforward be a Burthen to him, if not blessed with the Hopes of passing it with her; and concluded with conjuring him by all their Friendship to introduce him to her, if her Heart was not already engaged, and to favour his Pretensions with all the Interest Nearness of Blood gave him in her.

The Proposal was too advantageous for *Sabina* not to make her Brother highly satisfied with it, and he told her Lover with the same Frankness as he had declared himself, that nothing in the World that he then knew of would be capable of affording him so perfect a Joy as to see a Union between two Persons so dear to him.

He also assured him, that he had several Times talked to his Sister on the Subject of Marriage, and she had always answered him in such a Manner, as knowing her Sincerity, and the Confidence she had in him, made him positive she had not yet entertained any Thoughts of it, or given any Man the least room to flatter himself she preferred him above others.

To this he added, that he would go directly to her Lodgings, and prepare her to receive the Honour of a Visit from him that very Afternoon.

Luellin embraced, and thanked him in Terms which testified the Fervency of his Passion, and after having, according to the Custom of Lovers, a thousand Times over renewed his Entreaties that he would be zealous in his Cause, and appointed the Place where he should meet about the Hour of Tea-drinking, took his Leave with a Heart full of the most flattering Ideas of a speedy Success in his Desires.

The Brother of *Sabina,* on the other hand, had never undertaken an Office more pleasing to him; and not doubting but the Affair would be easily accomplished, as there was not the least Exception could be made, either as to the Family, Fortune, Character, or Personal Accomplishments of *Luellin,* gave himself not much Trouble to furnish himself pre-

---

1. **Discovery:** revelation.

viously with Arguments to convince her of what he imagined she would have Sense enough to distinguish without the Help of Perswasion.

In this Opinion he went to her Apartment, where finding her at Breakfast in a loose Deshabille,[1] "I am glad," said he, "I am come before you are dressed, for I expect you will equip yourself in the most becoming Manner you can, in order to rivet more strongly those Charms you have already thrown over a Heart I take upon me to recommend to your Acceptance."

She looked earnestly at him as he finished these Words, and finding a Mixture of Seriousness and Gaiety in his Countenance, knew not well how to understand the Meaning of what he said, or in what Manner to answer, but after a short Pause, "You are either in a very merry Humour this Morning," replied she, "and talk in this fashion meerly to divert yourself, or else you want to prove that Vanity in me of which last Night you accused our whole Sex:—If it be the former, I shall be ready to join in any thing that gives you Pleasure, but if the latter, must assure you, I shall never think that Heart worthy of my Acceptance that is to be gained or preserved by outward Shew."

"Perfectly well judged indeed, my dear Sister," replied he; "but I expected no less from you, and spoke as I did only to give you an Opportunity of testifying that good Sense, which can never fail both of engaging and making happy whoever you desire to make so.—I hope also," continued he, growing yet more grave, "it will so direct your Choice as to establish a lasting Felicity for yourself."

After she had answered this Compliment in Terms suitable to the Occasion, he told her, he thought it was now Time to think on Marriage, and that the Person he should introduce that Afternoon, had all the Qualifications that a Woman could wish to find in a Partner for Life.—He proceeded to inform her, that he had begun an Acquaintance with him in *Italy,* that they had lived in the greatest Intimacy ever since, "Not a Secret in either of our Hearts," said he, "but what each communicated to the other:—I must therefore be allowed to be a competent Judge of his Principles, Humour, Fortune, and every

---

1. **Deshabille:** a negligent style; e.g., a dressing gown.

thing belonging to him, and can venture to assure you all are such as merit the Love and Esteem of as many as have the Pleasure of knowing him."

Such a Character[1] from the Mouth which she knew was incapable of deceiving her, rendered her more serious than she would otherwise have been at a Proposal of this Nature, and she seemed to relish it with as much Satisfaction as was becoming of her, or could be hoped for from a young Lady of her strict Modesty.

In fine, the Brother had all the Reason in the World to believe his Negotiation would be crowned with the Success he wished, and that he had inspired her with a Prepossession in Favour of this new Lover, which wanted nothing but the Sight of him to be ripened into Passion.

It is probable indeed his Conjectures would not have deceived him, had he not unhappily destroyed all he had been doing, by mentioning the Name and Country of the Person he recommended; an Error he could not be aware of, as he was wholly ignorant of that Weakness which his Sister had the Misfortune to be guilty of.

That Aunt with whom she had been educated from her most tender Years, had, I know not on what Account, a strong Hatred to every one that came out of *Wales,* which she was continually testifying, in speaking of that whole People in a most contemptible, opprobrious, and even scurrilous Terms; by this Means *Sabina* imbibed a Prejudice against them, which would not suffer[2] her to think there could possibly be any such Thing as Merit among them; and she no sooner heard her Brother say he was of that Country, than all her late[3] Sweetness of Behaviour was converted into Sourness and Disdain, and she cried out in Tone full of Scorn and Derision—"Heavens! Is it a *Welch* Man of whom you have been saying all these fine Things?"

The Brother was strangely surprized, as well he might, at a Turn so sudden, and which he was so little able to comprehend; but she soon unravelled the Mistery, by railing,[4] in the same Manner she had been

---

1. **Character:** characterization.
2. **suffer:** allow.
3. **late:** recent.
4. **railing:** scolding.

accustomed to hear her Aunt do, against that Country, and all the Natives of it.

It was in vain he represented to her the Injustice of having an Aversion to the People of any particular Country;—in vain he recited many Examples of great and worthy Persons who were born even in Climates where they could least have been expected, or that he endeavoured with all his Might to convince her, that *Wales* had many Things to boast of beyond any other Part of his Majesty's Dominions:—The Prejudice was fixed and inexorably rooted in her Heart, nor could any thing he alledged make the least Change in her Sentiments.

"Well, Sister," said he at last, "since I find my Arguments have so little Weight with you, I shall leave you to be convinced by your own Judgement, which I am very certain will direct you better when once you are acquainted with *Luellin,* whom notwithstanding all your Prejudice I shall bring this Afternoon, and insist on your receiving him as my Friend at least."

"Since you will oblige me to see him," answered she, "Decency compels me to treat him with Civility, if you had less Regard for him; but this you may expect, nor ought to take it ill of me, that if he makes any Declaration to me of the Kind you mention, I shall give him such a Reply as will put a Stop to any future Thoughts of me, and convince him that I am determined, whatever be my Fate, never to wear a Leek[1] in my Bosom."

It is utterly impossible to describe how much the young Gentleman was astonished and troubled to perceive so obstinate a Folly had Dominion over a Sister, whose Understanding till now he had a high Idea of:—He doubted not, however, but the Sight of *Luellin,* who is deservedly accounted one of the most handsome and best bred Men of the Age, would have the same Influence over her, as it had on all others who conversed with him.

He therefore offered no more in Opposition to her Humour, but flattering himself with the Pleasure he should afterwards have in rallying her on the Change in her Sentiments, took his Leave, with thank-

---

1. **Leek:** the national emblem of Wales.

ing her in an ironical Way, though gravely, for the Consideration she testified to have for him, in resolving to use[1] a *Welch* Man well because he had a Value for him.

The full Belief he had that an Acquaintance with *Luellin* would make her of a quite different Way of thinking, and entirely extirpate that ridiculous Prejudice which had been instilled into her against all of his Country, prevented him from acquainting *Luellin* with any thing that had passed between them on that Score, and indeed gave him rather Hopes of Success than the contrary; a Thing he afterwards very much repented of: But as he was deceived himself by a too good an Opinion of his Sister's Understanding and Penetration, he could not be blamed for deceiving his Friend.

He only told him, that in case he found *Sabina* at the second Sight of her worthy of those tender Inclinations the first had inspired him with, he thought it would not be proper for him, as she was of a Temper extremely reserved, to make any Declaration of his Sentiments on that Head, till by a Repetition of his Visit they should become better acquainted.

This seemed so reasonable, that, all impatient as the Lover was, he could not but approve of it, especially as the other assured him, that in the mean Time he would labour for his Interest.

It is certain, that the Brother of *Sabina* advised him to proceed in this Manner, as he thought it would be the most effectual way of succeeding in his Wishes, because as he found the Aversion she had conceived against all those of that Country *Luellin* was, he imagined, it must be some little Time before it could wear off, or even in case she should be convinced of her Error at first Sight of him, she would then be ashamed to confess it, and rather chuse to do a Violence to her own Heart, than suffer it to be said she could so easily pass from one Extreme to another.

What he thought on this Score was truly Nature, People do not care to acknowledge they have been to blame, and when they have appeared very tenacious in any Point, sometimes are apt to persist in it after their Reason gives the Lye to their Tongue.

---

1. **use:** treat.

He therefore acted for his Friend in the most prudent Manner imaginable; but, alas! what Wisdom is sufficient to combat against Prejudice! *Sabina* could not but confess her Lover was a very handsome and accomplished Person, yet the Thoughts of his being *Welsh,* prevented any good Quality she found in him from making an Impression in her Mind in favour of his Hopes.

She performed her Promise to her Brother, indeed, and received him with Civility; but her Behaviour was so distant, and all she said accompanied with such a gloomy Reserve, as might easily shew any one, who was the least acquainted with her Temper, how little she was pleased with his Company.

Luellin, however, was not unhappy enough to discover it; and imputing that extraordinary Shyness he could not help observing in her merely to her Modesty, proposed to her Brother several Parties of Pleasure for them there, but she absolutely declined making one in any of them.—When he mentioned *Ombre,*[1] she said she hated Cards.—If taking a little Excursion out of Town, a Country Ramble was her Aversion.—*Ranelagh*[2] gave her the Vapours.[3]—*Vaux-Hall* Gardens[4] were too cold.—The Fireworks at *Cuper's*[5] were shocking.—The Season for Plays was over for polite[6] People.—And a Concert always made her melancholly.

Besides all this, her Refusals were given in a Manner, which had so much of Disdain in it, as made her Brother bite his Lips with Vexation, and occasioned[7] him to shorten his Visit, very much to the Dissatisfaction of the other, who in spite of the Coldness, and, indeed, Ill-Nature of *Sabina,* thought her more charming at this second Interview, than he had done at the first, and consequently, was more in Love than ever.

---

1. **Ombre:** a fashionable three-handed card game.
2. **Ranelagh:** an amusement park in Chelsea, a borough of London.
3. **Vapours:** depression.
4. **Vaux-Hall Gardens:** a fashionable pleasure resort.
5. **Cuper's:** Cooper's Gardens, another London pleasure garden.
6. **polite:** fashionable.
7. **occasioned:** caused.

The Brother, to avoid entring into any Discourse with him, on a Topic which he could not answer to, without either deceiving, or giving Pain to his Friend, pretended an Engagement, an parted from him the Moment they left *Sabina*'s Lodgings.

As he had a very sincere Friendship for *Luellin,* and the most tender Regard for the Welfare of his Sister, to find she was likely to continue refractory to what afforded so great a Prospect of Happiness to her, rendered him extremely uneasy and perplexed.—Early the next Morning he went to her again, and after having taken the Privilege of a Brother in condemning her Conduct, and the foolish Prepossession which had occasioned it, the little Efficacy he found that had on her, made him once more have recourse to the Arguments he before had urged, and endeavour to reason her out of a Prejudice, which had not the least Foundation in Truth, or common Sense.

But had this Gentleman been endued with the Eloquence of an Angel, all he had said would have been lost on the perverse, the obstinate *Sabina.*—Equally deaf to his Remonstrances or Perswasions, all he could get from her was, an Intreaty to persecute her no more with any Discourse on so disagreeable a Subject, and to beg he would not take it ill, that, in this, she never could be brought to acquiesce with his Opinion.

On his asking her, if she found any thing disagreeable, either in the Person or Conversation of *Luellin,* she replied, that she could not but allow[1] he was handsome, genteel, had both Wit and good Breeding; but, notwithstanding all this, as he was *Welsh,* he was her Aversion.

In fine, there was no prevailing on her to receive a second Visit; and she protested solemnly that she would never be troubled with him any more; adding, "If you had that real Affection for me you pretend, and as I might expect from a Brother, you would be far from desiring I should put so great a Constraint upon myself, as to treat civilly, or even to sit in Company with a Man of his Country."

In answer to this peremptory Refusal, he could not help telling her, that he was sorry he had been deceived in the good Opinion he had of her Understanding:—That he blushed for her Folly, and that, from

---

1. **allow:** acknowledge.

this Time forward, he should look upon her, as utterly unworthy of the Happiness she rejected.

Such cruel Words from a Brother she tenderly loved, made her burst into Tears; but he was in reality too angry with her to be at all moved by them, and flung out of the Room, without even turning his Eyes on her.

Luellin, who little suspected his Misfortune, had been in search of this dear Friend and Confident,[1] while he was with his Sister, and not finding him at Home, went to every Place where they had been used to meet; but the other not knowing what to say to him, so industriously avoided him, that it was three or four Days before he could see him.

This made him imagine, that all was not so right as he at first had flattered himself with; that either the Brother did not sincerely approve of his Alliance, or that *Sabina* herself was against it.—Impatient to be convinced, he went to his Lodgings, and waited there till he came Home, though it was late at Night.

The Brother of *Sabina* was a little surprized to find him there; and not very well prepared how to behave on this Occasion, could neither deny that he had purposely shunned him, nor the Motive of his doing so.

He let him into Part of the Aversion his Sister had conceived against *Wales,* and owned he feared his being of that Country, would be an Objection not easy to be removed; but as he did not let him into the Whole of the Contempt she was possessed of, nor all the Discourse they had together on that Subject, the Lover still retained some Hopes of getting over the Difficulty.

After a great deal of Talk on the Affair, it was agreed between them, that *Luellin* should write to her; and, at the same time that he declared his Passion, give a Hint that he was not ignorant his Country was so unhappy as to be disliked by her; and an Assurance, that if he should be so fortunate as to suceed in his Pretensions, he never would desire her to set a Foot in *Wales,* nor would be there himself, but live with her either in *London,* or any other Place she should make Choice of.

---

1. **Confident:** confidant (one in whom he confided).

This being resolved upon, the Brother took upon him to be the Bearer, and also once more to exert all the Interest he had with her, in the Behalf of the Author, the truly devoted *Luellin,* as he subscribed himself at the Bottom of his amorous Epistle.

So faithful was he in the Cause of his Friend, that he not only performed the Promise he had made him, but also gave so high a Character of him, and the Advantages would accrue to their Family by an Alliance with him to all their Kindred, that *Sabina* could see none of them, without hearing something of the Merits of *Luellin,* and how happy she might be with him: To all which, she returned much the same Answers she had given her Brother, and sometimes with more Sharpness.

That Gentleman, however, had the hardest Task to prevail with her to hear him read the Letter he brought to her; for all he could say was ineffectual to make her look upon it herself. And what in the End did all his Endeavours avail? Before he had well concluded, she snatched the Paper out of his Hand, tore it, and stamped it on the Floor.

A second Quarrel now arose between them on this Score;—he left her in a very great Passion, and went no more to visit her; but her other Relations still continued to argue with her in favour of *Luellin,* though to no manner of Purpose, unless it were to give her greater Opportunities of discovering[1] her Obstinacy in this Point.

Luellin in the mean Time, to whom the Brother was obliged to relate the whole Truth, in order to cure him of a Passion which he was now convinced would never be returned, could not be perswaded to desist; and as there was no Possibility of bringing her to receive another Visit from him, pursued her to Church, watched her wherever she went, and would not be hindered from speaking to her in what Place soever he saw her, or whatever Company was with her, though the respectful Compliments he made her were never answered but with Slights, and frequently with Affronts.

At last, quite tired out with the Persecutions she received on all Sides, she went privately away into the Country, acquainting no one

---

1. **discovering:** revealing.

Person in the World, but a Servant who attended her, with the Place of her Retirement.

Her Brother, and all her Friends were very much troubled at her absconding in this Manner; but the passionate *Luellin* was inconsolable:—So truly did his faithful Heart resent this Usage, that it threw him into a high Fever, out of which he was not without great Difficulty recovered.

It is not to be doubted, but that great Enquiries were made after the fair Fugitive; but she had taken such Precautions as to render fruitless all Endeavours for that Purpose, nor did any body hear the least Word from herself, of what at first filled them with Astonishment, and very soon afterwards with Grief.

This young Lady, to amuse herself as well as she could in an Absence from all her Kindred, and those others she had been accustomed to converse with, went to all the little Diversions the Place she was in afforded: At one of these rural Entertainments, she happened to fall into the Company of a young Gentleman, who told her he had left *London* for a Time, meerly to shun the Solicitations he was plagued with to marry a Person for whom he could have no Inclinations.

This Parity, as she thought, of Circumstances, made her conceive a kind of Good-Will for him, which on his addressing her, as he soon did, on a more tender Score, grew up into a kind of an Affection.

She was so free as to tell him she came into the Country on the same Account he did; and also to acquaint him with her real Name and Family, which till then she had disguised under a fictitious one.

Whether he at first intended this as a serious Affair, or only to divert himself, is uncertain, but it is not so that after he knew who she was, he left nothing unsaid, or undone, that he thought might engage her.

Not that, as she has since declared, she was absolutely in Love with him, but she saw nothing where she was, beside himself, that seemed a fit Companion for her:—He pretended an Extremity of Passion for her, and that he had an Estate superior to what her Fortune could expect; and all this joined with the Consideration of silencing any Overtures that might be made by her Friends in the Behalf of *Luellin,* or any other she might happen equally to dislike, prevailed on her to listen to the Proposals of this new Lover with a favourable Ear, and at length to give herself and Fortune entirely to him.

In fine, without consulting one Friend, without the least Enquiry into his Character and Circumstances, or without any Settlement or Provision, she married him, and in a few Days after came up a Bride to *London,* to the Surprize, as I have already said, of all that knew her.

As her Husband's Affairs were not immediately discovered, the disinterested Part of her Acquaintance paid their Compliments of Congratulation; but those of her Kindred and intimate Friends, especially her Brother, could not approve of her having taken so precipitate a Step, and were very fearful of the Event.[1]

But not to prolong the Narrative beyond what is necessary, the unhappy *Sabina* had not been married a Month before she found her whole Fortune was obliged to go for the Payment of her Husband's Debts;—that it had been really to avoid his Creditors, not a disagreeable Match, as he had pretended to her, that brought him to that Part of the Country, where it was her ill Fortune to become his Prey;—and that he neither was in Possession of, ever had been, or was born to inherit a single Foot of Land, but had always lived a loose idle Life, and in fine, was looked upon, and in effect was no other, than a common Sharper[2] of the Town.

Difficult would it be for me to represent the Miseries of her Condition, which were rendered yet more severe by the Consciousness of having, in some Measure, merited them by a Folly which she could now find no Excuse for.

After having lived for about half a Year with a Husband whom she could no longer have the least Regard for, and from whom, besides the Deception he had been guilty of to her, she received only ill Usage, and experiencing all the Vexations of Reproaches from Abroad, and Want at Home, she at length got rid of him:—He quitted her, and went to *France,* in quest, as it is supposed, of new Adventures.[3]

---

1. **Event:** outcome.

2. **Sharper:** gambler.

3. **Adventures:** sexual adventures.

This fine, gay, obstinate Lady, now is glad to accept of a Contribution made by her Friends[1] for supporting her in a mean[2] plain Way, visited by few, respected yet by fewer, and caressed by none; she has Leisure to reflect upon, and regret the unhappy Prepossession which made her so industriously fly the Good Heaven proffered, in a wealthy, generous, and accomplished Man, and throw herself into the Arms of an abandoned Villain and Impostor.

Had that Aunt been living, who had inspired her with so fatal a Prepossession, she would doubtless have repented her of it; but Death, sometime before *Luellin* had commenced his Suit, prevented her suffering any thing, either from Remorse within herself, or from the Reproaches of others.

But while I truly commiserate the Fate of *Sabina*, I cannot forbear accusing *Luellin* of Want of Judgement, in persisting in his Suit, after being acquainted with the obstinate Prepossession of his Mistress: In my Mind, it is a Kind of *Quixotism*,[3] for Merit to combat against Prejudice.—In vain does Beauty, Wit, Bravery, Virtue, Courage, or every other excelling Qualification, that Nature, joined with Education, can bestow, oppose itself against the Sails of that stupid Windmill[4] in the Brain; and though the Poet says,

> The Brave and Virtuous conquer Difficulties,
> By daring to oppose them;[5]

Yet I am of Opinion, that great Author thought not of Prejudice when he wrote these Lines, since that is a Difficulty not to be surmounted by any Services, any Deservings, not even any Considerations of Self-Interest whatsoever; but is, at the same Time, an Enemy to the Hap-

---

1. **Friends:** relatives.

2. **mean:** low, poor.

3. **Quixotism:** practice resembling that of Don Quixote, protagonist of the novel *Don Quixote* (1605, 1615) by Miguel de Cervantes: striving after high ideals in a visionary and futile way.

4. **Sails . . . Windmill:** One of Don Quixote's adventures involved fighting with a windmill.

5. **The Brave . . . them:** quotation unidentified.

piness of the Person who harbours it, as much, if not more, than to those who vainly endeavour to overcome it.

As for *Luellin,* however, he recovered of his Fever, and his Passion at the same Time; and soon after had the good Fortune to be married to a young Lady of great Merit herself, and truly sensible of his, with whom he now lives in all the Happiness the World can give.

I Heartily wish that Examples of the ill Consequences attending an unreasonable Prejudice, were less frequent; but I fear there are few into whose Hands this Piece may fall, who will not rather think it too common a Case to be inserted, than too extraordinary to be believed.

Many, indeed, may laugh at the unfortunate *Sabina,* and plume themselves on a superior Understanding, which enables them to avoid either a too great Attachment, or too great an Aversion for any particular Place, or the Natives of it, and cry, "They wonder the Woman could be so infatuated.—There certainly are worthy and unworthy Persons born in all Climates." And yet these very Persons, who talk in this Manner, are, perhaps, no less biassed, than the Lady they condemn, though on different Subjects.

If we could be sensible that strong Liking or Disliking we feel within ourselves was Prejudice, that very Sensibility would go a great Way towards curing us of it; but the Mischief, as I have already observed, but cannot too often repeat, is, that we mistake the most blind Partiality for the most quick-ey'd Judgement, and think every Body in the wrong, who does not see as we do.

It is therefore the Business of all who would wish to think or act like rational Creatures, on the first Emotions of an Inclination to favour or disfavour any particular Person or Thing, to ask themselves the Question, Why they do so?—To examine nicely[1] into the Merits of the Cause, and weigh them in the Scale of Reason.—How would then what seems most ponderous often be found light as Air, and that which appears but of a feathery Substance, prove of more Weight than Gold!

Without this we never can be sure of forming a right Judgement, or be capable of acting with even common Justice.

---

1. **nicely:** precisely.

Justice, the Queen of Virtues!

(says our excellent *Waller*,[1] in one of his moral and instructive Poems,)

> From our *Complexion* we are *chaste* or *brave;*
> But *this* from *Reason*, and from *Heav'n* we have.
> All *other* Virtues dwell but in the *Blood;*
> *This* in the *Soul*, and gives the Name of *Good!*[2]

Would one not think that Man was mad, who should go all his Life in Leading Strings;[3] yet what is it else than to adhere to any thing in Age, merely because we were taught it in our Youth?

I am very sensible, however, that all that can be said by me, or any one else, on this Subject, would have as little Efficacy, as preaching to the Winds or Waves.—There is no turning the impetuous Tide of Prejudice.—It bears down every Thing before it, and overflows all the Boundaries of Reason.

But wherefore has it this mighty Force?—Why, by giving Way to it at first.—By suffering our nobler Faculties to be immerged in its bottomless Depth, for Want of taking a little Pains in the Exertion of them.

Difficult it is to prevail on young Persons to apply themselves seriously to an Examination of themselves, I mean their Passions and Inclinations: They are, for the most part, too volatile to fix the Mind in that State of Reflection which is absolutely necessary to accomplish so great a Work; and those who are arrived at a more advanced Age, are generally too obstinate and too proud, to recede from an Opinion they have for a long Time entertained.

It is not, therefore, so much the Persons who are prejudiced, as those who like the Aunt of *Sabina*, inspire that Prejudice, on whom the Blame lies of all the Ills arising from it.

---

1. **Waller:** Edmund Waller (1606–1687), lyric poet.

2. **Justice . . . Good:** quotation unidentified.

3. **Leading Strings:** strings used to guide and control toddlers.

I would therefore, methinks, fain prevail on those who unhappily are governed by Prejudice, to keep it so far to themselves, as not by Example, or Precept, to render others guilty of the same.—To let the young and unbiassed Mind take its own Bent (excepting always in Matters of Religion and Morality) and let Reason freely operate.— The Almighty has given every one a sufficient Share of that Divine Emanation to direct them to form a true Judgement of the Things of this World, or at least so far as relates to his own Affairs, or the Good of Society in general.

As these Lucubrations[1] are intended for the Good of the Publick, and the Advice contained in them flows from a sincere Heart, and the warmest Wishes for the true Happiness and innate Peace of all my Fellow-Creatures, I flatter myself there is nothing I have urged on this Head will give Offence to any.

*   *   *

FROM BOOK XXIII

I come now to a Letter which I am certain none of my Readers will be surprized to find inserted in a Work of this Nature, because of the Service it may do to young unmarried Ladies, if rightly attended to.

To the FEMALE SPECTATOR.
WORTHY MADAM,

That tender Regard you express for the Happiness and Reputation of Human-Kind in general, but particularly for those of your own Sex, emboldens the most unfortunate of Women to give you a Detail of the Sorrows she labours under, and that fatal Error in Conduct, which has but too justly brought them on her.

In disburthening myself this Way, I taste the first Interval of Ease I have known for a long Time; but that is the least Motive which

---

1. **Lucubrations:** studies.

induced me to write: The main View I have to desire the Publication of my Case, is to warn all young Girls, of what Rank or Degree soever, from being guilty of the Fault I have been.

But on perusing this melancholy Epistle, you will be Judge how far it may deserve the Attention of the Public, as to the Subject it contains; for as to the Stile, I have no Pretence to Wit or Elegance, and in my present Situation, cannot be supposed to range my Thoughts in that Order which the Press requires, and must therefore intreat the Favour of you to render them more methodical.

Be pleased therefore, Madam, to permit me, in my plain Manner, to inform you, that I am the only Daughter of a Gentleman who makes no inconsiderable Figure in the World. Tho' I had the Misfortune of losing my Mother, she dying when I was very young, I had not that of seeing any other in her Place; and my Father, tho' naturally stern, seemed to take so much Delight in me, that he would frequently say, that as I had a Brother who would rob me of the Estate,[1] he would take Care that I should have a Portion,[2] which should intitle me to marry to a greater.

His Fondness of me was so well known, that scarce had I attained the Age of fourteen, before there were several who desired his Permission to make their Addresses to me;[3] but he, who it seems had higher Expectations for me, refused them, and the first Declaration of Love that was made to me, was by a young Gentleman, whom, unhappily for both, I became acquainted with at a Ball.

The Passion he professed for me was, alas! but too sincere, as he afterwards gave fatal Proofs of.—My Heart was sensibly[4] touched with the affecting Things he said to me, and being too young, or at least too indolent, to consider the Consequences, I encouraged his Hopes, as far as was consistent with Modesty and Honour.

---

1. **Brother . . . Estate:** By the prevailing law of primogeniture, the eldest son of a family inherited the entire estate.

2. **Portion:** dowry; money that a woman takes to her marriage.

3. **make their Addresses to me:** court me.

4. **sensibly:** appreciably.

As he was a younger Brother, and had a very small Fortune, it would have been Madness in him to apply to my Father.—Our Intercourse[1] was therefore obliged to be kept extremely private, nor did any one, but the Maid who waited on me, and was in the Secret from the Beginning, know any thing of my Acquaintance with him.

It would be too tedious to relate the Contrivances I had to meet him: Sometimes I had the Vapours,[2] and must have a Walk betimes in the Morning in the Park.—Sometimes I had a Fancy to see a Play *incog.*[3] and must go to *Burton*'s Box[4] muffled up.—Sometimes affect to be a great Œconomist, and go to Sales, in order to buy Bargains.— Nobody with me in these Excursions but my Maid; because, as I said, taking a Fellow in a Livery[5] would discover[6] who I was, and frustrate my Intentions; and a Thousand other such Pretences, which were not in the least suspected, either by my Father, or any of the Family.

Yet would you believe it, Madam, with all this Pains I took, I had in reality no settled Affection for him.—The Novelty of the Thing pleased my Vanity, and the Secrecy of it my Pride, in being able to circumvent my Father.—I was, however, deceived myself, for I imagined that my Passion was equal to that of any Heroine in Romance, and the Confessions I sometimes let fall of this ideal Flame[7] were such as might well deceive the Person in whose Favour they were made.

Nothing is more to be wondered at, however, than that the Whim, for I can call it no other, did not transport me[8] so far as to consent to a private Marriage, which he was continually pressing for; but

---

1. **Intercourse:** exchange of thoughts and feelings.

2. **had the Vapours:** suffered from depression.

3. **incog.:** incognito, in disguise, unknown.

4. **Burton's Box:** A Mrs. Burton (fl. 1722–30) long served as middle gallery boxkeeper at Drury Lane Theater. Twenty years after her time, the center box in the middle gallery was still referred to as "Burton's Box."

5. **Fellow in a Livery:** servant in uniform.

6. **discover:** reveal.

7. **Flame:** passionate love.

8. **transport me:** carry me away.

whether I ought to impute it to my good or evil Fortune, I know not, that I could never be perswaded to that, since I went so far as to promise, and to bind that Promise with many repeated Vows and Imprecations, never to be the Bride of any other Man.

O, how thoughtless is Youth! How little capable of judging for themselves, or of themselves!—*Silvius,* for so I shall call him, imagined he had gained a great Point in having engaged me in this Manner; but, alas! I considered little on it, and tho' it is certain at that Time I intended to keep it, I never reflected how many Difficulties lay in the Way.

But soon the Trial came. An Overture was now made to my Father, which he found too advantageous for me to be rejected by him. It was in favour of a young Gentleman, to whom I shall give the Name of *Celander.* He was descended of a noble Family, had a very great Estate, and was possessed of all the Accomplishments that can endear a Person of his Sex to one of ours.

I had often heard him spoke of by several Ladies of my Acquaintance, and never without such Praises as I must confess he merits.—I had seen him, too, but it was only *en passant,*[1] or at the Opera; but that was enough to make me know he was handsome, well made,[2] and perfectly genteel.—This, whenever any Discourse happened concerning him, I always allowed,[3] but indeed thought no farther on him, till my Father told me he had given him Leave to visit me, and that he expected I would receive him as a Man whom he intended for my Husband.

Impossible is it for me to express the Agitation of my Heart, when I heard my Father speak in this Manner. To be told a Man so much admired by the whole Town had singled me out as the only Object worthy of his Affection, was too flattering to my Vanity not to be pleasing; but yet the Thoughts of marrying him, and abandoning my *Silvius,* gave a most terrible Alarm.

---

1. **en passant:** in passing.
2. **well made:** shapely.
3. **allowed:** acknowledged.

In fine,[1] I know not whether I was rejoiced or grieved. A Mixture of Pain and Pleasure at once invaded me, and so hurried my Spirits, that I was unable to make any direct Answer to what my Father said. He interpreted my frequent Change of Colour and incoherent Speeches, however, only to the Bashfulness which a first Proposal of that Kind might naturally occasion, as I had with much ado drauled out that I should always be obedient to his Will, he was perfectly satisfied, and said no more to me at that Time.

The next Day *Celander* dined with us.—The Grandeur of his Equipage,[2] and every Thing that appeared about him was sufficient to dazzle so young a Heart as mine, but his Politeness could not but charm the most experienced one.—In the Afternoon, my Father took an Opportunity of leaving us together; and I must own that I found so infinite a Disproportion between the Manner in which he addressed himself to me, and that of *Silvius,* as made me even then wonder how I could ever think the other worthy of my Attention.

This, I say, I thought while I was with him, but when I was alone the Tenderness of *Silvius,* the Ardors he expressed for me, and all the Assiduities he had paid to me, turned the Balance of my Inclinations again on his Side, and I cryed to myself I never would be so ungrateful as to throw into Despair a Love I had encouraged and sworn to recompence.

For some Days I continued in this fluctuating State of Mind, loving both, yet neither as I ought to do, and therefore, in Fact, little deserving myself of the Love of either.

But it was my Fate to find more Sincerity than I merited. I am but too well convinced that the Professions made me by each of them did not in the least exceed the Dictates of their Hearts, and this it is that makes my Unhappiness.

Pardon, Madam, these Interruptions from the Thread of my Narrative, which the Remembrance of those Times renders it impossible sometimes to forbear; but I will now be as little tedious as possible, and hasten to the sad Catastrophe.[3]

---

1. **In fine:** in short.

2. **Equipage:** carriage.

3. **Catastrophe:** outcome.

Celander at last gained an entire Conquest over me, and all that remained for *Silvius* was Pity.—The Promise I had made him, indeed, gave me Shocks, but they wore off, in the Consideration that as I was not at my own Disposal,[1] a Vow of that Kind could not be looked upon as binding.

My Father was highly satisfied on perceiving my Inclinations were conformable to his Desires, and my Lover transported[2] at the Concessions I made him.—There now remained nothing but the Drawing up the Marriage Articles,[3] and New-Cloaths, and Equipages for the Solemnization of our Nuptials,[4] and all those Things were ordered, by both Parties, to be prepared with the greatest Expedition.[5]

Silvius was soon informed of what passed in our Family, and not doubting the Truth of his Misfortune, by not having seen me in a much longer Time than we were accustomed to be absent, wrote a Letter to me full of Complaints, and prevailed upon my Maid to deliver it, and endeavour to obtain an Answer.

I could not help being a little moved at reading it, but hearing *Celander* was come in just as I had finished, prevented all the Effects it might otherwise perhaps have had on me. I absolutely refused to write, and to hinder him from doing so any more, bad the Maid tell him plainly that there was nothing farther for him to hope:—That my Father had insisted on my giving my Hand to *Celander,* and that I had resolved not to run the risque of disobeying him.

Some few Days after this, as I was in the Coach with *Celander* and a young Lady, going to take the Air in *Hide-Park,*[6] it was my ill Fortune to see him in a Street we passed through: He saw me too, and gave me a Look in which I know not whether Despair or Rage was most predominant, and suited exactly with the Description the

---

1. **at my own Disposal:** in marriage, because her father had legal control over her.

2. **transported:** ecstatic.

3. **Marriage Articles:** legal documents mainly concerning financial arrangements.

4. **Solemnization . . . Nuptials:** marriage ceremony.

5. **Expedition:** speed.

6. **Hide-Park:** Hyde Park, a large and fashionable park in West London.

Maid had given me of him, at the Time of her relating the Message I had sent by her, in Answer to his Letter.

The unexpected Sight of a Person whom I had used so ill, gave me a very great Shock for the present; but I was too young, too gay, and indeed too well satisfied with my own Fate to be long under any Concern for that of another, whatever Obligations I had in Honour, Conscience, or Generosity to be so.

Celander, who thought every Minute an Age, till he could call me his Wife, hastened all the Preparations for our Wedding on his Part, and my Father, equally impatient for the Completion of a Union he no less wished, being equally industrius, every Thing was got ready much sooner than could have been expected, and we were married in the Presence of the greatest Part of the Kindred on both Sides, who all seemed to take Interest in our mutual Felicity.

Three Days were spent in Rejoicings at my Father's House; after which we set out for a fine Seat[1] *Celander* has at about forty Miles distant from *London*.—There I received the Compliments and Congratulations of all the Gentry of the Country;—the Homage and almost Adoration of my Husband's Tenants and Dependants, and every Day, nay almost every Hour, presented me with something new, wherewith to flatter my Vanity and Pride.

Yet all this was nothing to that ravishing[2] Content, which the excessive Tenderness of *Celander* afforded:—He was, if possible, more diligent in searching out Ways to please me, than before our Marriage.—The Name of *Husband* robbed me of nothing of the Obsequiousness of the *Lover;* nor our Familiarity of the Respect he had always treated me with. A Happiness, alas! too perfect to be permanent; yet might it have been lasting as my Life, had I never been guilty of any Thing to render me unworthy of it.—But it seemed as if Heaven, to punish my Breach of Faith the more severely, had bestowed on me such a Profusion of Bliss only to make my succeeding Miseries fall with the greater Weight.

---

1. **Seat:** estate.

2. **ravishing:** extraordinarily pleasing.

While these pleasing Scenes continued, I never thought on *Silvius,* nor durst my Maid, who I still kept with me, ever presume to mention him to me, as I had strictly forbad her the contrary, till one unhappy Time—O, that she had died before the Arrival of it, that so the fatal Secret of my Crime might have been buried with her! Then had I been preserved from the Sorrows I endure, and the most excellent of Men, and best of Husbands, not deprived of his Tranquility.

We had been in the Country, as near as I can remember, about six Weeks, when as I was alone one Morning in my Dressing-Room, this ill-starr'd[1] Creature came in, and with a Look which expressed somewhat more than ordinary, begged I would give her Leave to reveal a Secret to me, which, she said, she had long smothered in her Breast, but was now so uneasy, that she was sure she should run mad, if she were not permitted to divulge it.

I, who imagined it was only some foolish Affair relating to herself, fell a laughing at her serious drawn-down[2] Countenance, and bad her speak what she had to say at once.

She then, after having afresh begged my Pardon, told me that in five or six Days after our coming into the Country, she was sent for to a neighboring Inn, where they said a Relation of hers just arrived from *London* desired to speak with her; but that on her being shewed into a Room, she found the Person who waited for her was no other than the unfortunate *Silvius.*

I no sooner heard his Name, than I endeavoured to stop her from going any farther, by telling her I would hear nothing of him, and that knowing, as she did, my Mind, it was very impudent, and what I never would forgive in her, to mention him to me.

The poor Wench trembled while I spoke, but told me she would not have disobeyed me for the World in any other Circumstance, but that she could not sleep in her Bed, and was so tormented in her Mind, that it was now impossible for her to refrain any longer.— "Well, then," said I, scornfully, "what is this mighty Business?"

---

1. **ill-starr'd:** ill-fated.

2. **drawn-down:** melancholy.

She then proceeded to relate a Tale too melancholy not to have touched the most disinterested Heart: She said that he seemed rather a Spectre than real Flesh and Blood; and that there was nothing but the Accents of his Voice by which she could have distinguished him.— That after having given Vent to the tumultuous Passions which raged within him, in Terms which testified the unmost Horror and Despair, he took a Letter out of his Pocket, and at the same Time drew his Sword, and pointing it to her Breast, said that Moment should be her last, if she did not swear to deliver it into my Hands.

It was in vain she repeated to him the Injunction I had laid her under of never speaking of him.—In vain she urged that no Remonstrance made to me could be of any Service to him, and would only give me Pain, as I was married, and could now do nothing for him. All she said served only to make him more vehement; and he insisted on her Oath, which she was at last obliged to give, with the Addition of the most solemn Curse upon herself, if she fulfilled it not.

She then told me, that the Fears of my Displeasure had made her all this Time conceal it from me; but that, for a Week past, she had dreamed continually of him, and had such Terrors upon her Spirits on his Account, that she verily believed he had laid violent Hands upon himself, and that his Ghost haunted her in this Manner for her Breach of Vow.

I could not keep myself from being very much affected with what she said, but was much more so, when taking the Letter out of her Hand, I found it contained these Lines.

To the fair perjured LAVINIA.

If I thought that what I am about to write would be capable of giving you any Pain, false, cruel, and ungrateful as you are, I could not have been enough Master of my Heart to send it; but I doubt not that you will be rather pleased to know you are going to be rid for ever of the Person whose most distant Looks would upbraid your Guilt.—Few are there, O most unjust *Lavinia!* who would not have taken Advantage of the Contract between us.—You know that you are mine, bound by the most solemn Vows, in Presence of your Maid, whom I could compel to bear Testimony of the Truth; but the Generosity of my Nature sets me above all mercenary Views, and the Sincerity of my Love from doing any thing that should expose, or render you unhappy. May Heaven be as forgiving, and you never have Reason to regret your Breach of Faith!

To ease you of all Fears on my Account, and myself of the Discontent of breathing the same Air with one who has so cruelly deceived me, I quit *England* for ever. I cannot be worse treated in the most barbarous Lands, than I have been in that which gave me Birth; and I leave my dearest Friends without Reluctance, since by doing so, I leave also my bitter Enemy.—But who, besides your faithless Self, knows whether I am the only Man has been betrayed by your Allurements! You may perhaps have practiced the same bewitching Arts on others as well as me, and Numbers be involved in the same Despair I suffer. Even *Celander,* he who now lies in your Arms, ought not to depend on a Heart so inconstant, so little capable of a true Affection. But I have done with my Reproaches, and in spite of the mighty Cause I have to hate you as my bitter Ruin, have still Love enough to wish you happy, if you can be so.—You see, tho' you have made me wretched, it is not in your Power, however, to make me ungenerous, and therefore ought to remember, with some Compassion at least,

> *Your once Adoring*
> SILVIUS.

Such a Letter as this you will own would have shocked any Woman, conscious as I was, of deserving all the severe Things contained in it; but I felt besides an inward Terror, which, at that Time, I could not account for, but have since thought a Presage of my approaching Disaster.

I had read the fatal Scroll twice over, and was going to lock it into a Cabinet, when, on hearing *Celander*'s Voice, and thinking he was that Instant coming in, I fell into a Trembling, and thrusting it hastily into the Wench's Hand, bad her run and put it into the Kitchen Fire, there being none above Stairs;[1] on which she went out of the Room to do as she was ordered, and I sat down endeavouring to compose myself.

But *Celander* not coming, and Palpitation of my Heart rather increasing than diminishing, I got up again, and ran down Stairs after the Maid, designing either to charge her to burn it directly, or to give it me again; I know not well what was in my Thoughts in the Confusion I then was;—But, O good God! What became of me, when, as I set my Foot into a Parlour, thro' which I was to pass, I saw my Husband with that Letter in his Hand, the Maid on her Knees before him, beseeching him to return it to her, and the Countenance of both so wild and distracted, as left me no room to doubt the Truth of my ill Fortune.

"I have stumbled on a Secret, Madam," said *Celander,* as soon as he perceived me, "I little expected to find; but you may easily, and *Silvius,* too, forgive my Curiosity, since I shall suffer more than either of you."

There needed no more to deprive me of all the little Senses I was Mistress of; and whether he added any thing farther I cannot say, for I fell into a Swoon that Instant.—*Celander,* as I afterwards heard, attempted nothing for my Recovery, but went out of the Room, still keeping the Letter in his Hand. The Maid was also in a Condition little capable of assisting me; however her Screams drew in other Servants, who, among them, brought me to myself, and carried me to my Chamber,[2] where, being laid on the Bed, and every Body but she who had been the Cause of this unhappy Accident being withdrawn, I was made acquainted with the Means by which it happened.

That foolish Creature, it seems, had the Curiosity to examine the Contents of the Letter before she destroyed it; and seeing Nobody in the Parlour, went in there and read it. She happened to stand before a great Glass[3] just opposite the Door, and *Celander* passing by, in order

---

1. **above Stairs:** on an upper floor.

2. **Chamber:** bedroom.

3. **great Glass:** large mirror.

to come up to my Chamber, seeing her in this Position, and the Tears all the Time she was reading running down her Cheeks, stopped to look at her.

As he was perfectly gay and facetious in his Nature, and knew she was a Favourite with me, he would be very often pleasant with her,[1] and finding she continued so intent on the Paper, he stepped softly behind her and snatched it out of her Hand, thinking to divert himself with the Fright he should put her in.

He had no Intention of reading it, it is certain, but had[2] returned it to her, after having laughed a little at the Concern he gave her, if unhappily my Name had not struck his Sight. That indeed occasioned a different Turn, and he thought he had a Right to see what it contained.

Thus, dear *Female Spectator,* was the whole Secret of my Crime discovered[3] to him, from whom I had most Reason to wish it might be eternally concealed.

What to say to evade, or to palliate the Matter, I was utterly incapable of resolving: Sometimes I was for[4] denying every thing, and pretend I never knew any such Person as *Silvius.* At others, thought it best to confess ingenuously the Truth, and lay the Blame on Youth and Inadvertancy.

Celander, however, was not in haste to put me to the Trial: He went Abroad[5] directly, returned not Home till very late at Night, and then ordered a Bed to be prepared for him in another Chamber.

This Behaviour gave me the most terrible Alarm: I thought it denoted an Indifference more cruel than the severest Reproaches could have been; and as I truly loved him, chose to suffer every thing his Rage could inflict on me, rather than continue in the Suspence I now was.

---

1. **be . . . pleasant with her:** chat with her, tease her.

2. **had:** would have.

3. **discovered:** revealed.

4. **for:** in favor of.

5. **Abroad:** out.

I flew therefore to the Room where he was, and in the utmost Distraction conjured him to let me know the Cause of his forsaking my Bed. I was obliged to repeat the same Words, or others to the like Purpose, many Times, before I could prevail on him to speak, tho' all the Time he seemed to look upon me with Eyes more full of Grief than Anger. At last, "I knew not," said he, with a deep Sigh, "till this unhappy Day, that I was the Invader of another's Right, or that *Lavina* could not make me blest without a Crime."

On this I threw my Arms about his Neck, and told him, as well as I could speak for Tears, that none but himself had any Right either to my Heart, or Person;[1] and that if, when I was a Girl, incapable of judging for myself, I had been guilty of some foolish Words in Favour of another, it merited not to be called a Crime.

But wherefore should I trouble you, Madam, with a Detail of what I said, or his Replies; it is sufficient to inform you, that he has an over Delicacy in his Nature, which all my Arguments, neither then, nor ever since, tho' a whole Year is now elapsed, could overcome.

He not only censures me as guilty of Injustice, Ingratitude, Inconstancy, and Perjury to *Silvius,* but also of Dissimulation to himself; and will not be convinced that I preferred him to his Rival on any other Score than that of Interest.[2] He often laments, in Terms which stab me to the Heart, that I have not a *Soul* full of as many Charms, as he still continues to think are in my *Person*.

To render me yet more unhappy, the public Papers gave an Account, that the Ship in which the despairing *Silvius* had embarked, was cast away, and every Soul on Board perished in the Waves.—My Husband, on hearing it, presently cried out, "Ill-fated *Lavinia!* born for the Destruction of all who love thee!"—Troubled as I was for a Man to whom I found I had been but too dear, I found some Consolation, in the Hopes that *Celander* would, by his Death, be eased of those Scruples which had so long made him a Stranger to my Bed; but, alas! a fixed, inexorable Opinion of my Unworthiness had taken

---

1. **Person:** body.

2. **Interest:** self-interest (financial).

sole Possession of his Mind, and neither Vows, Tears, nor every En-
dearment that Woman can put in Practice, have the least Power to
alter it. The most gloomy Sadness dwells upon his Brow.—He eats
little,—speaks yet less,—avoids Company,—takes no Diversions, and
sometimes breaks into such Starts of Horror, as give evident Testimony
of his being in Danger of falling into a Condition more deplorable
than Death itself.[1]

As I love him with the utmost Sincerity and Tenderness, judge how
great my Distress must be even at seeing him thus, and how infinitely
more in the Consciousness of being the Occasion: But why do I appeal
to you? It is not in the Power of your Spectatorial Capacity to make
you conceive the thousandth Part of what I feel; my Misery is such
as only can be truly judged by one in the same wretched Circumstances.

But I will dwell upon the melancholly Theme no longer.—It was
not the Imagination that my Story might be of some Service to our
too unthinking Sex, that was the only Motive which induced me to
write to the *Female Spectator;* I had indeed another, and more selfish
one, and that is, if you do not think my Fault too great to be forgiven
by Heaven, or commiserated by Earth, to intreat you will say something in Mitigation of it. *Celander* is a Subscriber to your Books, and
constantly reads them.—He will find the Truth of my Heart in the
Account I have given you; and that, joined with some perswasive Arguments from your agreeable Pen, may, it is possible, retrieve some
Part of the Blessings I once enjoyed, and preserve from a total Despair
her who is at present the most unhappy of all created Beings; yet, with
the utmost Respect,

MADAM,
Your most humble,
and most obedient Servant,
LAVINIA.

St. *James's,*
Feb. 20, 1745–6.

P.S. Madam, Diseases of the *Mind,* as well as those of the *Body,*
if neglected, gather Increase of Strength every Day: I therefore beseech

---

1. **Condition . . . itself:** madness.

you to delay the Publication of this, and what you shall think fit to say upon it, no longer than is consistent with those Rules you have established.

That Person must have a very obdurate Heart indeed, who is incapable of being moved at the Afflictions of this Lady; but yet, notwithstanding all the Pity we have for her, we cannot so much, as she may wish, or perhaps expect, excuse the Fault for which she suffers.

It is a great Misfortune, when young Ladies, who have scarce quitted the Nursery, think themselves Women, and imagine they have a Right to act as they please, chuse what Company they will, and are fond of having Secrets of their own; when, in reality, nothing can be for the Advantage of their Interest, or Honour, that is not fit to be communicated to their Parents.

Nothing methinks is so becoming as that modest Timidity, which all our Sex are born with, and is only in a Manner forced from us, by the Example of other more experienced. A Girl, who accustoms herself betimes[1] to talk of Love and Lovers, will become an easy Prey to the first Offer.—It is therefore the Business of those who have Charge of them, to keep their Minds employed on other Things, and never to let them hear any discourse or read any Books, which may rouse that Vanity of making Conquests, which, we must confess, is but inherent to us all when very young, and in some remains even to old Age.

I am afraid *Lavinia,* having the Misfortune to lose her Mother, and being so much the Darling of her Father, was permitted to have too much of her own Will; and that though *Silvius* was the first who had the Temerity to address her,[2] yet doubtless she had heard a great many Things said of her Beauty.—How common a Compliment is it to the Parents, to cry, "Miss grows a Lovely Creature!—Well, she'll kill all the Men in Time!—What Eyes she has!—How delicate her Shape!" and such like Speeches, which poison the Mind of the poor Girl, and make her think there is nothing she has to take Care on, but to

---

1. **betimes:** early.

2. **to address her:** as a lover.

embellish her Person, so that her better Part is wholly neglected, and every Precept for improving the Mind grows irksome to her Ear, and makes not the least Impression on her Heart.

Whereas if she heard only Praises for the Progress she made in those laudable Accomplishments she was allowed to be instructed in, her Thoughts would be wholly turned that Way.—She would consider Knowledge as the most valuable Charm in *Woman* as well as *Man,* and not plume herself on those Attractions which the Small-Pox, or any other Fit of Sickness, may destroy even in the Spring of Youth, and which in a few Years will infallibly fade.

It is greatly owing to these ill-judged Encomiums, that makes so mighty a Difference between the Understanding of the Sexes, and I may venture to say, because I am pretty certain of the Truth of it, that if when Girls we were dealt with as Boys are we should be much more on an Equality with the Men, when we come to be Women.

Neither ought even Wit to be too lavishly indulged; for Wit without a due Balance of Judgment which cannot be expected from very early Years, is apt to degenerate into Pertness and a sawcy Contempt of our Elders, than which nothing is more dangerous both for the Manners and Morals.

A mixture of this perhaps might also have been infused into *Lavinia,* or she would not have dared to encourage a clandestine Courtship; much less as she herself acknowledges, took a Pleasure in deceiving her Father.—She must certainly have utterly renounced all Duty and Affection when she could go so far as to dispose of herself,[1] not only without his Permission, but to one who she knew very well he never would be brought to approve.

She is notwithstanding greatly to be pitied even for her Faults, since doubtless they arose from the Mistakes I have mentioned in those about her, and which by giving a wrong Bent to her Humour rendered her incapable of judging for herself.

Happy had she been if she had seen *Celander,* whom it is very plain she truly loves, before her Acquaintance with *Silvius,* who it is as plain she only imagined herself in Love with: Many there are, who like her

---

1. **dispose of herself:** promise herself in marriage.

have been thus self-deceived, and it therefore behoves every young Person to be upon her Guard against these false Emotions of the Heart, which are seldom indulged without drawing on some fatal Consequence.

As this unfortunate Lady was, however, so far swayed by them, as to enter into a solemn Engagement with her first Lover, I know not how, if she had reflected at all on it, she could answer[1] to herself the Violation of it:—It is true she never could have fulfilled it, at least during her Father's Life, without involving both herself and *Silvius* in all the Miseries of Poverty; and as she after loved another must have been yet more wretched in sacrificing her Passion to her Promise; yet still I am surprised that she could be even for a Moment happy in giving to one those Endearments which were the Right of another.

But her extreme Youth, and the Flatteries I have already said, which without all Question attended her Situation in Life, must plead her Excuse; and the just Sense she now seems to have of the Error she has been guilty of hinder us from being too severe.

Celander, methinks, should be no less forgiving.—Her greatest Fault was Inadvertency and Want of a due Examination into her own Heart; and few, alas! there are, who at her Years, are capable of doing it.— If any Suspicion ever entered his Head, that her real Inclination kept Pace with her first Vow; that she married him meerly for the Sake of Grandeur; and that *Silvius* had been[2] the happy Man, had his Estate been equal; that Suspicion ought to vanish on the Proofs she now gives him of an unfeigned Affection.—Her Griefs and her Distress at his estranged Behaviour should convince him that it was *Himself* and not his *Fortune,* which prevailed on her to break through her Engagement and abandon his Rival to despair.

Besides, he should consider that whether at their Marriage she was truly his Wife, as another had received her Faith, which indeed I am not Casuist enough to determine; yet she is now unquestionably so, as the Death of *Silvius* has released her from all the Obligations she rashly had laid herself under to him; and I know not whether living

---

1. **answer:** justify.

2. **had been:** would have been.

with her in the Manner he does, is not an Error equal to that she has been guilty of.

That he still loves her, she seems to believe, and if so, as she may easily judge, his Behaviour can only be owing to an over Delicacy, which may be called a Virtue in extreme, or Honour strained to too high a Pitch; and in supporting which, he suffers himself, perhaps, greater Pains than he inflicts. It is as one of our Poets says,

> A raging Fit of Virtue in the Soul,
> 'Tis *Pride*'s Original, but *Nature*'s Grave.[1]

And our inimitable *Cowley*[2] complains of it in these pathetic Terms:

> Have I o'ercome all real Foes,
> And shall this Phantom me oppose?
> Noisy Nothing! Stalking Shade!
> By what Witchcraft wer't thou made?
> Empty Cause of solid Harms,
> Foe to Peace, and Pleasure's Charms.[3]

On the whole, it is my Opinion, he ought to take the mourning Penitent to his Arms, pardon and endeavour to forget what is past;— the sad Mistake, for which she so much suffers, was made before she ever saw him.—Him she has never wronged: *Silvius* alone has Reason to complain, and Heaven to resent her Breach of Vow. *Celander* has nothing wherewith to accuse her on his own Part, and has no Pretence to make himself the Avenger of a Crime not committed against him.

Let him no longer, therefore, be the Cause of his own Unquiet, and of that of one so dear to him. Enough already has he sacrificed to a Niceness,[4] which, tho' the Token of a Mind rich in Virtues is no more

---

1. **A raging . . . Grave:** quotation unidentified.

2. **Cowley:** Abraham Cowley (1618–1667), poet and essayist.

3. **Have I . . . Charms:** Abraham Cowley, "Honour," ll. 11–16 (l. 16 actually reads, "But I shall find out Counter-charms").

4. **Niceness:** scrupulosity.

than a Weed springing from a too luxuriant Soil, which ought to be plucked up, lest it should choak the nobler Plants.

But, if the Admonitions of a *Female Spectator* may want[1] sufficient Force to expel those Clouds of Melancholy, which it seems invelop this Gentleman, let him hearken to what Mr. *Dryden* says,

> What then remains, but after past Annoy,
> To take the good Vicissitude of Joy:
> To thank the gracious Gods for what they give,
> Possess our Souls, and while we live, to live.[2]

As to *Silvius,* Death screens him from the just Censure we otherwise should be obliged to pass on his Behaviour; but tho' the Grave is sacred, and shuts out all Reproaches, those who are living, and act as he did, must not escape untold the Error of their Conduct.

When a young Gentleman sees a Lady whom he is inclined to love, he certainly ought, before he indulges the growing Passion, to reflect on all the Circumstances between them, and be able to say to himself at least, that the Attainment of his Wishes is neither a Thing impracticable, or would be attended with worse Consequences, than the Deprivation of them could be.

There is a Story very currently reported of a Journeyman Taylor,[3] who seeing Queen *Elizabeth* go in her State Robes to the Parliament House, became so violently in Love with her, that he run mad upon it.—I think every Man is as little in his Senses, who encourages an amorous Inclination, where there are no reasonable Hopes of Success; or if there are of gratifying his Passion, must inevitably be the Ruin of both their Fortunes.

This was evidently the Case of *Silvius,* and is of many more such Inconsiderates; but I know what they alledge in their Excuse: They tell you Love is a Passion which no Human Reason can controul:—That it is not an Impulse of their own Will, but is forced upon them

---

1. **want:** lack.

2. **What then . . . to live:** John Dryden, "Palamon and Arcite" 3.111–14.

3. **Journeyman Taylor:** a tailor past his apprenticeship who works for another for day wages.

by the irresistable Influence of the charming Object; and therefore whatever Disparity there may be between them and the Person they love, yet still they must love on whatever shall ensue.

These Enamoratoes[1] have ever in their Mouths some Piece of Poetry or other, which they imagine favours their Enthusiasm; and so great an Idol do they make of their Passion, that they even set it above all Laws, both Human and Divine. The following Lines are great Favourites with them, and never fail to be quoted when any Remonstrances are made to them:

> —No Law is made for Love;
> *Law* is for Things which to *free Choice* relate;
> *Love* is not in our *Choice* but in our *Fate*:
> Laws are but positive; Love's Power we see
> Is Nature's Sanction, and her first Decree.
> Each Day we break the Bond of Human Laws
> For Love, and vindicate the common Cause.
> Laws for Defence of civil Right are plac'd;
> Love throws the Fences down, and makes a general Waste.
> Maids, Widows, Wives, without Distinction fall,
> The sweeping Deluge Love, comes on, and covers all;
> For Love the Sense of Right and Wrong confounds;
> Strong Love, and proud Ambition have no Bounds.[2]

Well, indeed, may it be called, as another great Author has it:

> The Frenzy of the Mind.[3]

Yet will I take upon me to maintain, that in its Beginning, it may easily enough be subdued, by any thinking and discreet Person; but the Mischief is, that some young People are so infatuated, as to imagine it a mighty pretty[4] Thing to be in Love; that it adds to their Character,

---

1. **Enamoratoes:** lovers.

2. **No Law . . . no Bounds:** John Dryden, "Palamon and Arcite" 1.326–36, 3. 808–09.

3. **The Frenzy of the Mind:** Benjamin Hawkshaw, "The Fever," l.14.

4. **pretty:** fine.

and affords room for them to say, and be said to, a great many fine Things.—How have I seen several of both Sexes, who, without feeling the Passion, having dressed their Eyes in Languishments, sighed by Rote, and affected all the Symptoms of the most dying Love; some of whom, by long counterfeiting the Infection, have at last caught it in Reality: As *Cowley* describes it in a most admirable Manner:

> Unhurt, untouch'd, did I complain,
> And terrify'd all others with my Pain,
>   But now I feel the mighty Evil:
>   Ah, there's no fooling with the Devil!
> So wanton Men, when they would others fright,
>   Themselves have met a real Spright.[1]
>   Darts, and Wounds, and Flame, and Heat,
> I nam'd but for the Rhyme, or the Conceit:
>   Nor meant my Verse should raised be
>   To the sad Fame of *Prophecy.*
> *Truth* gives a dull Propriety to my Stile,
>   And all the Metaphores does spoil.
>   In Things where Fancy much does reign,
> 'Tis dangerous too cunningly to feign.
>   The *Play* at last a *Truth* does grow,
>   And *Custom* into *Nature* go.
> By this curst Art of Begging I became
>   Lame, with counterfeiting lame.
>   My Lines of amorous Desire
> I wrote to kindle, and blow others Fire.
>   And 'twas a barbarous Delight,
>   My Fancy promis'd from the Sight:
> But now, by Love, the mighty *Phalaris*,[2] I
>   My burning Bull, the first do try.[3]

---

1. **Spright:** spirit, ghost.

2. **Phalaris:** Sicilian tyrant (d. 554 B.C.) who allegedly had his enemies roasted alive in a bronze bull.

3. **Unhurt . . . do try:** Abraham Cowley, "The Dissembler," ll. 1–6, 13–30.

But as to those whose Hearts are insensibly[1] attracted by the Perfections of a Person they may happen to see, and feel in themselves the sincere Tokens of a growing Passion:—Even those, I say, if any material Impediments lie in the Way of their Desires, may, if they will attempt to do it, conquer the Impulse, powerful as it is.—Let them forbear all farther Interviews with the dangerous Object.—Let them shun the softening Conversation of all who either are Lovers, or pretend to be so, and endeavour to fill their Minds with the Study of some Science or Art.—Absence, Time, and Employment, will infallibly work a Cure, tho' I will not argue but at first the Patient must undergo some Pain.

A young Sailor, who was passionately in Love with a Maid that had but one Eye, after having been a three Years Voyage, went to visit her on his Return, and imagined he found her quite different from the Person he so much doated on at his Departure:—"Bless me!" cry'd he, "how you are altered since I went away! Why you have lost one of your Eyes!" On which she laughed, and replied wittily enough, "No, but I perceive you have found both yours."

While the Passion lasts, it doubtless gives Charms where there are none, and highly magnifies those it really finds; but when it ceases, we see without a Mist before our Eyes, and often are surprized at ourselves for having been so much deceived.

But supposing the Object of our Affections to be in Fact possessed of the most consummate Perfections; if those Perfections cannot be attained, without Prejudice either to ourselves or the Person we love, is it not the extremest Folly to pursue the Aim?—What Ideas could *Silvius,* who truly loved, or *Lavinia,* who imagined she did so, form to themselves of Happiness in Life, by encouraging an Inclination for each other? What likelihood of compleating the Union they had vowed? Or if madly they had resolved to enter into it, what but Misery had[2] attended it?—The Husband, unable to support his Wife as she had been bred, must have been doubly wretched, to see the Idol of

---

1. **insensibly:** by imperceptible degrees.
2. **had:** would have.

his Soul languish under Wants he had not Power to relieve, and which he had brought her under; and the Wife, grown wiser by Calamity, would certainly have repented the Error of her Choice, and hated the Author of her altered State.—Discontent, Grief of Heart, Reproaches, would soon have usurped the Place of fond Endearments, and he that loved, and she that did not love, have been equally unhappy.

I believe, if we look into the World, we shall find no greater Evils in private Life, than what Marriages, whether clandestine, or openly solemnized, in Defiance of the Will of those who ought to have the Disposal of us, have occasioned.

Obedience to Parents is an indispensible Duty.—No one, how great soever, ought to think himself exempt from paying it. Decency and Good Manners require it. Natural Affection obliges to it. The Laws of Man enjoin it, and the Law of God not only commands it, but annexes to the fulfilling it a Promise of long Life in the Land which he shall please to give us.

Yet, notwithstanding this, when a Parent through Avarice, Caprice, or Partiality, would force his Child to marry utterly against Inclination, I cannot think Disobedience a Crime, because we are not to obey our Parents in Things which are in themselves unlawful; and certainly there is nothing more opposite to the Laws of God, and more contradictory to the Institution, and even to the very Words of Marriage, than to vow an everlasting Love to a Person for whom one has a fixed Aversion.

But tho' we are not always bound to marry according to the Direction of our Parents, we ought not, however, to think ourselves at Liberty to chuse for ourselves.—If we cannot bring our Hearts to correspond with their Desires, we must not be so wholly guided by our own, as to bring into their Family a Person whom they do not approve of.

In short, it is the Opinion of the *Female Spectator,* that he, or she, who cannot marry according to their Parents Liking, ought not to marry at all, at least till the Decease of those Parents leaves them free to dispose of themselves.

It is, however, a very great Misfortune, methinks, that so many Places where young People may meet and undo themselves for ever at

Pleasure are tollerated.—The Custom of calling the Banes[1] in the Parish Churches, as old fashioned and vulgar as it is now esteemed, prevented many a worthy Family from being brought into Affliction by the Folly of one inconsiderable Branch of it.

Marriages also in private Chambers,[2] tho' with the Consent of Friends, and never so many Persons present, seem to me to lose great Part of their Solemnity.—If the Ceremony is allowed to be a Divine Institution, and the Union of Hands and Heart, to be a Type of the Mystical Union of *Christ* and his Church, certainly the most proper Place for the Celebration of it, is that which is consecrated and set apart for Religious Rites

I have the Honour to be entirely of the same Way of thinking with a late noble Lord, who said *he could not look on any Marriage as perfect which was not celebrated before the Altar,* and obliged his Daughter, and the Bridegroom he had made Choice of for her, to be married at the Parish Church, though both of them were somewhat reluctant, as it was against the Mode.[3]

The main Reason I have heard alledged against it is, that it is too great a Shock to the Modesty of a young Lady to be given to a Man in the Presence of so many People as generally crowd into the Church on such Occasions; but I could wish there were more of Sincerity and less of Sophistry in this Argument, and that the Brides of this Age would in other Respects discover an equal Share of Timidity with their Great-Grandmothers, who were not ashamed to go to Church with the Man they loved, and was authorized by their Parents, or such who had the Disposal of them.

Some too, in order I suppose to prove themselves good Protestants, will say, that a Marriage before the Altar makes it look too much like a Sacrament, and savours of the Church of *Rome;* but all who talk in

---

1. **Banes:** banns; proclamations of an intended marriage. By old custom, a forthcoming marriage was announced on three successive weeks from the church pulpit so that anyone knowing of an impediment could say so in advance.

2. **private Chambers:** rooms in private houses.

3. **against the Mode:** unfashionable.

this idle Manner, I am afraid, are of the Number of those who, to fly from *Popery*,[1] run into *Prophaness,* and rather than put too great a Stress on any of the Ordinances of the Church, despise and ridicule every Thing it enjoins,

I am sorry to say, that of these there are not a few; but as this is a Matter quite foreign to my present Purpose, and indeed I must acknowledge out of the Province of a *Female Spectator,* I shall add no more upon it.

All I would endeavour by this Animadversion on *Lavinia*'s Letter is to perswade the *younger* Part of my Sex, that it is highly unbecoming of them to entertain any Thoughts of Love or Marriage, till it is proposed and recommended to them by those under whose Government[2] they are; and the *elder* to avoid all such silly Compliments and Discourses as may contribute to put into the Minds of those under their Care, Ideas which otherwise perhaps they would have very little or no Notion of.

The Small-Pox is not half so great an Enemy to the Face as Flattery is to the Mind of a young Virgin.—It empoisons all the noble Propensities, turns every thing to Vanity, and makes her, instead of pleasing others, look on nothing but herself as worthy of being pleased— She flies the Conversation of all those who deal sincerely with her, and is in Raptures with such as tend to the Praises of her Beauty.— She swallows greedily the most gross and absurd Encomiums, believes them all, and that she merits even more than can be said.—In this Imagination, blown up[3] with Self-Conceit, she grows above all Controul.—Her Words, her Actions are wholly under the Direction of her own Will, which influencing her only to the Gratification of her Passions and Humour, what but Ruin in its worst Shape can be expected to ensue!

Of all the Virtues, there are none ought more to be inculcated into the Mind of a young Girl, than Modesty and Meekness.—Vanity and

---

1. **Popery:** Catholicism.

2. **Government:** control, guidance.

3. **blown up:** swelled.

Pride are perpetually endeavouring to force their Way into the Heart, and too much Care cannot be taken to repulse their Efforts:—The more she has of Beauty, the less she ought to be told of it, and the stronger Argument made Use of, to convince her of the little Value she should set upon it.

Nothing gives me more Pain than to see a Mother encourage her Children in what she calls *Spirit,* and be rather pleased than offended at any pert Behaviour they may be guilty of, especially when they are very young.—Poor Woman, she does not consider how this same Spirit will grow with their Years, and to what dangerous Lengths it may one Day transport them.

It is a Spirit not easily quelled when once raised, and I would have no Parents flatter themselves with the Power of doing it; for when too much Lenity[1] finds itself provoked to Austerity, the Person it is exercised upon, instead of being humbled by the Change, becomes more perverse, and not seldom flies into open Rebellion.

*   *   *

FROM BOOK XXIV

There is no one Virtue that more demonstrates a truly noble Soul than Fortitude.—It is, indeed, the utmost Dignity of Human Nature, and brings it very near Angelic.

On the other Hand, there is nothing so much betrays a mean Mind and weak Capacity, as to repine and fret ourselves at every little Event that may happen to cross[2] our Inclinations, or Expectations.

The one commands the Respect of all who know us:—The other exposes us to their Contempt:—The one sets us above *ill* Fortune.—The other renders us unworthy of *good.*

---

1. **Lenity:** gentleness.

2. **cross:** run counter to.

I know very well that this is a Maxim much easier recommended to others than put in Practice by ourselves; yet as there have been Instances of Persons who labouring under the most severe Calamities, have brought themselves to such an Evenness and Steadiness of Temper, as not to discover[1] any Dejection, every one ought to exert their utmost Resolution to imitate the Model.

Monsieur the *Abbe de Bellgarde*[2] says, that in scorning to do a base Action, and in being above shewing ourselves moved at those done to us, consists the only laudable Pride of a reasonable Being.

That great Author himself met with many Things, which would have shocked any Man of less Philosophy.—He was ill-treated by his Father, who gave away to a Son he had by a second Marriage, that Patrimony the *Abbè* was born to inherit.—He was coolly looked upon by a Prince whom he loved, and from his Youth had served with the greatest Fidelity, and was most cruelly deceived by one he took to be his Bosom Friend, to the Ruin of almost all his little Fortune; yet Monsier *de Pont*, who wrote his Life, tells us, that he was never seen with a clouded Brow, nor heard to complain of the Injustice he sustained; and it is for this greatly bearing his Misfortunes, that he bestows higher Encomiums on him, than for all his other Virtues, and a Stock of Wit and Learning which very few Men of his Time could equal, and, if we may depend on Character, none be said to excell.

Who would not therefore endeavour to attain that happy Composedness of Mind, which renders us so easy within ourselves, so much endears us to our Friends, and makes our Enemies ashamed of being so.

It is a very great Reflection, and I am sorry to say too just a one, upon the *English* Nation, that we have more *Suicides* among us in a Year, than in any other Place in an Age.—Whence can this unnatural Crime proceed, but from giving way to a Discontent which preys like a Vulture upon our very Vitals on every Accident that displeases us,

---

1. **discover:** reveal.

2. **Abbe de Bellgarde:** Jean Baptiste Morvan de Bellegarde (1648–1736), at one time a Jesuit priest, was well known as a translator and moral essayist.

fills us with black and dismal Thoughts, and at length precipitates us into the utmost Despair!

Like all other ill Habits this must be suppressed in the beginning, or it will grow too mighty for Controul, if in the least indulged.—To that end we should never put the worst Colours on Things, but rather deceive ourselves with imagining them better than they are.

Of this I am perfectly convinced, both by Observation and Experience, that an easy and unruffled Mind contributes very much to the preventing many ill Accidents, and to extricate us out of those Difficulties we are actually involved in: Whereas a Person of a fretful and discontented Disposition is bewildered, as it were, amidst his Troubles. His Thoughts are in a Maze, and Reason has no Power to point him out the Path he ought to take for his Redress.

Besides, as I have already hinted, every Disappointment is not a real Misfortune, though blinded by our Passions we may think it so. I know a Gentleman, who, by the strangest Accidents in the World, was twice prevented from going a Voyage which had the Prospect of great Advantage to him: He thought himself the most unhappy Man that ever was, and could not help complaining in all Companies, how averse Fortune was to his Desires; but in a short Time after, News arrived that both those Ships, in which he had intended to embark, were lost, and every Soul on Board them had perished in the Waves. This compelled him to acknowledge himself happy in the imaginary Disappointment, and bless the Goodness of that Divine Power, he had so lately, under the Name of Fortune, accused of Cruelty.

Another, who was passionately in Love with a very beautiful young Lady, behaved himself in the most extravagant Manner on a Rival's being preferred by her Father.—All his Acquaintance trembled, lest some Act of Desperation should ensue; and it is much to be feared, they would not have been mistaken, if in two or three Days after the Loss of all his Hopes on her Account, he had not providentially discovered she had been made a Mother two Years before by one of the Helpers in the Stable.

A Lady of my Acquaintance, who was brought near the Brink of Distraction for the Death of a Husband to whom she had been married but two Months, and tenderly loved, soon found a Consolation for her Loss, in the Discovery that he had been an Impostor, had not an Acre of Land in the World, though he pretended himself in Possession of a large Estate; and what was yet worse, that he had been contracted to a Woman who was about to sue him for half the Fortune he had received with her; and that if he had lived but a very little Time longer, she must have been inevitably ruined.

The least Observation may convince us in daily Instances, that what we most desire, is in reality our greatest Happiness to miss; but tho' all see, and confess it in the Affairs of others, few can be perswaded it is so in their own, till Time and Accidents open the Eyes of Reason.

Blind to our own Good, as to our Faults, we hurry on precipitately to whatever Phantom Fancy sets before us,—adore it as a Deity,— sacrifice our *all* to it, and push from us with Vehemence and Contempt, the friendly Hand that aims to pull us back, though by Heaven itself directed.

I am not insensible[1] that to be of a Disposition not over anxious nor eager in the Pursuit of any Thing, is looked upon to savour too much of the *Stoic,*[2] and by some is accounted even Dulness, Stupidity, and Sluggishness of Nature; it may indeed betray a Want of that Vivacity which is so pleasing in Conversation, and renders the Person who possesses it, more taken Notice of than otherwise he might be; but then, if those who argue in this Manner, would give themselves the Trouble to reflect how dear[3] sometimes People pay for exerting that Vivacity, or rather, as the *French* term it, a *brusque* Behaviour, none would wish to exchange the solid, serious, and unmoved Temper for it.

I am always extremely concerned, when I see People place their whole Happineis in the Attainment of any one Aim.—I scarce ever knew it to succeed without being productive of very great Mischiefs.— We are so little capable of judging for ourselves, that when the Almighty, offended with our Presumption, gives his Fiat to our Wishes,

---

1. **insensible:** unaware.

2. **Stoic:** The Stoic school of philosophy, founded in Athens ca. 200 B.C., was thought to advocate enduring all contingencies without visible emotion.

3. **dear:** expensively.

they seldom come uncharged with Ills, which we then pray as earnestly and with much more Reason to be delivered from.

Upon the whole, therefore, we ought to look on all the little Calamities of Life as things unworthy of wholly engrossing our immortal Part.—*Virtue* and *Wisdom* are the two only Pursuits where Ardency is reconciled with Reason: For the acquiring these, we cannot indeed be too eager. All the Zeal, all the Warmth we testify for them is laudable. The more we are possessed of *them*, the less we shall feel of any *other* Wants: Besides, we have this Reflection to encourage our Endeavours, that whoever is happy enough to arrive at any Degree of Perfection in the *one*, cannot fail of being in a great measure possessed of the *other* also.

Our inimitable *Shakespear,* who, of all the Dramatic Writers, in my Opinion, seems to take most Pains to inculcate those Ideas, which alone can make us truly happy, advises us to remember,

> Our Lives are short, but to extend that Span
> To vast Eternity, is Virtue's Work.[1]

But now it is Time to quit the *Spectatorial* Function, and thank the Public for the extraordinary Encouragement these Lucubrations[2] have received; to those who have favoured us with their Correspondence, and who express a Desire of having the Work continued yet a longer Time, our Gratitude is particularly due: Though on a Consultation of our Members, it is judged more for the Advantage of our Reputation, to break off while we are in the good Graces of the Town, than become tedious to any Part of it.

As we have more than once expressed our Intention of concluding with this Book, the Authors of several ingenious Letters, which came too late to be inserted, will not, we hope, think themselves neglected; since, as the Number of our Correspondents has every Day greatly multiplied, it is likely the *Female Spectator* might be prolonged till we

---

1. **Our Lives . . . Work:** No concordance indicates that these lines are by Shakespeare. Haywood evidently often quoted from memory, and her memory sometimes fails her.

2. **Lucubrations:** studies, and the products of study.

ceased to be, if a *Finis* to the Undertaking were not to be put, till either Matter[1] failed us to write upon, or kind Assistance to it failed from other Hands.

But though we think convenient to drop the Shape we have worn these two Years, we have a kind of hankering Inclination to assume another in a short Time; and if we should do so, Notice shall be given of it in the public Papers, flattering ourselves, that those who have testified their Approbation of the *Female Spectator,* either by their Subscriptions, or Correspondence, will not withdraw their Favour from the Authors, in whatever Character we shall next appear.

Close as we endeavoured to keep the Mystery of our little Cabal, some Gentlemen have at last found Means to make a full Discovery of it. They will needs have us take up the Pen again, and promise to furnish us with a Variety of Topics yet untouched upon, with this Condition, that we admit them as Members, and not pretend to the World, that what shall hereafter be produced, is wholly of the *Feminine* Gender.

We have not yet quite agreed on the Preliminaries of this League, but are very apt to believe we shall not differ with them on Trifles, especially as one of them is the Husband of *Mira.*

In the mean time, should any one, from this Hint, take it into their Head, to publish either Book or Pamphlet, as wrote by the Authors of the *Female Spectator,* it may be depended on that whether we do any Thing ourselves or not, we shall advertise against whatever shall come out that Way, and lay open the Imposition.

End of the TWENTY-FOURTH *and last* BOOK.

---

1. **Matter:** material.